This book is a valuable contribu question of the nature of the unit of the diversity of its threefold historical function. It demonstrates how the finality of the person and work of Christ is the crux of the matter and how the atonement has law as its background. A readable presentation of the biblical data relevant to the subject that leaves no stone unturned.

Paul Wells,
Dean of the Faculté Jean Calvin, Aix-en-Provence, France

The question dealt with in this book is the relationship between the laws and requirements of the Old Testament and those of the New. Are these still obligatory? In dealing with this question, very important for lovers of the Scriptures, the author suggests as the *Westminster Confession* did, a three fold classification, and provides a very full analysis of the arguments in favour of that classification from many authors down through the centuries, as well as of those who write against that classification. I commend it to all who wish to live by the Scriptures.

Lord Mackay of Clashfern,
Lord Chancellor, 1987-1997

It is a given for scholars in a variety of allied disciplines (e.g., biblical studies, systematic theology, Christian ethics) that the ancient Christian distinction between the civil, ceremonial, and moral laws is without foundation. Philip Ross dissents from the consensus and he does so thoughtfully, lucidly, and wittily. Those who are new to the question and those are willing to reconsider their views will find in Ross an able guide through the labyrinth.

R. Scott Clark,
Professor of Church History and Historical Theology,
Westminster Seminary California, Escondido, California

Whenever biblical theology is rediscovered or the Gospel of Christ is proclaimed, Paul's question 'Why then the law?' always follows. Although it was already answered by Jesus in the Sermon on the Mount, by Paul throughout his letters, and by the Fathers of the Church in their own days – whether Early Fathers, Reformers, or Confession authors – it is once again being raised in our day.

The question of the role of the law is a major theological issue. But as pastor, hymn-writer and spiritual counselor par excellence John Newton long ago noted, it is of immense practical importance. For, if wrongly answered, the spiritual implications may prove to be disastrous.

Against this background Philip Ross's new book *From the Finger of God* is to be welcomed with open arms. It is a serious and careful work, and leads to deeply satisfying conclusions. Dr Ross treats us to a fine example of careful, readable biblical, theological, and historical scholarship. But more than that, he has given us a book of great relevance with an immensely important message for the contemporary church. I for one hope that it will be carefully studied by scholars, students and ministers and prove widely influential in the life of the Christian Church worldwide.

Sinclair B. Ferguson,
Senior Minister, First Presbyterian Church, Columbia, South Carolina

Philip Ross has dealt with issues lying near the heart of the Christian life (and indeed, of the healthy functioning of any human society) in this careful, fair, and, at times, humorous (or at least, entertaining and attention-holding) study of the continuing valid-ity of God's law. He surveys exegetically and in terms of the history of theology, the teaching of the *Westminster Confession of Faith* that from the point of view of the New Testament, there is a threefold division of the law of God: moral law, ceremonial law, and civil law. Over the years I have seen strong praise of this distinction, as well as stout denunciation of it, but never have I seen such judicious exploration of it, biblically, theologically, and pastorally. His scholarship is of a high quality, and shows thoughtful research in relevant sources, both ancient and modern, and a grasp of the biblical languages. He knows how to get to the point of an argument, without being deterred by the long pages of professional jargon that one so often finds in some exegetical studies dealing with biblical law and with the Apostle Paul. And yet he does so honestly and fairly. He provides the clearest explanation I have seen so far of the significance of the deliverances of the Jerusalem Council (in Acts 15), and also probably offers the most thorough and intelligible discussion of both the concept of 'the general equity of the law', and also of what is meant by the generally neglected category of 'judicial law.' His discussion of 'natural law' in terms of Romans 2 makes eminent sense: both for the universality of the law, and for the call to missions in light of the final judgment of all humanity. I will be frequently referring to his volume in my classes, and warmly commend it.

Douglas F. Kelly,
Richard Jordan Professor of Theology,
Reformed Theological Seminary, Charlotte, North Carolina

In recent times, little has weakened biblical theology more than the tendency to collapse all the rules and statutes of the Old Testament into one uniform corpus of law material. In this timely and extremely helpful study, Dr Philip Ross demonstrates not only that the division of the law into moral, civil and ceremonial categories arises out of a natural reading of the biblical text, but that its adoption in Patristic, Reformed and Puritan literature shows it to have been the orthodox position of the church. To lose this confessional distinctive is to drive an unbiblical wedge between the Testaments, and to eviscerate the gospel itself. Unless the moral law is still in force, how can we define sin? And unless we can define sin, what gospel can we preach? Dr Ross's work is an important corrective to much misunderstanding on the nature and place of God's law in the Bible, and a reliable guide both to the primary and secondary literature on the subject.

Iain D. Campbell,
Minister, Point Free Church of Scotland, Isle of Lewis

Like me, you may never have thought that the division of the Law into the categories of civil, ceremonial and moral needed prolonged enquiry. When you read this book you will be glad that Dr Ross thought otherwise. The book would be worthwhile if only for the discussion of the Decalogue or of the fulfilment of the Old Testament in the New, but there is something for the Bible lover on every page, as well as a demanding but readable opening up of a huge area of biblical enquiry, that takes us with profit from Genesis through to the Lord Jesus and his apostles. A real and rewarding mind-opener!

Alec Motyer,
well-known Bible expositor and commentary writer.

Elegantly written, this work is an impressive achievement in biblical studies combining systematic clarity with exegetical analysis.

Theodore G. Stylianopoulos,
Archbishop Professor of Orthodox Theology and Professor of New Testament (Emeritus),
Holy Cross Greek Orthodox School of Theology, Brookline, Massachusetts

This is one of the most important theological books to be published for several years. It is desperately needed and should be read by pastors and church leaders worldwide as a matter of urgency.

The book is important because it addresses and argues for the crucial teaching concerning the three-fold division of God's law. This teaching is increasingly and widely rejected by Evangelicals today, despite the fact that Christians from many traditions over the centuries have embraced it, including the majority of Reformed Confessions. What is distressing is sometimes the disparaging and dismissive manner in which Evangelicals have written about, and reacted to, the three-fold division of the Law. For these reasons alone the book is timely and important.

A second reason for the book's importance is that it is an extremely practical subject involving vital questions. For example, is the Law of God permanent and binding on us today; if so, which parts of it? These questions need to be answered correctly and biblically.

The third reason for arguing that this book is important is the way in which he addresses the subject. This is not a polemic but a thoroughly biblical and historical approach in which the author uses his grasp of the biblical languages and biblical as well as systematic theology to search the Scriptures. Consequently, he provides a persuasive biblical and theological basis for the three-fold division of the Law.

I appeal to Christians to give priority to the prayerful and diligent study of this challenging book.

D. Eryl Davies,
Head of Research, Wales Evangelical School of Theology

In this remarkable work Dr Philip Ross studies the threefold Division of the Law as traditionally held by the Reformed, Orthodox and Catholic Churches and establishes this framework to be scripturally based. Ross's study is a welcome contribution to this topic especially in the context of challenges to this formulation from several modern authors who reject it as non-biblical, challenges which this study effectively refutes. This study is to be commended not only for its scholarly rigor but also for its ecumenical relevance.

George Keerankeri, S.J.,
Reader in Sacred Scripture, Vidyajyoti College of Theology, Delhi

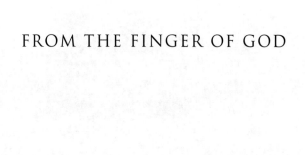

FROM THE FINGER OF GOD

FROM THE FINGER OF GOD

The Biblical and Theological Basis
for the Threefold Division of the Law

Philip S. Ross

MENTOR

In memory of the saints
whose dust lies in the burial grounds
of Lochcarron and Kishorn.

Several of them preached Christ to me;
many of them prayed for me;
all of them longed to live according
to the perfect rule of righteousness.

Now perfect in holiness,
they behold the face of God, in light and glory,
waiting for the full redemption of their bodies.

Copyright © Philip S. Ross 2010

ISBN 978-1-84550-601-8

Published in 2010

in the

Mentor Imprint

by

Christian Focus Publications Ltd.,

Geanies House, Fearn,

Ross-shire, IV20 1TW, Scotland

www.christianfocus.com

Cover design by Daniel Van Straaten

Printed and bound by
Bell & Bain, Glasgow

Mixed Sources
Product group from well-managed forests and other controlled sources
www.fsc.org Cert no.TT-COC-002769
© 1996 Forest Stewardship Council

FSC

CONTENTS

ABBREVIATIONS

ANF	*Ante-Nicene Fathers*
CBQ	*Catholic Biblical*
ERT	*Evangelical Review of Theology*
ETR	*Etudes théologiques et religieuses.*
HTR	*Harvard Theological Review*
JBL	*Journal of Biblical Literature*
JETS	*Journal of the Evangelical Theological Society*
JR	*The Juridicial Review*
JSNT	*Journal for the Study of the New Testament*
JSOT	*Journal for the Study of the Old Testament*
LCL	*Leob Classical Library*
SBET	*Scottish Bulletin of Evangelical Theology*
SJT	*Scottish Journal of Theology*
TB	*Tyndale Bulletin*
TDNT	*Theological Dictionary of the New Testament*
TDOT	*Theological Dictionary of the Old Testament*
TWOT	*Theological Wordbook of the Old Testament*
VT	*Vetus Testamentum*
WBC	*Word Biblical Commentary*
WCF	*The Westminster Confession of Faith*
WLC	*Westminster Larger Catechism*
WSC	*Westminster Shorter Catechism*
WTJ	*Westminster Theological Journal*
ZNW	*Zeitschrift für die Neutestamentliche Wissenschaft*

ACKNOWLEDGMENTS

A multitude of friends helped me in a variety of ways during several phases of this work—from the team at Christian Focus to those who suggested resources—but I will restrict my acknowledgments to those who have had most involvement in critiquing the content. Several people read every word and made suggestions that I have tried to follow. Beyond several of those who have commended this book, these include Professor Donald MacLeod, Dr Paul Middleton, Dr Kathy Ehrensperger, Iwan Rhys-Jones, Dr Tom Holland, and Rev. John van Eyk, plus two real doctors, Philip John Stewart and Roland William McCallum. In particular, I must thank Dr D. Eryl Davies who not only urged me to persevere, but persevered with me to the end.

ACKNOWLEDGMENTS

1

A CATHOLIC DOCTRINE

> I believe...in the holy catholic church.
>
> *The Apostles' Creed.*

Doctrine divides. Or so they say. But this book is about a doctrine that has united Christians in every century and across denominations. Not uniquely Eastern or Western; Roman Catholic or Protestant; conservative or liberal; Patristic or Puritan; Thomist, Calvinist, or anything else; the threefold division of the law is catholic doctrine. Throughout history, the church's most prominent theologians expounded, maintained, and defended its teaching. It was 'well known' and adopted by the 'ancients', says Calvin.[1] Most Reformed[2] confessions likewise adopt the division and even those that do not declare it work within its framework.[3] We will return to consider the historical roots of this doctrine, but what is the threefold division of the law?

---

1   John Calvin, *Institutes of the Christian Religion* (Grand Rapids: Eerdmans, 1995), 4:20:14.

2   I use 'Reformed' in an historical sense to refer to churches that have their roots in the Reformation, particularly those influenced by Calvin and Swiss Protestantism as opposed to Luther and German Protestantism. Contemporary Reformed denominations incorporate a variety of theological opinion.

3   For example, *The Three Forms of Unity,* that is *The Heidelberg Catechism, The Belgic Confession,* and *The Canons of Dort.*

NO MINOR THREAD

The division exists not just to explain a doctrine of biblical law; its practical-theological teaching answers the Christian's question, 'Am I still bound to obey the Mosaic Law?' The threefold division of the law says, 'Yes and no.' The Mosaic Law does not apply without exception to the Christian, but nor can we dispense with it altogether. One part of the law is non-binding, another binding in its underlying principles, and another ever-binding.

The non-binding laws were exclusively 'ceremonial'. They regulated the Israelite sacrificial system and matters such as ceremonial cleanliness. Although they hold forth moral duties, they were typical of Christ's sacrifice and since he has fulfilled all that they typified, they are abrogated and non-binding upon those who follow Christ.

Laws concerning everyday civil matters in the Israelite community are binding in their underlying principles. The Christian is not bound to obey the Mosaic civil code in detail, but the moral principles at the heart of the civil law still bind.

The only laws that are, without exception, ever-binding are the laws of the Decalogue. Those Ten Commandments reveal the demands of God upon all people, not just those in ancient Israel. From the beginning, they were the basis upon which God judged mankind. The coming of Christ and the incorporation of Gentiles into the church did not nullify the Decalogue; it remains binding upon Christians and non-Christians alike.

The threefold division of the law has been expressed in various ways throughout the centuries, but this non-binding, binding in underlying principles, and ever-binding distinction captures the practical essence of the division. In this book I will take *The Westminster Confession of Faith* formulation as a primary example of the division, not because I plan to have a uni-focal emphasis on seventeenth-century theology, but for three reasons. First, it represents one of the most recent and expansive confessional restatements of the threefold division. This not only allows for comparison with the theological arguments used to support the framework in periods of church history unaffected by Puritan concerns, it also reveals some of the rationale behind the widespread acceptance of the doctrine. Second, the wording in *The Westminster Confession of Faith* is almost identical with that of *The Thirty Nine Articles* and *The Irish Articles*, so it may be viewed as representative of the theology that shaped Protestantism in Britain, Ireland, and those countries where Presbyterianism and Anglicanism dispersed their children.[4] Third, although terms of subscription vary, those documents remain the subordinate standards for many Reformed denominations throughout the world.

The Westminster Confession's Chapter XIX, 'Of the Law of God', reads as follows:

I. God gave to Adam a law, as a covenant of works, by which he bound him, and all his posterity, to personal, entire, exact, and perpetual obedience; promised life upon the fulfilling, and threatened death upon the breach of it; and endued him with power and ability to keep it.

II. This law, after his fall, continued to be a perfect rule of righteousness; and, as such was delivered by God upon mount Sinai in ten commandments, and written in two tables; the first four commandments containing our duty towards God, and the other six our duty to man.

III. Besides this law, commonly called moral, God was pleased to give to the people of Israel, as a church under age, ceremonial laws containing several typical ordinances; partly of worship prefiguring Christ, his graces, actions, sufferings, and benefits; and partly holding forth divers instructions of moral duties. All which ceremonial laws are now abrogated under the New Testament.

---

4   For a summary of statements in some of the earlier Rerformed confessions see Robert Letham, *The Westminster Assembly: Reading its Theology in Historical Context* (Phillipsburg: P&R Publishing, 2009), 294–5.

IV. To them also, as a body politick, he gave sundry judicial laws, which expired together with the state of that people, not obliging any other now, further than the general equity thereof may require.

V. The moral law doth for ever bind all, as well justified persons as others, to the obedience thereof; and that not only in regard of the matter contained in it, but also in respect of the authority of God, the Creator, who gave it. Neither doth Christ in the gospel any way dissolve, but much strengthen this obligation.

VI. Although true believers be not under the law as covenant of works, to be thereby justified or condemned; yet it is of great use to them, as well as to others in that as a rule of life, informing them of the will of God and their duty, it directs and binds them to walk accordingly; discovering also the sinful pollutions of their nature, hearts, and lives; so as examining themselves thereby, they may come to further conviction of, humiliation for, and hatred against sin; together with a clearer sight of the need they have of Christ, and the perfection of his obedience. It is likewise of use to the regenerate, to restrain their corruptions, in that it forbids sin; and the threatenings of it serve to shew what even their sins deserve, and what afflictions in this life they may expect for them, although freed from the curse thereof threatened in the law. The promises of it, in like manner, shew them God's approbation of obedience, and what blessings they may expect upon the performance thereof, although not as due to them by the law as a covenant of works: so as a man's doing good, and restraining from evil, because the law encourageth to the one, and deterreth from the other is no evidence of his being under the law, and not under grace.

VII. Neither are the forementioned uses of the law contrary to the grace of the gospel, but do sweetly comply with it; the Spirit of Christ subduing and enabling the will of man to do that freely and cheerfully which the will of God revealed in the law requireth to be done.

In this citation, section III explains the non-binding 'ceremonial laws' and section IV deals with the 'judicial laws' of which only 'the general equity' still stands. The remaining five sections discuss the ever-binding 'moral' law: It was 'delivered by God upon

Mount Sinai in ten commandments', having first been given to Adam 'as a covenant of works'. Nevertheless, 'true believers be not under the law as covenant of works' and such uses of the law 'sweetly comply' with the grace of the gospel.

This was how the *Westminster Confession* answered the Christian's question, 'Am I still bound to obey the Mosaic Law?' In a context where 'the Reformers were at odds, not with the Catholic tradition, but with its immediate repsentatives,'[5] the Westminster Divines subjected their approach to the law to biblical scrutiny like any other doctrine. They debated the exegetical foundations, not in isolation, but 'self-consciously as part of the great tradition of the church.'[6] Thus, the *Westminster Confession of Faith* restated the catholic view of the law.

A few centuries on, not all subscribers to their confession appreciate that restatement. According to Tim Keller, nearly all Presbyterian Church in America presbyters subscribe to *The Westminster Confession of Faith* 'with only the most minor exceptions (the only common one being with regard to the Sabbath).'[7] If, however, such an exception amounts to a wholesale rejection of the confessions's approach to the Sabbath, its authors might have judged Keller a master of understatement. Were the *Westminster Confession* a garment, you would not want to pull this 'minor' thread, unless you wanted to be altogether defrocked. And perhaps the reason that some people pull at this thread is because they regard the confession as more of straightjacket than a garment. Unbuckle the Sabbath, and you are well on your way to mastering theological escapology.

If this seems overstatement to rival Keller's understatement, let me say that biblical law, with its Sabbath, is no easily dispensable

---

5   Letham, *Westminster Assembly*, 96.

6   Ibid., 97.

7   Tim Keller, 'How Then Shall We Live Together? –Subscription and The Future of the PCA.' Accessed on-line, 22 March 2010, http://web.archive.org/web/20050328000226/http://www.tnpc.org/ga/GAKeller.PDF.

part of the Reformed doctrinal infrastructure. And what applies
to the theology of the Reformed churches often applies to wider
Protestant theology. Attempts at performing a precision strike
on the Sabbath produce an embarrassing amount of unintended
damage. Strike out the Sabbath and you also shatter the entire
category of moral law and all that depends on it.

If the *Shorter Catechism* represents Reformed theology in one
of its most practical forms, it seems that any expurgation of
biblical law from the theological framework it expounds, should
lead to its complete unravelling. Nearly half of the catechism's
107 questions[8] deal with the demands and consequences of ever-
binding moral law. The *Westminster Confession* itself gives fewer
words to the subject, yet law remains integral to the theology of
the documents. From the beginning, law was written on the heart
of man.[9] 'Sin is any want of conformity unto, or transgression of,
any law of God, given as a rule to the reasonable creature.'[10] My
'every sin deserves God's wrath and curse, both in this life, and
that which is to come.'[11] The moral law leaves me 'inexcusable'[12]
and without escape apart from receiving Jesus Christ and resting
upon him alone,[13] the one who offered himself as 'a sacrifice
to satisfy divine justice'.[14] Should I refuse this 'freely offered'[15]
salvation, I will, on the day of judgment, 'give an account of'
my 'thoughts, words, and deeds'[16] and be convicted 'upon clear
evidence',[17] but if the Holy Spirit persuades and enables me to

---

8   Questions 39–84.
9   *WCF* IV.2.
10 *WLC* 24.
11 *WSC* 84.
12 *WLC* 96.
13 *WSC* 85.
14 *WSC* 25.
15 *WSC* 31.
16 *WCF* XXXIII.1.
17 *WLC* 89.

embrace Jesus Christ[18] I will have every transgression of the law pardoned. God will accept me as righteous in his sight.[19] This is the confession of presbyters and office bearers across many Reformed denominations. It broadly encapsulates the instinctive confession of Christian believers throughout Reformed and evangelical churches. But as Hugh Martin asks in *The Atonement*, 'What instrumentality or efficiency towards any thing like this can possibly be ascribed to the Incarnation of God's Son, if there be no strictly moral and authoritative juridical law?'[20] And he goes on to say that, 'So long as philosophy and theology shall conserve the distinctive peculiarity of Moral Law… the Westminster doctrine, which is the Catholic doctrine, of Atonement is impregnable.'[21]

In an article entitled, 'Why Is the Doctrine of Penal Substitution Again Coming Under Attack?', D. A. Carson lists five 'developments that have contributed to this sad state of affairs'.[22] It is a brief piece in which he could hardly cover every possibility, but perhaps there is a sixth development that Carson does not mention—the rejection of the threefold division with its view that moral law and sin are defined by the Decalogue. Perhaps there is a coherent explanation for penal substitution without moral law, but the issue Martin raised is not inconsequential to the integrated body of catholic doctrine. For that reason alone, an investigation into the biblical and theological basis for the threefold division of the law is not a trivial pursuit.

This makes the often perfunctory dismissals of the threefold division that have proliferated in recent decades all the more

18   *WSC* 31.
19   *WSC* 33.
20   Hugh Martin, D.D., *The Atonement: in its Relations to the Covenant, the Priesthood, the Intercession of Our Lord* (Edinburgh: Lyon and Gemmell, 1877), 274.
21   Ibid., 255.
22   From Google's cache of thegospelcoalition.org/articleprint.php?a=45. It is a snapshot of the page as it appeared on 18 Jun 2008 01:50:18 GMT.

remarkable. Let me give two examples. First, Tom Wells, co-author of *New Covenant Theology*, tells us that biblical evidence to support the Puritan approach to the Decalogue 'was always wanting'.[23] He goes on:

> As evidence for the wider sweeping conclusion that everything moral is comprehended in one of these ten commands, both the *Larger* and *Smaller* [sic] *Catechism* offer just three verses, Matthew 19:17, 18, 19. This is, surely, much too narrow a base from which to draw such a comprehensive conclusion. Further than that, assuming that Matthew 19 contains the best evidence for this opinion, we must note that it was not available to OT believers at all.[24]

Wells seems to imagine the divines took a similar approach to proof texting as a preacher I saw on the GOD Channel giving ten principles for business success, complete with proof texts. For his second point, 'Expand into international markets,' the preacher offered the text, 'Ask of me, and I will give you the nations for your inheritance' (Ps. 2:8). The Westminster Divines were a little more sophisticated. No reasonable person can dismiss their scholarship, breadth of knowledge, and sensitivity to biblical context. Most significantly, the first edition of the confession contained no proof texts. Apart from Parliament's insistence, it would have had none. A reluctant Assembly added proof texts not because they feared 'being unable to support the propositions of the Confession by Scripture' but because they realised 'that a complete presentation of Scripture proof would have required a volume.'[25] In this case, it is Wells' approach that is most obviously wanting.

The second example comes from a recent book by Jason Meyer, *The End of the Law*. He writes these words:

23   Tom Wells and Fred Zaspel, *New Covenant Theology* (Frederick: New Covenant Media, 2002), 72.

24   Ibid., 74.

25   John Murray, 'The Work of the Westminster Assembly', *The Presbyterian Guardian*, vol. II (1942). See also Letham, *Westminster Assembly*, 107, 137.

The NT itself does not make these three distinctions, and no one living under the law of Moses seriously thought they could pick which parts were binding and which were optional. God's law comes as a set with no substitutions. Therefore, exegetes should not read the three distinctions into NT texts that speak of the law as a singular entity. Furthermore, one will find it challenging to divide all laws into three neat, watertight compartments. [26]

So, as Tony Blair said on his last appearance at the dispatch box, 'That is that. The end.' There we have it, the orthodox view, two thousand years of Christian teaching, written off in seventy-five words—seventy-five words of tilting at windmills, seventy-five words that make one wonder if the author has ever read the confessional explanations of the threefold division. It is not necessary to read beyond *The Westminster Confession* 19.3 to see that the oft-repeated claim that the traditional view divides 'all laws into three neat, watertight compartments' is false. Ceremonial laws, says the confession, contain 'several typical ordinances, *partly* of worship, prefiguring Christ…and *partly* of divers instructions of moral duties.' Nonetheless, many who reject the threefold division do so because they do not believe it is biblical. The chapters that follow will therefore discuss the biblical and theological basis for the threefold division of the law. Before coming to that, however, I will summarise recent comment on the subject, sketch the historical roots of the doctrine, and say something about theological method.

FOR OR AGAINST? MOSTLY AGAINST

According to John Barton, 'Protestant moral teaching' differs from Catholic moral theology in that 'it has often only concerned itself with the right way of life for those who have made a decision

26   Jason C. Meyer, *The End of the Law: Mosaic Covenant in Pauline Theology* (Nashville: B & H Publishing Group, 2009), 282.

for God in Christ and therefore live within the fellowship of the church.'[27] Samuel Balentine similarly singles out Protestantism for special criticism, accusing Reformation theology (and Wellhausen) of leaving Protestantism with a negative view of the Law that led to 'the church's complicity in interpreting the Jewish legacy...as a "question" that prepared the sick of soul to seek a "final solution".'[28] Such assessments may be justified if Balentine is thinking of German Protestantism or an American Baptist setting, but areas mainly influenced by Genevan Protestantism have exhibited different tendencies. In the Highlands of Scotland, the context with which I am most familiar, the threefold division of the law had a practical impact on church and community. Not so long ago, the Ten Commandments were posted on the school wall and anyone seen working on the Sabbath might well be told to stop. Perhaps it was such attitudes that prompted William Still to accuse Free Presbyterians[29] of 'taking the whole Bible and filing it down to one fine point, like a pyramid, cone, or spinning top, so that you can poise the whole on one all-important, all-exclusive and all-inclusive point, namely the Sabbath Day. This is the whole law; there is no other. You can sin as much as you like against all the other nine commandments.'[30] Although this is an absurd overstatement, Sinai's shadow undoubtedly fell over the Highland church and community.

27   John Barton, *Ethics and the Old Testament* (Harrisburg, Trinity Press International, 1998), 60.

28   Samuel E. Balentine, *The Torah's Vision of Worship* (Minneapolis: Fortress Press, 1999), 73.

29   The Free Presbyterian Church was formed in 1893 by ministers and students of the Free Church who objected to the Declaratory Act passed by the Free Church General Assembly in 1892. For a brief account of these events and the Highland origins of the Free Presbyterian Church see: James Lachlan MacLeod, 'The Second Disruption: the Origins of the Free Presbyterian Church of 1893', *SBET* 16 (1998): 5–18.

30   William Still, *The Work of the Pastor* (Fearn: Christian Focus, 2010), 72.

The confessional teaching on the threefold division of the law became an issue at the Free Church of Scotland[31] General Assembly in 1997. A committee report called on the Assembly to declare that the teachings of Theonomy[32] 'contradict the Confession of Faith'.[33] The basis for this was that 'Theonomy is clear in its rejection of a distinction between civil and moral' but 'the Confession teaches a threefold distinction in the Law.'[34]

Anyone reading the literature that debates those issues may notice that the threefold division comes under censure from recent writers. The validity or invalidity of the division concerns those bound to uphold it by their subscription to certain Reformed confessions, while some Evangelicals[35] discuss it in the context of the debate between Dispensationalism[36] and Covenant Theology.

31   The Free Church was formed in 1843 by ministers who separated from the Church of Scotland. Today, her congregations are mainly in the Highlands and Islands. See G. N. M. Collins, *The Heritage of Our Fathers—The Free Church of Scotland: Her Origin and Testimony* (Edinburgh: Knox Press, 1976).

32   Theonomists believe that all Old Testament law (with the exception of ceremonial law) is still binding today.

33   'Theonomy and the Confession of Faith', *Reports to the General Assembly of the Free Church of Scotland: 1997, 40.*

34   Ibid., 36. The Assembly eventually voted for the committee's report.

35   What is an evangelical? For the secular media, an evangelical is a Bible-basher—the kind of fellow who makes Silvio Berlusconi sound sensible. I will use the term to refer primarily to North-American Baptists and British Anglicans who maintain the supreme authority of Scripture on its own terms, although it is tempting to answer the question with David Wells and say, 'Well, that all depends' (David Wells, 'On Being Evangelical: Some Theological Differences and Similarites' in Mark A. Noll, David W. Bebbington, and George A Rawlyk (eds.), *Evangelicalism: Comparative Studies of Popular Protestantism in North America, the British Isles, and Beyond, 1700–1990*, (Oxford: OUP, 1994), 407).

36   Dispensationalists believe God's dealings with man are made up of several dispensations. Although dispensationalism is changing, most think there are between four and eight dispensations, normally seven: Innocence, conscience, human government, promise, law, grace and kingdom. Dispensationalism stands in contrast to covenant theology which emphasises the unity of God's dealings with man in the covenant of grace.

Writing in 1955, Maurice Wiles acknowledges the division 'has been basic to almost all Christian interpretation...right down the ages', yet rejects it:

> I do not believe that there can be found any trace of such a distinction in the mind or writings of St. Paul....Nor does it appear that such a distinction was common to contemporary Judaism...Those who have later emphasized the writing of the Ten Commandments by the finger of God as evidence of the especial closeness of at least that part of the law to the perfect divine will are indulging in an argument which is the exact opposite of that employed by St. Paul.[37]

Chapter eight will consider the claim that Paul knew nothing of this distinction, while the following chapters will show that Wiles was wrong to suggest first century Judaism was oblivious to distinctions in the law and particularly to suggest the elevation of the Decalogue was a later emphasis.

Claiming to hold a 'modified Lutheran view'[38] of the law, Douglas Moo is a more recent critic of this 'hallowed theological tradition'. Its divisions are simply 'too neat',[39] it 'does not hold up under close scrutiny...it is not easy even within the Ten Commandments to distinguish clearly between what is "moral"...and what is not.'[40] He too thinks that first century Jews did not divide the law, but saw it as a unity.[41]

37   M. F. Wiles, 'St Paul's Conception of Law', *Churchman* LXIX (1955–6): 148.

38   Douglas J. Moo, 'The Law of Christ as the Fulfillment of the Law of Moses: A Modified Lutheran View', in *The Law, the Gospel and the Modern Christian: Five Views*, ed. Wayne G. Strickland (Grand Rapids: Zondervan, 1993), 319. According to Moo, 'Luther himself saw Law and Gospel as discontinuous and made the distinction between these two basic to his theology. This distinction has continued to be central to Lutheran theology, and I think that is both biblical and important. But I also think that the traditional approach needs to be modified by greater attention to the salvation-historical perspective of the Scriptures.'

39   Ibid., 343.
40   Ibid., 336.
41   Ibid., 337.

Moo appeals for support to Richard Longenecker who asserts that not even a division between 'the ethical kernel and the ceremonial husk' can be substantiated from Paul's writings. There 'is no real reason for believing that Paul differed from contemporary Judaism in its insistence that the ethical and ceremonial aspects of the Law together make up one indivisible whole.'[42] It is unclear if Longenecker's rejection of a distinction between ethical and ceremonial mirrors Wiles' and Moo's rejection of the Decalogue's distinctiveness, but first century Jews could hold that as a revelation of the divine requirements, the law was an indivisible whole, yet at the same time recognise distinctive aspects of that indivisible whole, such as the Decalogue.

O'Donovan agrees that the threefold division is inadequate, but finds criticism of it on the basis that Judaism did not follow it unimpressive. His argument is not that Judaism recognised the distinctiveness of the Decalogue, but that such a criticism 'betrays a misunderstanding. The threefold distinction was never supposed to be "descriptive ethics", an account of the way Israel interpreted its obligations.'[43]

Writing in 1989, Norman Geisler gives a Dispensationalist view of the threefold division. He struggles with the idea that the 'moral' part of the Mosaic Law still binds Christians, arguing that at no point does Scripture categorise the law in this way:

> The Law of Moses was a unit. There were civil aspects to the moral law, and moral dimensions of the civil law. Indeed there were moral aspects of the ceremonial law...nowhere in the New Testament does it declare that only the ceremonial aspects of the Law of Moses have been abolished.[44]

42   Richard N. Longenecker, *Paul, Apostle of Liberty* (Grand Rapids: Baker, 1980), 119.
43   O. M. T. O'Donovan, 'Towards an Interpretation of Biblical Ethics', *Tyndale Bulletin* 27 (1976): 60.
44   Norman L. Geisler, 'Dispensationalism and Ethics', *Transformation* 6 no. 1 (1989): 8.

Quoting James 2:10 as his proof text for the unity of the law, he gives well-rehearsed Dispensationalist arguments against Christians being bound by any part of the law.

Noted for his writing on Old Testament ethics, Christopher Wright thinks approaching the law from those traditional categories is 'not a very fruitful way in to discovering the ethical relevance of the law as a whole'.[45] His classification of the laws extends not to three groups, but five, which are not 'designed to answer the question, "Which laws are, and which are not, still relevant to us?" Rather, it will enable us to work out the moral relevance of the whole in an authentic context.'[46] The merits of Wright's fivefold division will be examined in chapter three, but the implication that proponents of the threefold division saw some law as irrelevant is unfair. Even if the ceremonial law was non-binding it was still 'relevant to us'.[47] Wright goes on to argue that it is 'futile…to think of isolating a separate category of "moral law". There is too much overlap between the categories. Some laws can be a combination…and there are moral principles to be found in all the categories. Not even the Decalogue is "simple moral law".'[48] In this case also, if he is implying that proponents of the threefold division have recognised 'moral principles' only in the Decalogue, he is misrepresenting their view. It is intrinsic to the threefold division that the 'judicial laws' contain 'general equity', that is 'moral principles'.[49]

Gordon Wenham notes that despite Paul's insistence that 'all Scripture is inspired and profitable', for many people only the moral law is binding. He views the threefold division as

45   Christopher J Wright, *Living as the People of God* (Leicester: IVP, 1983), 152.
46   Ibid.
47   See *WCF* XIX.3.
48   Wright, *Living as the People of God*, 158.
49   For an account of the historical development of the term 'general equity' see Harold G. Cunningham, 'God's Law, "General Equity" and the Westminster Confession of Faith.' *Tyndale Bulletin* 58.2 (2007), 289–312.

a 'convenient framework', yet 'arbitrary and artificial'; unjustifiable
from the New Testament, difficult to apply, and weakened by
the civil law's grounding in the moral.[50] Nevertheless, Wenham
argues the personal ethics of Old and New Testaments are
in 'broad agreement'. Law forms part of the covenant God
makes with his people in both cases (Gen. 17:1; 2 Sam. 7:14;
Matt. 5:17–48). Although he does not accept the threefold
division, he believes 'some injunctions are broad and generally
applicable to most societies, while others are more specific and
directed at the particular social problems of ancient Israel…the
principles underlying the OT are valid and authoritative for the
Christian, but the particular applications found in the OT may
not be.'[51] There is a similarity between his view and the threefold
division in that he recognises certain parts of the law as universal
in scope and authoritative (at least for the Christian), but also
dissimilarity in that those parts of the law are not necessarily
the Ten Commandments. On the matter of ceremonial law, he
is convinced it is of considerable importance as the theological
model for the atoning work of Christ.

Until his death in 1995, Greg Bahnsen was Theonomy's
chief exegete. Curiously, he tried to uphold his subscription to
The Westminster Confession while arguing for what amounted
to a twofold division of the law. On the one hand he commends
Samuel Bolton, one of the commissioners to the Westminster
Assembly, for recognising 'that the Old Testament corpus of
law was easily categorized into moral, judicial and ceremonial
laws'.[52] Arguments for the unity of the law are, wrote Bahnsen,
'simplistic and fallacious'.[53] The curiosity is that earlier in the same
book he proposes the 'most fundamental distinction to be drawn

50   Gordon Wenham, *Leviticus* (Grand Rapids: Eerdmans, 1979), 32–3.
51   Ibid., 35.
52   Greg L. Bahnsen, *By This Standard* (Tyler: Institute for Christian
Economics, 1985), 174.
53   Ibid., 315.

between Old Testament laws is between *moral* and *ceremonial* laws'.[54] He then finds two subdivisions within the moral laws: the Decalogue and laws that bring out its full meaning 'by way of illustrative application'; the latter being what he at another point classifies as the 'judicial' law. The only certainty about Bahnsen's position is that he believed the law had divisions.

Knox Chamblin, a professor at Reformed Theological Seminary, believes the threefold division 'can be misleading, because both OT and NT normally use the term 'law' to speak of the *whole* Mosaic Law', but the 'distinctions remain useful, if we do not allow them to become *divisions* and if we speak of *three dimensions of the one law* rather than of three kinds of law.'[55] This, however, is to take the term 'division' out of its theological context and make more of it than necessary. While 'division' generally describes this framework for interpretation of the law, it need not be interpreted in the strongest terms. Whether the reference is to the law or to an army, 'division' does not necessarily imply disunity. In some contexts, it merely highlights different categories and functions of the one thing.

Vern Poythress, of Westminster Theological Seminary,[56] seems unenthusiastic about this element of his confession. Distinctions are not useless, yet 'the simple distinction between moral and ceremonial does not reveal the full richness of God's law.'[57] Such a 'neat, pure separation...is not to be found in Matthew as a whole or in Matthew 5:17–20 in particular.'[58]

54   Ibid., 135.

55   Knox Chamblin, 'The Law of Moses and the Law of Christ' in *Continuity and Discontinuity*, John S. Feinberg, ed. (Wheaton: Crossway Books, 1988), 183.

56   It prepares men 'to propagate and defend, in its genuineness, simplicity, and fulness, that system of religious belief and practice which is set forth in the Westminster Confession of Faith and Catechisms.' *Catalog for the Academic Years 1994–1996* (Philadelphia: Westminster Theological Seminary), 5.

57   Vern Poythress, *The Shadow of Christ in the Law of Moses* (Brentwood: Wolgemuth & Hyatt, 1991), 100.

58   Ibid., 283.

Poythress' former colleague, Sinclair Ferguson, does not welcome the dismissal of the threefold division. 'The wholesale rejection of the value of this categorisation is premature...only given
this premise does Jesus' insistence that he fulfils rather than abolishes the law make sense (Mt 5:17–20).'[59] Such a categorisation,
he suggests, is an underlying assumption in both Testaments.[60]

For D. A. Carson, 'legitimate distinctions may be deduced from
Scripture even though they may not be explicitly taught',[61] but this
does not lead him to endorse the threefold division. Like Meyer
and others, he imposes the idea of neatness on the classification,
writing, 'it is not self-evident that either Old or New Testament
writers neatly classify Old Testament law in those categories in
such a way as to establish continuity and discontinuity on the
basis of such distinctions.'[62] The 'problem' with the division, he
says in a more recent article, is that 'it attempts to construct an
a priori grid to sort out what parts of the law Christians must
keep or do, and holds that Paul must have adopted some such
grid, even if he does not explicitly identify it.'[63] Even so, 'we may
still usefully speak of the tripartite division from an *a posteriori*
perspective: *after* we have observed the patterns of continuities
and discontinuities that Paul establishes'.[64]

59 Sinclair Ferguson, *The Holy Spirit* (Leicester: IVP, 1996), 164.
60 Ibid., 165. Dan Lioy of South African Theological Seminary is
another rare advocate: 'The tripartite division of the Mosaic Law is not new,
unwarranted, or foreign to the Hebrew Scriptures. Rather it is a convenient
and valid interpretation of the data present in the Old Testament.' Dan Lioy,
The Decalogue in the Sermon on the Mount. (New York: Peter Lang, 2004), 21.
61 D. A. Carson, *The Sermon on the Mount.* (Grand Rapids: Baker Book
House, 1978), 35.
62 D. A. Carson, 'Jesus and the Sabbath in the Four Gospels' in *From
Sabbath to Lord's Day*, ed. D. A. Carson (Grand Rapids: Academie, 1982), 68.
63 D. A. Carson, 'Mystery and Fulfilment: Toward a More Comprehensive
Paradigm of Paul's Understanding of the Old and New' in D. A. Carson,
Peter T. O'Brien, and Mark A. Siefrid, eds., *Justification and Variegated Nomism,
Volume II, The Paradoxes of Paul* (Tubingen: Mohr Siebeck, 2004), 429.
64 Ibid.

If these statements seem paradoxical, they should be read in the context of his comments about 'Pauline terminology' and what 'may safely be labeled "moral"'.[65] We will return to some of Carson's statements and to questions of methodology, but for now we may note that the threefold division is no impersonal, self-constructed framework. It is a doctrine that theologians saw in Scripture and it is wrong to suggest that they set out to establish it as an *a priori* hermeneutical grid. Interpreters throughout the ages regarded the threefold division as an *a posteriori* framework derived from the patterns that Scripture as a whole establishes.

Walter Kaiser contradicts many when he produces evidence to show that Judaism divided the law. The Rabbis distinguished between 'heavy' and 'light' commands, moral commands being 'heavy'. They did not see the law as 'a monolithic unity', while Jesus spoke of the 'weightier matters of the law' (Matt. 23:23–4).[66] The threefold division catalogues the 'constituent elements' of the Old Testament, functioning 'like our catalogue of literary genres…which were also unknown to the Old Testament writers and readers.'[67]

> Let the interpreter beware, however, for the distinction was not so odd that the ancient hearers missed the fact that the 'Covenant Code' had a heading that referred to its laws as מִשְׁפָּטִים, 'judgments' or 'cases' for the *judges* to use as precedents (Exod. 21:1). Furthermore, they could see that the Decalogue carried no socially recognizable setting with its laws, and that the tabernacle material from Exodus 25 through Leviticus 7 (at least) had an expressed word of built-in-obsolescence when it noted several times over that what was to be built was only a model ('pattern', תַּבְנִית, e.g., Exod. 25:9, 40) — the real had not yet emerged, but was as Hebrews 10:1 argues, 'only a shadow of the good things that are coming — not the realities themselves.'[68]

65   Ibid.
66   W. C. Kaiser, *Toward Old Testament Ethics* (Michigan: 1983, Zondervan), 45–6.
67   Ibid., 46.
68   Ibid, 46–7.

In this quotation he does not categorically state that the
מִשְׁפָּטִים, the Decalogue, and the 'tabernacle material' would have
corresponded to the civil, moral, and ceremonial categories for
the 'ancient hearers', but he appears to consider it a possibility.
In a later article, Kaiser repeats the argumentation above and
adds to it, suggesting the frequent Old Testament call for 'mercy
and not sacrifice' (Hos. 6:6; Isa. 1:11–7; Jer. 7:21–3; Mic. 6:8;
1 Sam. 15:22–3; Ps. 51:17) points to 'a deliberate priority and
ranking in the legal injunctions that had been given by Moses.'[69]
He also raises this objection to the view that the law is a unity:

> This argument that the *tôrâ* is a unity can also be used against the
> position that seeks totally to disengage the gospel from any relationship
> to the law. That same law of Moses in Genesis to Deuteronomy
> includes the promise as well as the legal aspects. Therefore if Paul's
> *nomos* is not just an aspect of the 'law' he refutes, then Paul abolishes
> the promise aspects of *tôrâ* as well. We cannot have it both ways.[70]

TRACING THE 'ORTHODOX POSITION'

In several Reformed confessions, the threefold division appears as
an established doctrine,[71] but when did its inclusion in the body
of divinity become common? Did the hermeneutical structure it
provides come from a single individual? Perhaps the most popular
idea is that it is the product of Thomas Aquinas (1225–74),[72]

69   W. C. Kaiser, 'God's Promise Plan and His Gracious Law', *JETS* 33.3 (1990): 291.

70   Ibid., 292.

71   *The Irish Articles of Religion* (84), *The Methodist Articles* (VI), *The
Reformed Episcopal Articles* (VI), *The Thirty Nine Articles* (VII), *The Second
Helvetic Confession* (XII).

72   Bernard S. Jackson, 'The Ceremonial and the Judicial Biblical Law
as Sign and Symbol', *JSOT* 30 (1984): 26; Carson, D. A., *The Sermon on the
Mount* (Grand Rapids: Baker Book House, 1978), 35; I. John Hesselink, *Calvin's
Concept of the Law* (Allison Park: Pickwick Publications, 1992), 102.

although Justin Martyr (100–165)[73] and Origen (185–254)[74] have also been credited with its creation. Although those claims are often unsupported, it is clear that the threefold division predates Reformed confessions. It is therefore necessary to survey the views of key figures in church history and to compare anything found in their writings with later formulations of the division.

Kaiser suggests that any search for the origins of the threefold division that ends with the church fathers does not go back far enough. While stopping short of claiming that it originated with the Rabbis, he cites Montefiore's and Dalman's testimony to the Rabbis' distinction between 'heavy' and 'light' commands. If Montefiore is correct, the Rabbis 'were familiar with the distinction between ceremonial and moral commands, and on the whole they regarded the "moral" as more important and more fundamental than the "ceremonial",'[75]—they accepted a twofold division. This may have laid the foundation for the approach favoured by some church fathers and later chapters will show that the primacy of 'moral' law was a well-established view.

What is at least a twofold division appears in the writings of Irenaeus (2nd–3rd century):

> For God at the first, indeed, warning them by means of natural precepts, which from the beginning He had implanted in mankind, that is by means of the Decalogue (which, if any one does not observe, he has no salvation).[76]

> The words of the Decalogue…remain permanently with us, receiving by means of his advent in the flesh, extension and increase, but not abrogation.[77]

73 Theodore Stylianopoulos, *Justin Martyr and the Mosaic Law* (Missoula: Society of Biblical Literature, 1975), 51–76; O'Donovan, 'Biblical Ethics', 58–61.
74 Christopher J. Wright, *Walking in the Ways of the Lord* (Leicester: Apollos, 1995), 93.
75 Quoted in Kaiser, *Old Testament Ethics*, 44.
76 'Against Heresies', vol. I, ch XV, *ANF*, 479.
77 Ibid., ch XVI.4, 482.

The laws of bondage, however, were one by one promulgated to the people by Moses, suited for their own instruction or for their punishment…for bondage and for a sign to them, He cancelled by the new covenant of liberty.[78]

Contrary to Frend's claim that Irenaeus did not accept 'the contemporary validity of the stark prohibitions of the Decalogue',[79] the above citations suggest he believed its observation was necessary for salvation. The remainder of the Mosaic Law is what Irenaeus apparently refers to as the 'laws of bondage', which were for 'instruction' or 'a sign'. It is not clear whether he is attributing multiple functions to all the 'laws of bondage' or if he is sub-dividing them into categories that might equate to judicial and ceremonial.

Clement of Alexandria (150–211/216) provides a small catalogue of divisions for the interpreter of Moses. 'The Mosaic philosophy' is, in his scheme, divided into four parts:

> The historic, and that which is specially called the legislative, which two properly belong to an ethical treatise, and the third that which relates to sacrifice, which belongs to physical science; and the fourth, above all the department of theology, 'vision', which Plato predicates of the truly great mysteries.[80]

A further threefold division of the 'sense of the law' follows this dividing of the 'Mosaic philosophy'. It is either 'exhibiting a symbol, or laying down a precept for right conduct, or as uttering prophecy'.[81]

While his ordering of the 'Mosaic philosophy' appears, as the term suggests, to be semi-scientific or philosophical, his three senses of the law are hermeneutical. The later threefold division

---

78   Ibid., Ch XVI.5, 482.
79   W. C. H. Frend, *The Rise of Christianity* (Philadelphia: Fortress, 1984), 248.
80   *ANF*, vol II, Ch XXVIII, 340.
81   Ibid., 341.

reflects those senses, yet they do not foreshadow it precisely. The symbolic and prophetic are combined in the ceremonial division and the preceptive are found in the moral and civil divisions. He did argue at one point that the Decalogue was not to be interpreted allegorically, but later he interpreted it symbolically.[82] Tertullian (155–230) agrees with Irenaeus when he writes, 'before the Law of Moses, written in stone-tables, I contend that there was a law unwritten, which was habitually understood naturally and by the fathers was habitually kept.'[83] This is demonstrated in 'Noah "found righteous"...Abraham accounted "a friend of God"...Melchizedek named "priest of the most high God".'[84] He argues Abraham's faith 'is itself inconceivable apart from the prior existence and acknowledgement of a basic natural or moral law.'[85] Even in the 'law' given to Adam that he should not eat of the tree, 'we recognise in embryo all the precepts which afterwards sprouted forth when given through Moses.'[86]

Tertullian 'is careful to insist that it is the ceremonial aspect of the law only that is finished with; the moral aspect is fulfilled in the sense of being retained and even amplified....The moral law was original and absolute; the other was secondary and only because of the hardness of Jewish hearts.'[87] Andrew Lincoln thinks that Tertullian may have most fully developed the distinction between moral and ceremonial,[88] but he did not explicitly proclaim more

82   Robert M. Grant, 'The Decalogue in Early Christianity', *HTR* XL, no. 1 (January 1947): 16.

83   *ANF*, vol III, Ch II, 153.

84   Ibid., 153.

85   M. F. Wiles, *The Divine Apostle* (Cambridge: CUP, 1967), 68.

86   *ANF*, vol III, Ch II, 152.

87   Wiles, *Divine Apostle*, 67, 69. Also R. P. C. Hanson, 'Notes on Tertullian's Interpretation of Scripture.' *JTS* 22 (1961), 273–9. For Gösta Claesson's English translation of *De Pudicitia*, the document Hanson discusses see www.tertullian.org/articles/claesson_pudicitia_translation.htm.

88   Andrew T. Lincoln, 'From Sabbath to Lord's Day: A Biblical and Theological Perspective' in Carson, *Sabbath to Lord's Day*, 380.

than a straightforward two-fold distinction. 'The importance of this distinction between the moral and ceremonial law in the whole succeeding tradition of exegesis can hardly be exaggerated', writes Wiles, 'It is to be found universally.'[89] Pelagius (354–420) is an example. He opposed allegorical interpretation of the entire law because it undermined morality and because Paul's comments about the law's inability to justify referred only to the ceremonial law.[90] Wiles is correct so long as he is not implying that this was the only distinction they made within the law.

Heikki Räisänen claims that Ptolemy (late 2nd century) 'was the first to make explicit critical distinctions within the OT law itself'.[91] Although Räisänen is mistaken about that, Ptolemy's *Letter to Flora* includes what may be the first unambiguous example of a threefold division in the Patristic period.

(VI,1)…God's law falls into three categories: first the one completed by the Savior, for the commandments, 'you shall not kill, you shall not commit adultery, you shall not swear falsely', are included in his prohibition of anger, lust, and swearing [Matt. 5:21–37]. (2) The second category is the one which is totally abolished. For the commandment, 'an eye for an eye and a tooth for a tooth', entangled as it is with injustice and in itself leading to injustice, was abolished by the Savior through its opposite; (3) opposites cancel each other: 'For I say to you: do not in any way resist the one who is evil; but if anyone strikes you, turn to him the other cheek also' [Matt. 5:39]. (4) Finally, there is the category of that which has been transferred and changed from the physical to the spiritual, the symbolic legislation ordained in the image of higher things. (5) For images and symbols pointing to things beyond themselves were valid as long as the truth had not come. Now that the truth is here, however, one must do the works of the truth, not the works of an image. (6) His disciples made this clear, as did the apostle Paul. The latter pointed to the category of images…by speaking of the Passover for us and of the

89   Wiles, *Divine Apostle*, 68.

90   Ibid., 69.

91   Heikki Räisänen, *Jesus, Paul and Torah: Collected Essays*, trans. David E. Orton (Sheffield: JSOT Press, 1992), 276.

unleavened bread. He pointed to the category of the law entangled
with injustice by saying: 'He abolished the law of commandments
and ordinances' [Eph. 2:15]. He pointed, finally, to the category not
entangled with anything inferior by stating: 'So the law is holy, and
the commandment is holy and just and good' [Rom. 7:12].[92]

The letter comes from the Gnostic Valentinian School and
Richard Bauckham notes Ptolemy's three parts 'correspond to
the now traditional division into moral, judicial, and ceremonial
law'.[93] With specific reference to the Decalogue, Robert Grant
maintains: 'From the time of Ptolemaeus (although he was
rejected as a heretic) we no longer find "double-mindedness"
over the Decalogue, at least within the Christian church.'[94]
Karlfried Froehlich also states: 'The appropriation of the Jewish
Scriptures in a Christian framework was...a main interest
of Christian Gnostics to whom Christian exegesis in general
owes a considerable debt.'[95] Could it therefore be that the
threefold division is indebted to Ptolemy's Gnosticism?

Certainly, Ptolemy's threefold division carries the same
outward form as the division found in later centuries, but the
correspondence is inexact. Even assuming his categories prove
identical to those of later writers, his hermeneutic is different.
None of the Reformed confessions, would support the view that
the civil law was 'entangled with the inferior and with injustice'
so that 'the Savior abolished it because it was incongruous with
his nature.'[96] Later proponents of the threefold division might
also have balked at Ptolemy's declaration that the Decalogue

92   Ptolemy, 'Letter to Flora' in *Biblical Interpretation in the Early Church*,
Karlfried Froehlich (Philadelphia: Fortress, 1984), 41–2.
93   'Sabbath and Sunday in the Post-Apostolic Church' in Carson, *Sabbath
to Lord's Day*, 268.
94   Grant, 'Decalogue', 13.
95   Karlfried Froehlich, *Biblical Interpretation in the Early Church*
(Philadelphia: Fortress, 1984), 11.
96   Ptolemy, 'Letter to Flora', 40.

'needed completion by the Saviour since they [the ten words] did not possess perfection'.[97] Unlike Ptolemy who thought 'some precepts…were ordained by human beings',[98] they saw the law as God given. Even in his own day, his doctrine was problematic:

> A principle of division involving a ceremonial section of the law of only temporary validity was one thing; but a principle of division involving a section of the law…which (in the words of Ptolemaus) included an element of unrighteousness was altogether another matter.…By going so far it had overstepped the mark and offended against the basic principle of all—the unity of divine origin of law and gospel.[99]

Like his contemporaries, later advocates of the division would also have found his approach 'entirely unacceptable'.[100] Apart from this, it is not possible to assume that his categories mirror those of the threefold division. Frances Young claims that Ptolemy's letter 'only differs from what became the orthodox position [the threefold division] in its view of the source of each type of law'.[101] That he differs in his view of the source is clear:

> The first part must be attributed to God alone, and his legislation; the second to Moses—not in the sense that God legislates through him, but in the sense that Moses gave some legislation under the influence of his own ideas; and the third to the elders of the people, who seem to have ordained some commandments of their own at the beginning.[102]

It seems, however, that she has misinterpreted Ptolemy as his three sources do not correspond to his three types. Having

97 Ibid.
98 Ibid., 38.
99 Wiles, *Divine Apostle*, 69.
100 Ibid.
101 Frances M. Young, *Biblical Exegesis and the Formation of Christian Culture* (Cambridge: Cambridge University Press, 1997), 127.
102 Ptolemy, 'Letter to Flora', 38.

expounded the sources, Ptolemy goes on to say, 'This part, the Law of God himself, is in turn divided into three parts', which he delineates as the Decalogue, laws interwoven with injustice, and symbolic laws. Most confusing is that Ptolemy applies the division according to source and the division into types directly to the Pentatuech. Flora could be forgiven if Ptolemy's letter left her baffled as it appears that his letter either presents a fivefold division, three parts of which have an external correspondence to the threefold division, or that it presents a threefold division, which in no way corresponds to the orthodox threefold division, except for one part which has a subdivision that has an external correspondence to the standard division. It is therefore a mistake to see Ptolemy as the source of the now-familiar threefold division. It is perhaps more likely that he was reworking 'the orthodox position' to fit with his view of an 'intermediate' god who gave the law.

For an approach that is closer to the formulation of later centuries, and marginally more ancient than Ptolemy, it is necessary to turn to Justin Martyr, who in the face of 'such speculations', says Young, 'insists on one God...the source of both Law and promises....It was all a matter of discerning the right references.'[103] Referring to *Justin's Dialogue*, O'Donovan points out what Justin considered the 'right references': Justin discerned on the one hand, 'that which was ordained for piety and the practice of righteousness' and on the other, that which was 'either to be a mystery of the Messiah or because of the hardness of the heart of your people.'[104] Yet he considers it 'doubtful whether Justin really intended to distinguish three categories.'[105] Stylianopoulos, however, maintains that in this passage 'we find a tripartite division of the Law....Justin divides

---

103   Young, *Biblical Exegesis*, 127–8.
104   O'Donovan, 'Biblical Ethics', 59.
105   Ibid., 59, n. 7.

the Law and, in some way, all of Scripture into the following parts: (1) ethics, (2) prophecy and (3) historical dispensation.'[106] The quotation selected by O'Donovan and Stylianopoulos come from Justin's summary statement in a chapter now entitled: 'The Jews in Vain Promise Themselves Salvation, Which Cannot Be Obtained Except Through Christ.'[107] He is not at this point specifically presenting the Christian view of the Mosaic Law, but if it contains a distinction, is it threefold or merely two-fold? Is 'that' which was 'a mystery of the Messiah or because of the hardness of the heart' one or two categories? When he uses the terms 'mystery' and 'hardness of heart' they are used concerning laws, some of which, according to the later expression of the threefold division, belong to the one category of ceremonial law.[108] Nonetheless, Stylianopoulos argues that the evidence from the *Dialogue* supports a threefold division for three reasons:

> Justin 'does not include the same acts and same commandments in both the historical and predictive interpretation of the Law.'

> He keeps the categories separate dealing with them in different sections of the *Dialogue*.

> 'Justin in no case interprets the same legal precept or same act as referring both to the mystery of Christ and to what he calls the hardness of heart of the people.'[109]

If this is correct, Justin worked within the framework of a threefold division that had the same basic categories as the division of later writers, yet their content was not identical. What 'was ordained for piety and the practice of righteousness' was, for Justin, not restricted to the Ten Commandments. Even if 'ethical law' deals with Decalogue commandments such as murder and adultery,

106 Stylianopoulos, *Justin Martyr*, 55.
107 Justin Martyr, *Dialogue of Justin* XLIV., Available from ccel.wheaton. edu/fathers2/ANF-01/anf01-48.htm#P4043_787325; accessed 8 Apr. 1999.
108 Ibid., XL, XVIII.
109 Stylianopoulos, *Justin Martyr*, 61–2.

and expresses universally binding principles,[110] Justin 'does not associate the ethical law exclusively with the Decalogue, as Ptolemy and Irenaeus do. In fact he does not even mention the Decalogue.'[111] This does not indicate a substantial difference with later writers who themselves might not always give the same content to the categories since varying exegetical methods may lead to different conclusions about the category of individual laws. For Justin, Jesus 'spoke well' when he summed up all righteousness in the two great commandments.[112] This reference to the two love commandments is significant as they have a long history of being interpreted as a summary of the Decalogue.

Noting Justin's 'stratification of moral, civil, and ceremonial elements in the Mosaic law', Jaroslav Pelikan writes that it 'proved difficult to maintain with any consistency and the fathers could not make it stick'.[113] Given that the stratification has braved nearly twenty centuries of ecclesiastical and doctrinal history, they may have been more successful than Pelikan admits. Similarly, O'Donovan comments that the 'hint of a threefold distinction was ignored by Justin's successors, who made a simple two-fold distinction between the moral commands, valid for all time, and those which prophesied the coming of Christ.'[114] Even where the division appears to be only two-fold, however, it is unsafe to assume that patristic writers would not have expounded what would have been a threefold division had they felt the need to expand. An example of the risk of making such assumptions

110   Ibid., 57.

111   Ibid., 59.

112   Justin, *Dialogue*, XCIII

113   Jaroslav Pelikan, *The Christian Tradition: A History of the Development of Doctrine*. vol. 1. 'The Emergence of the Catholic Tradition (100–600)' (Chicago: University of Chicago Press, 1971), 16–17.

114   O'Donovan, 'Biblical Ethics', 59. He does not reveal what successors he has in mind, but moves to 'a 5th century work known as the *Speculum 'Quis ignorant'*, which may, or may not, be by St. Augustine.'

might be found in the 1559 *French Confession of Faith*, which presents no more than a straightforward two-fold division,[115] yet this does not reflect the whole view of the Reformed church or of that confession's probable authors: Calvin, Bizet, and Viret.[116] In summary, the categories of Justin's threefold division compare to those of later theologians such as the Westminster Divines. Where they differ is in the Pentateuchal content he places within those categories. Whether the division originated with him or he was using an accepted framework, it is possible that the threefold division of later centuries shares its roots.

Moving to the fifth century, it is clear that Augustine did not believe Christians should obey the ceremonial law, since it consisted of 'signs of future things which were to be fulfilled in Christ'.[117] He also agreed that 'Christians are unquestionably bound to obey...that precept of the law, "Thou shalt not covet",'[118] apparently stating a general principle of the continuing validity of the Decalogue. That such teaching would have been widespread is confirmed by Augustine's inclusion of it in the catechetical manual he composed at Deogratias' suggestion.[119] He writes that Christ sent the Holy Ghost so that his disciples 'might be able to fulfil the law not only without its being a burden but even with delight. Now this law was given to the Jews in ten

---

115   'We believe that the ordinances of the law came to an end at the advent of Jesus Christ; but, although the ceremonies are no more in use, yet their substance and truth remain in the person of him in who they are fulfilled. And moreover, we must seek aid from the law and the prophets for the ruling of our lives, as well as for our confirmation in the promises of the gospel.' 'The French Confession of Faith, 1559' (XXIII) in Cochrane, *Reformed Confessions*, 152.

116   Cochrane, *Reformed Confessions*, 138.

117   Augustine *LETTER LXXXII*. (AD 405) II 15, Available from www.newadvent.org/fathers/1102082.htm; accessed 6 Oct. 2010.

118   Ibid., II 20.

119   S. Avreli Avgvstini, *Catechizandis Rvdibvs*, trans. Joseph Patrick Christopher (Washington DC, The Catholic University of America, 1926), 2.

commandments, which they call the Decalogue.'¹²⁰ Christians must not imitate those who 'lead any life that the Decalogue condemns and punishes.'¹²¹ Again, in response to the 'nonsense' of Faustus he sums up his position, 'The moral precepts of the law are observed by Christians; the symbolical precepts were properly observed during the time that the things now revealed were prefigured. Accordingly, those observances, which I regard as no longer binding, I still look upon as a testimony, as I do also the carnal promises from which the Old Testament derives its name.'¹²² Like others before him, he viewed the Decalogue as 'the unwritten or natural law given originally to man'.¹²³ He makes no mention, however, of Israel's judicial laws, unless 'carnal promises' incorporated such precepts.

The popular conception that the threefold division of the law can be traced back to Thomas Aquinas is not entirely baseless. Like his predecessors in the church, he saw a connection between natural law and the Decalogue.¹²⁴ The 'old law' contained moral precepts¹²⁵ all of which 'belong to the law of nature, but not all in the same way'¹²⁶ and 'all the precepts of the Law are so many parts of the precepts of the Decalogue.'¹²⁷ When Thomas asks whether

120   Ibid., 99.

121   Ibid., 119. Christopher translates *lex* as Decalogue, which leans more towards interpretation than strict translation.

122   Augustine, *Reply to Faustus the Manichaean* X.II, Available from www.newadvent.org/fathers/140610.htm; accessed 1 Feb. 2003.

123   Patrick Fairbairn, *The Revelation of Law in Scripture* (Edinburgh: T. & T. Clark, MDCCCLXIX), 45.

124   For an historical and theological account of 'natural law' see the published account of a Roman Catholic–Protestant discussion held in 1996 published in Michael Cromartie, ed., *A Preserving Grace: Protestants, Catholics, and Natural Law* (Grand Rapids: Eerdmans, 1997).

125   Thomas Aquinas, *Summa Theologica* I–II. 99. 2., Available from www.newadvent.org/summa/209902.htm; accessed 5 Dec. 1998.

126   Thomas Aquinas, *On Law, Morality, and Politics*, eds Richard J. Regan and William P. Baumgarth. (Indianapolis: Hacket Publishing Company, 1988), 85.

127   Ibid., 88.

the old law comprised of ceremonial as well as moral precepts, he answers yes and presents scriptural proof for his position rather than simply developing a system of interpretation. The text he uses is Deuteronomy 4:13–14, which refers to the stone tables and then 'the ceremonies and judgements'.[128] He completes the categorisation by arguing there was a third category of judicial precepts. He appeals for support to Deuteronomy 6:1 and its reference to 'precepts and ceremonies and judgments', claiming the 'judgments' are judicial precepts.[129] Aquinas finds further evidence when Paul writes that 'the commandment is just, and holy, and good' (Rom. 7:12). 'Just' refers to the judicial precepts; 'holy' to ceremonial precepts (since the word *sanctus*—'holy'—is applied to that which is consecrated to God); and 'good,' i.e. conducive to virtue, as to the moral precepts. Nevertheless, he accepts those judicial precepts 'have something in common with moral…and…ceremonial precepts', causing them to be categorised together in Deuteronomy 5:1 and Leviticus 18:4.[130]

Although some scholars argue that Thomas found 'in the God of revelation a free Lord who can bypass any moral order among men',[131] it seems more likely he taught 'that God cannot dispense anyone from any of the Decalogue's precepts'[132] and that he held to a threefold division of the law, which did not differ in any substantial way from that of later interpreters. Even so, this does not mean that Aquinas is the originator of the framework. The objections he raises, and later answers, at the beginning of

---

128   Aquinas, *Summa Theologica* I–II. 99. 3.

129   Ibid. 99. 4.

130   Ibid.

131   John G. Milhaven, 'Moral Absolutes in Thomas Aquinas', in *Absolutes in Moral Theology?* ed. Charles Curran (Washington Corpus, 1968), 164; quoted in Patrick Lee, 'Permanence of the Ten Commandments: St. Thomas and His Modern Commentators', *Theological Studies* 42, no. 3 (1981): 425–6.

132   Patrick Lee, 'Permanence of the Ten Commandments: St. Thomas and His Modern Commentators', *Theological Studies*, Sep 1981, Vol. 42. 3, 441.

every article suggest he was answering standard objections to an established theological position. Certain theologians, for example Isidore (556–636),[133] may figure prominently in his discussion,[134] but at no point does Aquinas imply that his interpretative framework was taken directly from an earlier theologian, such as Justin Martyr. To say, like Carson, that Thomas 'fleshed out'[135] the threefold division is probably to say too much. It implies that the Dominican friar made the threefold division more than it had previously been, yet his overriding concern was to faithfully preserve and appropriate 'the insights and arguments of earlier philosophers and theologians'.[136] He was not in the business of plumping out the creed. It is therefore more accurate to say with Casselli that Aquinas' task was 'one of synthesis and clarification'.[137] He 'is not breaking new ground with his threefold division of the Old Law, but he is clarifying and organizing disparate streams of thought found throughout history.'[138]

This section has given an overview of the interpretative frameworks for the Mosaic Law used by a sample of key figures in church history. Although this is not an exhaustive account, it has uncovered the roots of a threefold division that acquired fixed categories in the early Christian church. Its creation cannot be attributed to one individual. More likely, it was an

133   In I–II. 90–108, Aquinas often refers to Isidore's *Etymologies*, Book 5, 'On Laws and Times'. For a recent translation see *The Etymologies of Isidore of Seville*. trans. Stephen A. Barney, W. J. Lewis, J. A Beach, and Oliver Berghof. (Cambridge: Cambridge University Press, 2006), 117–34.

134   For an account of influences, see Stephen J. Casselli, 'The Threefold Division of the Law in the Thought of Aquinas,' *WTJ* 61:2 (1999), 175–207.

135   Carson, 'Mystery and Fulfillment', 429 n. 108.

136   Eleonore Stump, 'Biblical commentary and philosophy' in Norman Kretzmann and Eleonore Stump, eds., *The Cambridge Companion to Aquinas* (Cambridge: CUP, 1993), 256. Also James A. Weisheipl, *Friar Thomas D'Aquino: His Life, Thought, and Work* (New York: Doubleday, 1974), 163–4.

137   Casselli, 'Threefold Division', 177.

138   Ibid., 205.

uncontroversial 'orthodox position' that was restated with increasing precision in theological writings and confessions.

BEYOND THE CONFINES OF HERMENEUTICAL UTOPIA

The first time he delivered a lecture in a German university, Rowan Williams recalls being asked, 'What is your methodological starting point?' 'It may be thought', he writes, 'by insular souls to be a peculiarly Germanic question; British theologians are a good deal more inclined to begin haphazardly and let the methodology look after itself.'[139] No doubt, sound, though unintended, methodology could emerge from haphazardness, but in the absence of guarantees it is preferable to determine aims and methods in advance.

Two factors that make the threefold division of the law particularly worthy of investigation are relevant to methodology: its catholicity and the manner of its recent dismissal. As the preceding discussion has shown, this doctrine is not the product of ecclesiastical sectarianism. The threefold division defies pigeon-holing. But for its easy dismissal at the hands of contemporary theologians, who give little more than a few sentences to this 'hallowed theological tradition', it would almost remain a catholic doctrine. Although it is not without its defenders, scholars who mention it, particularly those belonging to North-American or Anglican evangelicalism, generally regard it with disfavour (regardless of formal subscription to confessions that affirm it). Should a doctrine that has been taught by the church for centuries be so easily set aside? And is it not paradoxical that those who are most keen to do so often belong to churches that vigorously defend conservative morality or Mosaic practices like tithing? This approach to an ancient doctrine calls for a thorough examination of the subject—an examination that considers not

---

139   Rowan Williams, *On Christian Theology* (Oxford: Blackwell, 2000), xii.

only the arguments of recent writers, but also those of historical figures as diverse as Thomas Aquinas and Thomas Boston.

Scripture—the Source of Systematic Theology

The threefold division is normally expressed within the systematic, dogmatic, and catechetical works that express the Christian faith. This places it within the domain of systematic theology, even if it would not always have been called 'systematic theology'. Just as terms like 'trinity' or 'original sin' are younger than the doctrines they describe, the term 'systematic theology' is younger than the discipline it describes. John of Damascus' eighth century *Expositio de fide orthodoxa* may be one of the earliest Greek works to be characterized 'by fairly complete dogmatics'[140] (even if it concentrates on Christology[141]), Augustine's *De doctrina christiana* may have given Latin theology its 'first systematic summary',[142] and some may judge it anachronistic to apply terms such as systematic theology to writers that predate the widespread technical use of the term, but it would be pedantic to claim that it did not exist before then. The existence of doctrines such as those mentioned above, or of creeds and catechisms, shows that from the earliest times theologians were willing to summarize and systematize Christian theology. Their methodology has much in common with that of later systematic theologians.

Since this study will range across two thousand years of history, we need to uncover the common presuppositional threads that motivated theologians and scholars, past and present, to argue for the threefold division. The pre-eminent, chronologically

140   Emilo Brito, 'Dogmatic Theology' in Jean-Yves Lacoste, ed., *Encyclopaedia of Christian Theology*, vols. 1¬3 (New York: Routledge, 2005), 453.

141   Ken Parry, 'John of Damascus' in Ken Parry, David J. Melling, Dimitri Brady, Sidney H. Griffith & John F. Healy, eds., *The Blackwell Dictionary of Eastern Christianity*

142   Brito, 'Dogmatic Theology', 453.

unrestricted, unifying feature of the discussions is a desire to be biblical, to present coherent doctrine and consistent teaching derived from the Old and New Testaments. Those who first adopted the division as a hermeneutical framework and those who enshrined it in confessions, along with church officers and scholars who sought to uphold it, did so because they believed it was biblical teaching. Differing approaches to the authority of Scripture over the 1,800 years (or more) that the threefold division has existed have been less significant than common assumptions about Scripture and a common desire to submit to its authority. For example, despite differences between Eastern Orthodoxy, Roman Catholicism, and Protestantism on the relationship between Scripture and tradition, all those branches of the church have held to a notion of textual coherence and claimed to submit to biblical authority (even if they have not always convinced one another). Like the threefold division, those features have their roots in the Church Fathers. Orthodox scholar, John Behr, sums up the Patristic approach:

> Christianity involves a book. But what is established as normative Christianity in the second century takes this in a much stronger sense: If God acts through His Word, then that Word needs to be heard, to be read, to be understood—the relationship with God is, in a broad sense, *literary*.[143]

For the early church, the 'unity and inerrancy' of this book would have been, says Young, 'unsurprising dogmas'.[144] To Justin's mind, 'because scripture is the word of God, it is infallible and indubitable.'[145] In view of his significance so far, it is worth noting how this dogma shapes his approach to Scripture:

---

143   John Behr, *The Formation of Christian Theology*, vol. 1, 'The Way to Nicea' (New York: St Vladimir's Seminary Press, 2001), 23.

144   Young, *Biblical Exegesis*, 10.

145   Eric Francis Osborn, *Justin Martyr* (Tübingen, J. C. B. Mohr, 1973), 87. [D 29.3 and D 68.1].

Scripture is thought of as one whole, homogenous work. Given the uniqueness of the revelation of God in Christ, to which the whole of Scripture testifies, it is impossible, moreover, that there could be any contradiction in Scripture or that any part of it does not have significance. If Trypho presents him with an apparent contradiction Justin simply admits his inability to understand the passage fully.[146]

Similarly, despite the passing of ten or eleven centuries, Aquinas, whose exegetical arguments I have already mentioned, held that 'the primary author of Scripture is God, or more precisely the Holy Spirit.'[147] Aquinas takes his famous 'literal sense to be that which refers to the intention of the author—who, in the case of Scripture, is God'.[148] Even if 'literal' does not have precisely the same meaning in Thomist discourse as in modern usage, his argument for the possibility of 'more than one literal meaning of a scriptural text'[149] does not allow for incoherence, since, in his own words, 'the teaching of God is a single unified science.'[150]

Acceptance of Scripture's authority and dependence on Scripture as the source of theology continues in Reformation-era writers. It also finds expression in *The Westminster Confession of Faith*, which provides the formulation of the threefold division under consideration here. Despite the turmoil that marked the Puritan era, their statement on Scripture reflects consensus and continuity with tradition—'a tenet passed on from an earlier patristic consensus which found acceptance among Roman

---

146   Behr, *Formation of Christian Theology*, 97.

147   Stephen Fowl, 'The Importance of a Multivoiced Literal Sense of Scripture: The Example of Thomas Aquinas.' in A. K. M. Adam, Stephen E. Fowl, Kevin J. Vanhoozer, Francis Watson, *Reading Scripture with the Church: Toward a Hermeneutic for Theological Interpretation* (Grand Rapids: Baker, 2006), 40.

148   Williams, *On Christian Theology*, 48.

149   Thomas Aquinas, *Summa Theologicæ: A Concise Translation*, ed. Timothy McDermott (London: Eyre and Spottiswode, 1989), 4.

150   Ibid., 2. Incoherence could flow from Fowl's 'retooled literal sense'. See Vanhoozer, *Reading Scripture*, 136.

Catholics and Protestants alike'.[151] The statement commits the framers of the confession and those who subscribe to it, to submit doctrines (including their approach to biblical law) to the sixty-six books of the Old and New Testaments:

> The Old Testament in Hebrew (which was the native language of the people of God of old), and the New Testament in Greek (which, at the time of the writing of it was most generally known to the nations), being immediately inspired by God, and, by His singular care and providence, kept pure in all ages, are therefore authentical; so as, in all controversies of religion, the Church is finally to appeal unto them.[152]

Little has changed in recent centuries so far as arguments about the threefold division are concerned. Those who have argued for it have done so on biblical grounds, while those who explicitly reject it almost universally do so because they do not believe it is a biblical framework.

We therefore need to examine the biblical data used by all parties in this debate with the aim of uncovering the biblical foundations, or lack of them, for the division. Did it survive as an unscrutinized assumption for nearly two thousand years? Have proponents of the threefold division falsely claimed biblical authority for an unbiblical view of the permanence of the Decalogue? Alternatively, are its modern critics simply unwilling to bear the weight of their own theology of Scripture? In his attack on 'fundamentalists', James Barr ridicules those who in attempting to understand Genesis 1 'twist and turn'[153] rather than admit that 'the only natural exegesis is a literal one, in the sense that this is what the author meant.'[154] Barr's accusation may

---

151 Theodore P. Letis, *The Ecclesiastical Text: Text Criticism, Biblical Authority, and the Popular Mind* (Fairhill: The Institute for Renaissance and Reformation Biblical Studies, 2000), 76.

152 *WCF* I.VIII

153 James Barr, *Fundamentalism* (London: SCM Press Ltd, 1995), 40.

154 Ibid., 42.

or may not be just, but what if, in a similar way, many of those who reject the threefold division because of the authority it gives to the Decalogue are twisting and turning to avoid admitting the obvious? Only by subjecting the threefold division of the law to biblical and theological scrutiny can such questions be answered.

In view of the vast amounts of literature dealing with law in the fields of Old Testament, New Testament, and Theological Studies, the aim of scrutinising the biblical and theological grounds for the threefold division might seem optimistic, but many issues that occupy discussion in these fields, such as strictly philosophical matters, are not directly relevant. The variety of approaches to Scripture throughout Christian history and within scholarship could appear to be a further complication. The combined effects, however, of the need to avoid anachronism and of developments in biblical interpretation make the task easier. It might be entertaining to speculate, but it would be incongruous to begin discussing Justin Martyr's view of Wellhausen's Documentary Hypothesis, Thomas Aquinas' attitude to the Third Quest for the Historical Jesus, or the Westminster Divines' approach to Q. The question, therefore, is not whether the confessional statements of a threefold division are sustainable in the light of historical-critical methodology or recent interpretative theories, but whether it can be upheld from the perspective of the common convictions about the Scriptures upon which it is supposed to have been based. This does not mean that the insights of twentieth-century scholars who have adopted a different approach are irrelevant (many of them will feature in the pages that follow). Nonetheless we may not judge the views of the 'ancients' according to exegetical arguments that depend entirely on the assumptions of a later era.

Apart from the need to avoid anachronism, the biblical studies environment is subject to change. The reign of historical-criticism has gradually come to an end with various scholars arguing for a return to pre-critical methodology or a move to post-critical methodology (the difference between the two is not always clear). Peckham, for instance, declares these 'post-critical times'—the era of 'historical-critical theory when literature was thought to reflect reality and when the sequence of literary works was taken as the image of historical-development' is 'past'.[155] Scholars challenge notions that scholars themselves have taken 'for granted',[156] not least the idea of editors, which John Van Seters dismisses as 'highly anachronistic',[157] such that 'all talk of "redactors" and "redactions" should be scrupulously avoided in biblical studies.'[158] Not everyone accepts such assessments,[159] but when academics like Peckham and Van Seters are willing to make unreluctant dismissals of once-assured scholarly consensus, it indicates that they are no longer consensus. In this environment, uncritical acceptance of statements like Crüsemann's, that 'today it is no longer disputed that we have the book [Deuteronomy] in...a later exilic form',[160] might be regarded as what Delitzsch called 'a rash concession to the heaven-storming omnipotence which is supposed to reside in the ink of a German scholar.'[161] As Weinfeld notes, such opinions were under review almost a century ago: 'The contention that the Ten Commandments bespeak a prophetic morality and are therefore the product of a later age has been discarded for some

155   Brian Peckham, 'The Function of the Law in the Development of Israel's Prophetic Traditions', in *Law and Ideology in Monarchic Israel*, eds. Baruch Halpern and Deborah W. Hobson (Sheffield: Sheffield Academic Press, 1991), 109.

156   John Barton commending John Van Seters, *The Edited Bible: The Curious History of the "Editor" in Biblical Criticism* (Winona Lake: Eisenbrauns: 2006), back cover.

157   Ibid., 18.

158   Ibid, 398.

159   See Eckart Otto's review of Van Seters. *RBL* 05/2007, [database on-line]; www.bookreviews.org/bookdetail.asp?TitleId=5237; accessed 29 Aug. 2008.

160   Frank Crüsemann, *The Torah* (Edinburgh: T & T Clark, 1996), 204.

161   F. Delitzsch, *Isaiah*, Commentary on the Old Testament in Ten Volumes, by C. F. Keil and F. Delitzsch, vol. VII (Grand Rapids, Eerdmans, 1978), 195.

time now, ever since Hugo Gressmann submitted the theory
to critical analysis in 1913, in his book *Mose und seine Zeit*.[162]
Contrary to Crüsemann, it seems that almost everything is
disputed. So perhaps it is unsurprising that Rodd judges certain
questions about the Decalogue 'impossible to answer, given the
present confusion in Pentateuchal criticism and the extent to
which presuppositions control the conclusions of scholars'.[163]

It is some of those controlling presuppositions that mean
there is not an absolute divorce between modern scholars and
pastor-theologians of old. James Bruckner writes of a 'general
shift'[164] towards an interpretative methodology with 'a focus on
the final form of the text'[165] and which 'accepts the references to
law as part of the narrative and seeks to understand them in that
context'.[166] Even if ancients might disagree with many moderns
on the historical accuracy of the text, Justin, Aquinas, and the
Westminster Divines would gladly 'assume the unity of the text'.[167]
When assumptions that operate as controlling presuppositions
for modern scholars match the controlling presuppositions of
the ancients, common interpretative conclusions may result
despite differing views of biblical authority.

In a similar way, views about New Testament interpretation
that created a divide between twentieth century scholars and pre-
critical writers have also been eroded. One example is the notion

162   Moshe Weinfeld, 'The Uniqueness of the Decalogue and Its Place in
Jewish Tradition', trans. Gershon Levi, in *The Ten Commandments in History
and Tradition*, ed. Ben-Zion Segal, trans. ed. Gershon Levi (Jerusalem: the
Magnes Press, The Hebrew University, 1990), 3.

163   Cyril S. Rodd, *Glimpses of a Strange Land: Studies in Old Testament
Ethics* (Edinburgh: T & T Clark, 2001), 78.

164   James K. Bruckner, *Implied Law in the Abraham Narrative: A Literary
and Theological Analysis*, JSOT Supplement Series 335, ed. David J. A. Clines
and Philip R. Davies (Sheffield: Sheffield Academic Press, 2001), 51.

165   Ibid.

166   Ibid., 60–1.

167   Ibid., 61.

that each Gospel was written for a particular local community, with its particular distinctives and concerns. For Richard Bauckham this should not be accepted as self-evident. There is 'a perfectly obvious alternative possibility' that 'an evangelist writing a Gospel expected his work to circulate widely among the churches, had no particular Christian audience in view, but envisaged as his audience any church…to which his work might find its way.'[168] We need not assume that 'all readers without exception before the mid-twentieth century missed the (alleged) hermeneutical relevance of the Matthean community to the interpretation of Matthew. Historical scholarship does not, after all, require us to suppose that they were all mistaken.'[169]

Perhaps the reality is, however, that historical scholarship did require us to suppose that all pre-critical readers were mistaken in their controlling presuppositions. The result was a great gulf fixed between textual and theological studies. Divinity was dismembered as a discipline. Yet in the process of this 'disciplinary fragmentation',[170] biblical theology emerged in Europe.[171] At its zenith in the distinct, though not disconnected, 'Biblical Theology Movement' of post-world-war-two America[172] that emphasised the unity of the Bible and redemptive history, this movement is itself now giving ground to other approaches: A 'child of modernity', it is 'subject to the limits modernity attempted to set on intellectual activity more generally and

168   Richard Bauckham, 'For Whom Were the Gospels Written?' in *The Gospels for All Christians* (Grand Rapids: Eerdmans, 1998), 11.

169   Ibid., 47. For a response to Bauckham see David C. Sim, 'The Gospel for All Christians? A Response to Richard Bauckham.' *JSNT* 84 (2001): 3–27.

170   Stephen Fowl, *The Theological Interpretation of Scripture: Classic and Contemporary Readings* (Oxford: Blackwell, 1977), xvi.

171   Ibid. He finds its 'formal beginning' in 1787 with J. P. Gabler's address to the University of Altdorf.

172   For a history of the 'Biblical Theology Movement' see Brevard S. Childs, *Biblical Theology in Crisis* (Philadelphia: The Westminster Press, 1970), 13–31.

theology in particular'.[173] The re-legitimization of reading biblical texts as a unity will remain part of its legacy, but the canonical approach is now just one of many. Werner Jeanrond sums up the situation at the end of the twentieth century:

> The defenders of a purist historical-critical approach have seen themselves confronted by a host of new attempts to approach the Bible from literary, sociological, psychological, canonical, feminist, liberationist, structuralist, and deconstructionist perspectives. All aspects of critical attention which are applied to the reading of literary texts have now also been tried in efforts to interpret the Bible.[174]

To Jeanrod's catalogue may be added the attempt to approach the Bible from postcolonial[175] or queer perspectives.[176] Any approach that aims to be 'disruptive of both sex-gender-sexuality norms and academic conventions'[177] will startle some, but is it disruptive of academic conventions? If Fowl and Jones are correct, there is no reason why, within the context of modern universities and professional societies,[178] it should be so:

> The only ostensible reason for adopting one interpretive interest over another is that it is interesting to sufficient numbers of scholars to sustain its practice....A liberal institution such as a university has a very limited stock of arguments to draw on in refusing to recognize and support a particular interpretive interest if it is not to transgress its own principles of pluralism and act arbitrarily.[179]

173   Fowl, *Theological Interpretation of Scripture*, xvi.

174   Werner C. Jeanrond, 'After Hermeneutics: The Relationship Between Theology and Biblical Studies' in Francis Watson, *The Open Text: Directions for Biblical Studies* (London: SCM Press Ltd, 1993), 87.

175   e.g., Fernando F. Segovia and R.S. Sugirtharajah, eds. *A Postcolonial Commentary on the New Testament Writings* (London: T&T Clark, 2007).

176   For example, Deryn Guest, Robert E. Goss, Mona West, and Thomas Bohache, eds. *The Queer Bible Commentary* (London: SCM Press, 2006).

177   Guest, *Queer Bible Commentary*, xiii.

178   They give SBL, SNTS, and SOTS as examples.

179   Stephen E. Fowl and Gregory L. Jones, *Reading in Communion: Scripture and Ethics in Christian Life* (London: SPCK, 1991), 17–18.

Sufficient numbers of scholars may remain interested in historical-critical methodology to sustain its practice, yet because students of ancient texts are likely to emerge from religious communities that live in relationship with those texts, the concerns of those communities influence interpretive interests in academia, whether they be gender issues, matters of sexual equality, or simply 'dissatisfaction with the limitations of historico-critical research precisely because it yields no hermeneutic.'[180]

The interpretive interests of this book are at least not a minority interest—either historically or in contemporary scholarship—not least because the final development in biblical interpretation that makes this task more straightforward is the effort of theologians and scholars to reunify textual and theological disciplines. As this is a work of systematic theology that reunification is of particular interest. To call it a reunification is not to imply that everyone wholeheartedly accepts the situation any more than to call the 1707 Act of Union a union implies that every Scotsman is a Unionist; it is simply to acknowledge the new situation.

The call for the 'theological interpretation of Scripture'[181] constitutes, in part, a call from modern scholars to pay attention to premodern exegesis. According to Yeago, 'the exegesis underlying classical Christian doctrines is in certain crucial respects methodologically superior to the "critical" exegesis which has claimed to invalidate it.'[182] Shaped by the concerns

180 Young, *Biblical Exegesis*, 3–4.

181 This call had some things in common with the earlier demands from Karl Barth and Rudolf Bultmann that 'historical-critical researchers' adopt 'a more critical attitude towards their own exegetical method', Werner G. Jeanrond, *Theological Hermeneutics: Development and Significance* (London: MacMillan, 1991), 126. For a full discussion of their period and the 'New Hermeneutic', which Jeanrond places 'within the confines of Neo-orthodoxy' (158) see *Theological Hermeneutics*, 120–158.

182 David S. Yeago, 'The New Testament and the Nicene Dogma: A Contribution to the Recovery of Theological Exegesis' in Fowl, *Theological Interpretation of Scripture*, 88.

of Christian communities, theological interpretation resists 'the fragmentation of theology into a set of discrete disciplines', and is 'pluralistic in its interpretative methods; it will even use the interpretative methods of modernity to its own ends.'[183] For David Steinmetz earlier exegesis is superior: 'The mediaeval theory of levels of meaning in the biblical text, with all its undoubted defects, flourished because it is true, while the modern theory of a single meaning, with all its demonstrable virtues, is false.'[184]

Some caution is necessary in applying the principles of 'theological interpretation' to this investigation into the biblical and theological grounds for the threefold division of the law. For example, how 'levels of meaning' should be defined would require extended discussion as some pre-modern statements on interpretation are sometimes understood to imply a single meaning, not least *The Westminster Confession*'s assertion that 'the true and full sense of any Scripture…is not manifold, but one'.[185] This, however, may not be equivalent to Steinmetz' 'modern theory of a single meaning' if he understands that single meaning to be historically limited. Nonetheless, the interest of 'theological interpretation' in historical and modern exegesis, and its desire to bring inter-disciplinary wholeness to theological study, coincides with the constraints of this investigation.

The primary common denominator for most theologians and writers mentioned in this chapter, whether church fathers or twenty-first century scholars, is not simply a desire to recognise Scripture as a sacred text, but that they treat it as authoritative for theology and practice. Systematic theologians across the generations and across doctrinal boundaries have always held 'that

183   Fowl, *Theological Interpretation of Scripture*, xvi.

184   David C. Steinmetz, 'The Superiority of Pre-Critical Exegesis' in Fowl, *Theological Interpretation of Scripture*, 37.

185   *WCF* I.IX. This clause was at the centre of a controversy regarding a lecturer at Knox Theological Seminary during 2007. See www.drsamlam.com/knox_seminary_and_dr_warren_gage_what_happened/; Accessed 29 Aug. 2008.

Scripture is to be treated as "authoritative" in some sense'.[186] For Christians, 'the final form of the biblical texts' is the 'normative standard for faith, practice and worship.'[187] It is possible that one group's approach may not be accepted as authoritative by another due to their interpretive methods. Some may even transgress 'carefully defined limits beyond which lies exclusion from the category "Christian reading" as such, and hence (in some cases) exclusion from the "Christian community".'[188] None of this, however, necessarily implies diminished authority for Scripture in any particular community, and it is 'fair to assert', with Stephen Holmes, 'that there can be no properly Christian theology that does not give at least [first place] to Scripture.'[189] Why? Because 'to do theology…we need, in short, to know those things that the church has found in the Scriptures, and that is why Scripture is "the" source of Christian theology.'[190]

Rejecting Methodological Schism

Inevitably, the Scriptural source that feeds into systematic theology today often travels via biblical theology. 'Systematic theology', wrote John Murray, 'will fail of its task to the extent to which it discards its rootage in biblical theology as properly conceived and developed.'[191] The difficulty with accepting this

186   Trevor Hart, 'Tradition, Authority, and a Christian Approach to the Bible as Scripture' in Joel B. Green and Max Turner, eds. *Between Two Horizons: Spanning New Testament Studies and Systematic Theology* (Cambridge. Eerdmans, 2000), 186.

187   Stephen E. Fowl, *Engaging Scripture: A Model for Theological Interpretation* (Oxford: Blackwell, 1988), 3.

188   Hart, 'Tradition, Authority, and a Christian Approach to the Bible', 186.

189   Stephen R. Holmes in Colin E. Gunton, Stephen R. Holmes and Murray A. Rae, *The Practice of Theology: A Reader* (London: SCM Press Ltd, 2001), 9.

190   Ibid.

191   John Murray, 'Systematic Theology' in *Collected Writings of John Murray,* vol. 4 (Edinburgh: Banner of Truth Trust, 1982),19.

defining statement today is that biblical theology is as hard to define as it is prominent. For Murray, biblical theology 'properly conceived' was exegetical theology that dealt with the 'process' of revelation as recorded in Scripture.[192] It is probably impossible to give a brief definition of biblical theology or systematic theology that will satisfy all of their claimed practitioners, but Krister Stendhahl's emphasis on the 'distinction between what it meant and what it means'[193] highlights some of the difference and reflects the true face of biblical theology in the church and academy.[194] It may be, as John Collins claims, that 'most scholars...would agree with Rudolf Bultmann that in biblical theology historical reconstruction stands in the service of the interpretation of the biblical writings "under the presupposition that they have something to say to the present."'[195] The reality is, however, that biblical theology is preoccupied with the descriptive and with what biblical passages meant within a predetermined literary or canonical context, while the scholarly output of biblical theologians studiously avoids saying anything to the present,[196] and pulpiteers who choose biblical theology as an all-

192   Ibid., 9.

193   Krister Stendahl, 'Biblical Theology' in George Arthur Buttrick, ed., *The Interpreter's Dictionary of the Bible* (New York: Abingdon Press, 1962), 420.

194   This is not to suggest that Murray was unaware of different approaches to biblical theology, only that Stendhahl's definition more accurately reflects biblical theology today. Murray in fact gives several pages to criticising alternative approaches. Murray, 'Systematic Theology', 10–12.

195   John J. Collins, *Encounters with Biblical Theology* (Minneapolis: Augsburg Fortress, 2005), 3.

196   In opposing Räisänen's argument for abandoning New Testament theology, Peter Balla is explicit about method and in his support of Stendhal: '...I would adopt that understanding of New testament theology in which the aim is a description of historical findings.' 'New Testament theology differs from systematic theology mainly in the realm of age-relatedness. The former is confined to biblical times whereas the latter includes theological thoughts up to the present.' Peter Balla, *Challenges to New Testament Theology: An Attempt to Justify the Enterprise* (Tübingen, Mohr Siebeck, 1997), 12, 46, 214–5.

exclusive paradigm rarely take their congregations beyond the hypothesized *Sitz im Leben* of whatever biblical passage lies open before them.[197] It may not be surprising then if 'biblical theology is a subject in decline.'[198]

This would alarm Michael Bird, the 'deeply concerned' former lecturer in New Testament at Highland Theological College, who in a posting on his blog seeks to defend the 'endangered species'[199] of biblical theology. He claims that 'a cohort of Reformed Theologians…are calling into question the validity or results of Biblical Theology'. In the event, he mentions only three—Robert Reymond, Guy Waters, and Tom Ascol—none of whom (on the basis of Bird's quotations) dispute the validity or results of biblical theology, but rather question its validity as the preeminent methodology. The most interesting feature of Bird's posting is his delineation of the relationship between biblical and systematic theology, along with the responses from other teachers and students of theology. He tells his cyber audience, 'I am not implying the priority of Biblical Theology over Systematic Theology, to the contrary, I am insisting on it!'[200] Following Millard Erickson, he also insists that theology must be done in three stages:

197 Biblical theology advocates, whether in the academy or the church, may not welcome the description, but James Barr's distinction between the Bible and God is a variation on this theme that also captures some of the real-world difference: 'Biblical theology has the Bible as its horizon…Doctrinal theology, however much it works with the Bible and acknowledges the Bible as authoritative, in not primarily *about* the Bible: it is primarily about God and its horizon is God. Its task is to elucidate, explain, and make intelligible and consistent the regulative principles which influence or control the action and speech of the religious community.' James Barr, *The Concept of Biblical Theology: An Old Testament Perspective* (London: SCM Press, 1999), 74.

198 Collins, *Encounters with Biblical Theology*, 11.

199 Michael F. Bird, 'Biblical Theology – An Endangered Species in Need to [sic.] Defence', Friday, January 18, 2008: available from euangelizomai.blogspot.com/2008/01/biblical-theology-endangered-species-in.htm; accessed 23 Jan. 2008.

200 Ibid.

1. Exegesis: analysis of the biblical texts in their historical and literary contexts.

2. Biblical Theology: situating exegesis in wider context of each body of literature…Importantly, Biblical Theology looks at the issues that the biblical authors raise in their own language and on their own terms without importing foreign ideas or issues.

3. Systematic Theology: the act of synthesizing key motifs and ideas as they relate to the mosaic of Christian belief done in dialogue with Philosophy, Scripture, and Tradition.[201]

Ben Myers responds that this three-stage model 'is completely wrong…there's definitely no one-way street from exegesis to dogmatics—the traffic always moves in both directions… theology is always there already—indeed, it's already inscribed in the texts themselves, and in the lexical tools which are used to translate the texts…'[202] The discussion is lengthy, but this snapshot illustrates the debate and highlights the key issue in the relationship between systematic and biblical theology.

Self-conscious purists may argue for a three-stage model where one stage is untarnished by the next, but this is a hopeless enterprise. Why should historic Christian doctrine comply with the self-authenticating strictures of academic biblical theology? Those who insist that theology must begin in a dogma-free exegetical laboratory, before the results are analysed by a closed-shop specialist in a subsection of a specific genre and only then passed into the contaminated hands of systematicians, are living in a fantastical hermeneutical utopia. Should a Christian interpreter actually come to the Pentateuch or the prophets without ever thinking about the 'one God in Trinity, and Trinity in Unity',[203] or Jesus Christ 'in two distinct natures and one person for ever,' they are probably more ignorant than brilliant. Exegesis

201   Ibid.
202   Ibid., Comments.
203   *The Creed of Saint Athanasius.*

without dogmatic presuppositions requires the interpreter to do an impossible mind-clearing exercise—only when the Christian exegete has abandoned the creeds of Christendom, set aside notions of creation, incarnation, redemption, and a multitude of other Christian dogmas, may their task begin.[204] Ironically, the three-stage model is not even biblical within the context of canonical interpretation unless intra-biblical exegesis is itself unbiblical. Neither the psalmists and prophets who interpreted the Pentateuch, nor the Jesus and his apostles who interpreted the law and the prophets, did so uninfluenced by systematic presuppositions. That there was a prototypical pattern of sound words to be held (2 Tim. 1:13) indicates that dogma-free exegesis was not even on the apostolic agenda. In contrast to Bird's idealism, Myers position reflects the reality of the two-way traffic between biblical and theological studies. Theologians who see Scripture as the 'source of Christian theology' will explore the exegetical and thematic works of biblical theology in order to develop, confirm, or transform the conclusions of systematic theology. Exegetes and biblical theologians who eschew systematic theology will approach the texts they study under the influence of dogmatic presuppositions—whether they like it or not.

What are the implications of this for the study of an ancient doctrine such as the threefold division? Even if Zachariae 'first gave "biblical Theology" its modern sense of the description of the theology of the Bible in the Bible's own terms',[205] or Gabler's lecture at the University of Altdorf in 1787 was an 'important turning point'[206] in the history of biblical theology, it would be

---

204 A non-Christian exegete would be no better placed, having to set aside a different set of presuppositions from their conscious or unconscious system of theology.

205 John Sandys-Wunsch and Laurence Eldredge, 'J. P. Gabler and the Distinction Between Biblical and Dogmatic Theology: Translation, Commentary, and Discussion of His Originality', *SJT* vol. 33.1 (1980), 149.

206 Ibid.

untenable to claim that no exegete throughout the preceding seventeen or eighteen hundred years aimed to have a theology of the whole Bible, to describe biblical concepts and themes, or to trace topics along a biblical plotline. This does not mean, however, that the dichotomy between the methodology of biblical theology and systematic or dogmatic theology is sealed with the approval of historical precedent.[207] Prior to this methodological schism, a theologian or interpreter who showed more concern for what the Scriptures meant than what they mean would have been regarded as an anomaly—like a surgeon who devoted his life to dismembering cadavers without ever removing an appendix. For Christian theology, biblical theology that stops with what the text meant is no more useful than systematic theology that ignores what the text meant. The threefold division of the law was born and brought to maturity before the two were forced apart. Scripture was the source material from which the doctrine was fashioned. The question this book will address is whether that source was used or abused according to limits that were common across centuries of 'Christian reading' rather than the transient and anachronistic limits that would be established by taking sides on a post-Enlightenment dichotomy.

I have outlined the historical, theological, and methodological context in which this study takes place, not least because 'the search for a context-independent method for either ethics or interpretation is doomed to failure....There is no neutral or apolitical way of discussing ethics or doing interpretation'.[208]

---

207   Note that Gabler intended biblical theology to serve dogmatic theology. For discussion of Gabler's influence see: Philip F. Esler, *New Testament Theology: Communion and Community* (Minneapolis: Fortress Press, 2005), 16–17; Paul Beauchamp, 'Biblical Theology' in Jean-Yves Lacoste, ed., *Encyclopedia of Christian Theology*, vols. 1–3 (New York: Routledge, 2005), 212; Charles H. H. Scobie, 'History of Biblical Theology' in T. Desmond Alexander and Brian S. Rosner, eds., *New Dictionary of Biblical Theology* (Leicester, Inter-Varsity Press, 2000), 11.

208   Fowl and Jones, *Reading in Communion*, 21.

WHAT WOULD MOSES THINK?

> It is evident that the sentence is broken off abrubtly; the words. 'I will
> drive him out,' being suppressed: even as in the case of a father, with
> sighs, sobs, and tears, putting his son out of doors.
>
> *Thomas Boston on Genesis 3:24.*

Theologians and churchmen in centuries past held that Scripture
was the source of the threefold division. They therefore included
it in their writings and confessions. But did they fashion
Scripture in their own image? Could they justify their doctrine
from within the framework of their own beliefs about Scripture?
In beginning to consider those questions, this chapter focuses on
relevant issues in the Pentateuch. Several questions arise:

1. Is the Decalogue distinctive in a way that means we should
   treat it differently? Is there any evidence in the Pentateuch
   that suggests it should stand apart from the rest of the law
   as in *WCF* 19:1–2? Was it 'not so much a new law as an
   authoritative formulation of already existing instruction'?[1]
2. Does either the use of 'commands, decrees and laws' in
   Deuteronomy 6:4 (Aquinas[2]) or the heading מִשְׁפָּטִים in
   Exodus 21:1 (Kaiser[3]) point to a threefold division?

---

1 William Dyrness, *Themes in Old Testament Theology* (Carlisle: Paternoster,
1998), 147.

2 Aquinas, *Summa* I–II. 99. 4.

3 Kaiser, *Old Testament Ethics*, 43–7.

3. Can we distinguish between civil and ceremonial laws? Could all the civil laws simply be seen as a 'pattern' in the sense that at least some ceremonial laws were (Exod. 25:9, 40)?
4. Are there more than three divisions as Wright proposes?[4]

THE DISTINCTIVENESS OF THE DECALOGUE

The threefold division places the Decalogue in the distinct category of moral law, which the Reformed confessions define as the Ten Commandments. The first issue to address therefore is whether such a precise categorisation is warranted.

Was the Decalogue New Law?

In a lecture delivered before the Munich Faculty of Law, David Daube argued that some things in legal history are 'self-understood'. Something might be 'so much taken for granted that you do not bother to reflect on it or ever refer to it....actual rules of law which, because of their absolute familiarity, are passed over in silence when others are set forth...rules which are not, when it might be expected, elevated, or demoted from—custom to *ius scriptum* [written law].'[5] This is a feature of law codes from the Mishpatim to the German civil code, which declared certain things *selbstverständlich* (obvious).[6] When an institution is embedded in society it is more likely 'to be accepted without ado and remain unformulated.'[7]

Calum Carmichael adopts Daube's view in his argument that the Decalogue is not distinctive as an historical development:

---

4   Wright, *People of God,* 152.
5   David Daube, 'The Self-understood in Legal History', *JR* 18 (1973): 126.
6   Ibid., 127–8.
7   Ibid., 132.

Many of the rules in question are ageless. Those against murder adultery, false accusation, stealing, and coveting apply to every time and place. Of his some two hundred publications, David Daube's: 'The Self-Understood in Legal History'…is widely regarded as among his most insightful. In it he discusses why it is that in early law codes, for example, the Roman Twelve Tables and the Bible's Book of the Covenant, some of the most basic rules of law are not found and concludes that "The author is not motivated to lay down what no one questions." Everyone knows the laws. Only matters that require reform or about which there is doubt appear in these early compilations. From this perspective we cannot examine the decalogue as we would other early legal documents. We have to wonder why a lawgiver committed rules, such as those against murder, adultery, and stealing, to writing in the brief, unembellished even banal, form in which we find them in the decalogue.[8]

Carmichael is right to suggest that the enacting of such rules should lead to further investigation, but how far does he take this principle? Would he include the Sabbath as something that was 'self-understood' from the beginning, or does he restrict the 'self-understood' to rules that seem more socially oriented? It is not clear how he would answer this question, but at no point does he say the Decalogue in its entirety was 'ageless'.

The confessionists leave no such uncertainties. The idea that the Decalogue signalled a marked development in the history of law was foreign to them. As the substance of the 'covenant of works', which God gave to Adam as a law, it 'bound him and all his posterity to personal, entire, exact, and perpetual obedience; promised life upon the fulfilling, and threatened death upon the breach of it' and 'after his fall, continued to be a perfect rule of righteousness; and, as such, was delivered by God upon Mount Sinai, in ten commandments.'[9] Paradoxically, this absence of

8   Calum M. Carmichael, *Law and Narrative in the Bible* (New York: Cornell University Press, 1985), 314.
9   Ibid., XIX.I–II

an express advance in the Decalogue made it distinctive for the confessionists. For them, the view that the Ten Commandments were distinctive and always binding rests partly on the conviction that they were the sum of natural law. We should therefore distinguish between distinctiveness arising from an historical development and distinctiveness within the biblical narrative.

Boston's thought is representative when he states that the 'law of the ten commandments, being the natural law, was written on Adam's heart on his creation…it became the law of works, whereof the ten commandments were, and are still the matter.' This natural law 'can never expire or determine'—it 'is obligatory in all possible states of the creature, in earth, heaven or hell'.[10]

According to Fairbairn, we misunderstand Boston if we suppose he meant 'that there was either any formal promulgation of a moral law to Adam, or that the Decalogue as embodying this law, was in precise form internally communicated by some special revelation to him'.[11] This, however, may itself be a misunderstanding, for when Evangelista expounds this view to Nomista in *The Marrow of Modern Divinity* (upon which Boston is commenting), Nomista asks, 'But, sir, how could the law of the ten commandments be the matter of this covenant of works, when they were not written, as you know, till the time of Moses?'[12] Evanglista responds that this was so, for Adam was created in the image of God.[13] Nomista 'cannot but marvel' at this, yet Evangelista sharply rebuffs him and tells of a 'learned writer' who said, 'Adam heard as much in the garden, as Israel did at Sinai; but only in fewer words and without thunder.'[14]

Even if Genesis presents Adam as morally upright before the

---

10   Thomas Boston, 'The Law of the Ten Commandments' in Edward Fisher, *The Marrow of Modern Divinity* (Fearn: Christian Focus Publications, 2009), 50.

11   Fairbairn, *Revelation of Law*, 46.

12   Fisher, *Marrow*, 53–4.

13   Ibid.

14   Ibid., 54.

fall, these statements about natural law being written on Adam's heart, particularly Boston's declaration that the Decalogue 'is obligatory in all possible states of the creature, in earth, heaven or hell', have no explicit textual basis in the Pentateuch. Yet that does not mean there is no foundation for those views implicit in Genesis or in other parts of the Bible. The mere absence of a 'proof-text' does not render unbiblical the conviction that the Decalogue comprised of the 'matter' of natural law, nor does it strengthen the view of Wells and Zaspel that Moses 'advanced the law which God had "written on the heart" of man at creation.'[15] (Progressive revelation does not, as they claim, require progressive morality or an increase 'in the demands of God as reflected in his moral character.'[16])

This brings us back to Carmichael's point that the Decalogue is distinctive in that unlike other law codes, it lays down rules that are 'ageless' and 'everyone knows'. He asks why they are committed to writing in an 'unembellished even banal, form'. His answer is that they are written retrospectively, using 'the fictional device of prophetic anticipation—really a looking back on events'.[17] In a more recent work, he defends this approach:

> I avoid a burden other critics impose on themselves. When they encounter laws that are ascribed to Moses living at a certain period of time, they feel compelled to reject this ascription because their historical sense makes them sceptical....Instead I try to make sense of the fact that the text claims the rules all come from Moses (or, in the case of the Decalogue from God). I see the clue to the interpretation of the laws as lying in the observation that Moses, like God, knows the past, acts in the present, and uncannily anticipates the future. A sophisticated fiction has been created.[18]

15 Wells and Zaspel, *New Covenant Theology*, 118.
16 Ibid., 72.
17 Carmichael, *Law and Narrative*, 318.
18 Calum M. Carmichael, *The Origins of Biblical Law: the Decalogues and the Book of the Covenant* (New York: Cornell University Press, 1992), 5–6.

In discussing the precise relationship between laws and the narrative he argues:

> The salient features of such laws as are found in the *Misphatim*, in Deuteronomy, and in the versions of the decalogue are precisely those...that characterize the narrative portions of, for example, the Pentateuch. The formulators of the laws are only secondarily interested in real-life issues in their own time. Their primary focus is on the history of their own national traditions, the very stories and legends available to us in the books of Genesis, Exodus, Numbers, Joshua, Judges, Samuel, and Kings. *What the laws focus on is the first-time-ever occurrence of a problem and the recurrence of that problem in subsequent generations.*[19]

For Carmichael, the first four words (one tablet) are a response to the making of the golden calf,[20] so 'realistically (if fictionally), they anticipate what will happen in the future.'[21] The last four words inter-link with the golden calf narrative and the creation Sabbath.[22] This theme of creation is then picked up in the first of the last six words[23] (second tablet), which are shaped around the narrative of Genesis 2–4,[24] but obviously not using the same 'fictional device of prophetic anticipation' at this point. Cain's actions are the background to the pronouncements on honouring parents, murder, and adultery,[25] while the last three forbidding theft, lying and covetousness, spring from the story of Adam and Eve.[26]

---

19   Ibid., 11–2.

20   Carmichael *Law and Narrative*, 318.

21   Ibid., 317.

22   Ibid., 325. Joseph Bekhor Shor (France, 12th Century) also saw a connection between the commandments in Exodus 34 and the Golden Calf Narrative. Moshe Greenberg, 'The Decalogue Tradition Critically Examined', trans. Moshav Shorashim, in *Ten Commandments*, ed. Segal, trans. ed. Levi, 90, n. 10.

23   Ibid., 328.

24   Ibid., 326–7.

25   Ibid., 328–32.

26   Ibid., 332–7.

Taken together, those ideas suggest stronger links with the creation narrative than might normally be recognised. The 'ten words' of Sinai echo the ten Divine pronouncements of creation. What is incorporated in the Decalogue 'goes back to the beginning of time.'[27] The idea of God's voice declaring the words may convey 'the notion that the voice is an echo of God's voice at the time of creation.'[28] As Deuteronomy notes, no such thing had happened since creation (Deut. 4:32–3). Carmichael does not, like *The Westminster Confession*, boldly declare that the Decalogue was a later formulation of what was given to Adam, yet he sees a link:

> This explicit link between the decalogue and creation is far more significant than realized. The author of the myth of the origin of the decalogue has patterned it after the myth of the creation of the universe. The decalogue serves the same purpose. Everyone would have known the basic structure of the universe, but it was nonetheless felt necessary to elaborate on it in the Genesis story. So too, everyone would have known the basic rules of the decalogue, but they are set down because an explanation of how they had come into existence was deemed important.[29]

The parallel he draws appears to diverge. He assumes the knowledge of the 'basic structure of the universe' was inadequate to the extent that it required the elaboration of Genesis. On the other hand, the Decalogue (and presumably the surrounding narrative) was not an elaboration of the rules, but an explanation of how they came to be. They were already 'self-understood' and required no elaboration.

Like Carmichael, James K. Bruckner sees a link between creation and biblical law. Using the Abraham narratives of Genesis 18–20 as a test case, he aims to prove that 'creation is the first and normative context for biblical law', to the extent

27 Ibid., 337.
28 Ibid., 339.
29 Ibid., 340.

that 'a full range of law is implied and operative in the Genesis narrative.'[30] The data in Genesis 1 to Exodus 18 'is an *ipso jure* (by operation of law) argument for the operation of law from the beginning of the human community'.[31] This law is not 'consciously rendered. The text does not present legal codes. Law is not referred to as revealed, nor is it formally presented by the narrator or by the characters. It is implied. To this extent its context is the narrative, and the theological context of that narrative is creation.' Even so, this law emerges from the narrative in the form of 'oughts and ought nots' which, 'woven into the foundations of human experience', are 'akin to commands and prohibitions', implying 'knowledge of law, law-keeping, and law-breaking before Sinai'.[32]

Reformed theologians of generations past, with many who preceded them, would have recognised such an approach, although the same could not be said for Bruckner's claim that 'when law is implied in the pre-Sinai narrative it is almost never in the context of a covenant', even in the case of the Noachide commandments or the Abrahamic covenant.[33] Being 'part of the created order', law appears, rather, 'in the context of divine-human relationships, which are characterized by the Creator-created relationship'.[34]

Perhaps Bruckner accepts what Eichdrot calls the 'all too naïve criticism' that 'the crucial point is…the occurrence or absence of the Hebrew word בְּרִית (berit)',[35] so that he makes an unnecessary dichotomy between the context of covenant and the context of divine-human relationships. For Reformed theologians, that

---

30 Bruckner, *Implied Law*, 11.

31 Ibid., 199.

32 Ibid., 12, 203–6.

33 Ibid., 206–7.

34 Ibid., 207–8.

35 Walther Eichdrot, *Theology of the Old Testament - Vol 1* (London: SCM Press, 1961), 17.

relationship is a covenant relationship. The Adamic race was bound to God in a 'covenant of works' the 'matter' of which was the Decalogue, and although some theologians in this tradition, such as John Murray, recoiled from the term 'covenant of works', they continued to see law in the context of a divine-human covenant relationship. This view of the relationship between God and man means they could accept Bruckner's conclusion that: 'the creational context of law…frees the interpreter to speak of law as the basis for all cultures at all times…operative beyond the confines of a historical past or a single culture…the bone and flesh of created humanity'.[36] But for those who believe humanity descends from Adam, and is born into a covenant relationship with its Creator, Bruckner's argument that this universal authority is only possible because law 'transcends the specificity of the concept of covenant', is redundant.

Frank Crüsemann is more specific than Bruckner, when he asserts that the Decalogue was not the beginning of law. 'Torah begins with creation and early history.' It has an element of universality having 'a place *within* it for God's instructions to all people. The covenant and commands of Gen. 9 are directed to all people—post Noah.'[37] Another related feature makes the Mosaic laws distinctive: 'As in the ancient Near East, our laws are a function of the state, but in Israel the function preceded the state and thus is above the state.'[38]

In his criticism of efforts to approach the Old Testament not from the perspective of Genesis, but Exodus,[39] Terence Fretheim also establishes creation as the context of redemption and law. As part of God's redemptive activity, the law was in continuity with his work of creation because redemption restores the possibility

36   Bruckner, *Implied Law*, 209.
37   Crüsemann, *Torah*, 3.
38   Ibid., 15.
39   Terence E. Fretheim, 'The Reclamation of Creation: Redemption and Law in Exodus', *Interpretation* 45, 354.

of 'ordinary human life',[40] even to the extent that as Israel attends to the commands given at Sinai, she moves towards God's intention for the 'entire world'[41] Sinai does not introduce new legal principles; it draws on known law to show the community how to meet the 'demands of creation' in a new context. It is '*a regiving of the law implicitly or explicitly commanded in creation.*'[42]

This approach may seem to lead towards the conclusion that the entire Mosaic Law is a universal and ever-binding legal code because any move away from it would be to retreat from the 'creational end' of redemption towards chaos. Indeed, Fretheim argues that if 'law is given within the very creation for the sake of the preservation of God's creative work', then 'every human being as creature is related to the law by virtue of being a creature.' No one is free of the 'creational demand'. Yet, the law is 'dynamic' because it must connect with the constantly changing realities of creation, and although laws related to worship are in the context of creation theology, they are 'peculiar to Israel's life with God'.[43]

Scholars such as Carmichael and Crüsemann work out their theses in a framework that differs significantly from that of the confessionists. Carmichael's suggestion that the first table fictitiously anticipated the golden calf incident would not accord with their view of Scripture. He might have met with a warmer reception with his claim that the Decalogue contained nothing new, with his arguments to support that from the second table, and with his wish to make sense of the text's claim that the laws came through Moses, or directly from God.[44] The degree of intertextuality that he sees sometimes appears to stretch the text, yet the basic concept that the matter of the Decalogue can be seen in pre-Mosaic biblical history needs further investigation.

40   Ibid., 359.
41   Ibid., 362.
42   Ibid., 363.
43   Ibid., 363–4.
44   Carmichael, *Origins*, 6.

The Pentateuch does not directly state that the Decalogue was written on Adam's heart, but it may show that God acted upon the same principles in his dealings with the first family,[45] so that 'Sinai is simply a regiving of the law implicitly or explicitly commanded in creation.'[46] If so, support for the claim that by virtue of its biblical antecedence 'the moral law doth for ever bind all' could be found in the Pentateuch.[47]

According to Bruckner, 'general theological thinking about the law in the context of the covenant of Sinai has led to neglect of the first occurrences of law in the canon.'[48] There is truth in his observation and some conservative writers question long-established notions of law in the pre-Sinai narrative.[49] A more detailed survey of biblical history is therefore needed to identify examples of the law's antecedence, even for the Decalogue alone. The following pages will show that such examples do exist in the Pentateuch for each of the ten words (taking the breakdown of the Decalogue followed by the Reformed confessions),[50] right up to the point of the Horeb revelation.

YOU SHALL HAVE NO OTHER GODS BEFORE ME. The first of the ten words appears absent in pre-Mosaic history as there is no clear condemnation of polytheists or those who did not worship the LORD. Genesis 1:26 may be 'a counter-assertion'[51] to the gods of Exodus 32:4 and the reference to 'lights' rather than 'sun' and 'moon' (Gen. 1:14–16) could be similarly pejorative,[52] but did this

45 Carmichael, *Law and Narrative*, 339.
46 Fretheim, 'Reclamation of Creation', 363.
47 *WCF*, XIX.V.
48 Bruckner, *Implied Law*, 204.
49 See, for example, Harold Dressler and D. A. Carson's argument against the idea of a 'creation ordinance' in Carson, *Sabbath to Lord's Day*, 27–30, 64–5.
50 *The Westminster Shorter Catechism* 45, 49.
51 Carmichael, *Origins*, 48.
52 Gerhard von Rad, *Genesis* (London: SCM, 1972), 55.

detailed knowledge of creation exist from the beginning or was it later revealed?

Whatever way we answer that question, this could be a case of a law made conspicuous by its absence. Dale Patrick is right that the Pentateuch's way of representing the LORD is 'an application of the first commandment,'[53] although his conclusion that it could not be violated before Sinai is less persuasive.[54] At the beginning, eating of the fruit from the tree of knowledge of good and evil will make Adam and Eve like the only God who is mentioned (Gen. 3:5, 22). The heart of the serpent's enticement is the temptation to set up other gods before the LORD, namely themselves.[55] As Adam and Eve surrender to temptation, they grasp after equality with God, 'snatching at deity'[56] and 'godlike capacity'.[57] Further on, it is unimaginable that Noah, who 'walked with God' (Gen. 6:9), having had such direct experience of the LORD's preservation, could sacrifice to or worship another god before the LORD (Gen. 8:20–1). Similarly, Abraham, Isaac, and Jacob have no other gods before the LORD before he has even declared it should be so. The LORD is 'the only deity on stage.'[58] Closer to Sinai there is more recognition of the existence of other gods, but to choose them before the LORD would for Moses and the Israelites have been absurd following their experience of his omnipotence (Exod. 15:1–18). Hence they ask, 'Who among the gods is like you, O LORD?' (Exod. 15:11).

In such ways, the Pentateuch suggests the patriarchs and their descendants believed they should have no other gods before the LORD. It presents them as devoted only to the LORD. This is not

---

53   Dale Patrick, 'The First Commandment in the Structure of the Pentateuch', *VT* 45, 107.

54   Ibid., 115.

55   John Calvin, *Genesis* (Edinburgh: Banner of Truth, 1975), 151.

56   William J. Dumbrell, *Covenant and Creation* (Carlisle: Paternoster, 1984): 38.

57   Carmichael, *Origins*, 47.

58   Patrick, 'First Commandment', 112.

an innovative claim. There is, says Childs, 'a general consensus that Israel's adherence to one God alone is reflected in the earliest level of tradition.'[59] So when Jethro, a non-Israelite priest, confesses that the LORD is above all other gods (Exod. 18:11), there is 'an obvious polemic aimed at establishing the exclusive claim of Yahweh in the mouth of a pagan.'[60]

YOU SHALL NOT MAKE FOR YOURSELF AN IDOL. It is not surprising then that there is little mention of idolatry (as image worship) in the Pentateuch's history of the chosen people, yet there is enough to show that the principle of the second word was embedded in their minds. The first clear reference to idols comes in Genesis 31, which gives an account of Rachel's theft of her father's teraphim before Jacob flees to Gilead. From Laban's standpoint, the actual theft of his gods is the crucial issue, but assuming the narrator tells the story from God's viewpoint, he hints at the absurdity of having gods that can be sat on— they cannot even rescue themselves from beneath a supposedly menstrual woman (Gen. 31:34–5). This is 'a very sharp judgment' on 'the unholiness and nothingness of this "god"; a woman sat upon it in her uncleanness'.[61]

Following the confrontation with Laban, Jacob settled within sight of Shechem (the city) where his daughter Dinah was raped by Shechem son of Hamor (Gen. 33:18–34:4). Simeon and Levi exact bloody revenge upon the city and its inhabitants, leading Jacob to fear reprisals (Gen. 34:25–31). In this situation, God calls him to worship at Bethel and a renewed experience of the true God brings Jacob to call upon his household to 'Get rid of their foreign gods' (Gen. 35:2), a call that the leaders of Israel echoed after the Decalogue had been given (Josh. 24:23; 1 Sam. 7:3).

---

59   Brevard S. Childs, *Exodus* (London: SCM, 1974), 403.
60   Ibid., 329
61   von Rad, *Genesis*, 310.

As a result, Jacob's household buries the gods under an oak and as they turn from idolatry 'the terror of God' falls upon their enemies (Gen. 35:4–5)—a 'characteristic sign of Yahweh's revelation and his "zeal".'[62] This account of these idols, which left Haran under Rachel and which she left under an oak at Shechem, confirm the Pentateuch's presupposition of the antecedence of the second word.

We may find further evidence in Genesis 6, which repeatedly describes Noah's fellowmen as 'corrupt' (שָׁחַת Gen. 6:11–12). The verb שָׁחַת appears over 150 times in the Old Testament and most contexts require it to be translated *to destroy*, but several times it is best translated *to corrupt*. When this is the case it is invariably conjoined with an explicit or occasionally implicit reference to turning from the LORD to idols. This is true of the Pentateuch itself when God reacts to the golden calf incident (Exod. 32:7; Deut. 9:12) and when Moses comments on idolatry (Deut. 4:16, 25; 31:29; 32:5). Other parts of the Old Testament reveal similar findings (Judg. 2:19; 2 Chr. 27:2; Ps. 14:1; 53:1; Isa. 1:4; Ezek. 16:47; 20:44; 23:11; 28:17; Hos. 9:9;[63] Zeph. 3:7; Mal. 2:8). This raises the possibility that as the narrator contrasts the 'corruption' (שָׁחַת) of antediluvian humanity with 'blameless' (צַדִּיק) Noah, who 'walked with God', he hints that their corruption consisted of turning from the God of their fathers to idols, although he does not explicitly mention idolatry. It may also be that an awareness of this brings Ezekiel to use the example of Noah in the context of idolatry (Ezek. 14:1–20). If this is accepted, then one rule that 'Yahweh acted upon'[64] in dealing with not just Adam and Eve, but all of antediluvian humanity, was that which was later established in the second word of the Decalogue.

---

62   Ibid., 337

63   Hosea's use of the verb 'recalls the usages in Deut 4:25; 31:29; and 32:5, all of which predict the sort of corruption that will nullify the covenant.' Douglas Stewart, *Hosea—Jonah*, WBC, 31 (Waco: Word Books, 1987), 147.

64   Carmichael, *Law and Narrative*, 339.

YOU SHALL NOT MISUSE THE NAME OF THE LORD YOUR GOD. The third word forbids taking God's name in vain—that is to use the divine name (יהוה) as a curse, to call upon his name in empty worship as Aaron did before the golden calf,[65] or to swear falsely. The Pentateuch portrays the patriarchs as men who took God's name on their lips with a sense of awe, as when Abraham pled for Sodom (Gen. 18:27). Even men in general 'called on the name of the LORD' (Gen. 4:26). Noah and the patriarchs often have his name on their lips (e.g. Gen. 9:26; 15:8; 24:7; 27:27). Abraham named the place of his testing 'The LORD will provide' (יְהוָה יִרְאֶה Gen. 22:14) and to swear by his name was the ultimate oath (Gen. 24:3), even for the LORD himself (Gen. 22:16). The chosen people hold the name of God in increasingly high esteem as they get closer to Sinai. There is no evidence that the divine name was used flippantly.

REMEMBER THE SABBATH DAY, TO KEEP IT HOLY. The first clear reference to the Sabbath is in Exodus 16 where God promises the Israelites bread from heaven. They are to gather enough for each day except on the sixth day of the week when they must collect enough for the seventh day also (Exod. 16:4–5). The people are to follow this pattern because the seventh day will be 'a day of rest, a holy Sabbath to the LORD' (Exod. 16:23). The LORD sets a rhythm for work and rest in the Sabbath, which he too participates in by not raining down bread from heaven. Were it true that 'Israel learns of it [the Sabbath] only at Mt. Sinai',[66] why would the text assume its existence at this point? Does Exodus 16 not suggest that they were aware of an obligation to rest before they heard the Decalogue?

Superficially, it may appear that Israel was 'not acquainted

---

65   Ibid., 322.

66   Gerhard von Rad, *The Problem of the Hexateuch and other Essays* (New York: 1966), 101; quoted in Carson, *Sabbath to Lord's Day*, 28.

with any sabbatical observance at that time'[67] since some of them still went out to gather on the seventh day (Exod. 16:27). But if so, the LORD's complaint, 'How long will you refuse to keep my commands (מִצְוָה) and instruction (תּוֹרָה)?' (Exod. 16:28) is misplaced; it implies knowledge of מִצְוָה and תּוֹרָה, not least concerning the Sabbath.

Exodus 5 also infers awareness of the Sabbath when it links rest and worship as Moses passes on the LORD's word to Pharaoh: 'Let my people go, so that they may celebrate a festival to me in the wilderness.' Pharaoh, interpreting this as a desire to rest (שׁבת) from their labour, increases their workload, but 'the lawgiver, opposing such an attitude, recognizes the need for rest from labor in Israelite working life, a need served by the institution of the sabbath.'[68] This passage highlights that recognition of this need for שׁבת was acknowledged from the beginning.

The argument that there was consciousness of this need to keep the Sabbath since creation is well rehearsed and often contentious. For the confessionists, 'instituting the Sabbath' was a part of the 'providence of God toward man in the estate in which he was created' (WLC 20) and following his example, was to be obeyed (WLC 120), as he himself later declared (Exod. 20:11). Harold Dressler rejects this because there is no direct command to keep the Sabbath or give it religious significance in Genesis 2.[69] It is, however, mistaken to restrict the fourth commandment's antecedence to its call to rest. When it 'imposes in effect a double obligation, that of making holy the sabbath day (v. 12) and that of working for six days (v. 13)'[70] it incorporates the Edenic

---

67   C. F. Keil and F. Delitzsch, *The Pentateuch* Vol. II (Edinburgh: T & T Clark, MDCCCLXIV), 68–9.

68   Carmichael, *Origins*, 36.

69   Harold H. P. Dressler, 'The Sabbath in the Old Testament' in Carson, *Sabbath to Lord's Day*, 28.

70   Craigie, *Deuteronomy*, 156.

work ethic for which there is direct command and expectation (Gen. 1:28; 2:15).[71]

Paradoxically, for a volume that accuses Sabbatarians of reading Exodus 20:11 into Genesis 2,[72] Dressler goes much further when he says that we should understand Genesis 2:3 'in terms of the ultimate rest for the people of God' described in Hebrews 4:1–10—in other words, ultimately in terms of heaven.[73] He acknowledges that God's blessing (ברך) and hallowing (קדשׁ) of the seventh day is significant (Gen. 2:3), but only 'in terms of an eschatological, proleptic sign indicating some future rest'.[74] But why should God employ such a 'proleptic sign' when Adam's Edenic bliss is in some sense 'rest', which is shattered by the fall, and to which, from an overall biblical perspective, the 'ultimate rest for the people of God' is a restoration? Dressler notes that although God rested on the seventh day he 'needed neither rest nor refreshing'.[75] The same might be true of Adam. God's sanctifying the seventh day is indicative not of man's need, but of the Creator's transcendence. The 'ultimate rest' anticipated throughout Scripture brings God's people relief from their enemies, and the idea that God reveals rest from the pain, sweat, and death of Genesis 3 before the fall sits uneasily with the text of Genesis 1–2. The view of the confessionists and older writers such as Calvin[76] that the Sabbath was established at creation and known before Sinai is drawn from the text less tortuously.

HONOUR YOUR FATHER AND YOUR MOTHER. That honouring parents was a part of patriarchal and pre-Mosaic Israelite existence

---

71   For more on this theme see Iain D. Campbell, *On the First Day of the Week: God the Christian and the Sabbath* (Leominster: Day One, 2005), 48–53.

72   Lincoln, 'Biblical and Theological Perspective', 348.

73   Dressler, 'Sabbath' in Carson, *Sabbath to Lord's Day*, 29, 39 n. 67.

74   Ibid., 29

75   Ibid.

76   Calvin, *Genesis*, 105–6.

is a painless deduction; the headship of the father and obedience of children is woven into the fabric of society. Noah's sons go with him in the ark (Gen. 7:7), while Reuben and Judah plead with their father to allow Benjamin to go with them to Egypt (Gen. 42:29–43:13). Genesis often highlights the filial duty this commandment expects when 'brothers, even if long estranged, come together to bury their fathers.'[77]

Negatively, dishonouring parents is condemned. Genesis contrasts Ham's attitude towards his father's nakedness with that of his brothers and his father curses him (Gen. 9:20–7). The condemnation of Esau for despising his birthright could arise, in the first instance, from the understanding that in doing so he dishonours his parents (Gen. 25:34).

Expanding on the idea of a link between this fifth word and both the Sabbath and creation, Carmichael speculates with Rabbinic exegetes that 'a rule about honoring parents follows one about honoring the creator Yahweh on the sabbath because parents create children.'[78] Eve's words, 'I have produced a man [Cain] with the help of Yahweh' (Gen. 4:2),[79] show that Yahweh and parents have a shared interest in creation. Cain destroyed what they had created and dishonoured his parents because one's creation 'redounds to one's honour'.[80] His relationship to Adam and Eve is the key to understanding the promise attached to this word (Exod. 20:12). In slaughtering Abel, he dishonoured them, causing him to lose the hope of living long in the land (Gen. 4:12) and to become a wanderer in the earth.[81] Carmichael's arguments are partially speculative, but part of the narrative condemnation, or indeed the LORD's judgement upon Cain could be because his

---

77   Gordon J. Wenham, *Story as Torah: Reading the Old Testament Ethically* (Edinburgh: T&T Clark, 2000), 95.

78   Carmichael, *Law and Narrative*, 328–9.

79   Ibid., 329.

80   Carmichael, *Origins*, 38.

81   Carmichael, *Law and Narrative*, 328–9.

crime involved dishonouring his parents. In other words, Cain understood the obligation to honour parents and knew that in killing his brother he was failing to do so.

YOU SHALL NOT KILL. If Cain's moral awareness was sophisticated enough for him to know that he should not dishonour parents in this way, he must have known that he had no right to kill his brother. He at least became aware of this after the slaying when the LORD challenged him and later cursed him (Gen. 4:9–12). The LORD meets Cain's despondency at this (Gen. 4:13–14) with a promise of vengeance on anyone who harms him and the mark makes plain 'that he opposes such arbitrary killing.'[82] This is explicit in Genesis 9:6 where man receives the right to exercise capital punishment, in contrast to the exception made for Cain.

Cain is not the Pentateuch's only killer. To the distress of their father (Gen. 34:30; 49:5–8), Simeon and Levi also became assassins (Gen. 34:26). Moses too carried out a premeditated murder, which he sought to hide (Exod. 2:11–14), and became a fugitive like Cain (Exod. 2:15). Murder was therefore a crime before Sinai, among the chosen people and in heathen nations.

YOU SHALL NOT COMMIT ADULTERY. Adultery, defined as a man intruding into another man's marriage or a woman allowing a man to violate her marriage, is repeatedly abhorred in the early biblical history. Adam and Eve were one flesh and their offspring would become one flesh upon marriage (Gen. 2:23–5). 'Implicit in this description of marital union, as later Rabbinical interpreters also saw, was that it should not be violated.'[83] The first example is in Genesis 12:10–20 where Abraham's willingness to let Sarah disappear into Pharaoh's house leads to his expulsion from Egypt. Remarkably, Abraham repeats the ruse and when

---

82   Ibid., 330
83   Carmichael, *Origins*, 39.

God comes to Abimelech in a dream it is not to advise him that adultery is a transgression of the moral order—he knows that already—but so that he knows he will commit adultery if he touches Sarah (Gen. 20:3–7).

This fiasco in Gerar led to the closing of every womb in Abimelech's camp—a 'cosmologically appropriate consequence', says Bruckner, for an almost-transgressed 'law of creation'.[84] In Genesis, immorality 'may result in catastrophic convulsing of creation in the realm of that behaviour', and this narrative implies prohibitions of adultery and coveting a neighbour's wife.[85]

Violation of the marriage covenant was a serious offence, but adultery could include other sexual misdemeanours.[86] God's judgement came on Sodom and Gomorrah, at least in part, because of their sexual violence (Gen. 19:5). James Miller thinks that homosexuality is 'incidental at most'—it 'merely added color to the story of attempted rape.'[87] Whether he is right or wrong, the situation was so menacing that Lot offered his daughters as substitutes (Gen. 19:8) and the men of Sodom do not pretend their 'self-authenticating'[88] moral values are good or attempt to hide their violent intentions towards Lot's visitors. They are certainly unwilling to submit to the way of another and their threat to deal worse with Lot than with his guests (Gen. 19:9) is, in effect, a guilty plea[89] that leads to catastrophic divine judgement. Following their flight, Lot and his daughters find asylum in a cave. They may have left Sodom behind without looking back, but Sodom has not left them. Having stupefied Lot with wine, they have sexual intercourse with him (Gen. 19:30–8)—something he would not otherwise do.

84   Bruckner, *Implied Law*, 193.
85   Ibid., 198.
86   Childs, *Exodus*, 422.
87   James E. Miller, 'Sexual Offences in Genesis', *JSOT* 90 (2000), 41–53.
88   Bruckner, *Implied Law*, 135.
89   Ibid., 136.

Wenham notes 'striking parallels' between this story and that of the flood. In both stories, children disgrace a 'surviving righteous father'.[90] Miller sees the same parallel,[91] but rejects arguments that Noah's humiliation was a case of castration or rape, preferring to treat Ham's viewing of his father's nakedness as incestuous because 'viewing nakedness is a form of sexual contact.' He appeals for justification to Leviticus 18 and 20 where incest is euphemistically termed as 'uncovering nakedness',[92] but Noah uncovered himself and the text does not support the view that Ham's offence was sexually motivated. Furthermore, a general equation of 'viewing nakedness' with 'sexual contact' does not consider intent.

One of Miller's main arguments is that incest is acceptable in Genesis so long as it is intra-generational and not inter-generational.[93] He bases this partly on his view that in Genesis 20, 'Abraham, the father of the Israelite nation, surprises Abimelek… with his incest'.[94] Abraham's response to Abimelech (Gen. 20:12) is primarily meant to justify his claim that Sarah was his sister, but it could also reflect a shared ancient Near Eastern view that for the offspring of only the father to marry was acceptable. The classification of siblings as the offspring of both parents only emerges in the incest laws of Leviticus and Deuteronomy.[95] If Abimelech was surprised, it was by his near miss with Sarah. Yet,

90   Wenham, *Story as Torah*, 95.

91   Miller, 'Sexual Offences', 44.

92   Ibid., 45.

93   Ibid., 41.

94   Ibid., 46.

95   Levinson argues: 'The more comprehensive ruling [of Leviticus 18:9; 20:17; Deut. 27:22] seems to react against the assumption that intercourse with the half-sister was originally permited, as Abraham takes for granted in his self-serving exculpation (Gen. 20:12). Thus, the one context for the string—sibling + child of father + child of mother—is incest.' Bernard M. Levinson, 'Textual Criticism, Assyriology, and the History of Interpretation: Deuteronomy 13:7a as a Test Case in Method', *JBL*, 120/2 (2001): 228.

this does not mean Miller's first observation is wrong. The mere fact that Genesis begins with just one couple suggests that for the race to be 'fruitful and multiply' brothers and sisters of the first family will have to marry.[96] The point of this exercise, however, is to discover if the basic principles of the Decalogue were known before Sinai rather than to establish the antecedence, or not, of Levitical laws that may have been rooted in the Decalogue.

Past events are re-enacted when, to the horror of another Abimelech,[97] Isaac follows his father's example (Gen. 26). The account of Joseph's rejection of Potiphar's wife (Gen. 39) reveals not only his (8, 13) and his master's rejection of adulterous behaviour (9, 19–20) but also his clear conviction that adultery was a sin 'against God' (9). Not all the sons of Jacob were so quick to flee from sexual misconduct: Reuben lay with Bilhah his father's concubine (Gen. 35:22) and earned his father's disapprobation (Gen. 49:4), while Judah was tricked into lying with his daughter in law and then condemning her to death for prostitution (Gen. 38). Shechem's rape of Dinah was 'an outrage in Israel... for such a thing ought not to be done' (Gen. 34:7).[98] Simeon and Levi justified their revenge on the grounds that Shechem had treated their sister like a whore (Gen. 34:31).

96   Calvin, for example, assumes Cain's wife was his sister. Calvin, *Genesis*, 215.

97   Gershon Hepner thinks he could be the same Abimelech as in the Abraham narrative. This is because he hears in Abimelech's חסד the rare 'disgrace' meaning of Proverbs 14:34 and wishes to connect the story with the narrative about Judah and Tamar in Genesis 38:'By lying with Rebekkah he would lie with a woman he considered to be his daughter-in-law since he falsely claimed that Isaac, Rebekkah's husband, was his son and such a relationship would indeed be חסד, *disgrace!*' This argument, however, is not sufficiently compelling to abandon a plain reading of the text. Gershon Hepner, 'Abraham's Incestuous Marriage with Sarah a Violation of the Holiness Code,' *VT* LIII, 2 (2003): 149–50.

98   'Since the 1980s...there have been more and more voices claiming that the story should be read as the seduction of Jacob's young daughter by the prince of Shechem and not as a rape.' See Yael Shemesh. 'Rape is Rape is Rape: The Story of Dinah and Shechem (Genesis 34)' *ZAW* 119 (2002): 2–21.

Israel and other nations in the pre-Sinai days therefore judged adultery and other forms of sexual misconduct to be evil.

YOU SHALL NOT STEAL. The first recorded theft is Adam and Eve's stealing of the fruit,[99] although theft was not the full extent of their sin. The most prominent examples come in Genesis 30–1 where Jacob defrauds Laban (30:37–43), Laban defrauds Jacob (31:6–7) and Rachel steals from her father (31:19). Genesis 44, which describes the fiasco with Joseph's cup, also confirms that theft was in no sense acceptable before Israel heard the ten words.

YOU SHALL NOT BEAR FALSE WITNESS. Carmichael sees a connection between the ninth word and the response of Adam and Eve when God questioned them after their fall into sin. The narrative indirectly raises the issue of making false charges so a 'norm opposing false witness is readily derived'.[100]

If he is correct, it could be that Adam and Eve's untruthfulness partly leads to their banishment from Eden, as does that of Abraham when he tries to deceive Pharaoh about his wife (Gen. 12:10–20). In the repeat event at Gerar, Abimelech accuses Abraham of doing things to him 'that ought not be done' (Gen. 20:9), which, judging by Abraham's defence (Gen. 20:12) and Abimelech's later concern (Gen. 21:23),[101] referred to Abraham's deceitfulness. Some time later Sarah discovers that lies are not hidden from the LORD (Gen. 18:15) and deceitfulness becomes a feature in the life of her descendants (Gen. 26:7; 27:19; 34:14–17; 37:31–3). Jacob recognised it as something that would lead to curse rather than blessing (Gen. 27:12). In Genesis,

99   Carmichael, *Law and Narrative*, 332.

100   Ibid., 333

101   On the basis of 'verbal resonances' and 'intertextual links' Gershon claims Abimilech himself is lying by implying that he, not Abraham, was the father of Isaac. Hepner, 'Abraham's Incestuous Marriage', 149–50.

all this deceitfulness frequently accompanies other wrongdoing, which leads to judgement. It is a known and intentional sin.

YOU SHALL NOT COVET. As with theft and false witness, there is a natural connection between covetousness and the fall narrative. Such a connection may spring instinctively to the minds of Bible readers because of the link between the words חמד (to covet, desire) and תַּאֲוָה (desire, lust) used to describe the fruit of the tree (Gen. 3:6), which reappear in the last of the ten words (Exod. 20:17; Deut. 5:21). The link is not artificial for the narrator makes clear that from 'Yahweh's perspective the motivation…has to be condemned.'[102] Indeed the fall account chimes with the view that the last commandment 'functions as a kind of summary commandment, the violation of which is a first step that can lead to the violation of any one or all the rest of the commandments.'[103] So for Adam and Eve their covetousness led them to turn from the LORD and steal the fruit.

   In a similar way, it is after Cain 'envies God's pleasure in his brother'[104] that he turns from the LORD and murders him (Gen. 4:3–9). Abel was not the only one to suffer because of fraternal envy, Joseph too attracted the jealousy of his brothers (Gen. 37:11) which led to his sale and 'death'—as far as his father was concerned (Gen. 37:35; 42:36). In the various stories detailing the schisms that destroyed the unity of Abraham's family (Gen. 13; 27:41–3; 37) covetousness breeds strife. It is a 'constant theme.'[105]

GENERAL EXAMPLES OF THE DECALOGUE'S ANTECEDENCE. Those examples support the view that the Bible presents the laws of the Decalogue as antecedent to it, but more general references

---

102   Carmichael, *Law and Narrative*, 335

103   John I. Durham, *Exodus*, WBC, no. 3 (Waco: Word Books, 1987), 298.

104   von Rad, *Genesis*, 105.

105   Bruckner, *Implied Law*, 222.

also show that knowledge of law existed before its revelation in the Decalogue.

Although the Jewish Sages may not have been familiar with the idea of natural law,[106] some held that although Adam, Noah, and the Patriarchs did not receive the law, they still kept it. Therefore God loved them and 'likened their name to His own great name.'[107] This, they thought, was most obvious with Noah, after whom the seven Noachide laws, largely preserved in the *Didache*,[108] were named. Those laws were thought to be based on Genesis 9:1–7 and binding on all men,[109] but as Wolfson points out, Genesis 9 only mentions the laws against murder and against eating meat with its blood still in it. Although no biblical evidence existed for the others, later rabbis tried to find some in Genesis 2:16–17, 'by the usual homiletical method', and decided that they were discovered by '"reason" or nature.'[110]

Whether the rabbis were justified in their exposition of Genesis 2:16–17, this first revelation of God to man was a commandment, the transgression of which would result in death. The fall narrative refers to man gaining knowledge of good and evil through disobeying that command (Gen. 3:5, 22). This does not mean that if man ate the fruit he would know in a strict legal sense the difference between what is allowed and what is forbidden; he was already aware of the prohibition against eating the fruit. Rather ידע conveys that Adam would gain an experimental knowledge of already existent good and evil

106   Ephraim E. Urbach, *The Sages: their Concepts and Beliefs*, trans. Israel Abrahams (Jerusalem: Magnes Press, The Hebrew University of Jerusalem, 1990), 324.

107   *Seder Eliyyahu Rabba*. Quoted in Urbach, *The Sages*, 320.

108   David Flusser, 'The Ten Commandments and the New Testament', trans. Gershon Levi, in *Ten Commandments*, ed. Segal, trans. ed. Levi, 237.

109   Ibid.

110   Henry Austryn Wolfson, *Philo: Foundations of Religious Philosophy in Judaism, Christianity and Islam,* vol. 2 (Cambridge, Massachusetts: Harvard University Press, 1948), 183–4.

without specifying the extent of that knowledge. He would be able to exercise 'absolute moral autonomy, a prerogative which the Bible reserves to God alone.'[111] Hence, we may not conclude from this that Adam either had or gained knowledge of the entire content of the Decalogue 'as a law'. He did, however, come to experience the difference between what was pleasing to God and what was not, which would have incorporated laws found in the Decalogue. For some, the text does not even support that since good and evil is not used in a moral sense; it refers to the difference between what is 'beneficial' and what is 'detrimental'.[112] But this view does not do justice to the comparison of Adam and Eve to אֱלֹהִים. In what sense can אֱלֹהִים experience what is 'detrimental'?

We need not read much further in Genesis to realise that the Pentateuch portrays a world subject to universal moral government. This is prominent in the flood narrative, which states that the LORD saw how great man's wickedness had become (Gen. 6:5) and presupposes that existing moral laws define such wickedness. And 'since it is God who brings the flood…these moral laws reflect the mind of the creator God who stands behind our world.'[113]

Perhaps the most significant reference in terms of word usage is Genesis 26:5 where the LORD records that Abraham 'obeyed my voice and kept my charge, my commandments (מִצְוָה), my statutes (חֻקָּה), and my laws (תּוֹרָה)'. This is the first time the Pentateuch uses those words, which are of considerable significance later.

Twentieth century scholars like von Rad thought this description of Abraham misplaced: 'Not even the Priestly document has a special interest in describing Abraham from the viewpoint of exemplary obedience.'[114] But there is more common

---

111   Dumbrell, *Covenant and Creation*, 38.

112   von Rad, *Genesis*, 89.

113   Dumbrell, *Covenant and Creation*, 13.

114   von Rad, *Genesis*, 270.

ground between sixteenth and twenty-first century interpreters: Calvin's view was that Moses used those terms to 'show how sedulously Abraham regulated his life according to the will of God alone'[115] and Fretheim writes: 'This is no simple anachronism; it carries significance for understanding the place of law in the pre-Sinai period.'[116] Like ancient Jewish writers, they sought to take those words with 'full seriousness'. The Talmud understood them to mean that the entire Law of Moses was revealed to Abraham,[117] with *Tosefta Qiddushin* stating the Torah was revealed to him. He did not gain this knowledge himself; 'he was vouchsafed a prior revelation.'[118] The Cabbalah taught on numerological grounds that the Decalogue alone was in view.[119]

Sailhamer expresses concern that if this verse depicts Abraham as a model of obedience rather than of faith; then, the same composition stresses law at the expense of faith and vice versa.[120] His solution is to suggest that Genesis 26:5 is effectively trying to teach faith and not law-keeping, so that it says: 'Be like Abraham. Live a life of faith and it can be said that you are keeping the law.'[121] While the Talmud wrenches the text too far in one direction, Sailhamer pulls it too far in another, perhaps because he views faith and law as being more antithetical than the Pentateuch itself.

Referring to Abraham's response to Abimelech (Gen. 20:12), Hepner (who thinks that Abraham is defending himself against the charge of incest rather than deceitfulness) writes that 'Abraham's

115 Calvin, *Genesis*, 60.
116 Terence E. Fretheim, 'The Book of Genesis', in *The New Interpreter's Bible*, 1 (Nashville: Abingdon Press, 1994), quoted in Bruckner, *Implied Law*, 47.
117 John H. Sailhamer, 'The Mosaic Law and the Theology of the Pentateuch', *WTJ* 53 (1991): 250.
118 Urbach, *The Sages*, 318.
119 Sailhamer, 'Mosaic Law', 250, n. 31.
120 Ibid.
121 Ibid., 254.

explanation hardly excuses his conduct since in Lev. xx 17 the
Holiness Code explicitly forbids such a relationship.'[122] This,
however, overlooks that in Genesis, Abraham's marriage predates
his call (Gen. 12:1–5) and whatever Genesis 26:5 intends to convey
about Abraham's knowledge of the Mosaic Law, it does suggest his
life was in harmony with later revelation of law—'Elsewhere in
the Pentateuch [Deut. 11:1]' the same terms found in Genesis 26:5
denote 'the whole of the Mosaic Law.'[123] Nonetheless, none of
this is enough to support the Talmudic interpretation or to lead
to the conclusion that Abraham followed the detailed regulations
of the Mosaic Law. It is more likely that Genesis 26:5 refers to
'self-understood' and accepted laws. Moberly's comments on
Genesis 22 give further insight into the Pentateuch's view of
Abraham and are relevant to this discussion:

> The overarching concern of the story is God's test of Abraham (v. 1)
> which is completely resolved by Abraham's obedience (v. 12). The
> meaning of this is illuminated when it is appreciated that the two
> key words, test (nissâ) and fear (yārēʿ) occur in one other context
> of fundamental theological importance, that is Exod. xx 20. Here
> it is explained that God has given Israel his torah, supremely the
> ten commandments, to test (nissâ) them and so that the fear
> (yirʾâ) of God should be before them so that they do not sin…
> The remarkable verbal and conceptual similarity between Gen. xxii
> and Exod. xx suggests that…the passages should be interpreted in
> the light of each other. The likely significance, I propose, is that
> Abraham supremely exemplifies the meaning of living by torah. He
> as an individual demonstrates the quality of response to God that
> should characterize Israel as a whole.'[124]

When this is considered with the Pentateuch's frequent use
of דֶּרֶךְ ('way'; the term found in Genesis 18:19) to define the

---

122   Hepner, 'Abraham's Incestuous Marriage', 149.

123   Sailhamer, 'Mosaic Law', 253.

124   R. W. L. Moberly, 'The Earliest Commentary on the Akedah', *VT* 38
(July 1988), 305.

Decalogue,[125] the narrative anticipation of the Decalogue becomes clearer. God says he has chosen Abraham to 'keep the way of the LORD by doing righteousness and justice', making it possible that Abraham is presented as someone who, unlike the men of Sodom, kept to that 'way' in 'doing righteousness and justice'. Abraham lived in accord with the Decalogue and therefore with the whole law founded upon it. He did not need the Decalogue to know what God expected of him, confirming that, according to the Pentateuch, knowledge of its content predated its delivery.

'IN THE BEGINNING'. One final matter to consider concerning the distinctiveness of the Decalogue is the relationship of the Decalogue and the rest of the Mosaic Code to the first chapters of Genesis. In Genesis 3 Adam and Eve transgress several of the Ten Commandments when they fall, and the rationale for some of the ten appears, implicitly or explicitly, in the prelapsarian order of Genesis 1–2. The older writers who argued that the Decalogue was written on the heart of Adam could at least claim that Genesis 1–2 portrays a sin-free paradise. The first couple had no God but the Lord, they worshipped no idol, hallowed God's name, and it is unlikely that Adam worked the garden nonstop (Gen 2:3, 15). Had they been fruitful and multiplied before the fall, their children would have honoured them. In a death-free world there could be no murder. Where nakedness brought no shame a man would hold fast to his wife. In a world where all was good and pleasant, who would steal? Who would lie? Who would covet? It is easy for those who know the story to respond, 'Adam', but even if Genesis 2:16–17 raises the possibility, it makes no prediction. The Decalogue does include the concepts of punishment ('visiting the iniquity of the fathers on the children') and guilt ('the LORD will not hold him guiltless'), but stated

125   See the section on 'Commands, Decrees, and Laws' and Appendix I for a detailed discussion of Braulik's work on the terms for law in Deuteronomy.

positively, the ten words could be the charter of a sin-free creation. From this perspective, the ancient notion of a world where the laws of the Decalogue were 'implanted in mankind'[126] is in harmony with Genesis 1–2.

On the other hand, it is impossible to think of the Mosaic Laws outside the Decalogue in the same terms. The law codes of Leviticus or Deuteronomy only make sense in a postlapsarian creation. The laws of Exodus 21–3 would be incomprehensible in a world free of slavery, murder, kidnapping, cattle-rustling, arson, burglary, sorcery, bestiality, usury, lies, and lawsuits. If sin and guilt did not exist, if men felt no need for reconciliation with God, the sacrifices and offerings of Leviticus would be meaningless. Deuteronomy's legal provisions—concerning judges, boundaries, warfare, or divorce—can only fit in a world where, with eyes opened, man and woman know 'good and evil' (Gen. 3:4–7). Thus, the civil and ceremonial laws, which can only apply in a fallen world, give priority to the Decalogue, which is potentially applicable before and after the fall.

These examples and observations from the Pentateuch support the view that the Decalogue is distinct from the rest of the Mosaic Code by virtue of its antecedence. It is distinctive because it is not a distinct historical development.

'God Spoke These Words'

Unlike any other nation, Israel heard their God speaking to them from out of the fire (Deut. 4:33, 36). Nothing so great had happened on earth since God created man (Deut. 4:32) and the children of Israel were witnesses to it so they might know 'the LORD is God, there is no other besides him' (Deut. 4:35, 39). Jewish writers see the location of this event as significant: 'The universality of the

126   Irenaeus, *ANF*, vol. I, ch XV, 479.

Decalogue is accentuated by the fact of its being offered in turn to all the nations...in the desert territory ('hefker') which belonged to none exclusively (Mek., Yitro, 1).'[127] God is free, unhindered by human boundaries, and 'lying between Egypt and Canaan,' Sinai represents 'YHWH's unchallengeable mastery over both.'[128] It was, however, first to Israel that God loudly declared the 'Ten Words' from the blazing darkness of Sinai (Exod. 20:1, Deut. 5:5, 22), effectively creating an immediately binding covenant with them, as seen in his reaction to their law-breaking debauchery below the still-blazing mountain (Exod. 32:8; Deut. 9:9, 12).

David Clines does not believe such a thing ever happened and he 'would be surprised if any scholarly reader did either'.[129] Commentators avoid the issue that 'the text is telling us lies and trying to deceive us, and that is a strange state of affairs in a text that is in the business of laying down ethical principles.'[130] He 'can only gasp at the audacity'[131] of the Pentateuch's authors, but scholars of centuries past, Christian believers, and Jews for whom there is 'no voice more central...than the voice heard on Mount Sinai',[132] might well gasp at Clines' dismissive rhetoric (despite his acknowledgment that 'strange and wonderful things happen').[133] For them, God's speaking distinguished the Ten Commandments from the other laws that Moses conveyed to the people and from Ancient Near Eastern law codes that claimed to be from various royal authors. Hammurabi speaks possessively of his laws and places their authority in himself, even if he collected

127   Hirsch, 'Decalogue', *Jewish Encyclopaedia*, 496
128   Jon D. Levenson, *Sinai and Zion: An Entry into the Jewish Bible* (Chicago: Winston Press, 1985), 22–3. Similarly Balentine, *Torah's Vision*, 119.
129   David J. A. Clines, *Interested Parties: the Ideology of Writers and Readers of the Hebrew Bible.* (Sheffield: Sheffield Academic Press, 1995), 27.
130   Ibid., 28.
131   Ibid., 33.
132   Levenson, *Sinai and Zion, 86.*
133   Clines, *Interested Parties,* 27.

and publicised them on Marduk's commission. Unlike other ancient societies where law is 'a human construct', Israel's law is divine speech.[134] This, according to Nicholson, gives 'theological and apologetic significance to the direct transmission of the Decalogue to Israel at Horeb....It was a testimony also to his holiness and wholly otherness.'[135]

When he turns to Exodus, Nicholson builds on Childs' view that the Decalogue's position in Exodus emphasizes that 'theophany and the giving of the law belong together'.[136] Even so, he finds Childs' dependance on the Deuteronomic account mentioned above problematic (although for the confessionists such a method of interpretation would be commendable). But he goes on to suggest that Exodus 20:22–3 supports Childs' argument in that the LORD uses his heavenly speech to convince Israel they should obey the second word. So 'the theophany in both deed and word evokes Israel's "fear" but a "fear" which expresses itself not merely in the emotion of awe but also in obedience to the divine will.'[137]

Nicholson concludes that the divine utterance of the Decalogue 'testifies to the transcendence of Yahweh' and is a 'sign of Israel's election'. The commandments 'came to Israel as part and parcel of her election, as a good gift from God'.[138] These arguments are directly relevant since they consider the nature and theological implications of the Decalogue as a divine declaration. One of the practical-theological implications, highlighted by Levenson, is that the voice at Sinai 'confronts anyone who would live as a Jew with an awesome choice, which, once encountered cannot be

134   For a more extended comparison between Hammurabi and biblical law, see Crüsemann, *Torah*, 15.

135   E. W. Nicholson, 'The Decalogue as the Direct Address of God'. *VT*. Vol. XXVII, Fasc. 4 (1977), 426.

136   Ibid., 427.

137   Ibid., 428–30.

138   Ibid.

evaded—the choice whether to obey God or stray from him, of whether to observe the commandments or to let them lapse. Ultimately, the issue is whether God is or is not king.'[139] For subscribers to the threefold division, those who would live as Christians are confronted with the same choice. In addition, if theophany and law-giving are so intertwined, if unique events reveal the unique God,[140] and if the God revealed is immutable, how can we disentangle his uniqueness and immutability from the Decalogue, making it a merely situational revelation of his will rather than one that is normative and does 'for ever bind all'?

The Covenant — 'Ten Words' From the Finger of God

'Modern scholars are in fundamental agreement,' Crüsemann declares, 'that there were no stone tablets from Sinai, especially not those of Exodus 34. Contemporary explanations of the tablets range from understanding them as geological peculiarities...or purely theoretical constructions.' Until archaeology tells us the answers, we must accept the theories of modern scholars.[141] The Pentateuch, however, marks out the Decalogue from general legislation as 'the ten words' (Exod. 34:28, Deut. 4:13; 10:4), written with the LORD's finger on the stone tablets (Exod. 31:18; 34:1, Deut. 5:22; 9:10). At a deeper level those 'ten words' were the covenant or testimony itself (Exod. 25:16, 21; 34:28; Deut. 4:13).

Meredith Kline suggests that, despite similarities between the Mosaic covenant and ancient Near Eastern suzerainty treaties, the stone tablets are not comparable to a stele containing contemporaneous legal codes. 'The revelation they contain is nothing less than an epitome of the covenant granted by

---

139 Levenson, *Sinai and Zion*, 86.

140 As Wright puts it: 'Unique Events Reveal the Unique God.' Christopher J. Wright, *Deuteronomy*, New International Biblical Commentary, ed. Robert L. Hubbard Jr. and Robert K. Johnston, no. 4 (Peabody: Hendrickson, 1996), 54.

141 Crüsemann, *Torah*, 53–5.

Yahweh, the sovereign Lord of heaven and earth to his elect and redeemed servant, Israel.' It was more covenant than legal code.[142] Making a similar comparison with Hittite treaties, Anthony Philips goes to an opposite extreme, claiming that Israel saw the Decalogue as its criminal law code, although he balances this by saying that it was treated as criminal law since the Pentateuch does not create such a sharp dichotomy between law and covenant and it 'constituted the covenant stipulations'.[143] Kline is right, however, to highlight the danger of obscuring the covenantal-religious nature of the Decalogue, particularly concerning the laws in the so-called 'second table'.[144] According to the Pentateuch, the commandments on the tablets were not merely central to the covenant; they were the covenant (Exod. 34:25, Deut. 4:13).

The placing of the stone tablets beneath the feet of God in the ark (Exod. 25:21–2), instead of beside the ark like the book of the law (Deut. 31:24), further displayed their covenantal nature. This paralleled the ancient Near Eastern custom of placing treaty documents at the feet of the gods to show that the signatories were taking a solemn oath witnessed by the gods.[145] Yet, that God was a party to the covenant weakens the parallel, since it is hard to see how he could be a witness. Thus, Kline writes that while there may be a 'literary approximation to the invocation of oath witnesses in Deut. 4:26; 30:19; and 31:28',[146] 'there could be no thought of a realistic invocation of a third party as divine

142   Meredith Kline, *The Treaty of the Great King: the Covenant Structure of Deuteronmy* (Grand Rapids: Eerdmans, 1963), 16–7.

143   Anthony Phillips, *Ancient Israel's Criminal Law—A New Approach to the Decalogue* (Oxford: Basil Blackwell, 1970), 11–2.

144   Kline, *Treaty of the Great King*, 16, 24–5.

145   Moshe Greenberg, 'The Decalogue Tradition Critically Examined', trans. Moshav Shorashim, in *Ten Commandments*, ed. Segal, trans. ed. Levi, 89; Kline, *Treaty of the Great King*, 19–20; Phillips, *Criminal Law*, 6–7.

146   Kline, *Treaty of the Great King*, 15, n. 6.

witness.'[147] But could the parallel not be sustained by considering the cherubim on the ark as witnesses, at whose feet the covenant was placed? They represent the 'multitude of holy ones' who witness the giving of the Decalogue (Deut. 33:2).

One further correspondence thought to exist between the tablets of the Decalogue and those of secular treaties is that the two tablets were identical copies.[148] The commandments were not divided between the two tablets; instead, one copy was made for the LORD as suzerain and another for Israel as vassal. The distinctive feature with the Decalogue is that both copies were kept together in the Ark, symbolising that, unlike other suzerain, the LORD dwelt in the community.[149]

Those similarities between the stele of ancient Near Eastern treaties and the two stone tablets of the Decalogue, coupled with the Pentateuch's elevation of it, are further pointers to its uniqueness. Nowhere, does the Pentateuch suggest the ten words of the covenant were of temporary jurisdiction. On the contrary, they were words that, if obeyed, would bring everlasting (לְעֹלָם) well-being to the people (Deut. 5:29), and would prolong their days in the land they were to inherit forever (Gen. 13:15; Deut. 5:33). The LORD declared the fourth word and the sign of the covenant to be forever, in the context of his inscribing the tablets (Exod. 31:12–18). The ten words would ever be the basis on which the ever-reigning LORD (Exod. 15:18) would dwell with his people. Their being written in stone with his finger symbolised that.

This alone does not prove that the Pentateuch presents the ten words as universally binding for all, yet at least one aspect of the covenantal relationship between the LORD and Israel operated on a universal level. Obedience to the covenant would

---

147   Ibid., 15.
148   Kline, *Treaty of the Great King*, 17–18; Phillips, *Criminal Law*, 7.
149   Phillips, *Criminal Law*, 7.

maintain Israel's relationship to the land (Deut. 5:33); wickedness, particularly idolatry (Deut. 7:25–6), would cause its previous occupants to be expelled (Gen. 15:16, Deut. 9:4–6). In a similar way, wrongdoing caused Adam, Cain, Abraham, and Moses to be expelled from various lands. The implication is that the LORD reigned over the nations according to a universal moral standard. If Israel fell into the idolatry of the nations she would be destroyed like them (Deut. 8:19–20). The stone tablets laid down the basis on which the LORD would dwell among and be at peace with any people, not just Israel. He revealed the ten words to them not because he would judge only them by this standard, but because of his electing love (Deut. 7:7; 10:15).

וְלֹא יָסָף — 'And he added nothing more.'

Deuteronomy's rendering of the Decalogue is immediately followed by the statement: 'These words the LORD spoke with a loud voice to your whole assembly, at the mountain, from the midst of the fire, the cloud and the thick darkness; and he added nothing more' (5:22). The final clause, 'and he added nothing more', was probably at the heart of the debate between the Rabbis and the Minim over the uniqueness of the Decalogue. It is certain the Ten Commandments were recited every day in the second temple and were of greater liturgical importance than even the *Shema*, but this policy changed around the end of the first century.[150] When it was later asked why it was no longer lawful to recite the Ten Commandments, the answer given was: 'Because of the zeal of the Minim: so that they may not

150   Geza Vermes, 'The Decalogue and the Minim', in *In Memoriam Paul Kahle: Beiheft zur Zeitschrift für die alttestamentliche Wissenschaft* (Berlin: Verlag Alfred Töpelmann, 1968), 232; Ephraim E. Urbach, 'The Role of the Ten Commandments in Jewish Worship', in *Ten Commandments*, ed. Segal, trans. ed. Levi, 163; Urbach, *Sages*, 19–20.

say, only these were given to Moses on Sinai (Y. Ber. I. 5, 3c).'[151]
The identity of the Minim is debated, but Jewish writers have
generally classified them as Christians, 'the Nazerenes and their
like'.[152] Geza Vermes argues this is a case of mistaken identity:

> It seems a priori unlikely that they made a strong enough impact on
> Judaism so soon after the death of Jesus. More important still, none
> of the parties within the early Church taught an 'antinomianism' as
> radical as the complete denial of the divine origin of the Torah. The
> Jerusalem Church would certainly not have done so, and neither
> would the disciples of Paul, who merely preached that the Mosaic
> Law was not universally obligatory. The most extreme views expressed
> in the Syriac Didascalia and the Pseudo-Clementine writings are still
> mild compared with the doctrine attributed to the Minim.[153]

More likely, is the Friedländer and Mormorstein identifications
of the Minim as Jewish Gnostics[154] who, according to Vermes,
'were the ancient forebears of what is known today as »Liberal«
Judaism'.[155] He also argues the Minim's teaching created chaos
that led the Pharisees to embark on 'exegetical acrobatics', which
the Targums' reflect in their translation of Deuteronomy 5:22.
Instead of deriving the יָסַף of וְלֹא יָסַף from יָסַף they took it
from סוּף (to come to an end, to cease) or אָסַף (to remove, to take
away). This was a departure even from the Septuagint translation,
καὶ οὐ προσέθηκεν, so rather than reading 'and he added nothing
more' it now read 'and he ceased not', meaning 'that God did not
interrupt his peroration but »spoke the Decalogue with a single
utterance«.'[156]

151 Vermes, 'Decalogue and the Minim', 232; Greenberg, 'Decalogue
Tradition', 118; Urbach, 'Role of the Ten Commandments', 168.

152 L. Ginzberg, A Commentary on the Palestinian Talmud [Hebrew] (New
York: Jewish Theological Seminary, 1951), vol. 1, 166; quoted in Greenberg,
'Decalogue Tradition', 118; Urbach, 'Role of the Ten Commandments', 170.

153 Vermes, 'Decalogue and the Minim', 238.

154 Ibid., 238–9.

155 Ibid., 240.

156 Ibid., 236–7.

The adoption of this translation seems to have been an overreaction to the Minim, which probably gave them more credibility than they deserved. Certainly, the phrase 'he added nothing more' refers specifically to the ten words: it 'states plainly that God limited himself to the Ten Commandments in his direct communication with the whole congregation of Israel on Sinai'.[157] That, however, does not mean the LORD gave no more laws, only that nothing else of the lapidary, God-uttered status of the Decalogue was issued; thus, it is one more pointer to the distinctiveness of the Decalogue.

Apodictic Form and Sanctions

Albrecht Alt was the first to make the distinction between casuistic and apodictic law in the Old Testament. He wrote that 'the casuistic, is to be regarded as of Canaanite provenance; until the contrary is proved, the other [apodicitic], which intrudes itself in the shape of the *lex talionis*, may be regarded as Israelite.'[158] The contrary has been proved. Anthony Phillips, writing in a work published thirty-six years after Alt's original essay, sums up the argument against Alt's originally over-restrictive assessment:

> This can no longer be maintained, for a mixture of apodictic and casuistic laws as in the Book of the Covenant have been found over a wide area of the ancient Near East, not only in the third person as in the Laws of Eshnunna, the Code of Hammurabi, the Middle Assyrian Laws and the Neo-Babylonian Laws, but also in the second person as in the Hittite treaties and West Semitic inscriptional curses. Accordingly this distinction can tell one nothing about the foreign or indigenous origin of Israel's laws.[159]

157   Ibid., 236.
158   Albrecht Alt, 'The Origins of Israelite Law', in *Essays on Old Testament History and Religion*, trans. R. A. Wilson (Oxford: Basil Blackwell, 1966), 106.
159   Phillips, *Criminal Law*, 13.

M. Weinfeld gives a similar critique, but cautions that the casuistic formulation predominates in other ancient Near Eastern law, and Israelite law remains unique in expressing commands in the second person.[160] The true origins of apodictic law, he says, lie in the ancient Near Eastern literary type of 'Instructions'. These were royal laws imposed by oath on the servants of the Hittite King, which laws, being addressed mainly in the second person, are strikingly analogous with Biblical apodictic law.[161] Building on this, he points out that the Ten Commandments were viewed in a similar way—'as the orders of a divine King who had appeared before His subjects.'[162] Yet, he fails to mention a difference in that the Hittite or Assyrian laws concentrated on officials who had to instruct the people,[163] whereas the Decalogue was declared directly to all Israel.

Despite the novelty of Alt's terminology, the observation that the Decalogue is expressed in such a form is not recent. Philo, long ago, observed this and maintained it was given in this way so none could escape the divine imperatives.[164] Phillips, more recently, suggests the Decalogue used the apodictic form to stress the importance of obedience over a wider sphere of activity than in particular cases.[165]

There is an element of truth in both arguments, but neither are elements which in themselves make the Decalogue unique. Examples exist outside the Decalogue of biblical laws that adopt the direct personal approach observed by Philo, and

160 M. Weinfeld, 'The Origin of the Apodictic Law: An Overlooked Source', *VT* vol. XXIII, fasc. 1 (1973): 63.

161 Ibid., 64–5.

162 Weinfeld, 'Uniqueness of the Decalogue', 10–1.

163 Weinfeld, 'Origin of Apodictic Law', 64, 70; The single exception appears to be in connection with funerary rituals, 65, n. 3.

164 Philo. *De Decalogo*, vol. VII, *LCL* trans. F. H. Colson (London: William Heinemann Ltd, MCMXXXVII), 39.

165 Phillips, *Criminal Law*, 13.

of the apodictic form being used in numerous case laws. This distinction, however, between apodictic and casuistic law is relevant to this subject because the ten words are distinguished within Israelite law itself by their exclusively apodictic form: 'You shall', 'You shall not', 'Remember', and 'Honour'. Unlike the rest of the law, they are not a mixture of casuistic and apodictic.

Gerstenberger sought to restrict apodictic law to laws that do not specify any penalty, a feature that has often been recognised in the Decalogue.[166] Philo also saw this and, in language similar to Ptolemy's, he suggests it was given without penalties because 'the LORD He was good, the cause of good and nothing ill. So then he judged that it was most in accordance with his being to issue His saving commandments free from any admixture of punishment, that men might choose the best.'[167] This absence of sanctions in the apodictic form makes the 'categorical imperatives' of the Decalogue 'universally applicable, timeless, not dependent on any circumstances whatsoever'.[168] Whereas the other features of the apodictic form only make the Decalogue distinctive in its overall literary form, this makes it distinctive in its content.

Although the Decalogue does not specify sanctions, this does not mean it is free of sanctions. Yehoshua Amir highlights Philo's failure to mention the warning of punishment in the second word,[169] but this is pedantic. What is essentially a declaration of God's character is not comparable with the penalties stipulated throughout the rest of Israelite law (for the transgression of most laws contained in the Decalogue). Anthony Phillips went so far as to argue that as ancient Israel's criminal law code, the Decalogue carried the death penalty for the breach of any part.[170] Other parts

---

166   Ibid., 13, n. 51.

167   Philo, *De Decalogo,* 93.

168   Weinfeld, 'Uniqueness of the Decalogue', 8.

169   Yehoshua Amir, 'The Decalogue According to Philo', trans. Yvonne Glikson, in *Ten Commandments*, ed. Segal, trans. ed. Levi, 148.

170   Phillips, *Criminal Law*, 1.

of the law certainly specify capital punishment as the penalty for some of the Ten Commandments, but the law never demands death for theft or covetousness. Nonetheless, his observation highlights the way in which penology inevitably reflects the seriousness of offences in any law code. In the Pentateuch, laws are not equally significant simply because they share the same form—something Richard Bergen observes in his argument that the penalty for transgressing a law reflects its importance:

> To illustrate let us consider the following stipulations which bear a close formal resemblance:
>
> You shall not murder (Exod. 20:13).
>
> You shall not boil a kid in its mother's milk (Exod. 23:19).
>
> You shall not go about as a talebearer among your people (Lev. 19:16).
>
> Formally, each makes an equal claim to obedience and one might assume, from this formal resemblance, that they are of equal significance; but, the evidence of the Pentateuch is otherwise. Of the three, only for the first does the Pentateuch record the consequence of its breach:
>
> Whoever strikes a man mortally shall be put to death (Exod. 21:12).
>
> …Thus, the Pentateuch affords evidence that some laws were thought of as having a special significance in that, for their breach, punishment is prescribed or envisioned.[171]

This should be obvious—every society shows it regards some laws as more important than others by making some penalties more severe than others. (Parking on a double yellow line does not normally lead to life imprisonment.) It is, however, so obvious that it is missed by those who claim the Pentateuch, and the first century Jews who studied it, regarded the Mosaic Law

---

171   Richard Victor Bergen, *The Prophets and the Law* (Cincinnati: Hebrew Union College Press, 1974), 189–91.

as an indivisible whole. The existence of such distinctions need not be stated; that the laws of the Decalogue generally carried more severe penalties than statutes such as those cited by Bergen belongs as much to the self-understood of legal history as the laws themselves.

These two seemingly paradoxical features of the Decalogue, the apodictic, sanction-free form, and the self-understood, or elsewhere-stated penalties, are a further mark of its distinctiveness. They may not lead directly to the conclusion that it 'doth for ever bind all', but the independence of circumstances, universality of application, and self-understood penalties do suggest that the Decalogue was never intended to be land-locked or time-locked.[172]

The Constitution of the Universe

It is widely held that the Decalogue has a unique canonical function as a summary statement of the laws that follow it.[173] Patrick Miller illustrates this with an analogy between the Decalogue and the United States' Constitution, since neither is strictly legal. Both contain basic principles rather than exhaustive legislation. As 'constitutional law', they are an unchanging foundation on which a body of precedents and case law is built.[174] Each of the commandments has 'a kind of *trajectory*' as their scope is broadened out in the rest of the law. The Sabbath commandment, for example, hits its target in the fallow land and jubilee year laws (Lev. 25:2–8), while the commandment against adultery resurfaces in laws against incest.[175]

---

172   Dumbrell, *Covenant and Creation*, 92–3.

173   e.g. Rolf Rebdtorff, *The Canonical Hebrew Bible: A Theology of the Old Testament*. Tr. David E. Orton (Leiden: Deo Publishing, 2005), 481. Brevard S. Childs, *Old Testament Theology in a Canonical Context* (London: SCM, 1985), 54.

174   Patrick Miller, 'The Place of the Decalogue in the Old Testament and Its Law', *Interpretation* (1989): 231.

175   Ibid., 237, 240.

Rodd rejects such views, blasting Miller's claims as 'distinctly shaky' and his suggestion that the laws have trajectories as carrying 'little conviction', yet his 'most serious objection is that there are so few *direct* references to the Ten Commandments elsewhere in the Old Testament…the term 'the ten words' occurs nowhere outside Exodus 34.28 and Deuteronomy 4.13 and 10.4 in the rest of the Old Testament.'[176] This objection is flimsy—Rodd himself says the Decalogue has an 'exalted position' in Exodus and Deuteronomy,[177] and as Braulik's work on the expressions for 'law' in Deuteronomy shows, it is not only the basic term 'the ten words' that refers to the revelation of the Decalogue at Horeb.

To some degree, Miller echoes Philo, who in *De Decalogo* gives his view of the Ten Commandments as 'the constitution of the universe'.[178] In his own words, God gave 'laws and heads summarizing the particular laws, but those in which He spoke through the prophet all belong to the former class.'[179] For Philo, the relationship of the laws to the heads was not as volatile as the body of case law Miller envisaged. Instead, it was of the 'genus to the species',[180] but unlike the Minim, Philo had no wish to undermine non-Decalogue law. By summarising each statute under one of the 'heads' of the Decalogue, he sought to affirm the authority of the statutes.[181] This task was not straightforward:

> If the Ten Commandments are the ten vessels into which Philo sought to decant all the laws found in the Torah, then it must be admitted that some of the vast quantity overflowed the intended containers, to the point where he was finally forced to provide a number of auxiliary containers for those laws which he could not fit into the Ten Commandments.[182]

176 Rodd, *Glimpses of a Strange Land*, 81–2.
177 Ibid., 92.
178 Amir, 'Decalogue According to Philo', 128.
179 Philo, *De Decalogo*, 15.
180 Amir, 'Decalogue According to Philo', 126.
181 Ibid.
182 Ibid., 127.

Rabbinic tradition shows a similar understanding to Philo when it asserts that Moses was not idle during his two 40-day visits to Mount Sinai. 'The time was utilised…to enlarge on the Ten Commandments and to explain to Moses the whole of the Torah.'[183] *Canticles Rabbah* record the result:

> Hananiah the son of R. Joshua's brother said: Between each commandment (of the Decalogue) the sections and detailed interpretations of the Torah were indited. When R. Johanan expounded the Scriptures and reached the verse 'set with Tarshish'… he said: the son of the brother of R. Joshua gave me a beautiful interpretation of this: 'Just as in the case of waves, between one big billow and another there are small waves, so between one commandment and another the sections and detailed interpretations of the Torah were indited.'[184]

Jewish thinkers of the Middle Ages unhesitatingly restated this 'ancient view' that the Ten Commandments were the sum of the Torah.[185] As a Christian scholar of the Middle Ages, Aquinas agreed with such Jewish thinkers. He aimed to show that any other moral precepts found within the law 'are reducible to the precepts of the Decalogue as so many corollaries'.[186] Thus, 'to the Third Commandment [Remember the Sabbath Day] are added all the ceremonial precepts.'[187] He considers this commandment a moral precept, 'but not as to the fixing of

183   Myer Galinski, *Pursue Justice: the Administration of Justice in Ancient Israel* (London: Nechdim Press, 1983), 25, n. 19.

184   Urbach, *The Sages*, 361; Emil G. Hirsch, 'The Decalogue in Jewish Theology', *Jewish Encyclopaedia* vol. 4, 496. Urbach says a different point is being made. It is not that the Ten Commandments are the sum of the Torah, but 'every commandment forms the basis of interpretations and subtle inferences.' Greenberg suggests Urbach's comments 'reflect the ongoing polemic on the matter'. Greenberg, 'Decalogue Tradition', 119, n. 57.

185   Ibid., 119.

186   Aquinas, *Law, Morality, and Politics*, 110–1.

187   Ibid., 111.

the time, in which respect it is a ceremonial precept'.[188] The last
two commandments [You shall not covet] forbid 'all kinds of
evil desires'.[189] For the remaining commandments, he cites the
following 'corollaries':[190]

AQUINAS' COROLLARIES TO PRECEPTS
OF THE DECALOGUE

Commandment	Example
First	Deut. 18:10–11
Second	Lev. 24:15
Fourth	Lev. 19:32
Fifth	Lev. 19:16–17
Sixth	Deut. 23:17; Lev. 18:22–3
Seventh	Deut. 23:19; 25:13
Eighth	Exod. 23:2, 7

While Aquinas' use of terminology and categories can make his
framework difficult to determine, he was not offering a complete
categorization, but selected those texts as examples. This is
established from his comment that the seventh commandment
also includes 'universally all prohibitions relating to peculations
and larceny',[191] and more specifically his statement that 'it is
in virtue of their institution that the ceremonial and judicial
precepts are determinations of the precepts of the Decalogue.'[192]

This approach survives in twentieth century Roman Catholic
doctrine[193] and in the writings of Reformed theologians. Some

---

188   Ibid., 89.
189   Ibid., 112.
190   Ibid., 111.
191   Ibid.
192   Ibid., 112.
193   The commandment, 'You shall not kill', 'comprises all reverence for life.'
A New Catechism: Catholic Faith for Adults (London: Search Press, 1967), 372.

suggest Calvin was one of those,[194] but it is not plain in the obvious sections of his *Institutes* or *Sermons on Deuteronomy*.[195] Patrick Fairbairn, lecturing in 1868, stated the *judicial* law is subordinate to the Decalogue, but closely connected to it.[196] He justified this with respect to the *Mishpatim* and laws of Deuteronomy:

> A series of particular cases is supposed—by way of example and illustration, of course, not as if exhausting the entire category of possible occurrences—and, in connection with them, instructions are given as to what may or should be done, so as to preserve the spirit of the constitution.

> A considerable portion of the statutes and judgments are…a simple application of the great principles of the Decalogue to particular cases, intended at once to explain and confirm them.…They serve materially to throw light on the import and bearing of the Decalogue.[197]

There is no direct evidence in *The Revelation of Law* that Fairbairn was influenced by earlier Reformed writers or by German scholars such as Fr. W. Schultz whose similar views were published in 1859.[198] Yet as a Free Church of Scotland professor, he would have been familiar with the Reformation writers and he was also fully conversant with contemporary German scholarship.

During the twentieth century, this 'ancient view' came to new prominence, partly in response to the view that the laws of the Pentateuch are a shambolic muddle. Kaufman mentions

194   J. Gary Millar, *Now Choose Life*, Studies in Biblical Theology, series ed. D. A. Carson, no. 6. (Leicester: Apollos, 1998), 107, n. 9; Stephen A. Kaufman, 'The Structure of the Deuteronomic Law', *Maarav* 1 no. 2 (1978–79): 111.

195   John Calvin, *Sermons on Deuteronomy* (Edinburgh: Banner of Truth, 1990).

196   Fairbairn, *Revelation of Law*, 94. He also suggests that a more appropriate (but not more succinct) designation for the judicial law would be: '*Statutory directions and enactments for the practical ordering of affairs amid the complicated relations and often untoward events of life.*'

197   Ibid., 95–7, 99.

198   Kaufman, 'The Deuteronomic Law', 151, n. 36.

A. C. Welch's declaration, that whatever way the laws of
Deuteronomy are organised, 'none can be quite so bad as the
order in which they appear'.[199] A. E. Guilding proposed in 1948
that this supposedly chaotic arrangement does not exist. The laws
are not 'arranged at haphazard';[200] the codes of Exodus, Leviticus,
and Deuteronomy are orderly expositions of the Decalogue[201] as
Philo argued.[202] His categorisation of the laws depends upon
pairing some commandments and, like Philo, he has to provide an
'auxiliary' container (for the feasts). He gives a detailed exposition
of his arrangement, but also summarises it as shown below:[203]

GUILDING'S DECALOGUE FRAMEWORK
FOR THE LAWS OF THE PENTATEUCH

The Decalogue	Exod. 20:23–23:17	Deut. 13–25	Lev. 10–23
No other gods.	20:23a.	13.	10.
No graven images.	20:23b.	14:1–21.	11.
Reverence for the name.	20:24–6.	14:22–9.	12–15.
The Sabbath.	21:1–11.	15–16:17.	16.
Honour to parents. No murder.	21:12–36.	16:18–22:8.	17. 18:1–13.
No adultery. No stealing.	22:1–19.	22:13–24:7.	18:14–30.
No coveting. No false witness.	22:21–23:9.	24:10–25:16.	} 19.
The Feasts.	23:14–17.	Inc. under sabbath.	23.

199   Ibid., 107.
200   A. E. Guilding, 'Notes on the Hebrew Law Codes', *JTS* XLIX (1948): 43.
201   Guilding, 'Hebrew Law Codes', 43.
202   Ibid., 52.
203   Ibid.

KAUFMAN'S DECALOGUE FRAMEWORK
FOR THE LAWS OF DEUTERONOMY

Word	Chapters in Deuteronomy
I-II Right Worship	12:1-28 Eradication of pagan cults. Proclamation of the centralization of Yahweh worship (113).
III	13:1-14:27 Using the LORD's name in vain (122-9).
IV Sabbath	15:1-18 Sabbatical moratoria. 16:1-17 The pilgrimage festivals (113).
V Authority	16:18-20; 17:2-13 Appointment of judges and the operation of the judicial system. 17:14-20 The law of the King. 18:1-8 The law of the Priesthood. 18:9-22 The law of the Prophets (113).
VI Homicide	19:1-13 Accidental and intentional homicide *(resah)* and sanctuary cities. Chap. 20 The law of warfare. 21:1-9 The untraced homicide. 21:22-3 The public display of executed criminals. 22:8 Make a parapet for your roof, lest anyone fall from it and bring bloodguilt on your house (113).
VII Adultery	22:9-11 Prohibited mixtures. 22:13-23:1 Improper sexual relations. 23:2-9 Sexual wholeness and genetic purity. 23:10-15 Sexual purity and cleanliness in the military. 23:18-19 Prohibition of cult prostitutes (113-4).
VIII Theft and property violations	23:20-21 Prohibition of lending at discount. 23:22-4 Vows to God to be paid promptly. 23:25-6 What may be taken from neighbors crops. 24:1-6 Divorce, marriage and pledges (139). 24:7 The law of mantheft (114).
IX	24:8-25:4 Bearing false witness (141-2).
X*a*	25:5-13 Coveting a neighbor's wife (142).
X*b*	25:13-16 Coveting a neighbor's property (142-3).

Kaufman made a similar effort to prove that Deuteronomy 12–26 is carefully structured with its major subjects arranged to fit the Decalogue.[204] Indeed, 'anyone familiar with the history of the exegesis of Deuteronomy can attest, if there is in fact a systematic arrangement of that Law, almost all of the results of a century of scholarship point inexorably towards such a conclusion.'[205] He suggests the recognised distinction between chapters 12–14 as laws relating to God and chapters 15–25 as laws relating to fellow men reflect a similar distinction in the Decalogue.[206] The outline opposite is drawn from his confusingly arranged scheme and narrative section.[207]

Kaufman admits some of his explanations might puzzle the author of Deuteronomy and that his theory could be refined. If, however, the criticism is that his scheme is 'too neat', he sees no reason it should not be so. 'Everything in the ancient Near Eastern world points clearly towards the existence of system and structure in such literary works.'[208]

While Georg Braulik finds Kaufman's approach has 'methodological and exegetical deficiencies',[209] he too promotes the thesis that the Decalogue is 'a kind of large-scale or general framework'[210] for Deuteronomy 12–26. Chapters 12–18 bear only a vague resemblance to the Decalogue, but from chapter 19 the connections become clearer.[211] This is not an imposition on the text—the text itself promotes such a view with its use of

204   Kaufman, 'The Deuteronomic Law', 108–9.

205   Ibid., 109.

206   Ibid., 111.

207   Ibid. He follows Roman Catholic numbering. Pages in brackets.

208   Ibid., 144–5.

209   Georg Braulik, 'The Sequence of the Laws in Deuteronomy 12–26', in *A Song of Power and the Power of Song,* ed. D. L. Christensen. (Winona Lake: Eisenbrauns, 1993), 319.

210   Ibid., 321.

211   Ibid.

BRAULIK'S DECALOGUE FRAMEWORK
FOR THE LAWS OF DEUTERONOMY.

Word	Chapters in Deuteronomy
I	12:2–13:19 *The one temple and one God of Israel.*
II	14:1–21 *Taking the name in vain.* YHWH's holy people in its ritual difference from the peoples of other gods.
III	14:22–16:17 *Keeping the Sabbath holy.* Cult and brotherhood in sacred rhythm—Israel's gathering at three pilgrimage feasts.
IV	16:18–18:22 *Honoring parents.* Office in Israel.
V	19:1–21:23 *Preserving life.* Deliberate killing (with digressions). 22:1–12 *Transition from the topic 'preserving life' to that of 'sexuality'.* The topic of 'sexuality' is first introduced at 22:5 with the motif 'crossing over', while the subject of 'killing' is last clearly evident at 22:8.
VI	22:13–23:14 *Rape* and *Family.* Concentrates completely on the area of sexuality. 23:15–24:5 *Transition from the topic of 'sexuality' to that of 'property'.* The 'property' theme appears for the first time at 23:15–16 (escaped slaves), while the theme of 'sexuality' is found for the last time at 24:5 (excusing the newly-married from military service).
VII	(23:15–25) 24:6–7. *Property.* The theme of property will be taken up again at 24:19–22 and 25:4, but at 24:8 the next topic 'judgment' begins.
VIII	24:8–25:4 *[Truth in the face of] judgment.*
IX/X	25:5–16 *Coveting.* The closing frame of the legal corpus begins at 25:17, looking back to themes from Deuteronomy 12, and the two rituals in 26:1–15 are deliberately conceived as a conclusion of the body of laws.

the expression חֻקִּים וּמִשְׁפָּטִים ('statutes and ordinances').[212] This phrase frames the deuteronomic paranesis of 5:1–11:32 and the laws of 12–26. These 'statutes and ordinances' therefore include the Decalogue which begins at 5:6, but more specifically the laws of 12–26. Deuteronomy 5:1 is no more than an announcement, 11:32 points forward, not back, and 12:1 is the real introduction to the 'statutes and ordinances'.[213] The structure he sees for the 'statutes and ordinances' of 12:1–26:16 as an explanation of the Decalogue is outlined in the table opposite.[214]

A thorough assessment of the structures presented by Guilding, Kaufman and Braulik would require detailed exegesis of Deuteronomy, but even limited comparison of their structures shows they have reached similar conclusions about the precise relationship of the Deuteronomic Law to the Decalogue. Guilding starts with chapter 13 rather than chapter 12, but from chapter 15 onwards, his groupings are comparable to those of Kaufman (who overlooked his article).[215] Braulik's outline differs from Kaufman's in that he, like Guilding, ties chapter 13 to the first commandment. His outline is not as rigid as the others in that he sees transitional sections between the commandments. An example is 22:1–12, which smoothes the transition between the commandments about murder and adultery.

It is not easy to find glaring examples of mismatches between particular laws and commandments in the outlines. At face value, a law such as that of 23:3–6, which forbids the Moabites and Ammonites entering the assembly of the LORD, seems to have little connection with the commandment against adultery, but it relates to 'genetic purity'.[216] Such an argument is plausible

212   Ibid., 320.
213   Ibid., 314–5.
214   Ibid., 331–2.
215   Ibid., 318.
216   Kaufman, 'Deuteronomic Law', 138; Braulik, 'Sequence of the Laws', 332.

since the Moabites and Ammonites were the illegitimate children produced by the incestuous relations of Lot and his daughters (Gen. 19:37–8).

Millar tries to find a mismatch with his criticism of Kaufman and Braulik for linking 8:9–22 with the fifth commandment on the basis that it is to do with submission to those in authority. 'The legislation,' he says, 'is addressed to the leaders themselves, rather than to the people',[217] but it is hard to see how he reached this conclusion. Certainly, the legislation refers to leaders, but its aim is to teach the people how they may know if they should submit to a prophet as one who speaks with divine authority. There is no change of addressee in the passage (18:14). Millar has given considerable attention to the schemes of Kaufman and Braulik, but some of his criticisms, such as his comment that the Decalogue is not 'actually quoted' in chapters 12–26, appear to be criticism for criticism's sake. Ultimately, he accepts 'their combined arguments for seeing a Decalogue pattern in the laws are powerful'.[218] There may be mismatches in the schemes of Braulik and Kaufman, but Braulik acknowledges his proposals require further investigation, and he is also right to claim that there can be 'no retreat'[219] from this 'ancient view'.

Even if there is some snagging to deal with in these precise literary structures, it has been shown that all of the Ten Commandments except the last appear in other parts of the Pentateuch.[220] Wienfeld sees a particularly strong relationship between Leviticus 19 and the Decalogue.[221] Wenham joins him

---

217   Millar, *Now Choose Life*, 130.

218   Ibid., 107–8.

219   Braulik, 'Sequence of the Laws', 334.

220   See: Moshe Weinfeld, 'The Decalogue: Its Significance, Uniqueness, and Place in Israel's Tradition', in *Religion and Law: Biblical–Judaic and Islamic Perspectives*, eds. Edwin B. Frimage, Bernard G. Weiss, and John W. Welch (Winona Lake: Eisenbrauns, 1990), 4.

221   Ibid., 18.

in noting parallels between particular verses in Leviticus 19 and each of the Ten Commandments.[222] Rodd, however, protests: 'none of the parallels are exact' when, for example, the Decalogue speaks of a 'graven image' while Leviticus refers to 'idols.' It is 'impossible to suppose that the writer was picking up on the law of the Decalogue' when terms such as adultery or murder are not explicitly mentioned and, as far as covetousness is concerned, it is 'quite impossible to suppose' any parallel can be found with Leviticus 19.[223] But why should a parallel only be a parallel if it is a verbatim repetition? If any language or culture has ever required letter for letter correspondence between two sayings or laws in order to recognise they are parallel or of the same class, it is not Hebrew. Rodd leans on the self-declared 'incontestability' of Frank Crüsemann's view that the Decalogue applies only to 'adult men responsible for administering justice...farmers who possess land and cattle', with the main principle being 'the securing of the freedom of the independent farmer'.[224] In this, Crüsemann 'anticipated'[225] Clines' similar view that the Ten Commandments were written to serve the interests of 'a balding Israelite urban male with a mid-life crisis and a weight problem, in danger of losing his faith'[226]—the 'Volvo-driving, property-owning classes'.[227] Thus, for Rodd, all argument is ended. The matter is settled—the Ten Commandments' status is something akin to the constitution of the National Farmers Union. Paradoxically, Rodd states that the 'incontestable' is in fact challenged by the views of Westermann, Zimmerli, Childs, and Weinfeld.[228] Yet any challenge to his views appears redundant when he recognises any attempt to get

---

222   Wenham, *Leviticus*, 264.
223   Rodd, *Glimpses of a Strange Land*, 83.
224   Ibid., 86.
225   Clines, *Interested Parties*, 34, n. 14.
226   Ibid., 34.
227   Ibid., 43.
228   Rodd, *Glimpses of a Strange Land*, 87.

behind the present forms of the Ten Commandments as 'futile' for 'within the completed Pentateuch…it was probably assumed they applied to everyone'.[229]

In Leviticus 19, and the wider Pentateuch, the constitutional status of the Decalogue as a statement of ten programmatic and foundational words is a final indicator of its unique status. All else is 'an informative (5:31), or even more, an authoritative (4:14) interpretation of the Decalogue, in the sense of a set of directions for its fulfilment in given, concrete situations.'[230] In this respect, it is 'a sort of Israelite creed' like the *Shema*:

> Just as the monotheistic principle expressed in the *Shema* is realized in many legal particulars…so also the religious and moral principles of the Decalogue take form in various laws of the Pentateuch.[231]

The following sections will consider the other laws in more detail, but the immediate implication is that those laws, the statutes and ordinances, may be interpreted differently in various 'concrete situations'. Situations may change and new statutes and ordinances will be required, but the Decalogue will be their foundation. It 'is obligatory always and everywhere'.[232] Although directed to Israel, it declared certain unchangeable truths from and about God, which affected all humanity, whether they knew it or not. From the perspective of the Pentateuch, as well as the confessions, it 'doth for ever bind all'.

Section Summary

Many contemporary theologians assume that the Decalogue is indivisible from the rest of the law and reject the traditional view

229   Ibid., 90–1.
230   Braulik, 'Sequence of the Laws', 314.
231   Weinfeld, 'The Decalogue', 26.
232   Ibid.

that the Decalogue stands in the theologically distinct category of 'moral law.' In this section I asked if the Pentateuch recognised the Decalogue as a distinct element within the law and concluded that several factors point to its distinctiveness.

First, it was not a marked historical development or new law. The Ten Words express morals that the Pentateuch indicates were 'self-understood' from the beginning. The patriarchs knew that the LORD's dwelling with them was linked with their acceptance of those 'self-understood' things.

Second, God spoke these words. Sinai was as much a revelation of the unchangeable Holy One as it was of his immutable will. In this unique Divine utterance he made a perpetual declaration of his requirements for individuals who heard the Decalogue then and for those who would hear it repeated in the future. It was binding in the wilderness, in the land, or wherever his people might find themselves in coming generations.

Third, these words came from the finger of God. He framed these self-understood truths in the Decalogue and declared them to be the 'covenant'. They were the basis upon which he would dwell among his people and the basis upon which Israel would maintain her relationship with the LORD and the land. They also revealed why the other nations were expelled.

Fourth, He added nothing to those words and no other part of the law had that 'binding foundation-scroll'[233] status.

Fifth, unlike the 'foundation-scroll', the rest of the law was not in an exclusively apodictic form or addressed to the individual throughout.

Sixth, only the Ten Words function as the 'constitution' upon which 'all else is but commentary'. They were the foundation for the laws that would govern Israel 'in the land'. It was their constitution—a constitution rooted in creation and anticipating new creation. Ultimately, it was the 'constitution of the universe'.

---

233   Weinfeld, 'The Decalogue', 37.

Those features uncovered in the Pentateuch support the traditional view that the Ten Commandments were a distinctive part of the law. They were not only the basis upon which God judged Israel, but also the standard by which he would always measure all men everywhere. For the Pentateuch, they 'for ever bind all'.

'COMMANDS, DECREES, AND LAWS'

In the previous chapter, I noted that Thomas Aquinas offered a text in support of the threefold division of the law. He used Deuteronomy 4:13–14 to prove that the law consisted of ceremonial as well as moral precepts. He also supposed that the reference in Deuteronomy 6:1 to 'statutes', which translates מִשְׁפָּט, specifically referred to judicial precepts.[234] More recently, Kaiser has argued that the heading מִשְׁפָּטִים in Exodus 21:1 would have suggested a distinction to the ancient hearers.[235]

In this section I will examine those suggestions because if the Pentateuch uses specific words or expressions to classify different types of law, it will be necessary to ask if those classifications support the threefold division. To do this, we need to consider the meaning of the various words and expressions for law, as well as their use in headings or section markers to distinguish particular categories of law.

The three Hebrew words in Deuteronomy 6:1, the text in which Aquinas found moral, civil, and ceremonial precepts, are מִצְוָה, חֹק, and מִשְׁפָּט. They are among the most frequently used words for law and occur together four times in Deuteronomy (5:31; 6:1; 7:11; 26:17). An example of the definitions given for those words in a standard lexicon[236] can be summarised as follows:

234   *Summa* I–II. 99. 3–4.

235   Kaiser, *Old Testament Ethics*, 43–7.

236   Whitaker, Richard. *Whitaker's Revised BDB Hebrew-English Lexicon* in BibleWorks Ver. 4.0.032c, BibleWorks LLC, Big Fork, Montana, 1999.

מִצְוָה—n.f. commandment -- 1. *commandment*, of man: king; 2. of God: a. sg. *the commandment*, code of law. b. pl. of *commands*; order c. of special *commands* of God. 3. *commandment*, sg., of code of wisdom.

חֹק—n.m. something prescribed, a statute or due -- 1. prescribed task. 2. prescribed portion. 3. action prescribed. 4. prescribed due. 5. prescribed limit, boundary: 6. enactment, decree, ordinace of either God or man: 7. pl. חֻקִּים enactments, statutes of a law.

מִשְׁפָּט—n.m. judgment -- 1. *judgment*: 2. attribute of the שֹׁפֵט, *justice, right, rectitude*. 3. *ordinance* promulgated by שֹׁפֵט: (law of king); Levit. ordinances; divine law in Gen. 4. *decision* of the שֹׁפֵט in a case of law. 5. one's (legal) *right, privilege, due*. 6. *proper, fitting, measure*; *custom, manner, plan*.

Such concise definitions may suit the task of basic translation, but more detailed investigation of word usage is necessary to judge if their primary reference is to specific categories of Mosaic Law. On the surface, their range of meaning is almost identical; any one of them could refer to any of the Mosaic laws. According to Lohfink the only determining principle for the word-selection in Deuteronomy is variety.[237] Van der Ploeg describes past attempts to give them different meanings as 'vain' since 'proof is wanting or fails to convince'.[238] The worthlessness of those attempts and the existence or non-existence of proof can, however, only be determined by examining them and the usage of the words in the Old Testament. Van der Ploeg does acknowledge that although there is not 'any noticeable shade of different meaning' this 'does not signify that the meanings are completely identical or that they have been so since the beginning'.[239]

237   See Georg Braulik, 'Die Ausdrücke für 'Gesetz' im Buch Deuter-onomium' (The Expressions for 'Law' in the Book of Deuteronomy), *Biblia* 51 (1970): 40.

238   J. van der Ploeg, 'Studies in Hebrew Law', *CBQ* 12 (1950): 248. He does not specify which 'vain attempts' he has in mind.

239   Ibid.

Although he maintains, 'Today I would write many things differently',[240] Georg Braulik's article 'Die Ausdrücke für 'Gesetz' im Buch Deuteronomium'[241] is a benchmark study[242] of the various Hebrew expressions for law. His article discusses the meaning of all ten expressions for law found in the Pentateuch and his observations are summarised in Appendix 1 of this book, but he concludes that no particular expression exclusively describes individual laws.[243] This does not mean, however, that we can instantly dismiss the suggestion that מִצְוָה, חֹק, and מִשְׁפָּט in Deuteronomy 6:1 should be equated with moral, civil, and ceremonial, since Braulik has shown that the individual words do refer to specific categories in certain contexts.

In Deuteronomy 4:10, 13, 36; 5:5, 22; 9:10; 10:2, 4, דְּבָרִים (words) refers to the Decalogue.[244] This does not prove that דְּבָרִים always means the Decalogue, yet it shows that it is a distinct element of the law which Deuteronomy sometimes recognises by the use of דְּבָרִים. It was not Justin, Aquinas, or the Westminster Assembly that first distinguished those laws as the Ten Commandments; Moses is entirely to blame (Exod. 34:28, Deut. 4:13; 10:4).

The previous section considered Braulik's argument that the double expression חֻקִּים וּמִשְׁפָּטִים 'ultimately refers only to 12:1–26:16'[245] and the idea that this legal corpus, although

240 'Manches wuerde ich heute etwas anders schreiben.' Georg Braulik, Katholisch-Theologische Fakultät der Universität Wien, to author, Email, 2 July 1999.

241 Braulik, 'Ausdrücke für"Gesetz"', 39–66.

242 Duane L. Christensen, *Deuteronomy 1–11*, WBC, ed. David A. Hubbard and Glenn W. Barker (General), John D. W. Watts (Old Testament), no. 6A (Dallas: Word Books, 1991), 79; R. Laird Harris, Gleason L. Archer Jr., and Bruce K. Waltke, eds. *TWOT*, vol. 1 (Chicago: Moody Press, 1980), 317.

243 Braulik, 'Ausdrücke für"Gesetz"', 66. Van der Ploeg also agrees that the Mosaic Law is not categorized by the use of specific Hebrew words. Van der Ploeg, 'Studies in Hebrew Law', 248–59.

244 Braulik, 'Ausdrücke für"Gesetz"', 45–6.

245 Braulik, 'Sequence of the Laws', 315.

distinguished from the Decalogue by the double expression, is based upon it. The words themselves do not possess a meaning that restricts them to a definition of the legal corpus (12:1–26:16), but in the context of Deuteronomy that is the purpose served by the expression חֻקִּים וּמִשְׁפָּטִים.

מִצְוָה was used in certain cases to refer to the Ten Words (Deut. 5:10, 29; 6:17; 7:9; 8:2; 13:5) and Aquinas may have been right to understand Deuteronomy 6:1 in that way. Deuteronomy 6:1–3 links the Horeb revelation and the teaching that begins at 6:4 with the *Shema*. So Christensen is correct when he writes:

> המצוה—the singular usage, *this is the commandment*, apparently refers to the principle underlying all the law (cf. 5:31). Thus, *the statutes and the judgments* stand in apposition, describing the general laws based on the first principle.[246]

He does not specify the underlying principle, but considering the connecting role of these three verses together with the observations that the חֻקִּים וּמִשְׁפָּטִים expand on the Decalogue and in chapter five מִצְוָה refers to the Decalogue, Aquinas could have found some textual basis for his argument. That he did not explain his linguistic reasoning may have been because, knowing 'very little Greek and virtually no Hebrew',[247] his appeal to Deuteronomy 6:1 reflected the linguistic insights of earlier generations rather than being a desperate attempt at proof-texting, even if it is not clear to what extent he (or they) believed those words always referred to specific categories of law.

This investigation shows that the individual Hebrew words for law do not divide the law into cast-iron categories. Even so, the Deuteronomy's use of the words sometimes makes a distinction between the Decalogue and the rest of the Mosaic code. That distinction does not force the practical-theological conclusion

---

246 Christensen, *Deuteronomy 1–11*, 135.
247 Stump, 'Biblical commentary and philosophy', 256.

that the Decalogue 'doth for ever bind all'. It does, however, further challenge the view that the Old Testament law was written, and always viewed, as an indivisible whole.

DISTINGUISHING CIVIL AND CEREMONIAL

The introduction to this book referred to Geisler's rejection of the threefold division because the 'Law of Moses was a unit. There were civil aspects to the moral law, and moral dimensions of the civil law. Indeed there were moral aspects of the ceremonial law.'[248] His rejection of the 'orthodox position' because it demanded a rigid approach to the law is inadequate as it does not reflect the traditional use of the threefold division.

Calvin, for example, held strongly to the threefold division yet recognised a ceremonial aspect in the Decalogue with the Sabbath commandment.[249] Similarly, Reformed theologians have not declared that civil laws can never have typical or ceremonial aspect. A cursory glance at almost any Reformed commentary on passages such as Hebrews 2:1 would show this.[250]

A further misconception is that the ceremonial law 'has been limited to the blood-sacrifices, priestly ordinances, and the ritual of the Day of Atonement'.[251] It is true *The Westminster Confession* refers to 'ceremonial laws containing several typical ordinances' but they are 'partly of worship' and 'partly of divers instructions of moral duties'.

---

248   Geisler, 'Dispensationalism and Ethics', 8.

249   R. J. Bauckham, 'Sabbath and Sunday in the Protestant Tradition', in *From Sabbath to Lord's Day*, ed. D. A. Carson (Grand Rapids: Academie, 1982), 316–7.

250   John Owen provides an example in his comment on the typical aspect of the penalties for transgression of the civil law when he writes that 'the sentence of the law against transgressors…argues unto the 'sorer punishment' that must needs ensue upon the neglect of the dispensation of the gospel.' *An Exposition of the Epistle to the Hebrews* Vol. III (Edinburgh: Johnstone and Hunter, M.DCCC.LIV.)

251   Wright, *People of God*, 156.

Nevertheless, the threefold division does distinguish between civil and ceremonial laws, and we must ask if that division can be justified. Can civil and ceremonial laws be distinguished from each other, or are the boundaries so blurred that any attempt at differentiation is bound to fail? Is it rather the case that the Pentateuch provides no basis for recognising differences between various laws?

Walter Kaiser has argued that the text of the Pentateuch does make such a distinction. The instructions about the tabernacle 'from Exodus 25 through Leviticus 7 (at least) had an expressed word of built-in-obsolescence when it noted several times over that what was to be built was only a model ('pattern', תַּבְנִית, e.g., Exod. 25:9, 40)—the real had not yet emerged, but was as Hebrews 10:1 argues, "only a shadow of the good things that are coming"—not the realities themselves'.[252]

Later chapters will consider the New Testament understanding of the Mosaic Law in detail, but the above quotation from Hebrews does not represent a radical reinterpretation of Exodus 25. The element of pointing forward from a present shadow to a future reality may not be obvious in Exodus, but the text clearly points from a present shadow to a present reality.

Following a meal shared with the elders of Israel on Sinai, during which they 'saw God' (Exod. 24:11), Moses spent forty days and forty nights with the LORD in the cloud. He then descended to make the tabernacle according to the 'pattern' (Exod. 25:9) so God would 'dwell among them' (Exod. 25:8). The tabernacle was to be a 'pattern' or 'model' (תַּבְנִית) of a greater reality just as an idol was an image (תַּבְנִית) of a real creature (Deut. 4:16–18) or god. When Moses was on the mountain God showed him a pattern from which he was to construct the tabernacle. According to Rabbinic exegesis, Moses saw the heavenly reality of the tabernacle, but Keil is correct that תַּבְנִית

---

252   Kaiser, *Old Testament Ethics*, 43–7

never refers to the original, leading to the conclusion Moses only saw a copy or plan of God's tabernacle.[253] Had he seen the reality of God in his dwelling place at this point, his prayer and the divine response on the second ascent would make little sense (Exod. 33:18–23). Even so, the tabernacle was to be the LORD's home while he dwelt among the Israelites, so it had to be a true pattern of his real abode.

This view of an earthly dwelling place as the home of deity was not unique to Israel; it was widespread throughout the ancient Near East. The earthly temple where the idol dwelt was a shadow of his heavenly palace.[254] In Mesopotamia and Canaan the temple of a god 'reproduced and made present the heavenly prototype'.[255] Goppelt suggests the idea extended beyond temples: 'Behind Exod. 25 stands the ancient oriental idea of a mythical analogical relationship between the two worlds…so that lands, rivers, cities and esp. temples have their heavenly originals.'[256]

In Exodus the extent of the plan goes beyond the overall shape of the tabernacle and specifies every detail. The ark and the cover where God will meet with Moses have primary place in the order of instructions (Exod. 25:10–22). This is followed by equally detailed specifications about the bread table (Exod. 25:23–30), lampstand (Exod. 25:31–40), overall design (Exod. 26; 27:9–19), altar (Exod. 27:1–8), priestly garments and work (Exod. 27:20–31:11). All these things have to be produced exactly as the LORD commanded (Exod. 31:11)—according to the

---

253   Keil & Delitzsch, *Pentateuch* II, 165. For a full discussion of possible meanings see William C. Propp, *Exodus 19–40: A New Translation with Introduction and Commentary* (New York: Doubleday, 2006), 376–7.

254   Jeffrey J. Niehaus, *God at Sinai* (Carlisle: Paternoster, 1995), 116.

255   R. J. Clifford, 'The Tent of El and the Israelite Tent of Meeting', *CBQ* 33, no. 2 (April 1971): 226; quoted in Niehaus, *God at Sinai*, 118.

256   Goppelt. 'τύπος as the Heavenly Original according to Exod. 25:40', In *TDNT* VIII (Grand Rapids: Eerdmans, 1972), 256.

'pattern.' They also had to be used according to specific commands (Lev. 1–9). The consequences of abuse were fatal (Lev. 10).

Furthermore, because the tabernacle was a copy of the heavenly temple it had to function according to heavenly norms. This called for many other laws relating to the tabernacle, its presence among the people, and ultimately to God's presence. No uncleanness or impurity could exist in the heavenly temple. The laws about ritual purity and separation reflected this. They dealt with food (Lev. 11), childbirth (Lev. 12), disease, infection (Lev. 13–14), and bodily discharges (Lev. 15). The people of Israel had to be kept separate from all such uncleanness lest they defiled the LORD's tabernacle and died (Lev. 15:31, Num. 19:13). Even if the tabernacle in those verses is understood to refer to the people themselves, the link between the laws and the tabernacle tent remains, for God's dwelling among them is bound up with the tabernacle (Exod. 25:8). The laws about purity were according to the 'pattern' of heaven in that they banned impurity from God's presence. Unlike the other laws, which ensured a well-ordered state, the laws about purity were necessary solely because of God's dwelling in the tabernacle and thereby among the people. Other laws sought to establish peace in a fallen world—prohibiting sin and specifying penalties. Such laws did reflect Israel's status and relationship with the LORD, but the Pentateuch does not present them as a duplicate of the heavenly order,[257] whereas the 'pattern' laws connected with the tabernacle reflected another world. We therefore cannot conclude that the laws outside the Decalogue comprise a mass of legislation that is beyond taxonomy. If the Mosaic Law is a unity, it is not in the sense that there are no distinct areas within the legislation.

A further distinction between the 'pattern' laws and the

257 It may be argued from a New Testament perspective that the non-ceremonial laws also had a typological aspect, but they are not termed a 'pattern' in the text of the Old Testament.

civil laws, as well as between the Decalogue and the civil laws, appears in the common qualification that the 'statutes and ordinances' (חֻקִּים וּמִשְׁפָּטִים) were to be observed 'in the land' (Deut. 4:5, 14; 5:31; 6:1; 12:1). No such qualification applies to the laws about sacrifice or purity. The tabernacle was established and filled with the glory of the LORD in the wilderness (Exod. 40). Aaron and his sons were anointed and began their ministry before Israel crossed the Jordan (Lev. 8–9). Therefore, the laws relating to the tabernacle were with immediate effect even if they did anticipate life in the land. This was not the case with the חֻקִּים וּמִשְׁפָּטִים which, as was pointed out in previous sections, mark out the Deuteronomic paranesis (5:1–11:32) and the law corpus (12:1–26:16), but Deuteronomy 4:14 also contrasts the Decalogue with the laws (חֻקִּים וּמִשְׁפָּטִים) that Moses mediated to the people.[258]

Braulik argues (elsewhere) that although the חֻקִּים וּמִשְׁפָּטִים are in contrast with the Decalogue that this 'does not, however, imply any difference of degree in the binding force of the law'.[259] The difference is 'in the range of validity: the Decalogue and in particular the first commandment remain binding for YHWH's people always and everywhere.'[260] This, he says, is established by the unconditional לַעֲשׂוֹת (to do, perform) in 4:13. The חֻקִּים וּמִשְׁפָּטִים, however, 'determine Israel's life only after the conquest of the land (4:5, 14)…it is only there that the law can be observed, the possession of the land is vital for Israel.'[261]

The qualification 'in the land' therefore restricts the binding force of the 'statutes and ordinances' to the Promised Land. In so doing, it distinguishes them from the Decalogue, which was

---

258   Braulik, 'Ausdrücke für "Gesetz"', 62.

259   Georg Braulik, 'Wisdom, Divine Presence and Law' (German title: Weisheit, Gottesnähe und Gesetz), in *The Theology of Deuteronomy*, trans. Ulrika Lindblad (N. Richland Hills: BIBAL Press, 1994), 7.

260   Ibid.

261   Ibid.

always binding, and from the 'pattern' laws, which were binding even in the wilderness. The Decalogue as the 'self-understood' 'constitution of the universe' was the unchanging basis on which God judges all men and nations. The 'pattern' laws were exclusively cultic and determined religious practice immediately and in any location. They would only ever be altered at God's own command (1 Chron. 28:12).

This view might appear to run into difficulties when the law corpus includes laws such as those dealing with clean and unclean food (Deut. 14). How can such 'pattern' laws be included in the law corpus, which will only be binding 'in the land'? The answer is that the 'pattern' laws are binding in the wilderness and 'in the land'. Braulik may be excessively restrictive to say the 'statutes and ordinances' are binding 'only after the conquest of the land', but even the 'pattern' laws that appear in Deuteronomy refer to the future setting of the land (Deut. 14:21).

We cannot say, therefore, that there is no overlap between the 'pattern laws' and laws for 'in the land'. On the other hand, we cannot ignore those distinguishing features; they show that the ancient threefold division of the law is not entirely unjustified even from the text of the Pentateuch. There may be overlap between those categories in the Pentateuch, but the threefold division allows such overlap and broadly reflects those distinguishing features.

A FIVEFOLD DIVISION?

The previous chapter listed Christopher Wright among critics of the threefold division. It is not that Wright rejects classification altogether; he proposes a slightly more elaborate scheme[262] derived from Anthony Phillips' 'basic functional division'.[263]

262 Wright, *People of God*, 152.
263 Ibid., 152, n. 3.

In view of Phillips' claim that Israel saw the Decalogue as her 'criminal law code',[264] it is not surprising that Wright's first category is 'criminal law', which deals with offences that are against the interests of the whole community. The state was the offended party, yet since the Israelite State was a product of God's redemptive work, he was 'the supreme authority'. Any rejection of that authority was a breach of the covenant, an offence against him, and so also against the state. Such misdeeds were therefore treated as crimes. The Decalogue is not pure criminal law, but it marks out serious crimes and all capital offences can be related to it, although not all transgressions of the Decalogue were capital offences. The Tenth Commandment is an example of a law that prohibits a 'morally "criminal"' offence against God.[265]

This summarises Wright's initial categorisation, for which he borrows the categories of modern statecraft from lawyer-turned-theologian Anthony Phillips, but Philips' categories are not obviously drawn from the Old Testament. If an 'offence against God was an offence against the state'[266] and therefore a crime, was not all transgression a 'crime' for it was all against God? The identification of crimes as sins against God in contrast to civil offences, which are 'concerned with private disputes between citizens,'[267] lacks support. The Pentateuch's record of Joseph protesting to Potiphar's wife—'My master has withheld nothing from me except you, because you are his wife, "How can I do this great wickedness, and sin against God?"' (Gen. 39:9)—suggests such transgression was against God and a fellow citizen.

Civil law (mentioned above) is Wright's second category—essentially casuistic law.[268] Here he focuses on the claim that

264   Phillips, *Criminal Law*, 11.
265   Wright, *People of God*, 152–3.
266   Ibid., 152.
267   Ibid.
268   Ibid., 153.

Israel's slave laws highlight 'the inadequacy of the "moral/ civil" distinction, if it assumes that…"civil law" was entirely contingent to Israel and ethically irrelevant.'[269] But it makes no such assumption. On the contrary, the traditional distinction assumes that the 'general equity' of the civil law is highly relevant and obliges universal obedience.

In Wright's scheme, family law follows on from civil law. Family law dealt with matters for which the head of the household had primary responsibility—matters like marriage (Exod. 22:16f.), the status of slaves (Exod. 21:5f.; Deut. 15:16f.), inheritance (Deut. 21:15f.), and redemption of land or people (Lev. 25:23ff.).[270] He presumes such laws would be classed as civil law under the threefold division. Most would, but the laws about redemption and jubilee in Leviticus 25 may also be considered to have a ceremonial aspect. Wright is not satisfied with the traditional categorisation because what he terms family law 'clearly needs a separate category, for sociologically it was a different kind of law'.[271] If, however, the criterion of categorisation is the text of the Old Testament then sociological analysis is not satisfactory. What textual evidence is there to prove that such laws were regarded as separate? Their authority derived from the same source as the other laws and to subdivide it like this is artificial. We could multiply such categories. Why not distinguish building control (Deut. 22:8), agricultural law (Lev. 19:19), and fiscal policy (Exod. 22:5)?

Wright's fourth category is cultic law, which upon examination is identical to the ceremonial law under what he calls 'the old division'.[272] In justifying this re-branding process, he claims 'many people's concept' of the ceremonial law, being

269   Ibid., 154.
270   Ibid., 154–5.
271   Ibid., 155.
272   Ibid., 156.

'controlled by the Letter to the Hebrews and limited to the blood-sacrifices, priestly ordinances, and the ritual of the Day of the Atonement',[273] does not account for other aspects of cultic life. 'Many people's concept' of the ceremonial law could be as limited as Wright claims, but the historic formulations of it cover every aspect of what he terms cultic law.[274] Hence, the contrast he makes between 'cultic' and 'ceremonial' law is non-existent.

The fifth and final category Wright presents is charitable law, which neither the Israelites nor we would 'regard as law at all, in the judicial sense', since it was not enforceable. Charitable law provided wide-ranging protection for the defenceless in society such as widows, orphans, and strangers. It was theologically motivated law with a humanitarian outcome: God redeemed the Israelites from slavery in Egypt, so they had to be gracious towards the weak and the enslaved.[275]

That Wright suggests this category of law is non-judicial and non-enforceable is puzzling, especially in the light of the laws he places in this category.[276] In the first passage he includes Exodus 22:21–7 where God commands the children of Israel not to take advantage of strangers, widows, or orphans, before warning them, 'If you do…I will kill you with the sword; your wives will become widows and your children fatherless.' Other statutes he mentions clearly define transgression of those laws as sin (Deut. 24:15) and even the curses declarations he includes (Deut. 27:18, 25) incorporate capital offences. Those laws therefore forbid actions that would result in God's wrath and curse as much as the laws that he defines as criminal. To

---

273   Ibid.

274   For example *The Westminster Confession* (19.3) speaks of 'ceremonial laws containing several typical ordinances; partly of worship prefiguring Christ, his graces, actions, sufferings, and benefits; and partly holding forth divers instructions of moral duties.'

275   Ibid., 157.

276   Ibid., 157, n. 6.

transgress those laws is as 'morally criminal' as transgression of the tenth commandment.

In summary, Wright's proposals are flawed since they arise from a desire to replace 'the old division' which he has not described accurately. His categories do not flow from the text and are an unworthy replacement for the 'old division'.

SUMMARY

So what would Moses think? If the Pentateuch represents what Moses thought, then the basic categories of the threefold division would not have left him in severe shock. The view that the laws of Moses are 'one indivisible whole'[277] finds no support in the Pentateuch. Its labelling of some laws as 'pattern' laws and others as 'statutes and ordinances' to be observed 'in the land' introduces discrimination, while the Hebrew expressions for law distinguish the Ten Commandments from the rest of the Mosaic code in certain contexts. Above all, the Decalogue's self-understood, divinely-uttered, lapidary, apodictic, and constitutional status marks it out as a distinctive collection of laws that in the Pentateuch 'for ever bind all'. Those who adopted this 'orthodox position' throughout the centuries did so because they believed it had a biblical and theological basis derived, in part, from the Pentateuch. Like all interpretations, it is open to challenge, but it should not be misconstrued or dismissed without consideration. Its legitimacy as an authoritative theological framework and its developed exposition in the Reformed confessions did not, however, depend solely on the Pentateuch, but also on the other sixty-one books in the Protestant canon. In the next chapter we will therefore consider relevant issues from the rest of the Old Testament and beyond.

277   Longenecker, *Paul*, 119.

III

LAW IN ACTION?

They got Christ's young love.

Samuel Rutherford on Israel

Having decided that the threefold division is not so out of
harmony with the Pentateuch as many writers suppose, the
next step is to examine issues concerning juridical process
and interpretation of the law in Israel as described in the rest
of the Old Testament and the Gospels. Reformed interpreters
have viewed the first part of the New Testament as being in
close continuity with the Old Testament regarding the status
of the law, since the hermeneutical turning point is the death
and resurrection of Christ, not a blank page found between the
testaments. From that perspective, I will deal with certain points
from the Gospels in this chapter, but because questions about
Jesus and the law are normally discussed separately, that will be
the matter of the next chapter.

JURIDICAL PROCESS

If the threefold division has some basis in the Pentateuch, we
might expect that any account of juridical process in the Old
Testament would lend further support to the idea. For Daniel
Friedmann, 'the first two trials of the Bible...are conducted from
beginning to end, by God, who serves as the investigator, the

prosecutor, and the judge.'[1] After the trials of Adam and Eve, then Cain, those roles 'passed into human hands.'[2] Galinski is less optimistic. In his exhaustive two thousand year history of ancient Israelite law courts, from Jethro (Exod. 18) to the Sanhedrin, he notes that according to Jewish tradition, juridical process can be traced almost to the beginning, being 'one of seven cardinal precepts of conduct promulgated to Noah and binding upon all future Mankind'.[3] This, however, is not clear from Genesis 9 and in general, he cannot do more than discuss bare legal structures without going beyond the Old Testament.[4] In another volume on Jewish legal history, Westbrook claims that in the book of Ruth 'the substantive law…does not differ radically from that found in other periods', yet 'there is no consciousness of a code of Mosaic law that has to be followed by the local courts.'[5] Given the law on levirate marriage in Deuteronomy 25:5–10, the latter point is probably overstated in this case. Irrespective of where the foundations of the first law court were laid in the Old Testament, any effort to systematise juridical process from any of its narratives, far less establish an underlying doctrine, is fraught with difficulty. Hans Jochen Bocker highlights this problem:

> It is more difficult than might appear at first sight to bring together OT data on the administration of law. There are no OT 'rules of court.' We must remember above all that in its basic message the OT is not interested in conveying a picture of legal processes in Ancient Israel. Its concern lies elsewhere. Its purpose is to report God's activity in and with Israel and to demonstrate Israel's answer

---

1   Daniel Friedmann, *To Kill and Take Possession: Law Morality, and Society in Biblical Stories* (Peabody: Hendriockson Publishers, 2002), 9.

2   Ibid., 10.

3   Galinski, *Pursue Justice*, 1.

4   Ibid., 42–86.

5   N. S. Hecht, B. S. Jackson, S. M. Passamaneck, D. Piattelli, and A. M. Rabello, eds., *An Introduction to the History and Sources of Jewish Law.* (Oxford: Clarendon Press, 1996), 3.

to this activity. This purpose is pursued in many ways, and in the course of it much is said about law, but unsystematically and in passing. This makes the matter so difficult.[6]

Bocker is right to highlight the intent of the Old Testament as an obstacle for anyone seeking to prove that the narratives present any authoritative way of administering the Mosaic Law. In addition, the purpose of courts in ancient Israel was not to establish underlying morals or constitutional matters, but to apply 'self-understood' and divinely uttered commands as they had been worked out in the Law of Moses. Thus, we should expect that any account of juridical process would focus on implementing 'civil' legislation rather than on distinguishing between fundamental principles or cultic laws.

If any theme stands out in the Old Testament narratives, it is not Israel's careful interpretation of the law, but her disregard for the divine statutes. Joshua ends his days urging Israel to 'do all that is written in the Book of the Law of Moses' (Josh. 23:8), yet on the passing of his generation Israel 'abandoned the LORD' (Judg. 2:12). Judges of varying piety come and go, but the dominant theme is that 'in those days there was no king in Israel. Everyone did what was right in his own eyes' (Judg. 21:25). When the days of kings in Israel and Judah appear, they are not marked by unfailing submission to the Law of Moses. The best of the kings do 'what is right in the eyes of the LORD' and to varying degrees, they follow the Law of Moses (2 Kgs. 23:24–5; 2 Chr. 30:1–16). Yet, even they stumble and fall (1 Sam. 11; 2 Kgs. 20:12–15). The worst of them simply 'do what is evil in the eyes of the LORD' and lead the people in refusing to hear the Law of Moses (2 Kgs. 21:1–9). Indeed, during Josiah's reign it transpires that the Book of the Law, which Israel was charged to keep,

6   Hans Jochen Bocker, *Law and the Administration of Justice in the Old Testament and Ancient East*, trans. Jeremy Moiser. (London: SPCK, 1980), 28.

had lain abandoned in the temple until Hilkiah rediscovered it (2 Kgs. 22:8). In the end, neither judges nor kings can keep the children of Israel faithful to the Law of Moses and the divided nations are united under judgment (2 Kgs. 17:6; 25:21). This occurred because the people of Israel and Judah 'sinned against the LORD their God' and 'did not keep the commandments of the LORD their God' (2 Kgs. 17:7–23). Thus, the Old Testament report of 'God's activity in and with Israel' presents 'Israel's answer to this activity', from the days of the judges to the days of Jehoiachin, as an overwhelming rejection of his interest in them.

This is not to say the narrative sections of the Old Testament suggest complete ignorance of the law. Nathan charges David the murderous adulterer with 'despising the word of the LORD' (2 Sam. 12:9), while Jezebel shows surprising concern for the Mosaic Law with her false charge against Naboth and in ensuring it is upheld by two witnesses (Exod. 22:28; Deut. 17:16; 1 Kgs. 21:10). Yet, none of this is intended to provide later interpreters with a framework for understanding the Mosaic Law; the authors of Old Testament narrative simply assume it has binding authority. We may observe that the nation's besetting sins are transgressions of the Decalogue, such as idolatry, murder, and adultery, but this is not enough to prove a division between moral and civil in juridical process.

The New Testament Gospels do not give further insight into Israelite juridical process, even though under Roman rule local law was maintained as much as possible.[7] The first significant juridical event is that of the woman 'caught in adultery' (John 8:1–11), which is not considered too important due to its absence from the earliest Greek manuscripts. Theonomists see this account as an example of Jesus upholding the two-witness rule (Deut. 19:15), since no witnesses remained after the departure

---

7   Carson, D. A., *The Gospel According to John* (Leicester, IVP, 1991), 599.

of her accusers.[8] This, however, is simplistic given that Jesus' call for those 'without sin' to cast the first stone probably pointed to the sin of her accusers. The other relevant event is that of Jesus' own trial when, like Jezebel, his accusers were remarkably concerned to uphold the two-witness rule (Matt. 27:59–60) even if it was a little frustrating (Mark 14:55–6). Ultimately, the two-witness rule was made redundant because for his accusers his 'I am' to the high priest (Mark 14:62) was a self-incriminatory lie and sufficient proof of his having committed a capital offence (John 19:7; Lev. 24:16).

This general lack of detail concerning juridical process in the biblical history of Israel would not have troubled those who argued for a threefold division. Keith Whitelam's comments, although dealing specifically with monarchs, highlight a possible reason for this:

> One of the major problems in dealing with the judicial functions of the Israelite monarchy has been a failure to distinguish between the ideal or theoretical position on the one hand, and its practical implications on the other. In general, the ideal position is presented in the Psalms and Prophets, whereas the historical books often witness to the practical problems involved in the administration of monarchical judicial authority and the failure to attain this ideal.[9]

This distinction may have something in common with the thinking behind the practical-theological threefold division. Its advocates were not concerned to ask, 'How was the Mosaic Law understood in the courts of Israel?' but rather, 'How should the Mosaic Law have been understood in Israel?' Their concern was to determine from Scripture what God himself regarded as 'the ideal position'.

8   Greg L. Bahnsen, *Theonomy in Christian Ethics* (Nutley, The Craig Press, 1977), 231–2.

9   Keith W. Whitelam, *The Just King: Monarchical Judicial Authority in Ancient Israel* (Sheffield: JSOT Press, 1979), 18.

In the opening words of Psalm 72 the psalmist combines the themes of kingship and justice:

> Give the king your justice, O God,
>   and your righteousness to the royal son.
> May he judge your people with righteousness,
>   and your poor with justice.
> Let the mountains bear prosperity for the people,
>   and the hills, in righteousness.
> May he defend the cause of the poor of the people,
>   give deliverance to the children of the needy,
> and crush the oppressor.

In 'observing all the words of this law…that he may not turn aside from the commandment', this king fulfils the divine mandate outlined in Deuteronomy 17:18–20 and becomes the 'ideal'. The prophets echo the same themes when they speak of a throne to be occupied by one 'who judges and seeks justice and is swift to do righteousness' (Isa. 16:5) or of a king who will 'deal wisely, and shall execute justice and righteousness in the land' (Jer. 23:5).

The same problem, however, appears in the Psalms and Prophets as in the narratives. Although the Law of Moses is enfleshed in the king as his piety overflows into the administration of justice, there is no account of juridical process or anything sufficiently specific to suggest a particular framework for the Mosaic Law. Thus, any expectations that references to juridical process in the Old Testament would lend support to the threefold division are not met. At the same time, nothing undermines the idea or its basis in the Pentateuch.

'MERCY AND NOT SACRIFICE'

An earlier chapter recorded Kaiser's suggestion that the Old Testament call for 'mercy and not sacrifice' (Hos. 6:6; Isa. 1:11–7; Jer. 7:21–3; Mic. 6:8; 1 Sam. 15:22–3; Ps. 51:17) 'points to a deliberate priority and ranking in the legal injunctions that had been given by Moses.'[10] What does this phrase, found in narrative, the prophets, and the gospels reveal about the interpretation of the law? Jesus relates the expression to the case of David eating the bread of the Presence (1 Sam. 21:6; Matt. 12:28–34), which might suggest that for him 'ceremonial' laws were a lesser division of the Mosaic Law. An earlier incident that may reflect 'deliberate ranking and priority' is the mass circumcision at Gilgal of all the people who had been born in the wilderness (Josh. 5). Does their uncircumcised state in the wilderness suggest the laws regarding circumcision in Leviticus 12:3 were less important?

Although 1 Samuel 15 does not use the phrase 'mercy and not sacrifice', that theme underlies this account of the LORD sending Saul to utterly destroy[11] Amalek. In a successful battle, Saul destroyed all the people, but he spared Agag the king with the best of their animals and claimed the people spared the best of the animals to sacrifice to God. Diana Edelman puts this down to Saul's 'desperate desire to fulfil the divine command to its last iota' and his presumption that 'the people acted under similar altruistic motivations.'[12] But Samuel was not convinced. When Saul came boasting of having carried out the LORD's instructions, he demanded to know why Saul had not obeyed the voice of God, asking:

> Has the LORD as great delight in burnt offerings and sacrifices,
>   as in obeying the voice of the LORD?
> Behold, to obey is better than sacrifice,
>   and to listen than the fat of rams.
> For rebellion is as the sin of divination,
>   and presumption is as iniquity and idolatry.

---

10   Kaiser, 'God's Promise Plan', 291.

11   חֵרֶם ban, devote to destruction.

12   Diana Vikander Edelman, *King Saul in the Historiography of Judah* (Sheffield: JSOT Press, 1991), 105. See page 102 for her basis for this interpretation.

Whether Saul, with his people, intended to offer sacrifice commanded by the Law of Moses, and whether that was their original plan or a panicky excuse, the crucial issue for Samuel was that Saul was seeking God's submission rather than submitting to God. Saul's willingness to sacrifice was not true worship, but 'hidden non-co-operation'[13] because he was disobedient to the clear command of the LORD. Samuel was not opposed to sacrifice (1 Sam. 10:8), but when Saul bolts towards the altar for the second time (cf. 1 Sam. 13:8–14) Samuel makes plain that such worship is not the kind of service God seeks. Unless accompanied by obedience to God's instructions it is vain hypocrisy—and worse—idolatry. Formal perfection in the worship of God, may mask rebellion against God, and thus be idolatry because instead of being directed to a God who seeks humble obedience, it is directed to a god made in man's own image whose favour can be bought with sheep and oxen.

The other Old Testament references to 'mercy and not sacrifice' occur outside narrative contexts. According to Davies, 'it is probably a mistake to look for a single viewpoint in all these passages',[14] but he does not explain why this should be so. A more likely error is that of rummaging for differing viewpoints in passages with a high degree of similarity in wording, vocabulary, and context. For Yehezkel Kaufmann, passages such as Hosea 6:6 have a common theme in 'the great new doctrine of prophecy' which 'was the primacy of morality over the cult....Whether or not the prophets objected to sacrifice on principle, it is plain that they considered morality the essence of religion and valued it over the cult.'[15]

Kaufmann sees the doctrine as new because in his judgement

13   Hans Wilhelm Hertzberg, *I & II Samuel* (London: SCM Press, 1960), 128.

14   G. I. Davies, *Hosea* (Grand Rapids: Eerdmans, 1992), 170.

15   Yehezkel Kaufmann, *The Religion of Israel: From its Beginnings to the Babylonian Exile*, trans. Moshe Greenberg (London: George Allen & Unwin Ltd, 1961), 160.

the Torah does not openly declare the primacy of morality, although he concedes 'there is but a step from the moral outlook of the Torah to the doctrine of the primacy of morality…but this step was never taken before prophecy.'[16] The lack of 'mercy and not sacrifice' phraseology in the Pentateuch does not mean, however, that they are 'given equal emphasis'.[17] Throughout the Pentateuch, 'sacrifice' is never the first choice. Nor is it an equally valid alternative to 'mercy'. The provision of sacrifice declares the need for atonement when 'mercy' fails and thus asserts the 'primacy of morality'. The prophetic calls for justice instead of offerings are more than sayings 'formulated under the shadow of Deuteronomistic theology';[18] they are direct applications, and as Bergen points out, the prophets considered themselves heirs, rather than founders, of a tradition that put mercy first.[19] He also highlights the way in which prophetic discourse reflects this approach to the Mosaic Law:

> It is noticeable that, in no case, does the accusation portion of any of the Prophetic Judgment-Speeches of our prophets correspond in content to any of the cultic requirements of apodictic law. None of the prophets says, "Because you have boiled a kid in its mother's milk, therefore…"; or, "You have not kept the feast of unleavened bread, therefore…"[20]

In his view, this does not merely reflect perfect obedience to cultic law among the people, or that the prophets considered cultic requirements 'mere accoutrements of religion',[21] but that 'the consequences ascribed by the Pentateuch to their breach set apart some [laws] as being more significant than others'.[22] He

16   Ibid., 160–1.
17   Ibid., 160.
18   Otto Kaiser, *Isaiah 1–12* (London: SCM Press Ltd, 1983), 28.
19   Bergen, *Prophets and the Law*, 216–7.
20   Ibid., 214.
21   Ibid., 215.
22   Ibid., 217.

finds further support in Noth's comment on the absence of cultic law from the Decalogue: the 'unique element in the relationship between God and Israel is not evident in the cultic sphere but in obedience to the one God and his demands which pertain to relationships. Even the sabbath commandment is no exception here...it was at all events not thought of as a cultic feast.'[23] Bergen is right to see such an approach to the Pentateuch in the prophetic mindset, but he overstates his case when he claims that for them 'the transgression of a casuistic law...would have no effect upon the covenant relationship',[24] since such laws reflected the 'mercy' the prophets demanded.

With respect to the threefold division, two opposing sentiments expressed in the prophetic 'mercy and not sacrifice' passages are worthy of particular consideration. They are most clearly expressed in Amos 5:21 where the LORD says, 'I hate, I despise your feasts, and I take no delight in your solemn assemblies', and in Amos 6:6 where he says, 'I desire mercy.' At a practical level, those statements are no more than further cases where 'not rite but right is demanded; devotion not devotions'.[25] At a deeper level, they reveal a 'deliberate priority and ranking' in that there is certain obedience (mercy) the LORD consistently desires and can never hate, while there is other obedience (sacrifice) he does not always desire and may sometimes hate—whenever 'Israel's altars are not a means of expiating sin, but a cause of sin.'[26] As the proverb says, 'The sacrifice of the wicked is an abomination to the LORD' (Prov. 15:8).

Nowhere does Scripture suggest that God ever hates obedience to any part of the Decalogue. The LORD cannot despise singular

23   Ibid., 216.

24   Ibid., 223, n. 1.

25   J. Alberto Soggin, *The Prophet Amos*, trans. John Bowden, 1987 (London: SCM Press Ltd, 1987).

26   Grace I. Emmerson, *Hosea: An Israelite Prophet in Judean Perspective.* (Sheffield: JSOT Press, 1984), 153.

devotion to himself, the rejection of idolatry, the honour of his name, or the sanctifying of the Sabbath. He does not hate respect for parents, life, marital fidelity, honesty, truth, or contentment, although there are times when the one God who can give life or take it away (Deut. 32:39), himself commands judicial killing (e.g. Gen. 9:6, Exod. 21:12, I Sam. 15:2–3). Not even in the case of the Sabbath commandment does he hate or not desire obedience. The prophets never direct their ire at genuine obedience to this commandment. It too has moral primacy over cultic laws. Thus, Jeremiah tells Israel that although the LORD has no time for their ceremonial obedience (Jer. 7:21–3), still he wants them to keep the Sabbath holy (Jer. 17:20–27). Isaiah condemns its 'misuse',[27] yet expects them to 'call the Sabbath a delight' (Isa. 58:13). Ezekiel repeatedly condemns Sabbath desecration (Ezek. 20:13ff., 22:8, 23:8) and Amos, who speaks of the LORD despising and hating their religiosity, prophecies judgement upon reluctant Sabbath-keepers (Amos 5:8). This high view of the Sabbath is not surprising if, as Balentine argues, the Sabbath commandment is the 'rhetorical center' in both versions of the Decalogue where 'the concerns of the entire Decalogue are drawn together in the command to keep the Sabbath day'.[28] Ironically, Balentine's own vision of the Old Testament reduces these prophetic emphases to criticisms of priestly ritual as 'an agent of social control'.[29] He leans on Nelson's observation 'that ritual provides "the backbone of religion, for it can be carried on even when faith is weak",'[30] but this is the very theology rejected by the prophets.

As with the Decalogue, no biblical examples portray God as hating obedience to the 'statues and ordinances' that flow from it (see previous chapter). Obedience to the 'judicial' as well as

27   J. A. Motyer, *The Prophecy of Isaiah* (Leicester: Inter-Varsity Press, 1993), 47.

28   Balentine, *Torah's Vision*, 187.

29   Ibid., 152.

30   Ibid., 176.

the 'moral' law of the classical threefold division was the 'mercy' desired by God. The category of 'ceremonial law' therefore finds support not only from the 'pattern' or 'model' dimension discussed earlier, but also from the 'mercy and not sacrifice' presupposition found in various parts of the Old Testament. Only obedience to the ceremonial laws may be hated and not desired by God. In asserting 'the primacy of morality', the threefold division integrates major Old Testament themes.

LAW AND PROPHETS

The connection between the ceremonial laws of the threefold division and 'sacrifice' is obvious, but how does 'mercy' relate to the moral and judicial categories? Does it encompass all the non-cultic laws of the Pentateuch? Should 'mercy' be more narrowly defined as the Decalogue? Or might 'mercy' and the law-breaking that prophets condemn have no direct connection with the Law of Moses?

Commentators often note a direct link between the prophetic message and the Decalogue in some passages. One example is the accusation in Hosea 4:2 of 'swearing, lying, murder, stealing, and adultery', which are breaches of five of the Ten Commandments. Douglas Stuart adds one more in translating the last phrase in the verse as 'idols crowd against one another.'[31] Defending a connection with the Horeb revelation, he notes that the violations of murder, theft, and adultery 'are given in the exact root vocabulary of the Decalogue'.[32]

Turning to Amos, Stuart finds the prophet's message in conformity to the Mosaic covenant. 'The crimes Amos identifies are those the Sinai covenant defines as crimes (e.g., oppression of the poor, denial of inheritance rights, failure to observe

31   Stuart, *Hosea—Jonah*, 70.
32   Ibid., 76.

sabbatical and jubilee laws, etc.). Moreover, the punishments Amos predicts for Israel all fit the curse categories established in the Pentateuch.'[33] This is his view of the prophets in general and he rejects the idea that they invented biblical social ethics.[34]

For John Barton, such an approach is 'basically unsatisfactory',[35] particularly when it comes to Amos' condemnation of the nations surrounding Israel in the opening section of his prophecy. It risks, he argues, 'suggesting that the nations are condemned for breaking an edict they were unaware of: for what reason was there to think that God's will had been revealed to them?'[36] The biblical writers, however, make no effort to avoid this 'risk' whether they are describing the flood, Sodom's destruction, or recording prophecy. This is unsurprising if the Pentateuch's presentation of the Decalogue as distinct by virtue of its antecedence is part of a Scripture-wide presupposition that the content of the Ten Words was 'self-understood' from the beginning. Barton therefore makes a false dichotomy when he writes that Amos 'is precisely not saying that the nations will perish because they have—all unwittingly for all he knows—broken the decree of Yahweh; he is saying they deserve punishment for contravening moral principles that even they should have recognised.'[37] For Amos, there is no difference. Habbakuk similarly makes no allowances when, in what Roberston describes as the 'fullest single application of the moral law to the nations', he condemns the Babylonians for 'plundering, killing, seeking unjust gain, shedding blood, forcing others to drink, and worshipping idols.'[38]

33 Ibid., 288.

34 Ibid., xxxi.

35 John Barton, *Amos's Oracles against the Nations: A study of Amos 1.3–2.5* (Cambridge: Cambridge University Press, 1980), 43.

36 Ibid.

37 Ibid.

38 O. Palmer Robertson, *The Christ of the Prophets* (Awaiting Publication), VI; 25.

Barton makes a further claim, that Amos only denounces the surrounding nations 'for offences against common humanity' and not sins such as idolatry, but this is also dubious. Amos' condemnation of Moab's magical burning of Edom's royal bones (2:1) and his mention of Kerioth (2:2) carry an implicit charge of idolatry. He was more than a campaigner for human rights. The same is true of other prophets: Ezekiel condemns the idolatrous pride of Tyre and predicts judgement (Ezek. 28:2–10) while Zephaniah denounces Nineveh's blasphemous idolatry by depicting her as taking to herself words that, according to Isaiah, only the LORD can utter (Zeph. 2:15; Isa. 45:21).

In a more recent article, Barton takes the same approach to Isaiah, attempting to show 'natural-law tradition…has roots not only in the classical world, but also in Hebrew tradition.'[39] It is not 'hopeless anachronism', he concludes, to see in Isaiah's denunciations 'a cast of mind that assumes something like natural law as its starting point.'[40]

> [Isaiah] begins with a picture of the world in which God is the creator and preserver of all things, and occupies by right the supreme position over all that he has made. The essence of morality is cooperation in maintaining the ordered structure which prevails, under God's guidance, in the natural constitution of things, and the keynote of the whole system is order, a proper submission to one's assigned place in the scheme of things and the avoidance of any action that would challenge the supremacy of God or seek to subvert the order he has established. Such is the basic premise from which all Isaiah's thinking about ethical obligation begins.[41]

In recognising the sovereignty of God over his creation, this statement has a ring of traditional orthodoxy. But what does

---

39   John Barton, 'Ethics in Isaiah of Jerusalem', in Robert P. Gordon, ed., *'The Place Is Too Small for Us': the Israelite Prophets in Recent Scholarship* (Winona Lake: Eisenbrauns, 1995), 80.

40   Ibid.

41   Ibid., 90.

he mean by 'the ordered structure which prevails' or 'proper submission to one's assigned place'? Is he referring to the structure and assignments of the original creation, of society in a fallen world, or of the new heaven and new earth promised by Isaiah? Barton's point is somewhat impenetrable, but the idea that Isaiah's morality was a matter of cooperation with the events of providence or something relative to circumstances is not supported by the text of Isaiah and as Palmer Robertson observes, 'In his effort to establish the role of natural law in Isaiah, Barton inadvertently echoes 8 of the 10 commandments.'[42] Isaiah is, in fact, straightforward in relating immorality to transgression of the law (5:24; 24:5; 42:24) and Jensen is correct that he always sees תּוֹרָה as 'deriving more or less immediately from Yahweh'.[43]

Barton shares his reasoning with Eryl W. Davies who writes:

> Not only the Decalogue but the law as a whole was such a limited and imperfect instrument that serious doubts may be entertained concerning the dependence of the prophets on Israel's legal tradition....The prophet's condemnation of the people's extravagance and luxury cannot have been rooted in Israel's legal tradition. Similarly, the law did not concern itself with sobriety, and consequently the accusations against drunkenness (Is. 5:11, 22) could have had no basis in any legal stipulation. Further, it is unlikely that Isaiah's condemnation of pride, self-gratification and vanity (Is. 3:18ff; 5:21) were rooted in the law, for it is difficult to see how such attitudes of mind could have been effectively controlled through legislation.[44]

None of this provides an adequate foundation for dismissing prophetic dependence on Israel's legal tradition. That there is no apodictic prohibition of drunkenness in the Mosaic Code is obvious, but the narrative sections of the law cannot be ignored.

42   Robertson, *Christ of the Prophets*, VI–1 n. 1.

43   Joseph Jensen, *The Use of tôrâ by Isaiah: His Debate with the Wisdom Tradition* (Washington: the Catholic Biblical Association of America, 1973), 67.

44   Eryl W. Davies, *Prophecy and Ethics: Isaiah and the Ethical Traditions of Israel* (Sheffield: JSOT Press, 1981), 26. cf. Barton, 'Ethics in Isaiah', 83.

For those whose theological framework has included the threefold division, there is no reason to think that Isaiah could not have been dependent on the stories of Noah's drunkenness where 'we are dealing with another fall'.[45] In addition, that Isaiah's condemnation of 'attitudes of mind' does not separate his morality from the Mosaic legislation merely because it could not 'effectively be controlled' is plain from the existence of the tenth commandment: 'You shall not covet.'

Barton suggests the 'natural law' of Isaiah is a 'remote ancestor' of Romans 1:19–25. If so, perhaps the risk that the 'nations are condemned for breaking an edict they were unaware of'[46] is no risk at all. Were the prophets the progenitors of the theology of Romans, they would not have considered the nations as unaware of moral truth, but of suppressing it (Rom. 1:18). In relation to the people of God themselves, Isaiah was not the only prophet to make a plain charge of breaking God's law (5:24; 24:5; 42:24). He was joined explicitly by Jeremiah (6:19; 9:13; 16:11; 44:10), Ezekiel (20:13; 22:26), Hosea (4:6; 8:1), Amos (2:4), Zephaniah (3:4), and Zechariah (7:12). Barton and Davies are therefore unconvincing in their attempts to distance the prophets from the Mosaic Law.

The opening paragraphs of this section referred to those who see a direct link between the prophetic message and the Decalogue. Like Stuart, many see a particular link between Hosea 4:2 and the Ten Words, but that does not constitute an explicit recognition of their uniqueness. Palmer Robertson argues for a general link between various passages where transgressions of the Decalogue are catalogued and the prophets apply 'each of the original "ten words" to their contemporaries'.[47] The following table outlines his chosen 'samples of these applications':[48]

---

45   Gordon J. Wenham, *Story as Torah: Reading the Old Testament Ethically* (Edinburgh: T&T Clark, 2000), 35.

46   Barton, *Amos's Oracles*, 43.

47   Robertson, *Christ of the Prophets*, 7.

48   Ibid., 7–17.

ROBERTSON'S EXAMPLES OF PROPHETIC APPLICATION OF THE DECALOGUE

Word	Prophetic Sample
I	Israel changing gods and digging their own cisterns (Jer 2:11–13).
II	Israel make idols for their own destruction (Hos. 8:4–6; 9:10).
III	Condemnation of Israel's empty worship (Amos 5:21–4). Insouciant oath taking (Isa. 48:1) and chatter (Zeph. 1:12; Jer. 5:12).
IV	Impatience towards the Sabbath (Amos 8:5). Attitude to the Sabbath leading to blessing or curse (Jer. 17:19–27).
V	Disrespect for parents (Ezek. 22:7; Mic. 7:5–6).
VI	Abounding strife and violence paralyze the law (Hab 1:2–4; Mic. 6:12).
VII	Trooping to brothels and neighing for neighbour's wives (Jer. 5:7–8; Amos 2:7).
VIII	Theft by oppressive lawmaking (Isa. 10:2, 1:23). Bribery and sharp practice (Hos. 11:8; Amos 8:5–6; Hab. 2:6–7).
IX	Lying and false promises (Hos. 10:4; Jer 9:3–11).
X	Insatiable appetites for the wealth of others (Isa. 56:11; Amos 4:1; 5:11; 8:4–7).

While this displays a link between the prophets and the Decalogue, it does not lend unique support to the threefold division, or tie 'mercy' exclusively to the Decalogue. Many of these condemnations could equally have been based on laws in the 'statutes and ordinances' of Deuteronomy. Yet, throughout the prophets, the sins condemned are transgressions of law that can be traced back to the Decalogue in much the same way as those 'statutes and ordinances'. The prophets need not give explicit support to a division between 'moral' and 'judicial' laws for it to be likely that, like the Pentateuch, their framework recognises the primacy of the Decalogue.

That the Ten Words have such primacy may be the assumption behind Amos' proclamation of a famine 'of hearing the words of the LORD' (Amos 8:11). The Masoretic Text's דִּבְרֵי יְהוָה (words of the LORD) is contested,[49] but there are good exegetical reasons to accept it as it stands and 'the plural itself is well established.'[50] Amos' reference to 'words of the LORD' reflects not indifference to the number of the noun, but a deliberate focus on the Decalogue. Andersen and Freedman find support for this in Exodus (24:3–4; 34:27–8) and in the possibility that Deuteronomy 5:5 uses the plural term, yet they acknowledge that the plural seems to 'describe the written code centred on the Decalogue'.[51] This qualification is necessary because the Hebrew expressions for 'law' do not consistently delineate particular sections of the law and there is no more compelling reason to accept the Septuagint's plural rendering in Deuteronomy 5:5 (τὰ ῥήματα κυρίου) than there is to accept its singular rendering in Amos. The textual features of Amos 8:11 reflect rather than determine the prophet's focus on the Ten Words. His call to Israel, 'Prepare to meet your God, O Israel!' (הִכּוֹן לִקְרַאת־אֱלֹהֶיךָ יִשְׂרָאֵל, 4:12), also echoes the language of Exodus 19—the only other passage that uses identical vocabulary in calling Israel to prepare to meet God (כּוּן, Exod. 19:11, 15; קְרָא, Exod. 19:17). Like his fellow prophets, Amos' focus on the 'words of the LORD' flows from his recognition of their programmatic role.

---

49   Some Hebrew texts prefer the singular, which is adopted in other translations (e.g. ⅏, Syriac, Vul.) and occurs almost universally in the prophets.

50   Shalom M. Paul, *A Commentary on the Book of Amos* (Minneapolis: Fortress Press, 1991), 265, n. 5.

51   Francis I. Andersen and David Noel Freedman, *Amos: A New Translation with Introduction and Commentary* (New York: Doubleday, 1989), 824

LAW AND THE SONGS OF GOD'S PEOPLE

The truism, 'Give me the making of the songs of a nation, and I care not who writes its laws' has been attributed to figures as diverse as Plato, the eighteenth century Scottish writer, Andrew Fletcher, and Bernard Shaw. Such a connection between song and the thought of cultures or religious communities is generally assumed. This is also true for ancient Israel although, unlike modern nations, their songs were often about their laws, precisely because they cared who had written them. As the hymnbook of Israel, the book of Psalms provides insights into Israelite piety and beliefs, revealing not only how the law functioned in personal religion, but also how it was viewed in the created order.

Concerning ceremonial laws, the Psalms espouse the same approach to sacrifice as other parts of the Old Testament (discussed above). Psalmists can speak positively of sacrifice and offering (4:5; 27:6; 66:13–15; 107:22), but they also insist that God desires mercy and not sacrifice (40:6; 51:16). This division is particularly noteworthy in Psalm 50 where God declares that 'their ritual offerings are all bogus.'[52] He is not hungry for meat (12–13), but he does seek obedience to the commandments of the Decalogue, making specific mention of theft, adultery, and lying (18–20). The connection with Horeb is made more explicit by the theophanic expressions in the opening verses: God 'shines forth' (2), 'a devouring fire is before him, and around him a mighty whirlwind' (3). This intertextuality extends to verse 7 where God's words are 'reminiscent of the preface to the Decalogue'[53] and resonant of the *Shema* (Deut. 6:4).[54]

52   Konrad Schaefer, *Psalms*, BERIT OLAM: Studies in Hebrew Narrative & Poetry, ed. David W. Cotter (Collegeville: the Liturgical Press, 2001), 127.

53   Peter C. Craigie, *Psalms 1–50*, WBC, ed. David A. Hubbard and Glenn W. Barker (General), John D. W. Watts (Old Testament), no. 19 (Waco: Word Books, 1983), 365.

54   Schaefer, *Psalms*, 127.

Similar features appear in Psalm 81 where language and content recall Sinai in much the same way (7–10). According to Theodoret, even the call to sound the trumpet (3) 'reminded the people of the trumpets used on the mountain'.[55] Schaefer envisages celebration in the opening verses until 'the majestic voice resounds, which chills the initial enthusiasm as it unveils the radical falseness of such musical celebration.'[56] In this light, Terrien's translation of חֹק לְיִשְׂרָאֵל (5) as 'law in Israel' is interesting because he sees this as referring not simply to the preceding imperatives, but 'together with its synonyms, ordinance and statute' it 'designates at first…the Decalogue, carved in stone'.[57] His translation, however, appears to represent a triumph of his individual strophic structure over straightforward exegesis. In any case, the role of the Decalogue as the fundamental legal basis for God's charges against Israel is explicit in the Psalm's repetition of its prohibition of other gods and idolatry (9). Overall, there is a marked similarity between Psalms 50 and 81. As with other Asaph psalms, 'readers…can hardly fail to be struck by the instances of Deuteronomic language'[58] and, like the prophetic writings, they assert the 'primacy of morality'.

Psalm 119 mentions no offering except that of praise (119:108), but it does reveal something of how the law functioned and was viewed in Israel. Described by Augustine as a psalm that 'does not seem to need an expositor, but only a reader and a listener',[59] it is full of love and longing for God's laws, which are from

55   Theodoret of Cyrus, *Commentary on the Psalms 73–150,* trans. Robert C. Hill (Washington: the Catholic University of America Press, 2001), 52.

56   Schaefer, *Psalms,* 199.

57   Samuel Terrien, *The Psalms: Strophic Structure and Theological Commentary* (Grand Rapids: Eerdmans, 2002) 584.

58   Michael D. Goulder, *The Psalms of Asaph and the Pentateuch: Studies in the Psalter, III* (Sheffield: Sheffield Academic Press, 1996), 31.

59   Quoted in Will Soll, *Psalm 119: Matrix, Form, and Setting* (Washington: the Catholic Biblical Association of America, 1991), 1.

everlasting to everlasting. But what are the laws in question? Because 'the concrete specifics of the law are never spelt out'[60] and there is a 'lack of definition of Torah,'[61] does this mean the laws referred to are beyond definition? Allen keeps his options wide open when he writes: '"Torah" seems to embrace not only the Pentateuch but also at least Isaiah and Jeremiah and Proverbs'.[62]

For Levenson, 'one of the programmatic discoveries of biblical criticism was the idea that large parts of the Pentateuch date from *after* the prophets, not before' which 'raises the possibility that biblical references to *tôrâ* need not refer to the Pentateuch at all.'[63] Although acknowledging that the psalmist is theologically 'closest to Deuteronomy'[64] he agrees with those who see a great degree of similarity with Isaiah, Proverbs, and Job. He asks, if the author of Psalm 119 is 'speaking of the Pentateuchal laws... then why does he never mention any specifics? Why does he not insist with Moses and Samuel, that he has never misappropriated property, or, with Ezekiel, that he has never eaten forbidden food? The utter lack of concreteness and specificity in his discussion of commandments is further evidence against the assumption that the Pentateuch is uppermost in his mind.'[65] But why should he mention specifics? Perhaps he sees no need to mention specifics because the last thing he imagined is that centuries later 'programmatic discoveries' would show that large parts of the law he was extolling were yet to be written.

60   John Day, *Psalms* (Sheffield: Sheffield Academic Press, 1990), 56.

61   Ibid.

62   Leslie C. Allen, *Psalms 101–150*, WBC, ed. David A. Hubbard and Glenn W. Barker (General), John D. W. Watts (Old Testament), no. 21 (Waco: Word Books, 1983), 141.

63   Jon D. Levenson, 'The Sources of Torah: Psalm 119 and the Modes of Revelation in Second Temple Judaism' in *Ancient Israelite Religion*, eds. Patrick D. Miller, Jr., Paul D. Hanson, and S. Dean McBride. (Philadephia: Fortress Press, 1987), 560.

64   Ibid., 563.

65   Ibid., 566.

Levenson's answer to his own question is that the usage of law in Psalm 119 is closer to Proverbs where it 'indicates the counsel of a sage rather than juridical or cultic norms'.[66] His chosen proof text is Proverbs 13:13, which he translates: 'The teaching (*tôrâ*) of a sage is a fountain of life'. Although he concedes that this is not seen as 'one person's opinion, but as a revelation of the will of God',[67] the usage of תּוֹרָה in Proverbs and Psalm 119 are not as close as Levenson implies. Proverbs' thirteen uses of תּוֹרָה are either tied to human beings or are impersonal, whereas the twenty-five occurrences in Psalm 119 always see תּוֹרָה as coming directly from God. Thus, even if Proverbs and Psalm 119 ultimately refer to the same 'will of God'[68] the connection with sages in Proverbs cannot be used to semi-detach the law of Psalm 119 from the direct revelation of the Pentateuch.

Depending on one's perspective, the Masoretes were either more restrained or more imaginative than modern scholars. They counted ten Torah terms in Psalm 119 that they considered to correspond to the Ten Commandments.[69] There is, however, debate as to the number of Torah terms in the psalm with most seeing only eight, although Levenson concludes that the psalmist wanted to use one of ten synonyms in every verse.[70] Whatever the correct count, most interpreters, including those who have held to the threefold division, would consider it fanciful that such terms might correspond with the Ten Commandments. Nonetheless, the Masoretic connection with the Decalogue may not be entirely misplaced. The psalmist speaks of the law coming from God's mouth (13, 72, 88), which could recall the Pentateuch's description of God proclaiming the Decalogue and adding

66   Ibid.
67   Ibid., 567.
68   Ibid., 567.
69   Soll, *Psalm 119*, 46.
70   Levenson, 'Sources of Torah', 562.

'nothing more' (Deut. 5:22). Further to that, the description of the law as settled in heaven (89–91) conveys the idea of fixity, if not 'a kind of revealed natural law', adding further weight to a connection with the Decalogue, in contrast to the other laws which were binding 'in the land'. If the law that is so precious to the psalmist is the Decalogue, this raises the possibility that his focus on the promises of God springs from the commandments in the Decalogue containing promises. Additionally, there is theological harmony between the psalm and the prioritisations in the Mosaic Law, discussed earlier. His devotion is not the prosecuting zeal of a self-righteous ceremonialist. Rather, conscious of his failure (176), the psalmist expresses the warm devotion of a servant for his master—devotion that goes beyond the laws to the lawgiver himself. In the light of this discussion, it is reasonable to conclude that when the framers of *The Westminster Confession* met reluctantly Parliament's demand for proof texts they did not act unthinkingly when they attached verses 4–6 to Chapter 19—'On the Law of God'.

One final issue to consider concerning the psalms is whether they describe the law as universally binding. It does not appear that they do so explicitly, but the idea is implicit in Psalm 94:10 when the psalmist asks: 'He who disciplines the nations, does he not rebuke?' Stewart Perowne saw this as referring to the 'moral government of the world',[71] while Schaefer writes that this 'recalls the prophetic oracles which teach that violation of the moral law is a recipe for disaster.'[72] Regardless of whether they take 'moral government' or 'moral law' to be connected with the Mosaic legislation, the psalmist does seem to view discipline in connection with תּוֹרָה. This emerges in verse 12, which uses the same word, יָסַר, to speak of the individual being disciplined at the

---

71 J. J. Stewart Perowne, *The Book of Psalms: A New Translation with Introductions and Notes Explanatory and Critical* (London: Bell & Daldy, 1868), 159.

72 Schaefer, *Psalms*, 235.

same time as he learns from God's law. Thus, if the psalmist writes with a Pentateuchal mindset, which regarded the Decalogue as the 'constitution of the universe', it is predictable that he should think of the nations as being disciplined according to the words God uttered at Horeb.

SUMMARY

No biblical narratives present a detailed historical account of juridical process. They give more attention to the reign of injustice and Israel's rejection of God's law. Their authors yearn for an Israel governed by a king who loves the law and whose people are holy, but the Israel they know is more concerned about sacrifice than obedience, to the extent that the prophets proclaim God's hatred of Israel's obedience to some of his laws. They also declare what God desires—certainly nothing less than obedience to all the laws of the Decalogue. The psalmists' approach is in harmony with this—some of their compositions evoking the words, events, and theology of the Horeb revelation.

Considered individually, none of these things stand as single comprehensive arguments for the threefold division of the law, although they do suggest a clear division between ceremonial and non-ceremonial laws. Viewed together, and in light of the Pentatuech's presentation of the Decalogue as distinct from other non-ceremonial laws, it is plausible that they fit within an interpretative structure which views the Decalogue, the statutes derived from it, and the cultic laws as distinct categories. An embryonic form of the threefold division therefore has a basis in the Old Testament; whether its full-grown practical-theological implications have a basis in the New Testament is the next issue to consider.

IV

WHAT DID JESUS DO?

> He, who had nothing in him deserving of death, was...appointed to pay death to the full, while owing it nothing.
>
> *Augustine (354–430), Tractate on John 14:29–31.*

Those who have accepted the threefold division of the law as an historic Christian doctrine generally considered Jesus' views, as recorded in the New Testament Gospels, to be authoritative. More than simply instructive about the practice and interpretation of the law in Israel during his lifetime, they reveal his attitudes to that practice and interpretation, and to the Mosaic Law itself. If Jesus' approach to the law conflicts with the view of the Old Testament outlined in preceding chapters, or if Jesus suggested that his death and resurrection would change the degree to which the Decalogue would remain binding, then that would have implications for the threefold division of the law.

The Westminster Divines, and their followers, believed that Jesus did not change the law or his attitude to the law in any way during his life. On the contrary, 'Christ humbled himself in his life, by subjecting himself to the law, which he perfectly fulfilled' (*WLC* 48). John Owen, who preached to Parliament the day after Charles I went 'from a corruptible to an incorruptible Crown, where no disturbance can be',[1] related this active obedience of Jesus to the Decalogue:

1 The final words of Charles I before he lost his head. Available from www.royal.gov.uk/output/Page76.asp; accessed 20 January 2006.

His obedience being absolutely universal, and absolutely perfect, was the great representative of the holiness of God in the law. It was represented glorious when the ten words were written by the finger of God in tables of stone; it appears yet more eminently in the spiritual transcription of it in the hearts of believers: but absolutely and perfectly it is exemplified only in the holiness and obedience of Christ, which answered it to the utmost. And this is no small part of his glory in obedience, that the holiness of God in the law was in that, and in that alone, in that one instance, as to human nature, fully represented.[2]

This view of the 'perfect obedience and full satisfaction of Christ' is elemental to the theology of *The Westminster Confession*, for sinners are only justified when this is 'imputed to them and received by faith alone'.[3] A later chapter will return to this issue, but for this section it is sufficient to note that their theological framework allowed no room for the idea that Jesus could have overturned any Mosaic Law during his lifetime. Rather, he was subject to it.

Set apart from their theological conclusions, the view that the gospels present Jesus as living in conformity to the Mosaic laws remains widely accepted by scholars of all shades. Frank Matera writes: 'Jesus acts in the light of the in-breaking kingdom of God; he does not blatantly disregard the law.'[4] Even with respect to the Sabbath, anti-Sabbatarian Lincoln says there is no suggestion that Jesus 'was less than careful to observe the actual requirements of the Torah'.[5] To the question of whether Jesus rejected the Mosaic laws, Vermes answers:

2   John Owen, *The Glory of Christ* (Fearn: Christian Focus Publications, 2004), 117.

3   *The Westminster Larger Catechism*, 70.

4   Frank J. Matera, *New Testament Ethics: the Legacies of Jesus and Paul* (Louisville: Westminster John Knox Press, 1996), 27.

5   Lincoln, 'Sabbath to Lord's Day', 361.

The Synoptic Gospels, our primary witnesses, give no support to such a theory. Moreover, since it is nowhere stated or implied in them that Jesus failed to pay his debts, beat up his opponents or committed adultery, it is reasonable to infer that he accepted, respected and observed the laws and customs regulating private and public existence which were in force among his compatriots in his age.[6]

The confessionists would differ from many contemporary exegetes in that they viewed the Gospels as harmonious accounts of Jesus' life. They did not expect to find different approaches to the law in the different Gospels—Matthew's Jesus was Mark's Jesus; Mark's Jesus was Luke's Jesus; Luke's Jesus was John's Jesus. But even on this basis, was their acceptance of the threefold division compatible with the Gospels? That is the question I will address in this chapter, focussing first on relevant passages, incidents, and literary structures in the Gospels that suggest Jesus' attitude to the law incorporated a view of the Decalogue as ever-binding and programmatic. Following this, I will examine key issues that might contradict the threefold division (and its associated theology of active obedience). For example, did Jesus take 'mercy and not sacrifice' further than the Old Testament, rejecting the ceremonial altogether? Was he hostile to the observance of any part of the Decalogue, particularly the Sabbath?

JOHN'S 'MORAL BANKRUPTCY'

In the following pages the Gospel that will receive least attention is the Gospel of John. Given the widespread view that Johannine ethics are 'problematic',[7] it might seem that John's Gospel is

---

6   Geza Vermes, *The Religion of Jesus the Jew* (London: SCM, 1993), 11–12.

7   Jan G. van der Watt provides a brief survey of views on Johannine ethics and the reasons why he considers any study of John's ethics a challenge. See 'Ethics and Ethos in the Gospel According to John.' *ZNW* 97 (2006): 147–76.

the wrong place to look for any influence of Old Testament ethics. If Jack Sanders is right to claim that 'weakness and moral bankruptcy'[8] are the hallmarks of Johannine ethics it might be better avoided altogether. He caricatures John as a personal worker for an ancient version of a twenty-first century American missionary organisation:

> Here is not a Christianity that considers that loving is the same as fulfilling the law (Paul) or that the good Samaritan parable represents a demand (Luke) to stop and render first aid to the man who has been robbed, beaten, and left there for dead. Johannine Christianity is interested only in whether he believes. "Are you saved brother?" the Johannine Christian asks the man bleeding to death on the side of the road. "Are you concerned about your soul?" "Do you believe that Jesus is the one who came down from God?" "If you believe you will have eternal life," promises the Johannine Christian, while the dying man's blood stains the ground.[9]

Given John's statement of purpose (20:31) Sanders ought not to be surprised if it does not read like a catechism of morals. His claim that the command to love 'one another' limits the scope of love to the congregation ignores the intention of the command, which was not to establish intra-congregational ethics, but to ensure witness to the world (John 13:35). His unwarranted conclusion that, for John, 'the supreme and only good that one can do for one's neighbour is to bring him to faith'[10] results from a superficial approach to the text that ignores the behaviour of characters within the Gospel, which, as Van der Watt points out, 'is based on the interpretation of 'rules' (commandments) and express what the underlying ethical informants of these commandments are'.[11] A survey of the 'action lines' within

8   Jack T. Sanders, *Ethics in the New Testament: Change and Development* (Philadelphia: Fortress Press, 1975), 100.

9   Ibid.

10   Ibid.

11   Van der Watt, 'Ethics and Ethos', 151.

the narrative make it 'evident that the full scope of the moral situations envisaged by the Decalogue is indeed present and addressed in this Gospel'.[12] While not suggesting that the author 'had the Decalogue as Decalogue in mind',[13] Van der Watt traces the following reflections of the Decalogue as he believes the value system in John could be related to Jewish law and tradition that comes from the Ten Commandments:[14]

    I. Jesus accused of blasphemy (10:33).
    II. Worship of the only true God (4:20–4; 17:33).
       Zeal for true worship (2:13–22).
    III. Jesus accused of blasphemy (10:33).
    IV. Contention over the Sabbath (5:9; 7:22ff; 9:14).
    V. The family metaphor is developed
       according to ancient social norms.
    VI. Murder is regarded negatively (5:18; 7:19; 8:44; 11:53).
    VII. Reflect Jewish convention of those
       days (4:16–18; 7:53–8:11).
    VIII. Negative remark about Judas thieving (12:6).
    IX. The devil is the father of lies (8:44).
    X. The tenth commandment lacks
       concreteness in determining trespasses,
       so no specific examples appear.

Although some of those examples point to the social conventions or values of others, there is no reason to believe that John's Gospel affirmed an alternative value system, even if it rejects an accusation such as that recorded in 10:33–8 and interprets things differently.

12   Ibid., 152. He adds in parenthesis 'except for the tenth commandment which is not explicitly dealt with'.
13   Ibid., 155.
14   Ibid., 153–4.

Jey J. Kanagaraj goes further than Van der Watt in that despite
the paucity of direct citations, he sees stronger evidence for the
Ten Words being foundational to the thinking of Jesus and his
disciples. John presents the Decalogue 'in unspoken language'
according to his 'art of communicating the truth in silence',
meaning that he uses 'certain words and concepts with a double
meaning: superficial and deeper levels'.[15] Foundational to
Kanagaraj's argument is that a connection between the two
great commandments and the Decalogue was ingrained in the
thinking of Jesus and his disciples:

> The first Christians treated love as a summary of the Law
> (Rom. 13:8–10), the root of which they rightly believed, goes back to
> Jesus himself (Mt. 22:35–40; Mk. 12:28–34; Lk. 10:26–28; cf. Lv. 18:5;
> 19:18). When they treated love for one's neighbour as fulfilment of
> the Law, they often understood 'Law' as pointing to the Decalogue
> (Rom. 13:9–10)…It is highly possible that John, like Paul, was
> brought up in such a tradition and that behind his doctrine of love
> stands the Decalogue.[16]

The following section will show that there are good reasons to
believe that this was a widely held approach, but the author also
points to John's use of terminology from the Pentateuch:

> The term τὰς ἐντολάς occurs in John along with the verb τηρεῖν
> to imply obedience as the expression of one's love for Jesus (14:10,
> 15, 21; 15:12). The same expression is used for 'keeping' the Ten
> Commandments (cf. Mt. 19:17–19; 1 Cor. 7:19) and the equivalent
> phrase τηρεῖν τὸν λόγον (14:23–24; 15:20; cf. 8:51; 1 Jn. 2:5) alludes
> to Exodus 20:1 and Deuteronomy 5:22 where the term τοὺς λόγους
> or τὰ ῥήματα means the Decalogue. As love was treated as the
> summary of the Law, particularly in Christian circles, both Jews and
> Christians acknowledged the Decalogue as the 'content of the Law'.

---

15 Jey J. Kanagaraj, 'The Implied Ethics of the Fourth Gospel: A
Reinterpretation of the Decalogue', *TB* 52.1 (2001), 60.
16 Ibid., 37.

This means that in the first century both love and the Decalogue were treated in complementary and identical terms.[17]

Although in Matthew 19:17–19 Jesus defines the commandments to be kept as those of the Decalogue, it is a slightly ironic choice of passage since the man's question to Jesus ('Which ones?') raises the possibility that the association of commandments with the Decalogue was not automatic. Kanagaraj may not be wrong to associate 'commandments of God' in 1 Corinthians 7:19 with the Decalogue, but he does not justify this. His arguments about the Greek terms τοὺς λόγους and τὰ ῥήματα are weak; both translate דְּבָרִים in the Pentateuch, which as Braulik has shown does not refer exclusively to the Decalogue, but also to the rest of the Mosaic Law. If these terms communicate anything 'in silence' it is probably 'Mosaic Law' in general rather than 'Decalogue', so they only help Kanagaraj's argument in a general sense. Most of his article is taken up with an analysis of the influence of each commandment on Johannine thought. The table on the following page sets out his references and a brief summary of his reasons for recognising the influence of individual commandments.[18]

With these observations and his subsequent conclusions, Kanagaraj is on firmer ground than with some of his introductory comments. Although John does not have 'a consistent and coherent presentation of the Decalogue in his Gospel...whenever his narratives and discourses require, he does echo the Ten Commandments individually,' reinterpreting 'the Decalogue in its positive, redemptive, and practical dimension,' thus betraying his 'belief in the abiding validity of the law.'[19]

Despite the supposed difficulty of finding ethics in John, Van der Watt and Kanagaraj are not the only scholars to hear

17   Ibid.
18   Kanagaraj, 'Implied Ethics', 38–59.
19   Ibid., 60.

KANAGARAJ'S DECALOGUE INFLUENCES IN JOHN

Word	References
I	5:44, 17:3. The word μόνος reflects Yahweh's exclusive claim. He can only be recognised through Jesus.
II	4:20-24. God is spirit and must be worshipped as spirit. 2:13-22. The cleansing of the temple proclaims the theme of worshipping God in his holiness by believing in Jesus.
III	17:11-12, 26. Jesus reveals the name and glory of God. 14:13-14; 16:24. Prayer is now made in his name.
IV	5:1-18; 7:23. Sabbath is the day to see God and experience him recreating and giving wholeness through Jesus.
V	2:1-12. γύναι is a term of affection used by Jesus as he honours his mother and his Father. 19:26-7. This is the climax of Jesus' obedience to the fifth word.
VI	8:34-44. Killing is the work of the devil. 13:34; 15:12. Love to the extent of self-sacrifice is a positive expression of the sixth commandment.
VII	4:16-17. Jesus' use of the singular ἀνήρ and his conversation with the woman show he considered it wrong to have more than one husband.
VIII	12:4-6. Pilfering is part of Judas' wickedness. 10:1-10. Thievery and destruction marks the hireling's activities.
IX	8:44-6; 14:6; 8:32-6. The devil is a liar, but Jesus embodies God's truth, fulfils the ninth commandment, and sets his followers free.
X	12:6, 42-4. Judas covets money, just as the Pharisees covet praise from men. John's idea of 'believing' touches on inner motive as fundamental to union with Christ.

echoes and restatements of individual commandments. Loader takes a similar approach:

> For John, the decalogue command not to commit murder doubtless still has validity.[20]

> Both partners in the argument [8:13–20] assume the validity of the decalogue command, not to bear false witness.[21]

> We should probably assume that basic ethical principles, such as those contained in the decalogue, are at no point abandoned.[22]

> Allusions to decalogue commandments indicate their validity is assumed, but not as enjoining cultic practices and not including the sabbath.[23]

The last quotation shows that for the fourth commandment, Loader's approach is less comprehensive. Although he notes that Mary Magdalene does not come to Jesus' tomb until the Sabbath is over, his remark that 'John makes no explicit link between her behaviour and Law observance' is not good reason to dismiss a connection. After all, he uses the word 'assume' in three of the above quotations.[24]

These observations do not provide a stand-alone argument for the primacy of the Decalogue, but they do suggest John was comfortable with such an approach and argue against any claim that Jesus had little regard for the Ten Commandments. They also show that although John is not critical to study of law in the Gospels that should not be taken as an indication of its 'moral bankruptcy'.

---

20   William R. G. Loader, *Jesus' Attitude towards the Law: A Study of the Gospels* (Tübingen: Mohr Siebeck, 1997), 467.

21   Ibid., 469.

22   Ibid., 478.

23   Ibid., 475.

24   Ibid., 482.

THE MOST IMPORTANT COMMANDMENT

According to D. A. Carson, 'Jesus never treats the Decalogue as the perfect sum of moral law…In this Jesus is like the rabbis and unlike Philo.'[25] If Carson is saying that the rabbis never gave primacy to the Decalogue, he is mistaken,[26] but is he also wrong about Jesus? To sum up the law or note priority within it was not foreign to Jesus' mindset. When asked by a scribe, 'Which commandment is the most important of all?' Jesus answered:

> The most important is, 'Hear, O Israel: the Lord our God, the Lord is one. And you shall love the Lord your God with all your heart and with all your soul and with all your mind and with all your strength.' The second is this: 'You shall love your neighbour as yourself.' There is no other commandment greater than these (Mark. 12:28–31; cf. Matt. 22:36–40).

The Westminster Divines saw similar prioritisation in the Decalogue, 'the first four commandments containing our duty towards God, and the other six our duty to man'. In this they follow a traditional interpretation similarly expressed by Aquinas:

> Now the precepts of the decalogue contain the very intention of the lawgiver, who is God. For the precepts of the first table, which direct us to God, contain the very order to the common and final good, which is God; while the precepts of the second table contain the order of justice to be observed among men, that nothing un-due be done to anyone, and that each one be given his due.[27]

He in turn is following earlier writers, such as Philo, who in *De Decalogo* says that the Decalogue was divided into two tables of five commandments each. In the first 'the most sacred duties to

25   Carson, 'Jesus and the Sabbath' in Carson, *Sabbath to Lord's Day*, 95 n. 136.
26   See Chapter 3, also Galinski, *Pursue Justice*, 25, n. 19; Urbach, *Sages*, 361; Hirsch, 'Decalogue', in *Jewish Encyclopaedia*, 496; Amir, 'Decalogue', 126; Greenberg, 'Decalogue Tradition', 119, n. 57.
27   Aquinas, *Summa* I–II. 100. 8.

the Deity are enjoined' and in the second 'obligations towards our fellow creatures'.[28] Likewise Josephus, although not stating the Godward/manward distinction, writes: 'ten commandments were written, five upon each table, and two and a half upon each side of them' (Ant. 3:138). This division was common to Jewish commentators and differs slightly from that of later Christian writers, such as Augustine and the Westminster Divines, who preferred a four/six split. Different numbering of the commandments also complicates the issue, but the important point is that interpreters over many centuries agree that no matter how the commandments are divided, the first table deals with love to God and the second with love to fellow creatures.

This discussion of the Decalogue is relevant because figures as diverse as John Calvin[29] and Raban Maurus, the ninth-century Archbishop of Mainz, applied it to Jesus' response to the scribe in Matthew 22. Maurus wrote: 'For to these two commandments belongs the whole decalogue; the commandments of the first table to the love of God, those of the second to the love of our neighbour.'[30] Dale Allison argues that we should not consign this view to history because first-century readers of Mark's similar account would have interpreted Jesus' statements in that way:

> We are not to imagine that correct or credible exegetical insights will be preserved in the commentaries. But with regard to Mark 12:38–41 and its parallels, we have seemingly forgotten what many before us, with good reason, took for granted: that the double commandment to love is a summarizing exposition of the decalogue.[31]

28   Philo, *De Decalogo*, 106–110.

29   John Calvin, *A Harmony of the Gospels: Matthew, Mark & Luke* (Carlisle: Paternoster Press, 1995), 36.

30   Quoted in Thomas Aquinas, *Catena Aurea*, Available from www.ccel. org/a/aquinas/catena/Matthew/ch22.htm; accessed 7 December 2004.

31   Dale C. Allison, 'Mark 12:28–31 and the Decalogue.' *The Gospels and the Scriptures of Israel*, eds Craig A. Evans and W. Richard Stegner (Sheffield: Sheffield Academic Press, 1994), 278.

Allison gives a catalogue of writers and documents to support his view. The earliest extra-biblical examples are from the *Apostolic Constitutions* (2:5.36)[32] and Ireneaus' *Adversus Haereses*.[33] His appeal to the former is not fully convincing, because although the *Constitutions* make a clear link between the first great commandment and the first table, they use the command to love one's neighbour to stress the importance of church-going and make no reference to the second table prohibitions of murder, adultery, and theft. Ireneaus, on the other hand, does appear to make a direct connection with Jesus' words when he paraphrases the two love commandments: 'the righteous fathers had the meaning of the Decalogue written in their hearts and souls, that is, they loved the God who made them, and did no injury to their neighbour.'[34] Allison could also have mentioned Augustine who is more explicit: the Ten Commandments 'are reduced to two, namely, that we should love God with our whole heart, and with our whole soul, and with our whole mind; and that we should love our neighbour as ourselves.'[35] According to Christopher, Augustine is the first writer on catechetics to point out this link.[36]

Not all modern writers are guilty of the forgetfulness noted by Allison. The idea is written into a twentieth century Roman Catholic Catechism,[37] and referring to Luke 18:22–30, Pheme Perkins assumes that the love commandments summarise the Decalogue.[38] Likewise, Heikki Sariola argues that Mark has a markedly positive attitude to the Decalogue and the love

32   Ibid., 277.

33   Ibid., 273.

34   Roberts and Donaldson, *ANF*, vol I, Ch XVI, 482.

35   Avgvstini, *Catechizandis Rvdibvs*, 99.

36   Ibid., 4.

37   *A New Catechism*, 376.

38   Pheme Perkins, *Love Commands in the New Testament* (New York: Paulist Press, 1982), 23.

commandments[39]—it is possible that they summarise the two tables of the Decalogue.[40]

George Keerankeri does most to explore the status of the double commandment as a précis of the Decalogue. His study of Mark 12:28–34 begins with an examination of the commandments in their original context. The 'most important' commandment quoted by Jesus is the *Shema* (Deut. 6:4–9) and Keerankeri considers it a call for the 'concrete execution' of הַדְּבָרִים (these words), which point to the Decalogue and what follows it in Deuteronomy 5. He is correct that 'love for Yahweh…means observance of the law'[41] and wise not to link הַדְּבָרִים exclusively with the Decalogue because, as Braulik has shown (see chapter three), דְּבָרִים can also refer to the rest of the Mosaic Law.[42]

The second love commandment comes from Leviticus 19:34 where, says Keerankeri, 'the imitation of Yahweh stands as the basis of love for the רע [neighbour]. Israel must love the רע and the גר [alien] in the way Yahweh has loved it first…Love of neighbour is the sign of the presence of God among his people, not an expression of natural solidarity.'[43] As long as this is not applied exclusively to the love commandment, Leviticus 19:34 may support the weight of Keerankeri's conclusion. The proclamation 'I am the LORD your God' follows several commands relating to the love of neighbour (Lev. 23:22; 24:22), but it is not restricted to that sphere (Lev. 18:30; 19:3–4, 36). The Mosaic Law envisages God's presence with Israel as concomitant with general obedience (Lev. 26:1–12) and the rationale behind 'for you were strangers in

39 Heikki Sariola, *Markus und das Gesetz: Eine redaktionskritische Unterschung* (Helsinki: Suomalainen Tiedeakatemia, 1990), 275.

40 Ibid., 207–8.

41 George Keerankeri, *The Love Commandment in Mark: An Exegetico-Theological Study of Mk 12,28–34* (Roma: Editrice Pontificio Istituto Biblico, 2003), 32.

42 Braulik, 'Ausdrücke für"Gesetz"', 49.

43 Keerankeri, *Love Commandment*, 57–8.

the land of Egypt', may be more 'whatever you wish that others would do to you, do also to them' (Matt. 7:12), than 'whatever I have done for you, do for others.'

Keerankeri's comments on the love commandments in their original context, do not therefore amount to a closed case for viewing them as a summary of the Decalogue. He continues, however, to argue that in Mark 'commandment' is almost synonymous with the Decalogue, so when Jesus refers to 'the commandment of God' (Mark 7:8–9) he 'means primarily the Decalogue'[44] because in Mark 7:10 he 'does not cite any of the other numerous OT prescriptions and ordinances.'[45] Actually, Mark 7:10b is normally understood as a citiation of Exodus 21:17, but if the statutes of the Pentatuech are derived from the Decalogue, Keerankeri's point is not weakened.[46] If Exodus 21:17 and its surrounding context flow from the fifth commandment,[47] Jesus' rebuke to the Pharisees may reflect such an underlying assumption; his restatement of the fifth commandment—the fundamental principle of respect for parents—being followed by the case law of Exodus 21:17. It certainly reflects 'a strong commitment to the Decalogue command to honour parents'[48] and suggests that Jesus associates 'commandments' primarily with the Decalogue.

Turning to Mark 10:19, Keerankeri submits that it 'reveals the gospel's conception of the Decalogue as practically a synonym for the commandments of God.'[49] Although he does not develop this, several observations add weight to his claim. In his response to the rich man Jesus unbundles the 'commandments' as five or

---

44   Keerankeri, *Love Commandment*, 108.

45   Ibid.

46   See chapter two and the discussion of Kaufman, 'The Deuteronomic Law', 113–43; and Braulik, 'Sequence of the Laws', 319–334.

47   Guilding, 'Hebrew Law Codes', 43.

48   Loader, *Jesus' Attitude towards the Law*, 74.

49   Keerankeri, *Love Commandment*, 109.

six of the Ten Words: 'Do not murder. Do not commit adultery. Do not steal. Do not bear false witness. Do not defraud. Honour your father and mother.' The command 'Do not defraud' could be a repetition of the eighth commandment or, following Jesus' consecutive recitation of commandments six to nine, it could be, as Wessel suggests, 'a substitute for the commandment against coveting, fraud being a manifestation of coveting.'[50] Morna Hooker finds that 'no satisfactory explanation of this has ever been given…but it is interesting to find it used in Mal. 3:5.'[51] She does not expand on this, but it may support Wessel's argument, since several Old Testament references connect חָמַד (to covet) with unlawful taking (Deut. 7:25; Josh. 7:21; Mic. 2:2). In addition, Malachi 3:5—where the LORD's words of judgement against 'adulterers…perjurers…those who defraud' echo the Decalogue—provides one of only two Septuagint occurrences of ἀποστερέω (to defraud). Indeed Horeb is mentioned a little later (Mal. 4:4). Thus when Jesus, the one who Mark sees coming after 'my messenger' (Mal. 3:1; Mark 1:2), responds to this rich young man, his recalling of the Decalogue and reference to defrauding may reflect Malachi. Furthermore, both Malachi 3:5 and Jesus' statement occur in contexts that envision great reversals—the rich and arrogant will be brought low; the righteous who have left everything will be first (Mal. 3:13–4:3; Mark 10:20–31).

Plainly, the Gospels make no explicit declaration along the lines that the Decalogue is 'summarily comprehended' in the two great commandments, but was it 'with good reason', as Allison claims, that many 'took for granted…that the double commandment to love is a summarising exposition of the decalogue'?[52] Those who demand a single proof text for everything will never think so. For

50   Walter W. Wessel 'Mark' in *Expositors Bible Commentary*, ed. Frank E. Gaebelein [Pradis Ver. 5.01.0035] (Grand Rapids: Zondervan, 2002).

51   Morna D. Hooker, *A Commentary on the Gospel According to St. Mark* (London: A & C Black, 1991), 241–2.

52   Allison, 'Mark 12:28–31 and the Decalogue', 278.

others, who see Jesus coming as a man subject to the law, or for those who see Jesus presented in the Gospels as a man saturated in the Old Testament, it is a natural conclusion. Thus far, there is no reason to believe that Jesus did not view the Decalogue as having a constitutional status and being fundamental to all other law. That being the case, it is not surprising that he should equate 'commandments' principally with the Decalogue.

Against this background, the arguments Keerankeri and others present are satisfactory. They need not prove that the two greatest commandments are a summary of the Decalogue without reference to underlying Old Testament theology. They confirm that Jesus gave the highest place to the commandments of the Decalogue and his response to the scribe reflected that, thus it is 'with good reason' that the two great commandments were considered a précis of the Decalogue.

A 'PITIFUL JOB' OF DOCTRINAL INCULCATION

A 2007 edition of the BBC Radio 4 program, *You and Yours*,[53] which focused on the Rowntree Foundation, invited listeners to call in with their analysis of the reasons for social deprivation and disorder in twenty-first century Britain. Television (especially Channel 4's ghastly *Big Brother*), poverty, the classification of cannabis, and illiteracy took most of the blame from callers. The final caller, Eleanor Hurd, took a different line. She blamed Britain's ailments on 'the marginalisation of the Christian faith and the morality that goes with it', which 'has left so many of our young people really not knowing which direction to go in.' An atheist on the panel agreed with her, Roy Hattersley stuck to his view that poverty was the root of all social evils, while the priest was silent. It is common to hear Eleanor Hurd's view expressed, even by those who have no interest in Christianity or

53   Broadcast 7 August 2007, 1200.

churchgoing: 'I'm not religious,' writes a reader of *The Scotsman*, 'but the Ten Commandments seem a good idea: simple, easy to understand, apply to all.'[54] Yet, a little probing often reveals that such keenness for the Decalogue quickly fades. As Goldberg says of the American context, 'posting unread copies of the Ten Commandments in government hallways is more popular than following them.'[55] Even churchgoers who express such opinions are inclined to hesitate a little, if not retreat from their pro-Decalogue stance, when the subject turns to the fourth commandment. Abraham Heschel may have considered the sabbath day 'like a palace in time with a kingdom for all',[56] but for many Christians and Jews[57] it is a stifling intrusion.

British popular opinion (secular and religious; sabbath-loving and anti-sabbatarian) tends to consider Puritans, particularly the kind of men who framed *The Westminster Confession of Faith*, responsible for establishing a sabbatarian tradition that must, depending upon one's position, be preserved or abolished. But this is an ill-informed view—the Puritans are neither worthy of the credit nor deserving of the demerit. Much of the responsibility for this view of history lies with Peter Heylyn, the seventeenth century anti-sabbatarian who claimed that those who argued for Sabbath observance in his day had erected 'paper-walls', which he was confident would be 'beaten down' by his publication:

54   Comment 31 [on-line] available from thescotsman.scotsman.com/index.cfm?id=258352007; accessed 10 Aug 2007.

55   Steven Goldberg, *Bleached Faith: the Tragic Cost when Religion is Forced into the Public Square* (Stanford: Stanford Law Books, 2008), 3.

56   Abraham Joshua Heschel, *The Sabbath: its meaning for modern man.* (New York: Noonday Press, 1998), 21.

57   'My impressions from extended visits to Israel...were that Israelis welcome Saturday night with greater joy than Friday night.' Dennis MacDonald, 'A Response to R. Goldenberg and D. J. Harrington, S.J.' in *The Sabbath and Christian Traditions* eds. Tamara C. Eskenazi; Daniel J. Harrington, S.J.; William H. Shea (New York: Crossroad, 1991), 58.

In all Ages heretofore, and in all Churches at this present, it [the
Lord's Day] neither was nor is esteemed of as a Sabbath day, nor
reckoned of so near a kin to the former Sabbath: but that all such
leisure times as were not destinate by the Church to God's public
service; men might apply their minds and bestow their thoughts,
either about their business, or upon their pleasures such as are
lawful in themselves...you did never suck these Doctrines from
your Mother's breasts... you have deserted the whole practice of
the Christian Church, which for the space of 1600 years has been
embraced and followed by all godly men.[58]

Heylyn's view, as summarised by Kenneth Parker, is that 'the
definitive position of the church, ancient and modern, was to
treat the fourth commandment as a ceremonial law, abrogated
by Christ along with other laws of the Old Testament.'[59] As far as
Richard Bauckham is concerned, 'Heylin's work on the Sabbath
was a competent historical survey.'[60] Parker disagrees. It may be
'long-established and cherished historiographical orthodoxy',[61]
but 'it is simply not possible to draw any fundamental theological
distinction between the medieval and post-Reformation doctrines
of the Sabbath. The moral obligation to keep the Sabbath
was a concept as familiar to the fifteenth-century Englishman
as the seventeenth-century protestant.'[62] He backs up his case
with a roll-call of those who argued for sabbath-keeping in the
pre-Reformation era: fourth century theologians, Ephraem Syrus
and Eusebius of Caesarea;[63] Eustace, a Norman abbot who came

---

58   Peter Heylyn, *The History of the Sabbath*. (London: Printed for Henry
Seile, and are to bee fold at the Signe of the Tygers-head in Saint Pauls
Churchyard, 1636), no page numbers, 5–7 of the preface.

59   Kenneth L. Parker, *The English Sabbath: A study of doctrine and discipline
from the Reformation to the Civil War.* (Cambridge: Cambridge University Press,
1988), 2.

60   Bauckham, 'Sabbath and Sunday', 330.

61   Parker, *English Sabbath*, 6.

62   Ibid., 23.

63   Ibid., 18.

to England in 1200; St Hugh, bishop of Lincoln; Simon Islip, archbishop of Canterbury; John Bromyard; various medieval councils and synods; even King Henry VI who issued a statute condemning Sunday markets and fairs as 'abominable offences against God and his saints.'[64]

It is equally misguided to think that the promotion of sabbath-keeping today is limited to a handful of extreme neo-Puritans whose 'Calvinist rectitude' makes a place like the Outer Hebrides the 'last bastions of strict Sabbatarian observance'.[65] If European shop-opening hours are any guide, whether a country has had a largely Protestant or Roman Catholic influence makes little difference.[66] The desire for a sanctified Sunday in one form or another is common to most Christian denominations. Indeed, in the past decade, the most high-profile call for sabbath-keeping has not come from Hebridean Calvinists, but John Paul II. He too would have contradicted Heylyn: 'The fundamental importance of Sunday has been recognized through two thousand years of history…This is a tradition going back to the Apostles.'[67] John Paul II also set this within the context of the Decalogue, and in language that presumes the threefold division of the law: 'The Sabbath precept…is set not within the context of strictly cultic stipulations but within the Decalogue, the "ten words" which represent the pillars of moral life inscribed on the human heart.'[68]

64   Ibid., 10–14.

65   Cahal Milmo, 'Silent protest greets first Sunday ferry as South Harris defends its way of life', *The Independent*, 10 April 2006.

66   Britain, Ireland, and Poland are at the top of the opening-hours league tables, while Austria, Italy, and Norway still shut up shop on Sunday. [on-line]; available from www.metrogroup.de/servlet/PB/menu/1012244_l2/index.html; accessed 8 August 2007. According to Goldberg, for Americans, 'Sunday is about as restful as Tuesday'. He suggests the growth of Sunday opening may have much to do with two-career families having no other time to shop or the growth of shopping malls. Goldberg, *Bleached Faith*, 38.

67   John Paul II, *Keeping the Lord's Day Holy: Apostolic Letter DIES DOMINI of the Holy Father John Paul II* (London: Catholic Truth Society, 1998), 5.

68   Ibid., 17.

The best known recent work to set itself against this mark of both 'Calvinist rectidue' and the Holy See is the volume edited by D. A. Carson, *From Sabbath to Lord's Day*, which began as a 'research project' sponsored by the Tyndale Fellowship in Cambridge.[69] More manifesto than dispassionate report, its main contributors come from a Baptist or Anglican background, and are tied together by evangelicalism—something that might puzzle journalists like Cahal Milmo (quoted above). Carson sums up their consensus:

> First, we are not persuaded that the New Testament unambiguously develops a "transfer theology," according to which the Sabbath moves from the seventh day to the first day of the week. We are not persuaded that Sabbath keeping is presented in the Old Testament as the norm from the time of creation onward. Nor are we persuaded that the New Testament develops patterns of continuity and discontinuity on the basis of moral/civil/ceremonial distinctions. However useful and accurate such categories may be, it is anachronistic to think that any New Testament writer adopted them as the basis for his distinctions between the Old Testament and the gospel of Christ.[70]

Their first two concerns are relatively unimportant to this discussion. Some hold to the threefold division, viewing the fourth commandment as still binding, yet do not accept the transfer of Sabbath to the Lord's Day,[71] therefore the issue of 'transfer theology' requires little attention. Their concerns about Sabbath as a creation ordinance were discussed in an earlier chapter of this book, which rejected Dressler's argument that the Sabbath is given in Genesis 2 only as 'a proleptic sign indicating some future rest'.[72]

69 Preface in Carson, *Sabbath to Lord's Day*, 11.

70 Introduction in Carson, *Sabbath to Lord's Day*, 16.

71 Samuele Bacchiocchi, *Divine Rest for Restlessness: A Theological Study of the Good News of the Sabbath for Today* (Rome: Pontifical Gregorian University Press, 1980), 45.

72 Dressler, 'Sabbath in the Old Testament,' 28.

For the contributors, the third item on the list is sabbatarianism's guilty accomplice—the threefold division. There are, of course, those who claim to hold to the threefold division while not accepting the traditional views about the contemporary relevance of each category[73] (and vice versa).[74] Dan Lioy argues for the threefold division whilst appearing to be anti-sabbatarian,[75] but this at least suggests a different understanding of the moral law category to that which is found in the Reformed confessions and the anti-sabbatarians are not wrong to see a link with the threefold division. Contrary to Carson's portrayal, however, and in common with many other systematic theology categories, those who use the threefold division do not view it as the basis upon which the New Testament develops patterns of continuity and discontinuity, but rather as itself based upon the patterns of continuity and discontinuity developed in the New Testament. So what if doctrines such as the threefold division, Trinitarian theology, or an *ordo salutis* have at times been anachronistically imposed upon biblical texts? That does not mean that those who developed those doctrines believed that each biblical writer 'adopted them as the basis for his distinctions'. Nonetheless, if it can be demonstrated that the Gospels present the Sabbath as a statute that Jesus made null and void then this undermines the framework of the threefold division with its practical-theological claim that 'the moral law doth for ever bind all.'

Several passages in the Gospels recount Jesus' Sabbath controversies with the Pharisees. Do any of them challenge the

73   Such differences of opinion have existed with Theonomists arguing that all judicial laws remain binding while at the same time claiming to hold to the threefold division.

74   Bacchiocchi, *Divine Rest*, 45.

75   The 'timeless principles connected with the fourth commandment' are still relevant, yet 'the New Testament does not teach either a change in the Sabbath's observance or the establishment of a new Sabbath day for the people of God....Christians are not obligated to observe the seventh day of the week as the Sabbath.' Lioy, *Decalogue in the Sermon on the Mount*, 48.

earlier conclusions in this chapter? Did Jesus break the Sabbath and so fail to love God with all his heart, thereby disproving that 'the double commandment to love is a summarising exposition of the decalogue'?[76] Did he fulfil the Sabbath law eschatologically and soteriologically, but show little concern for its moral fulfilment? If so, could he have shown such unconcern because obsolescence was written into the fourth commandment? Could it be that the Sabbath is one of those laws whose ongoing relevance is only by way of memorial and foretoken?

For S. G. Wilson, Jesus' teaching in Luke's Gospel undermines the position of the law and some of its specific commands. The Sabbath controversies provide the clearest examples,[77] since 'rules about the sabbath are no longer in force—for corn-picking can scarcely be described as a work of compassion.'[78] Yet, he says, Luke is ambiguous: Jesus is sometimes opposed to the law, sometimes not—'either conclusion is defensible', not least because 'criticism of the law is generally implicit and has to be read between the lines, whereas the affirmation of the law is generally explicit.'[79] It is difficult to square this with his view that no Mosaic Laws were transgressed,[80] but neither was it a 'Pharisaic-rabbinic' debate concerning 'fine points of sabbath law'.[81] In any case, Wilson has few supporters. The majority opinion remains that even concerning the fourth commandment Jesus did nothing less than give full obedience: he 'upholds Sabbath law';[82] 'acted in complete accordance with the law';[83] 'there is nothing to support

76   Allison, 'Mark 12:28–31 and the Decalogue', 278.

77   S. G. Wilson, *Luke and the Law* (Cambridge: Cambridge University Press, 1983), 56.

78   Ibid., 39.

79   Ibid., 57–8.

80   Ibid., 31–2. He specifically mentions Leviticus 23:15.

81   Ibid., 39.

82   Loader, *Jesus' Attitude towards the Law*, 35 (also 263, 312).

83   Jacob Jervell, 'The Law in Luke-Acts', *HTR*, 64 (1971), 29.

the view that abrogation of the sabbath was at the heart of his teaching';[84] although 'the disciples of Moses…are accusing him of being ἁμαρτωλός because of his persistent disregard for the Sabbath…they fail to prove their point'.[85] It may read like what under Scottish Law might be announced as a 'not proven' rather than a 'not guilty' verdict, yet even Carson upholds this view in his contribution to *From Sabbath to Lord's Day*: 'There is no hard evidence that Jesus Himself ever contravened any written precept concerning the Sabbath.'[86] Craig Blomberg agrees that Jesus 'nowhere clearly broke any portion of Torah'.[87] Both men, however, append similar cautions to their statements:

> Nevertheless, one must not make too much of this observation. One dare not conclude on this basis that Sabbath observance is still mandatory. The same argument would require that we continue to sacrifice in the temple. Jesus' attitude towards the Sabbath cannot rightly be assessed apart from the consideration of his relationship to the law [Carson].[88]

> This observation has often been used to promote Sabbath keeping for Christians, but the logic is flawed. Jesus obeyed Torah because he understood it to be binding for the period of history in which he lived. The question that should concern Christians is what is binding for the new period of history…Most of Jesus' teachings and actions regarding the Sabbath as recorded in the four Gospels simply do not address the issue, of how to behave at this later date [Blomberg].[89]

In a footnote, Carson makes an unreasonable criticism when he cites R. T. Beckwith as an example of someone who makes 'too

---

84   Banks, *Jesus and the Law*, 131.

85   Severino Pancaro, *The Law in the Fourth Gospel* (Leiden: E. J. Bill, 1975), 51.

86   Carson, 'Jesus and the Sabbath' in Carson, *Sabbath to Lord's Day*, 84.

87   Craig Blomberg, 'A Response to Bacchioicchi and Primus' in *Sabbath and Christian Traditions*, 124.

88   Carson, 'Jesus and the Sabbath,' 84.

89   Blomberg, 'Response to Bacchioicchi,' 124.

much of this observation'.[90] In the relevant section, Beckwith is arguing against Rordorf's claim that 'Jesus Christ rejected the Sabbath',[91] and the most he makes of it is to write: 'The ways in which Christ defends his actions on the sabbath never suggest he is rescinding the sabbath, and often suggest the contrary.'[92] In reality, sabbatarians and anti-sabbatarians agree that the main issue is not Jesus' obedience to the fourth commandment—he did not have a *laissez-faire* approach to its moral fulfilment.[93] Could it be, however, that his eschatological and soteriological fulfilment was such that any person coming after his time could be happily untroubled about its moral fulfilment?

'Yes,' say the anti-sabbatarians writing in *From Sabbath to Lord's Day*. Their overall arguments, though, are not always easily defined as the six authors struggle to speak with one voice without encroaching on other contributors' subjects. This is perhaps why in his chapter on 'Jesus and the Sabbath in the Four Gospels', which overlaps with Max Turner's on 'The Sabbath, Sunday, and the Law in Luke/Acts', Carson makes 'no attempt… to bring together all the relevant observations stemming from the exegesis.' He only aims 'to pick up the most important

---

90   Carson, 'Jesus and the Sabbath,' 97 n. 161.

91   Roger T. Beckwith, and Wilfrid Scott, *This Is the Day: the Biblical Doctrine of the Christian Sunday in its Jewish and Early Church Setting* (London: Marshall, Morgan & Scott, 1978), 21.

92   Ibid., 24.

93   Detailed arguments about whether or not Jesus broke Sabbath laws are liable to descend into absurdity even in scholarly works as the following extract of a discussion between two academics over whether or not the disciples plucking of grain was legal because they were in danger of starvation confirms:

'*Watson*: …If I were starving, plucking grain would not help me to live, because you cannot get all that many grains by simply plucking by hand. It does not work….

'*Maccoby*: I would only pluck grain if I was starving.'

A response to Alan Watson's contribution in John F. A Sawyer, ed., *Reading Leviticus: A Conversation with Mary Douglas*. (Sheffield: Sheffield Academic Press, 1996), 273.

threads of thought and weave them into a pattern that may be helpful as a background to chapter 12.'[94] It is therefore reasonable and simpler to take Lincoln's summarising twelfth chapter, particularly his five pages on 'The Gospel's Depiction of Jesus' Relationship to the Sabbath'[95] as a fair representation of Carson's and Turner's joint position.

There is much in common with Carson's views on Matthew 5:17–20 (discussed later), and Bank's idea of Christ transcending the law is to the forefront. So, 'Jesus' messianic claim in relation to the Sabbath pointed to a transcendence of the institution, just as Jesus' ministry as a whole anticipates the change to a new order.'[96] 'It is not Jesus' healings on the Sabbath that are the cause of offense but the claims that He makes for Himself.'[97] 'His hearers are to interpret the Sabbath in relation to His own person and work.'[98]

Understood in a restricted sense, Sabbatarians might agree with those statements about Christ's transcendence of the law. If Jesus is viewed as he is presented, for example, in the opening verses of John—'In the beginning was the Word, and the Word was with God, and the Word was God'—as no less God than the God who gave the Decalogue then it is a statement of the obvious that in some sense he transcended the law. This is true of any lawgiver except in so far as he, she, or they, voluntarily submit themselves to the law, and except in so far as the law is an expression of their character, so long as their character is also immutable. In this sense the God of Sinai transcended the law, yet that mere fact did not mean that it was subject to imminent change. Why should it be any different if the same were true of Jesus in the Gospels? Even so, that is not the case: the Gospels

---

94   Carson, 'Jesus and the Sabbath,' 84.
95   Lincoln, 'Biblical and Theological Perspective', 360–4.
96   Ibid., 345.
97   Ibid., 360.
98   Ibid., 362.

describe a man who voluntarily submits himself to the law, not as one grasping for transcendence. Without importing doctrines about the two natures of Christ, it is not clear how one person could simultaneously transcend the Sabbath institution and submit to it as a law. Lincoln looks to Banks to explain:

> What becomes clear about the Sabbath…is that Jesus 'takes a position above it so that it is incorporated into an entirely new framework and viewed from a quite different perspective. As a result, what is acceptable or unacceptable in the way of conduct upon it is defined in relation to an altogether new reference point, i.e. Christ's estimate of the situation.' This new Christological perspective to be brought to the Sabbath is also suggested in Mark and Luke by their placing of this Sabbath pericope immediately after Jesus' teaching that new wine must be put into fresh wineskins. The Mosaic Sabbath constitutes one of the elements of the old order that will have to change in the light of the new.[99]

This explanation only leads to confusion. Should transcendence mean that during his earthly life Jesus took 'a position above it', whether by addition, subtraction, intensification, or relaxation, then he was not subject to it. If, as Lincoln and the other contributors claim, Jesus 'kept the Sabbath law',[100] then 'what is acceptable or unacceptable' is either still defined by the law, or Christ's estimate of the situation is in harmony with the law, so Bank's statement is redundant. And if the Sabbath commandment is 'incorporated into an entirely new framework and viewed from a quite different perspective', how is it abrogated as a legal requirement? Does abrogation not exclude incorporation?

Lincoln's reference to the wine and wineskins does not help. Commenting elsewhere on the parallel passage in Matthew 9, Carson explains the new wine parallel as meaning that the 'new situation introduced by Jesus could not simply be patched onto

99   Ibid., 364. This is also quoted by Carson on page 76.
100   Ibid., 345.

old Judaism or poured into the old wineskins of Judaism.'[101] He rejects the 'extreme' Dispensationalist view 'that there is no connection whatever with what has come before' and that Jesus had come to supersede the legal dispensation with something that was entirely new.[102] 'Jesus' teaching and the kingdom now dawning must be poured into new forms'. It cannot be 'contained by traditions of Jewish piety'.[103] Lincoln's statement, however, has more in common with the Dispensationalist view that Carson rejects. If the Sabbath commandment is an element of the old order that must change in the light of the new then it is indistinguishable from the 'traditions of Jewish piety' and does not even achieve the status of incorporation into the new order. It is wineskin rather than wine.

This view of continuity and discontinuity is also out of place with Lincoln's earlier statement that the 'the Sabbath with its legislation was never meant to be a tyrant that enslaved people by its insufferable demands but a benefit and a privilege instituted for the sake of people and their enjoyment.'[104] Unless the contributors view the new covenant as a less generous administration with restricted privileges and fewer enjoyments then it is surprising that such concern for people and their enjoyment should be swept aside.

Lincoln ends his précis of his fellow-contributors' findings on Jesus and the Sabbath in the Gospels with a paragraph that raises questions about their entire enterprise:

> Jesus' personal claims whereby He transcends the Sabbath law provide the Christological key with which His followers could later interpret the Sabbath. But His own teaching does not provide any further explicit directions about the sort of changes the inauguration

---

101   Carson, *Matthew*, [Pradis Ver. 5.01.0035].
102   Ibid.
103   Ibid.
104   Lincoln, 'Biblical and Theological Perspective', 362.

of the new order will bring. This is only to be expected because of the veiled nature of His earthly ministry. Only after the consummation of his ministry in His death and Resurrection would the significance of both His person and work become clear. The hidden and transitional aspects of Jesus' earthly ministry account for the fact that no definite break with the Mosaic Sabbath is clearly set out in His teaching or actions and mean also that Jesus' Sabbath practices (e.g., regular attendance at synagogue if "as his custom was" in Luke 4:16 is a reference to this) do not necessarily provide any norms for the new order. The veiled nature of Jesus' ministry accounts for the slight ambiguity in regard to His relation to the Sabbath and for the fact that for a time in the early church there were those who continued Sabbath observance while the full implications of the entry to the new age accomplished by Christ were being worked out.[105]

Given that estimates for the dating of the four gospels vary from 50–150 this argument is unsatisfactory. If 'Jesus' personal claims' represented an interpretative key, why had the Gospel writers not worked out how to use it decades after his death and resurrection? Why did they choose to leave their readers in the dark on an issue that was so prominent in their accounts of Jesus' life? Such obfuscation would be inexplicable in view of their consistent willingness to unveil his earthly ministry. Whether in commenting on other issues of law—'Thus he declared all foods clean.' (Mark 7:19)—or in repeated declarations of his divine person (e.g. Matt. 16:16; Mark 1:1; Luke 1:32; John 20:31) they spelt out the significance of his person and work. Indeed, contrary to Lincoln, they speak of Jesus giving unambiguous directions about the new order[106] and the law. When Jesus so firmly upholds the commandments in various speeches and encounters (e.g. Matt. 4:10; 5:21–37; 15:4, 19) it is reasonable to expect that he might have been equally frank about the Sabbath

105   Ibid., 364.
106   For example, in spelling out how the disciples would be treated by all nations (Matt. 24:9–14; Mark 13:9–13) and how they should approach all nations (Matt. 28:18–20; Luke 24:44–9).

if it was no more to be enjoyed. Neither Jesus nor the Gospels are ambiguous about Sabbath. The ambiguity in this case, which is beyond 'slight', is produced by the contributors' anachronistic anti-Sabbatarian framework. Vermes is correct when he writes:

> If, as is often claimed, the evangelists aimed at inculcating, in a fictional account of the life of Jesus, Christian doctrine such as the annulment of the Sabbath legislation, to members of the Gentile church, they did a pitiful job which falls far short of proving their alleged thesis.[107]

That, however, was not their thesis. The evangelists represent Jesus as a Sabbath-keeper, not as one who undermines the fourth commandment either directly by word and action, or indirectly by yet-to-be-understood personal claims, which is why 'within the early Christian communities Sabbath observance *per se* was not in question.'[108] It is therefore unsurprising if 'ambiguity' handicaps an anti-Sabbatarian thesis built on what would have been a 'pitiful job'. Nonetheless, the issue cannot be settled as far as the threefold division is concerned without considering the apostolic approach to Sabbath.

JESUS AND PURITY LAWS

Unless one is devoted to the King James Version or the Vulgate, the Gospel of Mark is uniquely unambiguous about the impact of Jesus' ministry on laws concerning food and washings: Jesus 'declared all foods clean' (Mark 7:19).[109] For Alan Watson there is no doubt that in Mark, 'Jesus' hostility is not just to Pharisaical interpretation but to the laws of God themselves',[110] at least 'those commandments of God [in Leviticus] that had no obvious

---

107   Vermes, *Jesus the Jew*, 13.
108   Herold Weiss, 'The Sabbath in the Synoptic Gospels' in *New Testament Backgrounds* (Sheffield: Sheffield Academic Press, 1997), 120.
109   The KJV and Vulgate omit this statement.
110   Alan Watson, 'Leviticus in Mark', in Sawyer, *Reading Leviticus*, 269.

ethical content',[111] since, apart from divorce and the general
list in Mark 7:20–23, 'there is nothing about Jesus' attitude to
God's laws in Leviticus that might be regarded as having a moral
content'.[112] But do Mark or the other Gospels present Jesus as
'hostile' to laws without 'moral content'? Hostile or not, did his
attitudes reveal any acceptance of categories such as moral and
ceremonial, or of the distinctions highlighted in the previous
chapters between laws that were a pattern and those that were to
be obeyed 'in the land'? The Gospels record his physical contact
with lepers and corpses. Did this reflect a slaphappy unconcern
about uncleanness? All except John report the rending of the
temple veil. What was the significance of that event for the status
of ritual laws? This section will consider such questions.

Was Jesus Unclean?

On several occasions Jesus touches those who are unclean, or is
touched by those who are unclean—a leper (Mark 1:41), a bleeding
woman (Mark 5:27), or a dead child (Mark 5:41). The effect of Jesus
touching the leper was immediate healing, which he followed
with an instruction in Mark 1:44 that the leper show himself to
the priest and make the appropriate offering 'for a testimony to
them'—an apparently plain instruction upholding the Mosaic
Law of Leviticus 14:1–9. For Broadhead, this 'appears enigmatic,
even contradictory' since Mark 'presents Jesus as one little
concerned for traditional aspects of piety', particularly 'cultic,
external representation of piety'.[113] Rejecting other views, such
as that of Pesch, Schweizer, and others that this shows Jesus
upholding the law,[114] he presents his alternative, which is to view

111   Ibid., 271.

112   He gives the laws in Leviticus 18:6–19:14 as examples. Ibid., 270.

113   Edwin K. Broadhead, 'Mk 1,44: The Witness of the Leper.' ZNW 83
(1992), 258.

114   Ibid., 259.

this as a 'prophetic witness against cultic piety', which has its precedent in Old Testament prophecy where the 'cultic piety of the temple is mocked'.[115] The problem with this is that while prophets witnessed for 'the primacy of morality over the cult' and mocked the inverted piety of the people, they did not mock the temple or laws such as those commanded in Leviticus 14. If anything, the passage Broadhead cites (Jer. 7) suggests that Jeremiah counted the behaviour of the priests and people to be a mockery of the temple and what it represented. Broadhead's case rests largely on his argument concerning the translation of the final phrase in Mark 1:44, εἰς μαρτύριον αὐτοῖς. Banks presented the same case seventeen years earlier: the final phrase 'is most likely to mean a "testimony against Israel", so it does not highlight Jesus' faithfulness to the Mosaic Law, "but that through its observance its adherents might be brought face to face with their own failure and with the corresponding reality of Christ's power."'[116] This translation may be legitimate (cf. Mark 6:11), but the idea that Jesus cynically used the law in a way that essentially legitimized hypocrisy is unconvincing. If all he wanted to do was bring the priesthood to reckon with his power he might have left that to the leper's lack of restraint (Mark 1:45). Regardless of how εἰς μαρτύριον αὐτοῖς is translated, that Jesus instructed the leper to fulfil the law of Leviticus 14 is unavoidable. It does not represent a break with prophetic tradition or sit uneasily with Mark's approach to the law.

Jesus' command is not the only problem for interpreters in Mark 1:40–45. Touching the leper would, according to Witherington, 'certainly render Jesus unclean' and 'we are nowhere told that Jesus, like the man he heals, ever went through ritual cleansing after this encounter. What Mark will suggest in chapter 7 is that Jesus believed...rules about clean

and unclean…were obsolescent.'[117] Certainly, we are not told
that Jesus went through purification rites, but why should we be
told? 'If Jesus was brought up as a devout Jew,' we can assume
with Dunn that 'unless there is evidence to the contrary, that he
observed the laws of clean and unclean purity, and that when he
attended the Temple he naturally observed the required purity
ritual.'[118] The silence of the text implies observance rather than
non-observance, for 'had he repudiated them, there would have
been a clear case against him. Jesus was never charged with
non-compliance.'[119] As with some other assumed innovations in
Jesus' attitude to the law, they also exist in the Old Testament. If
Witherington's 'we-are-nowhere-told' hermeneutic is applied to
1 Kings 17:17–24 and 2 Kings 4:32–7, then whatever problem he
sees with Jesus' ritual uncleanness and its implications for the law
also exist in the stories of Elijah and Elisha. We are not told that
they went through ritual cleansing after touching dead bodies,
so does this imply that they held antinomian beliefs about clean
and unclean? More importantly, Witherington's point is trivial
because no purification was necessary under the law.

Unlike Witherington, Wojciechowski wants to preserve Jesus'
purity at all costs:

> Now, if Jesus voluntarily touched a leper, he had to feel that he
> would not contract any impurity. If he intended to cleanse him, he
> had to attribute an exceptional value to his own touch, to believe in
> its religious – and not only medical – healing effect. The touching
> should have defiled Jesus, but it cleansed the leper.[120]

117 Ben Witherington, *The Gospel of Mark: A Socio-Rhetorical Commentary*
(Grand Rapids: Eerdmans, 2001), 104.

118 James D. G. Dunn, 'Jesus and Purity: An Ongoing Debate.' *NTS* 48
(2002), 456.

119 Loader, *Jesus and the Law*, 520.

120 Markus Wojciechowski, 'The Touching of the Leper (Mark 1,40–45)
as a Historical and Symbolic Act of Jesus.' *Biblische Zeitschrift* 33 (1989), 118.

His concern is misguided. This may arise in part from an unnecessary equation between uncleanness and unholiness, which appears in the sharp dichotomy he makes between ritual impurity and holiness. A similar concern emerges in Neyrey's effort to prove that by such contacts with sinners Jesus was 'never rendered unholy himself.'[121] Regardless of whether touching a leper was out of line with 'the prevailing legal interpretation',[122] in strict terms 'it conveys an impermanent contagion. It is not sinful to be ritually impure, and ritual impurity does not result from sin.'[123] The repeated mention of a man's 'guilt' concerning touching human uncleanness 'of whatever sort' that appears in Leviticus 5:3 may appear to challenge this, and some commentators on Leviticus 5:1–4 understand the passage in that way: 'To become unclean is to become guilty.'[124] 'The point is that impurity is the basis of the offender's guilt.'[125] Milgrom takes a different approach: 'The sin rests only in his neglect to purify himself of his impurity within the prescribed one-day time limit (11:28, 31–40).'[126] This is a better interpretation, although Leviticus 11 refers to touching animal carcasses, not lepers. Likewise, the purification required in Leviticus 15:7 relates to touching someone with a bodily discharge, and not a leper. Even a priest who touched an unclean person, which presumably might have taken place when skin diseases were examined (Lev. 13), was unclean only until the evening. Bathing was not required unless he was to eat the

---

121 Jerome H. Neyrey, 'The Idea of Purity in Mark's Gospel.' *Semeia* 35 (1986), 112.

122 Thomas Kazen, *Jesus and Purity Halakhah: Was Jesus Indifferent to Purity?* (Stockholm: Almqvist & Wiksell International, 2002), 127.

123 Jonathan Klawans, 'Idolatry, Incest, and Impurity: Moral Defilement in Ancient Judaism.' *Journal for the Study of Judaism* XXIX, 4 (1998), 393.

124 Robert I. Vasholz, *Leviticus* (Fearn: Mentor, 2007), 56.

125 Baruch A. Levine, *Leviticus* (New York: Jewish Publication Society, 1989), 27.

126 Jacob Milgrom, *Leviticus 1–16* (New York: Doubleday, 1991), 298.

holy things (Lev. 22:6). A straightforward equation between uncleanness and guilt is also rendered incoherent by the concept of a guilty pot or building (Lev. 11:33; 14:36). For Jesus to have contracted uncleanness would therefore have implied neither guilt nor transgression of the law.

The reality under Levitical law was that no man born of a woman could possibly go through life devoid of ritual uncleanness since his mother was unclean for seven days after childbirth and her purification was only complete forty days after childbirth (Lev. 12:1–4). This is especially relevant to the account of the woman who touched the fringe of Jesus' garment, which is immediately followed by the raising of Jairus' daughter (Mark 5:25–43; Matt. 9:20–26; Luke 8:43–56). Amy-Jill Levine claims that 'students of Christian origins are obsessed with Levitical purity legislation' and may well 'worry more about such matters, particularly as they concern women, than did many Jewish women in the first century.'[127] This is a fair assessment, but her argument that the woman was not a menstruant per se as 'neither the Hebrew nor the Greek provides firm or even necessary indication that the flow is uterine or vaginal'[128] is not persuasive. Given that ῥύσις (Mark and Luke) and αἱμορροέω (Matthew) point to genital discharge in eighteen out of nineteen combined LXX references, her discharge was most likely menstrual. Concerning Jairus' daughter, Levine finds that the 'best intertexts' are the Elijah and Elisha stories of raising the dead and that the entire pericope (Matt. 9:20–26) therefore 'emphasizes Jesus' conformity to the Law',[129] locating him 'within

127   Amy-Jill Levine, 'Discharging Responsibility: Matthean Jesus, Biblical Law, and Haemorrhaging Woman.' in Amy-Jill Levine with Marianne Blickenstoff, eds., *A Feminist Companion to Matthew*. (Sheffield: Sheffield Academic Press, 2001), 72.

128   Ibid., 75.

129   Ibid., 84. She points to Jesus' instruction to the leper in Matthew 8:4, and to the fact that the fringes on Jesus' clothing complied with the Law (82–3).

Jewish tradition without undermining the Law in any way or, indeed, even here evoking it.'[130] Somewhat like Wojciechowski and Neyrey in the case of the leper, Evans claims a 'purity miracle' in the healing of the woman: 'Instead of conveying uncleanness to Jesus, whom she touches, cleanness is conveyed to her.'[131] Kazen objects to such claims that the instantaneousness of the healing avoided contamination for Jesus 'since the instancy, the εὐθύς belongs to a literary level, and is a Markan trait,'[132] but even if the εὐθύς were absent, the notion of instant healing would be the most natural reading, and that this might avoid uncleanness for Jesus is logically possible. Nonetheless, it does not matter. Debate over split-second timing, and whether the instantaneous nature of the healing might have avoided uncleanness, when the uncleanness would neither have been a transgression of the law, nor indicated Jesus' attitude to the law, is illustrative of the obsession that Levine highlights.

What Defiles a Man

If the incidents of contact with unclean individuals point to Jesus' conformity to the law rather than to a breezy disregard for the Levitical legislation, what do Mark 7 (and its parallel Matt. 15:1–21) suggest concerning his attitude to unclean foods and purity legislation? The gospels report that the Pharisees came to Jesus asking why the disciples rejected the tradition of the elders and ate with unwashed hands (Mark 7:5). He responded with an accusation that they put their traditions above the Law of Moses, giving a specific example of their disobedience to the fifth commandment as one of 'many such things' (Mark 7:9–13). For

130 Ibid., 77.
131 Craig A. Evans in Bruce Chilton and Craig A. Evans, *Jesus in Context: Temple, Purity, and Restoration* (Leiden, Koninklijke Brill, 1997), 368.
132 Kazen, *Jesus and Purity Halakah*, 138.

Morna Hooker, the example does not fit the argument because the Torah affirms that an oath is inviolable 'and the question is therefore not one of Law versus tradition at all, but rather of the relative weight to be given to different parts of the Law...'[133] Her analysis is partly correct. Handwashing was not required in the law (although practiced by some Pharisees[134]), and that relative weight may be given to different parts of the law (even within the Decalogue) could be reflected in this text as it is in various Old Testament narratives (e.g. Joshua 2; 1 Sam. 19–20). Nonetheless, the handwashing and associated rituals Mark 7:4 describes, along with the Corban of 7:11, cannot be divorced from the law since they represent misapplication of the law. Even the 'textually problematic καὶ κλινῶν [7:4] accurately reflects a first century Jewish practice',[135] according to Crossley. It is 'based on the interpretation of Lev. 11:32 and 15:12 and not the actual beds mentioned in Lev. 15.' In Mark 7:1–23 Jesus is not 'opposing any biblical law but the expansion of biblical purity laws, in particular the avoidance of transmitting impurity through hand washing' so that the comment in verse 19 is 'an attack on the validity of hand washing and not the biblical food laws as is usually thought.'[136] It is not difficult to read verses 1–13 in this way, seeing them as an account of Jesus' upholding the true meaning of the law against extra-Mosaic accretions, but whatever the connection with the preceding section, verse 19, along with Jesus' statement (Mark 7:15–19), is too explicit in its

133   Hooker, *Mark*, 177.

134   See Robert P. Booth, *Jesus and the Laws of Purity in Mark 7* (Sheffield: JSOT Press, 1986), 203:'The Pharisaic question is credible in the time of Jesus on the basis that the Pharisees concerned were *haberim* who did handwash before *hullin*, and were urging Jesus and his disciples to adopt supererogatory handwashing which they themselves practised...'

135   James G. Crossley, 'Halakah and Mark 7.4:"and beds".' *JSNT* 25.4 (2003), 447.

136   Ibid.

reference to food to be restricted to extra-biblical washings. Even
if the point of Mark 7 is to indicate that Jesus ranked moral
purity above ritual purity as a 'weightier matter of the law',[137]
these verses require explanation.

Consistent with his comments on the leper, Witherington
thinks that taken 'in a straightforward manner' Mark 7:15 'means
that Jesus saw a significant portion of the Levitical law as no
longer applicable.'[138] Menahem Kister rejects such radicalism
because according to rabbinic purity rules nonkosher food
'defiles a human being by touching it and "transporting" the food
to his mouth, if indeed not by the act of eating it per se.'[139] Only
the corpse of a clean bird could defile, so Jesus is talking about
'defiled kosher food…simply because kosher food is the only food
eaten by Jews.'[140] This interpretation may make excellent halakhic
sense,[141] but that is not how it is viewed in Mark 7, nor is the only
alternative to view it as 'the most radical antinomistic saying in
the Synoptic Gospels.'[142] More obvious objections to the view
typified by Witherington, are that if it was so straightforward
then the Jewish authorities would have had a clear case against
Jesus, and more importantly, his followers ought to have grasped
what he was saying. Sanders sums up this argument (which has
been used by several authors, before and after him, with respect
to this passage and Luke 10:8):[143]

137   Eyal Regev, 'Moral Impurity and the Temple in Early Christianity in
Light of Ancient Greek Practice and Qumranic Ideology.' *HTR* 97:4 (2004),
387; Menahem Kister, 'Law, Morality, and Rhetoric in Some Sayings of Jesus'
in James L. Kugel, ed. *Studies in Ancient Midrash* (Harvard University Centre
for Jewish Studies, 2001), 153.
138   Witherington, *Mark*, 227.
139   Kister, 'Law, Morality, and Rhetoric in Some Sayings of Jesus', 151.
140   Ibid., 151–2.
141   Ibid., 151 n. 21.
142   Ibid., 154.
143   Räisänen, *Jesus, Paul and Torah*, 134; Dunn, 'Jesus and Purity', 463.

If Jesus had declared all foods clean, why did Paul and Peter disagree over Jews eating with Gentiles (Gal. 2.11–16)? Or, put in terms of Acts rather than Galatians, why did it take a thrice-repeated revelation to convince Peter (or, rather, to leave him puzzled and on the way to conviction) (Acts 10.9–17)? And if Jesus consciously transgressed the Sabbath, allowed his disciples to do so, and justified such action in public debate, how could Paul's Christian opponents in Galatia urge that the Sabbath be kept (Gal. 4.10)?[144]

To this observation, Dunn says we should add the consideration 'that no memory of Jesus eating pork or non-kosher food is preserved in any Jesus tradition.'[145] Sanders believes it impossible that Jesus intended 'to oppose Sabbath, food and other "ceremonial" laws, but that the disciples did not get it,'[146] and overall, 'this argument is fatal to the view that Jesus openly and blatantly opposed the law.'[147] According to the gospels there are some things 'that the disciples did not get', yet this is a defensible approach. It does not, however, shed much light on Jesus' statement (7:15) or his explanation to the disciples (7:18–23).

Booth is convinced that the importance of how the οὐ...ἀλλά construction of 7:15 is translated 'cannot be over-stated, for upon it may depend whether Jesus is considered to abrogate, or merely depreciate the cultic law of Israel.'[148] It reflects a 'semitic idiom of negation', which may also be seen in Mark 9:37. 'Contextual evidence' also shows 'the unlikelihood of Jesus making an unqualified abrogation of the cultic law in response to a question about handwashing,'[149] therefore Booth favours a relative understanding of the statement. He also goes to some lengths to show that 'things going out of a man' does not apply to bodily

144 E. P. Sanders, *Jesus and Judaism* (London: SCM Press Ltd, 1985), 250.

145 Dunn, 'Jesus and Purity', 463.

146 Sanders, *Jesus and Judaism*, 268.

147 Ibid., 246.

148 Booth, *Jesus and the Laws of Purity*, 70.

149 Ibid.

discharges and that the defilement they produce is ethical rather than cultic.[150] As a result, he concludes 'that the logion is credible as a saying of Jesus in the form, "There is nothing outside a man which *cultically* defiles him as much as the things coming from a man *ethically* defile him".'[151]

It is at least clear that Mark 9:37 could make little sense if it were interpreted as an absolute statement that left Jesus saying, 'Whoever receives the one who sent me does not receive me.' This, coupled with the contextual evidence he cites, gives cogency to Booth's argument. If Jesus is making a statement according to a prophetic tradition that emphasised the primacy of morality, then it would explain why Peter needed a later revelation, since it would not have been interpreted as a rejection of cultic laws. But would it be problematic for Jesus to have said, 'Things that come out of a person defile him, but nothing going in can defile him', if defilement were understood as ethical in both cases?

One possibility is that behind Jesus' statement lies a theological presupposition that gives logical priority to creational norms, similar to what was reflected in his statement concerning divorce—'from the beginning it was not so' (Matt. 19:8). If God created every living creature that filled earth, sea, and sky, and proclaimed them 'good' (Gen. 1:20–25), if Noah saved clean and unclean from the flood (Gen. 7:2), then it would be surprising if no ancient Jew ever wondered how they could have become 'detestable' (Lev. 7:21 etc.). Although he rejects the possibility that Jesus is 'just holding a mirror up to nature, depicting what has always been the case,' Joel Marcus acknowledges that 'such a change in the purity laws is not without precedent; after all, from the postdiluvian period to the giving of the Law of Moses all animals could be eaten (Gen. 9:3).'[152] Wenham thinks

150   Ibid., 206–214.
151   Ibid., 214.
152   Joel Marcus, *Mark 1–8* (New York: Doubleday, 2000), 457.

this approach to Genesis is 'problematic'. We cannot 'assert that
total freedom is being given' because the distinction between
clean and unclean occurs earlier in the flood narrative.[153] It seems
doubly problematic, however, to assert that animals that God set
apart (בָּדַל) to be unclean (Lev. 20:25) to a people that he had
set apart (also בָּדַל) from other nations to be holy (Lev. 20:24–6)
were in fact always set apart for all nations.[154] Marcus' basis
for rejecting this view is that up until Noah, Adam and his
offspring were vegetarians (Gen. 1:29),[155] but Genesis does not
describe a vegetarian world (Gen. 4:4). This means that while
Jesus' statement was not intended to reflect what had been 'from
the beginning', it may, contrary to Marcus, have been a reflection
of what had always been the case in a post-vegetarian world. Just
as Noah and his family would not have been rendered unclean
by touching a dead body, they would not have been rendered
unclean by eating shellfish. Prior to Moses, every creeping thing
was 'good' and 'for food'—sufficient reason to say that those
creatures of themselves could not cause ethical defilement.

The Levitical law itself suggests that no animal was
intrinsically clean or unclean since contact with the carcass of
either an unclean animal or a clean animal that became unclean
by its cause of death, rendered Israelites unclean until evening
(Lev. 11:28; 39–40). Eating the meat of the latter would have
caused uncleanness until the evening, requiring the eater to
cleanse himself (Lev. 17:15). Even Deuteronomy 14:21, which
seems to take a harder line by forbidding all Israelite consumption
of anything that died naturally, allowed them to give it to
sojourners or sell it to a foreigner, something that would not have

153   Gordon J. Wenham, *Genesis 1–15* (Waco: Word Books, 1987), 193.

154   It is also noteworthy that טָמֵא, which Leviticus universally uses to
term things unclean does not occur in Genesis until it is used to describe the
defilement of Dinah in chapter 34. In addition, it is precisely those 'creeping
things' (רֶמֶשׂ) of Genesis 9:3 that are forbidden in Leviticus 11:44–6 (רֶמֶשׂ).

155   Marcus, *Mark 1–8*, 457.

been permitted if it caused ethical defilement of a universal pre-Noahic principle. The law demands no judicial penalty for those who ate unclean foods, nor does it lay down regulations about what should happen if someone unwittingly ate pork, unless the cleansing outlined for the eating of the unclean foods mentioned in Leviticus 17:15 could have applied to the consumption of all unclean foods. It is therefore possible that just as touching dead animals made one unclean, but not sinful, that swallowing the meat of unclean animals caused uncleanness, but not ethical defilement. Sin and ethical defilement could not come through the mere consumption of unclean food, only through the wilful rejection of the laws that God had established to emphasise the distinctiveness of Israel.[156]

Thus Jesus' statement and explanation is coherent. Contact alone does not defile; rejection of God's commands does, and such rebellion always comes from within. The expository catalogue of iniquities in verses 21–2 defines what comes from within, the outbound things, as transgressions of the Decalogue and other exclusively non-cultic evils. There was nothing innovative about this as the law declared that such sins would make Israel—people and land—unclean to the extent that the land would 'vomit them out' (Lev. 18:1–29; Num. 35:33–4). 'These acts,' says Klawans, 'bring about an impurity that *morally*—but not *ritually*—defiles the sinner.'[157] The Mosaic Laws support his argument (mentioned earlier) that ritual impurity is not sin (though rebellion against the purity laws would be), but it does not work so simply the other way. By that logic, a ritually clean, murderous, covetous, arrogant, impenitent fool was welcome to the tabernacle, whereas Leviticus 18 suggests that such a person had no place among the people (v. 29), and such people had no place in the land (v. 24–8),

---

156   This is not a hair-splitting distinction, but one common to most societies who know, for example, not to accuse a medic of adultery every time they touch someone in places ordinarily restricted to sexual partners.

157   Klawans, 'Idolatory, Incest, and Impurity', 394.

far less in the tabernacle. By the time such 'abominations' prevail, ritual cleanliness has become an irrelevance. This at least seems to be how the psalmist (Ps. 24:3–5) saw things. It also reflects how Jesus saw things, yet Booth's rendition of the text (above), though possible, is unnecessary. The defilement in view is most likely ethical in both cases making Booth's qualifiers redundant. It is not even required to translate the οὐ...ἀλλά construction with a relative form. In the light of Leviticus, for Jesus to say, 'There is nothing outside a person that by going into him can defile him, but the things that come out of a person are what defile him,' implies neither abrogation nor deprecation of the cultic law, but rather reflects its content.

This still leaves Mark 7:19, 'He declared all foods clean,'[158] which is the evangelist's interpretation of these events some decades later and not something that was 'straightforward' at the time. If Jesus is expounding the Pentateuch's perspective on certain foods as not intrinsically unclean, but as set apart for uncleanness for as long as Israel is set apart (Lev. 20:24–6), then it is inevitable for Mark, writing in a new era, that if Israel is

---

158 This statement, καθαρίζων πάντα τὰ βρώματα, does not lend itself to straightforward translation. This is clear from sampling the multiplicity of English translations: 'This he said, making all meats clean.' (ASV, ERV); 'Thus he declared all foods ritually clean.' (Complete Jewish Bible); '...purging all meats' (KJV); 'In saying this, Jesus declared all foods "clean".' (NIV). The older versions, such as the Authorised Version, see the purging as the product of digestion, which eventually cleanses all food from the system. There is logic to this in the context since unlike murder, adultery, envy, folly, and the other things that Jesus mentions, food does not ordinarily stick around an individual or leave a lasting stain. More recent translations prefer to make the participle agree with the subject of λέγει in the previous verse so that it is Jesus who cleanses all foods. Translations like the NIV go beyond this and turn the comment into either (a) a declaration of Jesus' immediate rejection of Levitical food laws, (b) a declaration of the intrinsic cleanness of all foods, or (c) a proleptic abolition of the food laws. If the older translation must be rejected (and it is not clear that it must), then perhaps it is best to render the phrase as 'he cleansed all foods'. This allows the possibility that this is a parenthetic comment reflecting on the total accomplishment of Jesus' life.

no longer set apart that the laws that were intimately bound up with her sacredness are no longer binding. This means that even an apparently extreme statement like Sariola's is correct—'Ritual purity is entirely rejected by Mark'[159]—so long as it is understood to be a rejection that arises from the completed ministry of Jesus and not one which occurred during his ministry. Matera's comment reflects this balance: 'From the point of view of the Markan Gospel…it is Jesus who upholds the law and the religious leaders who nullify it. … By commenting that Jesus declared all foods clean, Mark makes explicit what is implicit in the feeding narratives: Jew and Gentile may now share table fellowship because Jesus, the Shepherd Messiah, has fed both.'[160]

Rending the Temple Veil

That the completed ministry of Jesus matters more than his lifetime attitudes to purity laws is seen in an event that Matthew, Mark, and Luke report—the rending of the temple veil. Many views have been put forward concerning its significance,[161] most of which would have implications for the Mosaic Law. The most recent and exhaustive study of the '*velum scissum*' is Daniel Gurtner's, *The Torn Veil*. He concentrates on Matthew's account, but many of his observations are relevant to the topic in general. The following extract reflects his primary conclusions:

---

159 Sariola, *Markus und das Gesetz*, 275.

160 Matera, *New Testament Ethics*, 28.

161 Nolland lists God's distress, the destruction of the temple, the abrogation of the old covenant, new access to God, Jesus being destroyed, the opening of heaven, and an apocalyptic sign, as the alternatives. John Nolland, *Luke 18:35–24:53*, WBC, 35c. (Nashville: Thomas Nelson, 1993), 1157. Sylva proposes an eighth alternative, claiming that the image is 'of Jesus' communion at the last moment before his death with the Father, who is present in the temple.' Dennis D. Sylva, 'The Temple Curtain and Jesus' Death in the Gospel of Luke.' *JBL* 105/2 (1986), 243.

The veil's separation function was executed by its prohibition of *physical and visual accessibility* to God. If this function ceases at the *velum scissum*, then the barrier that prohibits one from physically entering the presence of God, as well as from seeing his face, is effectively removed (again, as a result of the death of Jesus). Yet, as we have seen, physical accessibility could only be accomplished when the entrant bore gifts on the Day of Atonement, and only if the intruder had a high priestly status, lest those present die. Surely for Matthew, though, the raising of the saints (27:52–53) and the profession of the soldiers (27:54) connote life in various senses, rather than death. He must then presume that the atonement necessary for physical accessibility to God and for the maintenance of this communal presence among his people has been accomplished (Matt. 28:20), which Matthew *inextricably links with the death of Jesus.* The accomplishment of atonement by the death of Jesus necessarily leads to the accessibility of humanity to God, depicted in Matthew not just as a person entering God's presence… but also as God's being 'with us' (Emmanuel, 1:23).[162]

This assessment takes proper account of Mosaic Laws concerning the tabernacle, and Gurtner's comments on the Emmanuel theme tie in with some of the observations in the next chapter. The rending of the inner veil, the 'only καταπέτασμα [curtain, veil] for which a particular cultic function is designated',[163] means 'that the temple is superfluous: What it was intended to accomplish is surpassed by Jesus.'[164] This also implies that all the 'pattern' (תַּבְנִית) laws of the Mosaic Code were also superfluous. Israel's sacredness and cultic distinctives have come to an end. Yet, this is more than a theological extrapolation based on the conclusion that atonement has been accomplished. From the outset, the veil is linked with the separation theme, not least by the common בָּדַל vocabulary. It separates (בָּדַל) the Holy Place

---

162   Daniel M. Gurtner, *The Torn Veil: Matthew's Exposition of the Death of Jesus* (Cambridge: Cambridge University Press, 2007), 189.

163   Ibid., 49.

164   Ibid., 190.

from the Most Holy Place (Exod. 26:33), the Lord separates (בָּדַל)
Israel (Lev. 20:24, 26), and also separates (בָּדַל) certain foods
to uncleanness (Lev. 20:25). Foods separated for uncleanness
were a sign of Israel's separation to a God whose separation was
marked by the veil. The implications of its rending extend to
everything touched by the theme of separation, including the
people and the purity laws. Divine separation gives way to
divine nearness—'I am with you always' (Matt. 28:20), ethnic
separation gives way to a universal welcome—'make disciples of
all nations' (Matt. 28:19), and the separation of certain foods to
uncleanness now symbolizes a past reality that gives way to the
intrinsic cleanness of all things.

Gurtner argues that, like Mark, Matthew 'identifies the veil
with the heavenly firmament'.[165] He also looks for LXX uses
of σχίζω that inform Matthew's use of the word, suggesting
that a 'prominent "splitting" text which is probably in the
background...is the splitting (σχισθήσεται) of the Mount
of Olives at the Day of the Lord (Zech. 14:4).' If, however,
the veil is identified with the heavens, then Zechariah 14:4 is
only a 'prominent "splitting" text' because it uses σχίζω. A more
obvious background text is Isaiah 64:1, where the prophet prays
for God to 'rend the heavens and come down'. The LXX in this
instance uses ἀνοίγω rather than σχίζω to translate קָרַע, but
since σχίζω translates קָרַע in Isaiah 36:22 and 37:1 there seems no
reason why it could not have been used in Isaiah 64:1. In any case,
the mere absence of σχίζω does not mean that the Isaiah passage
could not be a background text as the imagery of rent heavens,
which is absent from Zechariah 14:4, is present in Isaiah. It is
improbable that the rending of the veil represents the departure
of the Shekinah since Matthew's Emmanuel imagery suggests
the opposite. A more likely notion is that the veil being torn
from top to bottom, which 'depicts the origin and destination

165 Ibid., 176–7.

of the action of tearing',[166] is seen as the answer to Isaiah's plea that God would rend the heavens and come down. He lamented over a Jerusalem rendered desolate (64:10) because God had veiled his face (64:7) from a people so unclean[167] that their best deeds, like a garment defiled by a menstruant's blood (64:6), debarred them from his presence. The rent veil proclaimed the end of uncleanness and the return of the Shekinah in Jesus. From this point on no symbolic uncleanness, such as that represented in the purity laws, can separate them from Emmanuel.[168]

SUMMARY

The view that the Gospels present Jesus as living in conformity to the Mosaic laws remains widely accepted by scholars of all shades. John's Gospel raises the issue of law least frequently, yet even he assumes the validity of the Decalogue and does not present Jesus as an antinomian. He probably shared the view held by other Gospel writers, and the Jesus they speak about, that the two greatest commandments summarize the Decalogue—a view well established in the history of interpretation.

Attempts by evangelical scholars to show that for the evangelists the Sabbath commandment belongs to the old order that must change in the light of the new are, by their own admission, hampered by ambiguity. And contrary to the popular notion that they endorse, Sabbath-keeping is not a Puritan invention, but a catholic tradition.

Some Christians dismiss the fourth commandment because they group it with purity laws, but this too is misguided if the underlying assumption is that the Gospels see Jesus as a cultic antinomian. There is no basis to support claims that Jesus

---

166   Ibid., 186.

167   טָמֵא as throughout Leviticus.

168   Such an interpretation of Isaiah 64 is also reflected in 1 Corinthians 2.

disregarded the cultic laws of the Mosaic Code. Some New
Testament commentators reach this incorrect conclusion because
rather than interacting with Leviticus they make unwarranted
assumptions about Levitical laws, particularly a direct equation
between uncleanness and guilt. Even if Jesus were unclean the
arguments that he opposed purity laws are unconvincing. Jesus'
statement that nothing going into a man could defile him was in
harmony with the law and reflected the impossibility of acquiring
moral impurity from mere contact with food. The gospel writers
came to believe that with the rending of the veil, the realities
to which the pattern laws pointed had arrived. Jesus' death
accomplished atonement ending all cultic separation. Thus Jesus
made laws concerning clean and unclean foods bind no longer,
not by the words recorded in Mark, but by the totality of his life
and finished work. For those reasons, the confessional claim that
'ceremonial laws are now abrogated under the new testament'
represents fairly the teaching of the Gospels.

V

JESUS PREACHES ON THE LAW

> 'Sophie...remember, Jesus,' her mother said.
> 'Yes, but you too,' she replied.
>
> *Sophie Scholl (1921–43), executed by the Third*
> *Reich, in final conversation with her mother.*

The previous chapter highlighted passages in Mark that suggest Jesus associated commandments primarily with the Decalogue. Other Gospels include parallel passages (Matt. 15:1–20; 19:16–30; Luke 18:18–30) where Jesus recites a series of the Ten Commandments. This is so widely accepted that it does not merit extended discussion.[1] Jesus, or his followers, upheld each of the Ten Commandments by personal obedience, direct or indirect citation, and allusion. While not demonstrating that they considered 'commandments' synonymous with the Decalogue, the following samples show that they affirmed all of the ten:

---

1 For example: Klyne Snodgrass, 'Matthew and the Law' in *Treasures New and Old: Contributions to Matthean Studies*, eds. David R. Bauer and Mark Allan Powell (Atlanta: Scholars Press, 1996), 108, 123; William Carter, *Matthew and the Margins: A Socio-Political and Religious Reading* (Sheffield: Sheffield Academic Press, 2000), 320, 388; Roger Mohrlang, *Matthew and Paul: a comparison of ethical perspectives* (Cambridge: Cambridge University Press, 1984), 11, 95.

I Matthew 4:10
II John 4:24
III Matthew 5:33–7
IV Luke 23:56
V Matthew 15:4; Luke 2:51
VI Matthew 5:21–6, 15:19, 19:18
VII Matthew 5:27–32, 15:19, 19:3–9, 18
VIII Matthew 15:19, 19:18
IX Matthew 5:33–7, 15:19, 19:18
X Luke 12:15

Several of those affirmations are clustered in Matthew 5, which requires further investigation for that reason, but more importantly because it records a statement from Jesus that is critical to all Christian approaches to biblical law:

> Do not think that I have come to abolish the Law or the Prophets; I have not come to abolish them but to fulfill them. For truly, I say to you, until heaven and earth pass away, not an iota, not a dot, will pass from the Law until all is accomplished. Therefore whoever relaxes one of the least of these commandments and teaches others to do the same will be called least in the kingdom of heaven, but whoever does them and teaches them will be called great in the kingdom of heaven (17–19).

According to D. A. Carson, 'many argue that Jesus is here referring only to moral law: the civil and ceremonial law are indeed abolished, but Jesus confirms the moral law…Although this tripartite division is old, its use as a basis for explaining the relationship is not demonstrably derived from the NT.'[2] Apart from Dan Lioy, however, whose work[3] was published two years

2   D. A. Carson, 'Matthew' in *Expositors Bible Commentary*, ed. Frank E. Gaebelein [Pradis Ver. 5.01.0035] (Grand Rapids: Zondervan, 2002).

3   He rejects Carson's argument because 'Christ began to annul the ceremonial aspect of the law when He declared all foods to be clean (cf. Mark 7:19).' Lioy, *Decalogue and the Sermon the Mount*, 139.

after Carson's, it is difficult to find any, far less 'many', who use the threefold division as the interpretative key to these verses. Carson refers to David Wenham, but Wenham preserves a measure of tentativeness: 'In arguing this I am coming near to reviving the traditional distinction between the moral and ceremonial law.'[4] Even Calvin, who says of Matthew 5:19, 'Christ is expressly speaking here of the rules of life, the Ten Commandments',[5] does not mention the threefold division or force Jesus' statement into its mould. Nonetheless, it is correct that the division cannot be assumed as a basis for interpreting Matthew 5:17–19, especially when Jesus' command, 'Do not think that I have come to abolish,' appears to challenge the threefold division. For example, when *The Westminster Confession* says that all 'ceremonial laws are now abrogated under the New Testament,' does it contradict Jesus' assertion that every iota and dot will stand? 'Abrogated' cannot be understood as anything other than 'abolished', so is this a case of inappropriate wording, of unbiblical dogma, or can the confessional language of abrogation be harmonized with Jesus' teaching? To answer those questions (and many others) we must consider the interpretation of Matthew 5:17–48.

'I HAVE NOT COME TO ABOLISH...BUT TO FULFIL'

If Jesus' words appear to sit awkwardly with the abrogation language of the threefold division, they seem to form an outright assault on the view that the law is abolished as an indivisible whole and to kill any suggestion that he saw no abiding validity in the law. Carson suggests that comparison with Matthew's other 'do not think' in 10:34 means that we should not take 'abolish' absolutely: 'Few would want to argue that there is no

4   David Wenham, 'Jesus and the law: an exegesis on Matthew 5:17–20', *Themelios* 4 (1979): 95.
5   Calvin, *Harmony of the Gospels,* vol. 1, 181.

sense in which Jesus came to bring peace…Why then argue that there is no sense in which Jesus abolishes the law?'[6] This comparison, however, is too simplistic and does not extend much beyond the opening Μὴ νομίσητε ὅτι. It sets aside the qualifying 'to the earth', and ignores the context in Matthew 10 of Jesus sending out the twelve apostles as sheep among wolves. In addition, Jesus promises his disciples peace in a troubled and hostile world (John 14:27; 16:33), so the sense in which he comes to bring peace does not qualify Matthew 10:34, which can stand as an absolute statement. Even if Jesus had elsewhere promised peace on earth, there are no parallels, in some context outside of Matthew 5, where Jesus says of the law, 'I abolish'. Why then argue that Jesus' statement should not be taken at face value? As Klyne Snodgrass asks, 'Can we believe that Matthew thought that his reader would know that he really meant the opposite of the words he was writing?'[7]

What of the words Matthew writes? In Matthew 5:17–19, can καταλύω mean anything other than 'abolish'? Throughout the LXX it normally translates Hebrew words associated with cessation and destruction, such as לוּן (lodge, rest; Gen. 23:23–5), חָנָה (encamp; Gen. 26:17), שָׁבַת (to cease, rest; Ruth 4:14), and סְתַר (destroy (Aram.) Ezra 5:12). The New Testament reflects this Old Testament background, using it twice to refer to lodging (Luke 9:12; 19:7), and on every other occasion to point to cessation in terms of destruction or tearing down (e.g. Matt. 24:2; 26:61; 27:40; Acts 5:38–9; Rom. 14:20). Therefore given that the word universally refers to cessation, temporary or absolute, any claim that Jesus actually meant he was abolishing the law, or bringing it to any kind of sabbath, must be backed by arguments of overwhelming force.

For many exegetes, their understanding of 'fulfil' largely

---

6   Carson, *Matthew*, [Pradis Ver. 5.01.0035].

7   Snodgrass, 'Matthew and the Law', 113.

determines their understanding of 'abolish', and for some that amounts to interpreting Jesus' words to mean their natural opposite. Dispensational theologian, Wayne Strickland, writes: 'The prophetic statements of Scripture can be abolished only when they are fulfilled, and Christ perfectly fulfils the prophecies of the Old Testament. As long as this world exists, there will be no repeal of the Law and Prophets apart from fulfilment.'[8] If so, fulfilment means abolition or repeal, and Matthew 5:17 ought to read, 'I have come to abolish the Law and the Prophets by fulfilling them.' Whether by fulfilment or peremptory declaration, abolition is abolition. Such an interpretation inverts the meaning of Jesus' words. It makes nonsense of his saying, 'Do not think...' and differs little from the Marcionite conversion of the sentence to 'Christ came in order to tear down the law.'[9]

'Fulfil' translates πληρόω and discussion about the precise definition fills several pages in some commentaries. Rather than follow that pattern at this point, I will state the five main interpretations of πληρόω, with general conclusions, and relegate the detail to an appendix.

The proposals that πληρόω means (a) to confirm[10] or (b) to transcend[11] should be rejected. The first would be 'a queer, unexplainable exception',[12] while the second lacks lexical and textual support. πληρόω could mean (c) that Jesus in his person

8   Wayne G. Strickland, 'The Inauguration of the Law of Christ with the Gospel of Christ: A Dispensational View', in *The Law, the Gospel and the Modern Christian: Five Views,* ed. Wayne G. Strickland (Grand Rapids: Zondervan, 1993), 258.

9   Ulrich Luz, *Matthew 1–7: A Commentary,* trans. Wilhelm C. Linss (Edinburgh: T&T Clark, 1990), 261, n. 39.

10   Gustaff Dalman, *Jesus–Jeshua: Studies in the Gospels,* trans. Paul P. Leverhoff (London: SPCK, 1929), 58; Bahnsen, *Theonomy,* 50.

11   Robert Banks, *Jesus and the Law in the Synoptic Tradition* (Cambridge: Cambridge University Press, 1975), 210.

12   Vern Poythress, *The Shadow of Christ in the Law of Moses* (Brentwood, Wolgemuth & Hyatt, 1991), 377.

or by his teaching fulfils the law and the prophets,[13] yet not exclusively. It could imply (d) that Jesus fulfilled the law by obedience,[14] but not restricted to particular laws. Finally, πληρόω could suggest (e) that Jesus' teaching or the actualization of it in his followers fulfils the law.[15]

Some of the differences in the interpretation of πληρόω arise from the extent of the context used to determine its meaning. Should it be restricted to Jesus' teaching in Matthew 5 or expanded to wider Matthean and New Testament usage? Whatever approach interpreters take, there is still overlap between most of the definitions and it soon becomes clear why Sigal wrote, 'Many scholars have dealt with this and have imparted a legacy of little clarity.'[16] It is easy to agree with Meier: 'Obviously, the general meaning is "to fill completely," "fulfil." But any attempt to become more specific plunges the exegete into a veritable whirlpool of conflicting interpretations.'[17] That those interpretations are offered so assertively only deepens the sense of conflict. To follow Bauer's example and refuse to settle on an exact meaning[18] is, however, not an option as the interpretation of this text is programmatic to any framework for the law, including the threefold division. It is necessary to reach some conclusion about the meaning of πληρόω, but why should the context that determines its meaning

13 W. D. Davies and Dale C. Allison, *A Critical and Exegetical Commentary on the Gospel According to Matthew*, Vol. I (Edinburgh: T. & T. Clark, 1988), 487; Carson, *Matthew*, [Pradis Ver. 5.01.0035].

14 Luz, *Matthew 1–7*, 264.

15 D. A. Hagner, *WBC: Matthew 1–13* Vol. 33a, electronic ed. (Dallas: Word, 1998), Logos Library System.; Loader, *Jesus' Attitude towards the Law*, 167; Snodgrass, 'Matthew and the Law', 115–16; N. T. Wright, *Matthew for Everyone. Part I, Chapter 1–15*. (London: SPCK, 2002), 40–1.

16 Phillip Sigal, *The Halakah of Jesus of Nazareth According to the Gospel of Matthew* (Lanham, University Press of America, 1986), 19.

17 John P. Meier, *Law and History in Matthew's Gospel: A Redactional Study of Mt. 5:17–48* (Rome: Biblical Institute Press, 1976), 73.

18 Ibid.

be artificially restricted? And must the potential definitions be treated as mutually exclusive? In the pages that follow, I propose that the determining context is the Old Testament, specifically the context of passages that Matthew cites, and that the possible meanings for πληρόω (c, d, or e) should not be polarized.

INTERPRETING MATTHEW 5:17

Given that this book is about the biblical and theological grounds for an historic Christian doctrine it is worth considering how one of its leading exponents interpreted Matthew 5:17. Relative to modern commentaries, Calvin has little to say on the matter, simply interpreting Jesus' words in relation to Jeremiah's new covenant:

> 'I shall write', He says, 'my Laws upon their hearts, and I shall forget their sins' (Jer. 31:33): these words do not at all depart from the former covenant, but rather declare that it will continue to be firm and valid, when the new has come upon it. This is exactly the intention of Christ's words, when he says that He has come to fulfil the Law. Truly he fulfilled the deadness of the letter by reviving it with His Spirit, and eventually displaying in actual fact, what had till then been indicated figuratively.[19]

This connection with Jeremiah was not a Genevan innovation—Pope Leo the Great connected the two passages more than a thousand years earlier[20]—and it merits consideration today. Another fulfilment passage, Matthew 3:15,[21] has also been linked with Jeremiah. It is included, for example, in the list of citations and allusions to the Old Testament found in

19 Calvin, *Harmony of the Gospels,* vol. I, 180.
20 Leo the Great, 'A Homily on the Beatitudes', Available from www.newadvent.org/fathers/360395.htm; accessed 4 April 2006.
21 I discuss the use of πληρόω in this passage in Appendix 2.

the appendix of the Nestle-Aland Greek New Testament.[22] In his article, 'Jesus Standing with Israel: The Baptism of Jesus in Matthew's Gospel (Matt 3:13–17)',[23] Jeffrey Gibbs discusses this link between Jeremiah 31 and Matthew's Gospel. Gibbs' purpose is to challenge the view that Psalm 2:7 lies behind the Father's words, 'This is my beloved son, with whom I am well pleased.' He argues instead that, along with Isaiah 42:1, Jeremiah 38:20 (LXX) is the background: 'Ephraim is a beloved son to me', so that Matthew is not portraying Jesus as Servant and King, but Servant and Israel.[24] After chapters 1–2, Matthew's narrative 'emphasizes other christological themes, most notably that the infant Jesus is the antitype or recapitulation of Israel as a whole (Matt 2:15)',[25] and Psalm 2 does not include the 'beloved' found in Matthew's expression or speak in the third person.[26] Furthermore, in Jeremiah 38:20 (LXX), the verbal agreement with υἱὸς ἀγαπητός (beloved son) is 'precise', Matthew has already cited Jeremiah 38:15 (LXX) in 2:18, the new Exodus motif of Jeremiah 38:8–9 (LXX) is present in Matthew 3, and the 'Jesus-son-of-God as Israel-son-of-God' typology found in Matthew 2 and 4 carries 'similar freight in Matthew 3'.[27] Thus 'Matthew presents Jesus at his baptism as God's son, the "embodiment" of Israel, God's son.'[28]

John's baptism is a baptism for repentance, but Gibbs avoids suggestions of vicarious repentance:

22 Nestle-Aland, *Novum Testamentum Graece.* (Stuttgart: Deutsche Bibelgesellschaft, 1993), 794.

23 Jeffrey A. Gibbs, 'Israel Standing with Israel: the Baptism of Jesus in Matthew's Gospel (Matt 3:13–17)', *The CBQ*, 64 (2002), 511–26.

24 Ibid., 512.

25 Ibid., 513.

26 Ibid., 514–5.

27 Ibid., 516–8.

28 Ibid., 520.

Though without personal need of baptism, Jesus receives John's baptism and thus identifies himself, son of God, with sinful Israel. He quite literally stands with sinners. Jesus' baptism not only shows that he sums up Israel in existence and deeds; Jesus' baptism means also that he is with and for Israel to save.[29]

If one 'leans towards a salvation-historical understanding of Jesus' words' to John, then says Gibbs, his argument 'supports the general understanding of "fulfilling all righteousness" as "carrying out God's saving plan" or "enacting God's righteous salvation."'[30] He therefore agrees with F. D. Coggin that this fulfilment is 'eschatological and soteriological rather than primarily moral.'[31]

Up to this point, Gibbs has presented a convincing case, but this downplaying of the moral introduces an unnecessary dichotomy, which is undermined by the link he has made with Jeremiah 31. The failure of Israel as God's son, which the prophet speaks against throughout his prophecy, is nothing if not moral. Israel has changed her God (2:11) and embraced idolatry (44:17–19). The poor are oppressed (5:26–8) and sacrifice has become more important than morality (7:21–3). They must recognize their wickedness, the iniquity of their fathers, and their sin against God (14:20). Jeremiah warns, in language reminiscent of Deuteronomy, that without this they will experience the curses of the law (7:33, cf. Deut. 28:26; 19:9, cf. Deut. 28:53). The promises of restoration that fill the 'Book of Comfort' (Jer. 30–32) are interwoven with the expectation of moral renewal. Israel will return to the LORD (31:6); a 'father to Israel', he will make them walk unstumbling in a straight path (31:9). Their iniquity forgiven and sin forgotten (31:34), God's son will experience 'new covenant' blessings, not least of which will be that he will put his law within them and write it on their hearts (31:33).

29   Ibid., 521.
30   Ibid.
31   Ibid., 522.

If this is the background to Jesus' baptism then it is impossible to set aside the moral element as defined by the law. If 'Jesus, son of God, stands with Israel and in the place of Israel'[32] as the son in whom and through whom the promises of Jeremiah are fulfilled, then moral fulfilment is an element of his fulfilment no less significant than any other. Furthermore, when, with Coggins, Gibbs contrasts eschatological and soteriological fulfilment with moral fulfilment, he presupposes that eschatological and soteriological fulfilment are intrinsically not moral, an idea that is open to challenge and which would find no place in the theology of those who have held to the threefold division.

Jesus' fulfilment of the law and the prophets is one with his fulfilment of all righteousness. Must we segregate Matthew 3:15 from 5:17? Perhaps part of the reason that Matthew 5:17 has become 'a whirlpool of conflicting interpretations' is that an over-specialised academy expects an increasingly atomistic approach. Thus Hagner restricts the context and meaning of πληρόω to Matthew 5,[33] whereas the ultimate context and background is the Old Testament, specifically the context of the passages Matthew cites and to which he alludes. Looked at in that bigger picture, some of the meanings proposed for πληρόω need not be set in opposition. Jesus fulfils the law and the prophets in his person and teaching (c), by his obedience (d), and in all that he does to actualize them in his followers (e). His fulfilment is eschatological, soteriological, and moral—he brings salvation to Israel that will culminate in a new world (Matt. 19:28); he is Jesus, who will 'save his people from their sins' (Matt. 1:21); unlike Israel, this son will not fall in the wilderness (Matt. 4:1–17; cf. Ps. 78:17, 40)[34] and he demands moral integrity from his followers (Matt. 5:20).

32   Ibid.

33   Hagner, *WBC: Matthew 1–13*, Logos Library System.

34   Charles A. Kimball notes similar typology in Luke's temptation account, but sees Ps. 2 as the background to Jesus' baptism. *Jesus' Exposition of the Old Testament in Luke's Gospel* (Sheffield: Sheffield Academic Press, 1994), 88–90.

We may see further detail in this picture of Jesus' fulfilment of the law and the prophets by looking at it from the perspective of the new covenant promised in Jeremiah 31:31–4. This is not to present Jeremiah 31 as an all-exclusive interpretive key to Matthew; an examination of other prophetic allusions and references will lead to the same conclusions, but the 'Book of Comfort' plays a significant part in Matthew and provides an accurate sample of his approach.

'I will put my law within them'

The new covenant consists of four elements: the law written on hearts, God's presence, knowledge of God, and forgiveness of sins. The first of those, 'I will put my law within them, and I will write it on their hearts' (31:33), does not go beyond the expectations of the Mosaic Law itself (Deut. 30:14). According to the *Shema* (Deut. 6:6), God always intended that the law be internalized in the hearts of his people. Indeed, if they were to obey that command to love the LORD with all their heart and with all their soul, they needed his direct operation upon their hearts (Deut. 30:6). Jesus promotes this agenda with his definition of the first and great commandment (Matt. 22:37), in his frequent pinpointing of the heart as the source of Israel's moral failure and covenant breaking (Matt. 13:14–15; 15:18–19), and in his exposition of the law as a matter of whole-hearted obedience (Matt. 5:21–48).

Several exegetes stress Jesus' teaching, or authoritative interpretation, as that which fulfils the law. These observations support that idea, but not the view that fulfilment is restricted to his teaching. According to Bernard Robinson, texts in Proverbs that speak of the 'parental torah' written on the heart (Prov. 3:1–3; 4:1–21; 6:20–1) are relevant and support his suggestion that 'the new covenant is thought of in terms of parental affection.'[35]

---

35 Bernard P. Robinson, 'Jeremiah's New Covenant: Jer. 31,31–34', *Scandinavian Journal of the Old Testament* vol. 15 no. 2 (2001), 195.

Whatever the merits of Robinson's case, Jesus is the attentive son above all others; the law is written on his heart. He goes forward with a whole-souled determination to do his Father's will that goes beyond mere legal obedience, yet exemplifies what it means to live the *Shema*, while simultaneously fulfilling some of the typology of the law (Matt. 26:38–44; 27:51).[36] Had Jesus behaved in any other way he would not have been a son with whom the Father was well pleased, but would have been guilty of the hypocrisy for which he declared woe upon others. Jesus therefore fulfils the law and the prophets in fulfilling this first promise of the new covenant in himself and by bringing about its fulfilment in others.

'I will be their God and they shall be my people'

The second promise, 'I will be their God and they shall be my people' (Jer. 31:33), likewise echoes the promises of the Mosaic covenant (Exod. 29:45–6, Lev. 26:11–12). It is also found in Zechariah (8:8) and Ezekiel (11:20; 37:23–7), where, as in the Pentateuch, these words are bound up with themes of obedience to the law and of God dwelling in the midst of his people. Although Matthew contains no clear reference to any text from this family of verses, this fulfilment theme is not absent. Most notable is the reference to Isaiah 7:14 in 1:23—'they shall call his name Emmanuel, which means, God with us'—signalling that the Shekinah has moved from bush and tabernacle to dwell in flesh and blood. Luz rightly observes that this is not an isolated example:

> Allusions to God's being-with-us permeate the whole Gospel (17:17; 18:20; 26:29). But Matthew has especially through the last verse of his Gospel ("I am with you always, to the close of the age." 28:20) created

36 This idea is also in Heb. 10:5–7, which quotes Ps. 40:6–8, 'I have come to do your will, O my God,' but stops short of 'your law is within my heart.'

an inclusion which marks a basic theme: the presence of the exalted Lord with his community shows him as Immanuel, God with us.'[37]

In his work *Matthew's Emmanuel*, David Kupp moves beyond identifying allusions to conclude that there is 'enough evidence and gospel references to posit the existence of an "Emmanuel Christology" in Matthew'.[38] He bases his argument not only on verses such as those Luz mentions or on the birth and infancy account where YHWH's presence affects *'every character and event'*,[39] but also on the way that Jesus dominates the foreground throughout Matthew's narrative, repeatedly highlighting 'his Emmanuel stature'.[40]

The last verse of Matthew recalls the Emmanuel passage in Matthew 1 and, as if to stress that Jesus is 'God-with-us' in perpetuity, Matthew, unlike Mark and Luke, does not mention the ascension, but gives what Kupp calls 'Matthew's presence motif' the final word. In his judgment, Matthew is revisiting the Sinai paradigm where law, community, and the presence of God come together:

> That tabernacle-building instructions appear immediately alongside the terrifying presence of God on Sinai is no accident. Theophanic presence requires sacred space for God's people to remain his. In Matthew law is also life and sacred space is found in gathering around the risen Jesus. Jesus' law is not simply a behavioural guide, but its enactment brings into being and maintains community, into the midst of which Jesus' presence can come....Through obedience to Jesus the new community realizes the meaning of its existence and experiences the transforming presence of Jesus in its midst.[41]

37   Luz, *Matthew 1–7*, 121–2.
38   David D. Kupp, *Matthew's Emmanuel: Divine Presence and God's people in the First Gospel* (Cambridge: Cambridge University Press, 1996), 220.
39   Ibid., 54.
40   Ibid., 40.
41   Ibid., 216–17.

Although the notion of Jesus enacting new law is questionable, an echo of the theology found in the Old Testament passages mentioned above supports Kupp's observation that these old covenant strands remain intertwined at the end of Matthew. Christ's being with his people in fulfilment of the law and the prophets is the dominant strand here, yet moral fulfilment refuses to be quarantined since his words—'teaching them to observe all that I have commanded you'—presuppose ongoing obedience as an indispensable companion to 'God with us'. It may not be stated as plainly as in some of the Old Testament passages, but it is inconceivable that Jesus expected his disciples to teach obedience to commands that he disregarded, or while disobeying them themselves.

'They shall all know me'

Jeremiah's third promise is of knowledge of God: 'No longer shall each one teach his neighbour and each his brother, saying, "Know the LORD," for they shall all know me, from the least of them to the greatest, declares the LORD.' Robinson thinks that having spoken of a collective bond, the author now focuses on the individual and on 'inwardness',[42] but the key word is 'me' and an emphasis on inwardness is liable to move the focus from the LORD to the individual.

Palmer Robertson avoids this with his argument that the 'teacher's office'—notably filled by Moses, then priests and prophets—'was that of covenant mediator. But under the new covenant, no mediator would be necessary for the communication of the will of God to his people. From the smallest to the greatest, all would know the Lord im-mediately.'[43] Irrespective

---

42   Robinson, 'Jeremiah's New Covenant', 199. Similarly, Daniel J. Harrington S.J., 'The New Covenant', *America*, 27 March 2006, 31.

43   O. Palmer Robertson, *The Christ of the Covenants* (Phillipsburg: P&R, 1980), 293.

of whether it is best to say 'no mediator would be necessary' given the language and content of Hebrews 12:24–5, the idea of 'im-mediate' knowledge of God may function in Matthew's understanding of Christ's fulfilment of the law and the prophets, since throughout Matthew, it is Emmanuel who teaches (4:23; 5:2; 7:29; 9:35; 11:1; 13:54; 21:33).

In a sermon on Matthew 5, Leo connected Jeremiah 31:31–4 and Jesus' teaching. Jesus, he said, withdrew to teach his apostles 'the loftier doctrines…that what had been promised might be fulfilled when the Prophet Jeremiah says: "behold the days come when I will complete a new covenant."'[44] Nestle-Aland suggests a specific link between this third promise in Jeremiah 31:34 and Jesus' exhortation to his disciples following his condemnation of the title-loving scribes and Pharisees: 'But you are not to be called rabbi, for you have one teacher, and you are all brothers' (Matt. 23:8).[45] This may recall Jeremiah's promise in asserting a new covenant norm where there will be no prelacy among the brethren, for no class will become unique mediators of divine knowledge. If Jesus is 'God-with-us', and 'a teacher whose status is comparable to the one of the Father',[46] there can only be 'one teacher' and 'one instructor—the Christ' (Matt. 23:10). Samuel Byrskog highlights H.-J. Becker's suggestion that these verses allude to the *Shema*'s יְהוָה אֶחָד/κύριος εἷς ἐστιν ('the LORD is one') as shown below:

---

44   Leo the Great, 'A Homily on the Beatitudes', Available from www. newadvent.org/fathers/360395.htm; accessed 4 April 2006. Interestingly, he also makes a link with Moses, but for him it is not Jesus who is the 'new Moses'. If anyone stands in Moses' place it is the disciples for Jesus signifies 'from the very nature of the place and act that He it was who had once honoured Moses by speaking to him: then indeed with a more terrifying justice, but now with a holier mercifulness.'

45   Nestle-Aland, *Novum Testamentum Graece*, 65.

46   Samuel Byrskog, *Jesus the Only Teacher: Didactic Authority and Transmission in Ancient Israel, Ancient Judaism and the Matthean Community* (Stockholm: Almqvist & Wiksell International, 1994), 300.

⁸ ὑμεῖς δὲ μὴ κληθῆτε ῥαββί· εἷς γάρ ἐστιν ὑμῶν ὁ διδάσκαλος, πάντες δὲ ὑμεῖς ἀδελφοί ἐστε. ⁹ καὶ πατέρα μὴ καλέσητε ὑμῶν ἐπὶ τῆς γῆς, εἷς γάρ ἐστιν ὑμῶν ὁ πατὴρ ὁ οὐράνιος. ¹⁰ μηδὲ κληθῆτε καθηγηταί, ὅτι καθηγητὴς ὑμῶν ἐστιν εἷς ὁ Χριστός.⁴⁷

This is noteworthy given the obvious recalling of the *Shema* in Matthew 23:3–7, and Matthew's portrayal of Jesus as the epitome of 'true obedience to Israel's confession of faith, the Shema';⁴⁸ he stands in contrast with the Pharisees who love themselves more than the one Father. And it is not just a matter of Jesus' obedience, for if Jesus is the one who 'is one', then it is the words he commanded that must be on their hearts (Deut. 6:6). The words of the law are his words; he will reveal their true intention and effectually teach those who acknowledge him as the one instructor to love him with all their heart, soul, and strength. They will 'know the LORD'.

If any passage in Matthew expands on this and deals plainly with the issue of knowing God, it is 11:25–30 where Jesus states that he and the Father are not known by anyone except each other. Nonetheless, they reveal each other to those they choose. The Father reveals Jesus—the ultimate end of 'those things' (11:25)—to little children; Jesus reveals the Father to those he chooses (11:27), whereby they know the Father. Michael Knowles is not convinced that Jeremiah 31:31–4 lies behind Matthew 11:27. It does not focus 'on a widely available and unmediated divine knowledge like that of Jer. 31.34, but rather on a restricted and strictly mediated knowledge.'⁴⁹ The divine knowledge of Jeremiah 31, however, is only widely available and unmediated to 'the house of Israel', and although in Matthew 11 it is restricted to those Jesus chooses, the object of his mission, and therefore

47   Ibid.
48   Ibid., 301.
49   Michael Knowles, *Jeremiah in Matthew's Gospel: the Rejected-Prophet Motif in Matthaean Redaction* (Sheffield: JSOT Press, 1993), 214.

of his fulfilment of the new covenant, is the 'house of Israel'. Furthermore, it is not 'strictly mediated' in the sense that it is less first-hand than Jeremiah predicts. Certainly, Jesus, son of Mary, is a mediator, but he is the exclusive mediator since he claims to be the only one who can bring people to know God.[50] If this is how the promise of Jeremiah is fulfilled, in one sense Robertson is correct, there is no need for a mediator since Jesus is Emmanuel.

Immediacy also appears in Jesus' invitation to the heavy laden in 11:29, which stands out against Deuteronomic references to learning: 'Come...take *my* yoke...learn of *me*.' On one unique occasion Moses gathers the people so that they will hear God's voice and learn to fear him (Deut. 4:10), but otherwise they must learn this through the instruction of the Levites (Deut. 31:13–14). When Jesus teaches those who come to him, learning must likewise shape their attitude to God, but his teaching is joined with his ability to reveal the Father. This mutual revelation of Father and Son makes Jesus' yoke easy and his burden light.

Jesus' offer is widely viewed as a contrast with the burden of Pharisaic application of the law (Matt. 23:4), but with Davies and Allison we may 'wonder whether it is really necessary to be so exclusively specific'.[51] Psalm 119 does speak of the law 'as the delight of the pious Israelite', yet that does not force the conclusion that it was 'not the law itself that was burdensome... but rather the overwhelming nomism of the Pharisees'.[52] After all, the same psalm retains a consciousness of the struggle to obey (119:36–8; 67; 71; 133; 176), and with that, fear of judgment

---

50   If the biblical use of μεσίτης as applied to Jesus is considered a guide, then mediator need not be restricted to redemptive contexts. Although 1 Timothy 2:5 and Hebrews 9:15 use it in that sense, Hebrews 8:6 and 12:24 refer to Jesus as mediator in the context of overall new covenant fulfilment.

51   W. D. Davies and Dale C. Allison, *A Critical and Exegetical Commentary on the Gospel According to Matthew*, II (Edinburgh: T. & T. Clark, 1991), 288.

52   Hagner, *Matthew 1–13*, Logos Library System.

(119:120). Jesus' point is that without him the whole enterprise of knowing the LORD, which includes hearing and obeying the law, is burdensome—impossibly so.[53] No matter how earnestly neighbours and brothers say to each other, 'Know the LORD,' they cannot make that a reality. It takes Jesus' fulfilment of the law and the prophets to achieve that.

Davies and Allison argue that Matthew 11:25–30 recalls Exodus 33:12–14 where Moses' prayer of intercession and request to know the LORD leads to the promise, 'My presence will go with you and I will give you rest.'[54] This, notes Hagner, is against 'the mainstream interpretation of this passage' because it does not see Sirach 51 as the source of Jesus' words: 'Once it is granted that Matthew could think in terms of wisdom Christology, the similarities (if not the precise wording) are so many and so strong that Sir 51 remains the most likely influence.'[55] But it is no indisputable given that Matthew thinks in those terms or that Jesus was saturated in Sirach. For Laansma, the Wisdom interpretation 'has missed Matthew's interpretation in the OT'[56] and according to Marshall Johnson, 'it is best that the wisdom motif remain in the scholarly footnotes' where Suggs, author of the influential work *Wisdom, Christology and Law in Matthew's Gospel*, 'found it.'[57] Even if the idea of wisdom incarnate shaped Matthew's thinking the similarities in wording between his Gospel and Sirach do not equate to thematic uniformity. Sirach has nothing to say about the knowledge of

53   Some of the same themes are drawn together in John 6:44–6, which is thought to quote Isaiah 54:13, but Jeremiah 31:31–4 is also recognised as a likely source (see Nestle-Aland, *Novum Testamentum Graece*, 267).

54   Davies and Allison, *Matthew*, Vol. II, 286–8.

55   Hagner, *Matthew 1–13*, Logos Library System.

56   Jon Laansma, *'I Will Give You Rest': the Rest Motif in the New Testament with Special Reference to Mt 11 and Heb 3–4* (Tübingen: Mohr Siebeck, 1997), 14.

57   Marshall D. Johnson, 'Reflections on a Wisdom Approach to Matthew's Christology', *CBQ* 36 (1974), 60.

God and speaks favourably of burdens more heavy than light (Sir. 51:16–20). Beyond the confines of Sirach 51 the discord is jarring: 'In Matthew the "laborers" are those offered rest, while in Sirach "laboring" (after Wisdom/wisdom) is what we are called to in order to attain rest in the end (cf. Sir 6,19; 24,34).'[58] More fundamentally, all of Matthew's explicit quotations are, without exception, from the Old Testament. Why then should we expect a subtle allusion to a body of literature other than that which he regards as authoritative and to which he consistently refers? This alone favours the Davies and Allison proposal, but in the absence of an explicit quotation it is unnecessary to make an exclusive link with any text; Matthew is simply 'mixing in OT phraseology from the world of ideas associated with God's promise of redemptive rest to his people.'[59] Those ideas, prominent in passages such as Deuteronomy 12:1–12 and 2 Samuel 7 also feature in Jeremiah's book of consolation (31:25–6) where rest for souls is part of the new covenant package. Indeed, Jeremiah 31:25 is closer to Matthew 11:28–9 than anything in Sirach.[60]

For Matthew, Jesus delivers the rest promised in the law and the prophets. It is a rest not from mere Pharisaic casuistry, but from weariness and pressures that are 'shoots from the root problem (Mt 1,21)'.[61] He delivers, because knowing him, people know the LORD; he is the 'one' whose words were to be upon their hearts and now he will teach those words one to one.

'I will forgive their iniquity'

The final element of the new covenant in Jeremiah 31 is the promise of pardon: 'For I will forgive their iniquity, and I will remember

---

58   Laansma, 'I Will Give You Rest', 197.

59   Ibid., 228–9.

60   It is a matter for discussion whether Jeremiah 31:26 is an expression of Israel's corporate refreshment or it refers to Jeremiah's own experience.

61   Laansma, 'I Will Give You Rest', 244.

their sin no more' (31:34). The causal relationship implied by the preceding כִּי is correctly translated by the majority of English translations[62] as 'for'. Forgiveness of sin is the prerequisite of the first three promises.

The most widely recognised New Testament allusion to this promise is Matthew 26:27–8[63] where, having taken the cup, Jesus says to his disciples, 'Drink of it, all of you, for this is my blood of the covenant, which is poured out for many for the forgiveness of sins.' For Hagner, the inclusive reference to 'all' only signifies the importance of each disciple drinking the wine,[64] but that is to stop short of exploring the link with Jeremiah 31:34b, which he himself recognises. Having already echoed the universalising and equalising 'all...from the least of them to the greatest' (Jer. 31:34a) in Matthew 11:28 ('all who labour') and 23:8 ('all brothers'), it is possible that Jesus does so again in the command of 26:27.[65] He fulfils the prophets in pouring out his blood for the forgiveness of sins and all who obey his command to drink will 'know the LORD'. Those that exclude themselves from the 'all' who drink from the cup of new covenant blessing, refuse the forgiveness symbolised in it and cut themselves off from every blessing.

The promise of forgiveness stands alongside another of the new covenant promises. This first emerges in the naming of Jesus-Immanuel (Matt. 1:26–7). The fulfilment of God's promises to save his people from their sins and to be present with them will come about in one person. Now, in Matthew 26:27–9, Jesus himself speaks in one breath of fulfilling those two promises—first the forgiveness of sins through his outpoured blood, then

---

62   The *New Living Translation* (Illinois: Tyndale House Publishers, 2004) is the odd exception, which opts for 'and'.

63   Nestle-Aland, *Novum Testamentum Graece*, 794.

64   Hagner, *Matthew 14–28*, Logos Library System.

65   It is noteworthy that both Matthew 23:8 and 26:27 were used in the Protestant arguments against the Roman Catholic practice of calling clergy 'Father' and that of withholding the cup from the laity.

the full-orbed experience of 'God with us' in the table fellowship of the Father's kingdom. Those themes from Jeremiah 31:31–4 are also held together in other covenant passages such as Exodus 24, which is the only place in the Old Testament where the precise phrase 'blood of the covenant' occurs (24:8). On the occasion described in Exodus 24, the people responded to Moses' declaration of the LORD's words with a promise: 'All the words that the LORD has spoken we will do' (Exod. 24:3). After this they made offerings and Moses took the blood, sprinkling half of it on the altar and half of it on the people to consecrate them to the LORD. Then Moses, Aaron, Nadab, Abihu, and seventy of Israel's elders see the God of Israel. Under his feet is a pavement of lapis lazuli. They eat and drink in his presence. In Matthew 26:27–9, Jesus' blood likewise brings God and his people together, except this time it is not only the leaders that will see God and sup in his presence, but all who receive the blood of the covenant. In such ways Matthew traces those threads through the law and the prophets and draws them together to show how Jesus fulfils both.[66]

One of the most important issues relating to this fourth promise is the definition of sin. Jeremiah promises it will be forgiven and Jesus declares that is why his blood will be poured out, but what is it? Repeatedly in Jeremiah, sin and iniquity is connected with, or defined as, transgression of the laws of the Decalogue (9:5–6; 13:22–7; 16:10–12; 17–18; 18:23), and never as the transgression of any statute or decree outside the Ten Commandments. Likewise, on the few occasions in Matthew where sin is defined by the immediate context, it is linked with transgression of the Decalogue (5:27–30), or simply

66   Knowles argues that Matthew 26:28 'alludes both to the provisions of the "new covenant" in Jer. 31[38].34 and to the violent nature of Jesus' death in keeping with his identity as a rejected prophet.' The latter may well be a further way in which Jesus fulfils the prophets, but the purpose of this section is to concentrate on Jeremiah 31. Knowles, *Jeremiah in Matthew's Gospel*, 209.

lawlessness (13:41). Matthew gives his readers no reason to think that he understands sin any differently to Jeremiah—to sin is to transgress the law. When Jesus' blood is poured out, it is to clear the 'debt' created by this transgression and for which Jesus told his disciples to seek forgiveness (Matt. 6:12). Any argument that Jesus redefined the law inevitably leads to the conclusion that he also redefined sin. It must therefore explain not only why he went to such extravagant lengths to acquire forgiveness for what was only sin until his coming, but also to what this forgiveness applies for those who will believe when the apostles go to 'make disciples of all nations'. If Matthew's Gospel introduces new law in the Sermon on the Mount and then speaks of forgiveness in relation to transgression of the old law, its notion of atonement is incoherent and sin becomes a moving target. It is more likely that Matthew views the sin for which Jesus' blood acquires forgiveness as always traceable to transgression of constant 'self-understood' norms that are defined by the Decalogue. Once again, moral fulfilment cannot be extricated and isolated from fulfilment in general.

Viewed together, those aspects of new covenant fulfilment bring out a little more detail in the picture of the beloved son who fulfils the law and the prophets. He has the law within him and causes it to be written on the hearts of those he chooses. With them, he 'who dwelt in the bush' (Deut. 33:16) will now dwell. Emmanuel has come and will be with his disciples as they teach the nations to obey. All who learn of him will know the LORD. Jesus—the one who is one—will go with them and give them rest. Foretastes and foretokens of the Father's kingdom, these things are only made possible when Jesus' 'blood is poured out for many for the forgiveness of sins'. Thus he fulfils the law and the prophets in his person and teaching (c), by his obedience (d), and in making his followers obedient (e). His fulfilment is eschatological, soteriological, and moral.

It is in this wider context that Matthew 5:17 must be interpreted. The wedge-driving exegesis that arises from restricting the context and meaning of πληρόω to Matthew 5, or even to Matthew itself, is inadequate and unhelpful. Matthews's interaction with the Old Testament passages in their Old Testament context is a more complete way to discover the ideas behind Jesus' fulfilment of the law and the prophets. This means that the aim of Matthew 5:17 is not to settle controversy about the continuity or discontinuity of the law as legal code, but to affirm Jesus' fulfilment of the law and the prophets together. The samples from Jeremiah show that Matthew presents Jesus as holding the same assumptions about the law, sin, and covenant as the prophet, whose own assumptions were Pentateuchal. Jesus' fulfilment is therefore harmonious with the original intention of the Mosaic Law, as recorded in the Pentateuch, and with the prophets' hermeneutic and application of that law. Thus, while Matthew brings his readers forward by showing them what fulfilment looks like, he does not demolish and reconstruct the Law of Moses or use Jesus' words in Matthew 5:17 to undermine the Old Testament's view of the Decalogue. This leaves untouched the basic categories outlined in the preceding chapters of this book—some laws were a 'pattern', some were to be obeyed 'in the land', but the Decalogue was the controlling influence.

NOT A JOT OR A TITTLE

It is hard to avoid the conclusion that Matthew 5:18 does other than make Jesus' earlier statement that he did not come to abolish the law more absolute. If not a jot or a tittle passes away until heaven and earth pass away, and until all is accomplished, any notion of fulfilment that involves abolition becomes doubly untenable. Even if the time when all will be accomplished were read as a reference to the life and work of Jesus, that cannot be the case with the passing away of heaven and earth, especially if it is 'a popular circumlocution for "never"'.[67] Such an understanding would not have startled an audience that knew the Psalms, which speak of God's word and statutes as sure (Ps. 93:5), everlasting (Ps. 119:160), and fixed in the heavens (Ps. 119:89). Nestle-Aland cite Psalm 119:89 as finding an echo in Luke 21:33, which has Matthew 24:35 as a parallel. Although the point is the same— God's words, or Jesus' words, will always endure—the parallel is unlikely since the psalm uses the permanence of heaven (the dwelling place of God) to convey the eternity of God's word, while in Matthew and Luke, Jesus speaks of his words as outlasting heaven and earth (the created universe). It is, therefore, doubtful that Matthew's gospel refers on one occasion to the passing of heaven and earth as a certainty and on another picks up on it as a popular way of saying 'never'. Jonathan Pennington is correct: 'the phrase [heaven and earth] refers to all creation, following the common Jewish usage.'[68] Nonetheless, 'never' is effectively what Matthew 5:18 amounts to—as long as heaven and earth endure, the law stands irrescindable and unalterable.

Matthew 5:19 brings further intensification. Whether one obeys and teaches 'the least of these commandments', that is the laws of the Old Testament,[69] determines how one will be evaluated in the kingdom of heaven. This all seems to present a problem for any interpretive approach that speaks of the law being abolished

---

67   Luz, *Matthew 1–7*, 265.

68   Jonathan T. Pennington, *Heaven and Earth in the Gospel of Matthew* (Leiden: Koninklijke Brill, 2007), 200.

69   Carson and Hagner acknowledge that the Mosaic Law is in view, but promote an unnecessary dichotomy. It is the law as 'taken up and interpreted by Jesus' (Hagner, *Matthew 1–13*, Logos Library System), or the law as it 'pointed forward to Jesus and his teaching; so it is properly obeyed by conforming to his word' (Carson, *Matthew*, [Pradis Ver. 5.01.0035]). Wells & Zaspel push the distinction further: 'Apart from Jesus' interpretation of it [the law], it has precisely no enduring use' (Wells and Zaspel, *New Covenant Theology*, 118). It is, however, difficult to reconcile this with Matthew 5:17, which is the passage they are discussing.

in any way, including the threefold division, which describes the ceremonial laws as 'now abrogated under the New Testament'.

John Calvin tried to resolve the tension by arguing that 'Christ is expressly speaking here [Matt. 5:19] of the rules of life, the Ten Commandments.'[70] Coming from someone who regarded the Ten Commandments as anything but 'the least of these commandments' this is an odd solution, which forces an unnecessary division between verses 18 and 19. At the same time, Jesus' teaching may result in the dominance of the Decalogue whether or not he is 'expressly speaking' of it.

The issue for the threefold division is the one raised near the beginning of this discussion of Matthew 5—can the confessional language of abrogation be reconciled with Matthew 5:18–19? One answer to this is that it may be reconciled with Jesus' words because temporal jurisdiction or future abrogation was written into the Mosaic Law. Much of the debate about the abiding validity of the law, in this context, arises from the faulty presupposition that the Mosaic code was a catalogue of inflexible, ever-binding, always-applicable statutes, almost to the degree that we might suppose Moses would be aghast were he to read the Gospels or the Epistles. New Testament scholars take insufficient account of the argument, typified by Braulik, that 'binding force' is not the same as 'range of validity'.[71] Jesus could have said everything he says in Matthew 5:17–20 and still hold that the law did not have a universal 'range of validity' because that is what the law itself teaches. As our discussion of the Pentateuch in chapter three has shown, the Deuteronomic paranesis (5:1–11:32) and the law corpus (12:1–26:16), individually framed by the expression חֻקִּים וּמִשְׁפָּטִים, were to be observed 'in the land', while another body of laws served as a 'pattern'.

Apart from that broad framework, the Pentateuch provides

70   Calvin, *Harmony of the Gospels,* vol. 1, 181.
71   Braulik, 'Wisdom, Divine Presence and Law', 447–8.

at least one specific example that demonstrates that notions of temporal jurisdiction or future abrogation were not foreign to the law. Exodus 16 tells the story of the LORD raining down bread upon the grumbling Israelites. He says to Moses, 'the people shall go out and gather a day's portion every day, that I may test them, whether they will walk in my law [תּוֹרָה] or not' (Exod. 16:4). This is a test of Israel's willingness to obey God's instruction in general, but a test that hinges on their obedience to specific rules about collecting the manna. They were to 'gather a day's portion every day' except on the sixth day when what they gathered would be twice as much (Exod. 16:5). They failed the test. The hoarders woke up to a stinking, worm-infested breakfast (Exod. 16:20), while those who went out to harvest on the seventh day found nothing (Exod. 16:27). This disobedience is the cause of the LORD's complaint to Moses: 'How long do you refuse to keep my commandments [תּוֹרָה] and my laws [מִצְוָה]?' (Exod. 16:28). The Pentateuch does not present the manna laws as some kind of pre-Mosaic laws; they are as much part of the law as the חֻקִּים וּמִשְׁפָּטִים. Israel's infraction of those specific laws is therefore indistinguishable from rejection of God's instruction and law in general.

Although embedded in the Mosaic Law, the manna laws are of temporary jurisdiction. Exodus 16:35 records Moses as saying, 'This is what the LORD has commanded: "Let an omer of it be kept throughout your generations, so that they may see the bread with which I fed you in the wilderness, when I brought you out of the land of Egypt."' This jar set before the ark was to be a memorial to Israel of God's provision for them, but until it became a memorial it was a foretoken of future provision in the land flowing with milk and honey that was to follow the wilderness years. The command to preserve an omer revealed that manna would not be a perpetual provision (as Exodus 16:35 records) and the specific gathering laws were therefore limited in their validity by the law itself. This, however, did not mean that the constitutional principles behind those laws also passed away, something that is most obvious in the abiding validity of the Sabbath laws. Nor does it mean that the jots and tittles of the gathering laws pass away; they stand as a continual example of what it means to depend on the LORD in a specific situation, in a way that accords with the patterns of work and rest that he has established. More than that, they remain part of the law so that Israel will not forget that 'man does not live by bread alone, but man lives by every word that comes from the mouth of the LORD' (Deut. 8:3). Although the specific laws no longer have jurisdiction, they remain, to the jot and tittle, part of the legal framework that teaches Israel dependence upon the God before whom they are to have none other (Deut. 8:16–19).

Thus when Jesus says 'not an iota, not a dot, will pass from the law until all is accomplished' he includes laws that no longer have jurisdiction. Though abrogated in so far as they regulated specific actions, they remain embedded in a *corpus juris* that will stand until the end of time. Their ongoing relevance is by way of memorial and foretoken. In the end, there is no incompatibility between Matthew 5:18 and the confessional language of abrogation, so long as abrogation is defined by the 'built-in obsolescence'[72] and temporal jurisdiction written into parts of the Mosaic Law. Jesus' warning to those who relax the commandments, alongside his encouragement for those who do them and teach them (Matt. 5:19), must also be read in this light. His followers will follow and teach the commandments in a way that is in continuity with the law's intent, the prophetic oracles, and Jesus' teaching as recorded in Matthew 5. Their righteousness will then exceed that of the scribes and Pharisees (Matt. 5:20) because it will reflect 'the primacy of morality over

72   Kaiser, *Old Testament Ethics*, 43–7

the cult'[73] and a proper understanding of the law as memorial and foretoken.

ANTITHESIS & ADVANCE V.
CO-ORDINATION & CONTINUITY

One final question remains about Jesus' teaching in Matthew 5 and that is whether his statements in 5:21–47 are in continuity with the law's intent, or does he diminish the law? These verses contain what are generally classified as the 'antitheses', a designation almost universal in modern scholarly discourse, though, paradoxically, not universally endorsed. For Harrington 'the word "antithesis" fits the rhetorical pattern but not the content,'[74] while Allison judges from 5:17–20 that 'there are in the first place no antitheses because in the second place there is no overturning of the Torah.'[75] It is true that the repeated δέ (but) throughout those verses need not be taken as a strong adversative and that it could suggest 'more co-ordination or continuity'.[76] Gundry thinks '"antithesis" designates the material incorrectly', yet continues to use the term 'because it has become traditional in discussions of this passage.'[77] This approach might be sensible if 'antithesis' were a neutral label, but to call something that which you do not believe it to be is unusual. In this case it is also liable to establish the prejudice that whenever Jesus declares '…but I say to you…' he states the direct opposite of what the law declared. With few

---

73   Kaufmann, *The Religion of Israel*, 160.

74   Daniel J. Harrington (S.J.), *The Gospel of Matthew* (Collegeville: Liturgical Press, 1991), 90.

75   Dale C. Allison, *The New Moses: A Matthean Typology* (Edinburgh: T&T Clark, 1993), 182.

76   J. Andrew Overman, *Church and Community in Crisis: the Gospel According to Matthew* (Valley Forge: Trinity Press International, 1996), 81.

77   Robert H. Gundry, *Matthew: A Commentary on His Literary and Theological Art* (Grand Rapids: William B. Eerdmans, 1982), 83.

writers willing to argue for a degree of contrast that lives up to the strength of the antithesis terminology, or to support a claim like Mohrlang's that 'in some cases we must frankly acknowledge that the actual effect of an antithesis *is* to annul a precept of Torah,'[78] it is pointless to use 'antithesis' as a universal descriptor. Approaches to 5:21–48 are as varied as each interpreter's understanding of καταλύω and πληρόω in the preceding verses (5:17–20), and most view them as an outworking or illustration[79] of what is recorded there, so that notions of transcendence, intensification, and confirmation rather than abrogation are to the fore:

> The attempt to see in the antitheses a contrast between the word of God and the words of Jesus is unfounded and very difficult to reconcile with 5:17–20.[80]

> He comes not to abolish, but to uphold and expound Torah on the basis of the authority which is his....the specific applications do not come into conflict with Torah; they go beyond it.[81]

> The six so-called antithesis (5:21–48) are not understood by Matthew as changes in God's law, but as more penetrating appreciation of and obedience to the law. The actions encouraged are not violations of any biblical law; they uphold the law.[82]

> Jesus not only sharpens the commandments; he changes their character, and makes them into agape-demands.[83]

---

78   Mohrlang, *Matthew and Paul*, 19.

79   For example. Harrington, *Matthew*, 90; Snodgrass, 'Matthew and the Law', 120; R. T. France, *The Gospel According to Matthew: An Introduction and Commentary* (Leicester, Inter-Varsity Press, 1985), 117; Rudolf Schnackenburg, *The Gospel of Matthew* (Grand Rapids, Eerdmans, 2002), 53.

80   Snodgrass, 'Matthew and the Law', 120.

81   Loader, *Jesus' Attitude towards the Law*, 173; 177.

82   Anthony J. Saldarini, *Matthew's Christian–Jewish Community* (Chicago: University of Chicago Press, 1994), 162.

83   Birger Gerhardsson, *The Shema in the New Testament* (Lund: Novapress, 1996), 278.

Jesus contradicts neither the law nor current rabbinic interpretations of it. Rather he carries out its tendencies to their divinely intended ends.[84]

Jesus…does not want to abolish the commandments of the Bible, but he does abolish their formal authority…in the coming kingdom of God they will become the conditionally valid, unconditionally binding will of God.[85]

Since the previous section discussed those ideas[86] there is no merit in doing so again for each of the six issues raised in 5:21–47. Nonetheless, we need to ask if those verses are compatible with our interpretation of 5:17–20. If so, this would see Jesus' words as an expression of the law's original intent and scope, avoiding the difficulties of an argument like that of Luz (above), which makes a dichotomy between 'formal authority' and the commandments.

We need not enter a protracted discussion about whether Jesus' initial references are to the Torah or to the teaching of the Scribes and Pharisees, especially when 'one can find early Jewish rabbis who agree with Jesus at almost every point.'[87] Even if Jesus' repeated phrase, 'you have heard it said', indicates that he is not quoting texts from the 'it is written' category, but summarising a mixture of interpretation and misinterpretation, tradition and addition, it does not affect this discussion. We need only ask, Does Jesus challenge the threefold division's adoption of the Old Testament's presentation of some laws as a 'pattern', some that were to be obeyed 'in the land', and the Decalogue as the controlling influence? Does he say anything contrary to the original intention of the Mosaic Law?

84   Gundry, *Matthew*, 83.
85   Ulrich Luz, *Matthew 1–7* (Minneapolis: Fortress Press, 2007), 231.
86   Also Appendix 2.
87   Harrington, *Matthew*, 91. Also Luz, *Matthew 1–7*, 279:'…at least some antithesis contain nothing that could not be found also in Jewish tradition.'

Hatred and Lust

The quotations above showed that some think that Jesus went beyond the law, and further examples emerge in more specific treatments of the passage. Commenting on 5:21–26, Hagner writes, 'The horizon of what is addressed by the commandment not to murder is broadened to include even the harbouring of anger against another…Jesus' interpretation deepens the commandment, making the demand greater than it was usually understood to be.'[88] Wells and Zaspel take a similar view: 'No fair exposition of the sixth commandment could arrive at an equally weighty prohibition of hatred. Some sort of advance is involved.'[89] All this might have been a surprise for the author of Leviticus 19:17 who wrote, 'You shall not hate your brother in your heart, but you shall reason frankly with your neighbor, lest you incur sin because of him.' And no one remotely familiar with the Mosaic laws on manslaughter in Deuteronomy 19 would have been dumbstruck at the notion of an inextricable link between murder and hatred. Even if the Pentateuch stopped at Exodus 20, Wells and Zaspel fail to account for other Old Testament literature, such as the exhortation in Proverbs 25:21–2: 'If your enemy is hungry, give him bread to eat, and if he is thirsty, give him water to drink, for you will heap burning coals on his head, and the LORD will reward you.' If Jesus' words are an advance over the sixth commandment, then so too is the book of Proverbs.

These authors see a similar 'advance' in Jesus' prohibition of lust.[90] Banks agrees: 'By equating the covert desire with the overt act Jesus was demanding a new relationship which actually transcended the requirements of the law.'[91] Once again, Proverbs

88   Hagner, *Matthew 1–13*, Logos Library System.
89   Wells and Zaspel, *New Covenant Theology*, 105.
90   Ibid.
91   Banks, *Jesus and the Law*, 191.

with its prohibition of lust (6:25) undermines their argument. Jeremiah also views adultery and lust as inseparable bedfellows (5:7–9). On this occasion, however, it is not even necessary to go beyond Exodus 20 as the tenth commandment on any 'fair exposition' demands no less than Matthew 5. If Wells and Zaspel, with Banks, are correct, how should we understand 'You shall not covet your neighbour's wife'? Unless we are to view the average Israelite male as strangely under-sexed, he likely coveted his neighbour's wife not because she baked excellent cupcakes, but out of sexual desire. It is hard to imagine how such covetousness could be anything other than internal—'in his heart'.

Any attempt to portray the teaching of Matthew 5 as an advance or intensification of the law demands a selective approach to the Pentateuch and to the Old Testament. Andrew Overman is not being simplistic when he writes, 'while anger is not the same as murder, and lust is not literally the same as adultery, both actions and attitudes in their own way disrupt community and finally make a joke out of the laws that are to define and guide the people of God.'[92] To accept the viewpoint of Hagner, Banks, Wells, Zaspel, and others, means assuming not only that generations before Matthew made a joke out of the laws, but that the joke was written into a universal hermeneutic of biblical law. A more natural reading is that Matthew's Gospel does not have a 'radical, dismissive, or *de novo*' agenda for the law. Rather, 'from 5:21–48 Matthew gives specific instances of how the law should really work in concrete, communal settings.'[93] Murder and adultery are the only two Decalogue commands specifically mentioned in those verses. Jesus does not rescind or intensify them; he interprets them in the context of wider Mosaic Law and in harmony with other Old Testament literature.

---

92   Overman, *Church and Community in Crisis*, 82.
93   Ibid., 81–2.

Divorce

From verse 30 onwards, Jesus addresses issues touching on laws outside the Decalogue, so even if he had set them aside it would not have the same impact on the threefold division. Nonetheless, the way Matthew 5 handles them is still relevant to this discussion. They focus on actions rather than thoughts. The subject of divorce comes first (5:31–2). It has a thematic connection with the preceding verses on adultery and is best considered in conjunction with Matthew 19:3–12, where the same issues arise. Matthew records Jesus as saying that anyone who divorces his wife[94] except for sexual immorality (πορνεία) makes her commit adultery and whoever marries a divorced woman commits adultery.[95] This stance presumes the abiding validity of the Decalogue's seventh word, but according to some writers, it is also a straightforward case where Jesus abolishes other Mosaic laws: 'Whereas once God made concessions... Jesus now abolishes such concessions.'[96] 'Whereas Moses allowed divorce, Jesus disallows it.'[97] 'What Moses clearly allowed... Jesus expressly forbids. Here there is a tightening of the law at least,

94   Matthew 19:9 adds 'and marries another'.

95   Textual variants account for the differences between translations of Matthew 19:9 in English versions. Bruce Metzger explains: 'After μοιχᾶται several witnesses (including K W Δ Θ Π ƒ¹³) add καὶ ὁ ἀπολελυμένην γαμῶν (or γαμήσας) μοιχᾶται ("and he who marries a divorced woman commits adultery"). Although it could be argued that homoeoteleuton (μοιχᾶται ... μοιχᾶται) accounts for its accidental omission from ℵ D L 1241 al, the fact that B C* ƒ¹ al read μοιχᾶται only once (at the conclusion of the combined clauses) makes it more probable that the text was expanded by copyists who accommodated the saying to the prevailing text of 5.32.' A Textual Commentary on the Greek New Testament (Stuttgart: Deutsche Bibelgesellschaft, 2002), 39–40.

96   John Piper, 'Love Your Enemies': Jesus' love command in the synoptic gospels and in the early Christian paranesis: A history of the tradition and interpretation of its uses (Cambridge: Cambridge University Press, 1979), 89.

97   Hagner, Matthew 1–13, Logos Library System.

but it apparently involves an abrogation.'[98] But what did Moses allow? And do Jesus' comments on the effects of divorce really amount to an express prohibition?

The allowance vocabulary, which comes from the modern English translations of ἐπιτρέπω in Matthew 19:8, may convey more of a sense of wholehearted approval than intended. ἐπιτρέπω occurs only eighteen times in the New Testament, sometimes in the context of neutrality on the part of the object towards the subject (John 19:38; Acts 21:39–40), but in other cases neutrality is impossible. This is particularly so in Mark 5:13 and Luke 8:32 where Jesus' granting Legion's demons permission to enter two thousand pigs can hardly mean that Jesus wished to encourage demonic activity (even in unclean beasts). Thus Matthew 19:8 does not suggest that Moses was nonchalant about divorce, and perhaps the older translations' choice of 'suffered' is more appropriate.

This view finds support in that Matthew 5:31 is not a quotation from the Pentateuch and nowhere does the Mosaic Law sanction divorce. The King James Version's translation of Deuteronomy 24:1 as '*let him* write her a bill of divorcement' is unjustified. The pericope assumes the existence of divorce—a necessary evil to be 'suffered' rather than a wholesome feature of society. It says nothing more than that a divorcee who remarries only to be divorced or widowed may not return to her first husband. Piper is mistaken when he says 'God made concessions' since every piece of Mosaic legislation that touches on divorce and remarriage reveals God's total unwillingness to make concessions for divorcees (Lev. 21:7, 14; Deut. 24:1–4). For him to make a concession on the indissolubility of the marriage bond in Genesis 2:24 would be on the same level as a concession on parental respect, murder, or theft. John Murray gives an accurate summary of the Mosaic legal doctrine on divorce:

---

98   Wells and Zaspel, *New Covenant Theology*, 106.

Permission, sufferance, toleration was granted. But underlying this very notion is the idea of wrong. We do not properly speak of toleration or sufferance as granted or conceded in connection with what is intrinsically right or desirable....When we say that an intrinsic wrong is presupposed in the very sufferance accorded, it is not meant simply that a general or specific sinful condition is presupposed in the practice of divorce but also that in the very act of divorce itself there is an intrinsic wrong not compatible with the absolute standard of right.[99]

Jesus' response to the Pharisees when they ask why Moses 'commanded' divorce (Matt. 19:7) reflects such ideology. He corrects them, saying that Moses only suffered divorce because of the hardness of their hearts, but it was not so from the beginning (Matt. 19:8).[100] The permanency of marriage is 'a rule which is prior to and more important than divorce both logically and temporally'.[101] Jesus' response reflects more than the prophetic declaration of 'the primacy of morality'. It also reflects the same chronological priority that Daube, Carmichael, Bruckner, Crüsemann, and others, observe when they argue that part of the uniqueness of the Decalogue lies in its declaration of such 'self-understood' laws (discussed in chapter 3). If 'Sinai reiterates for those redeemed the demands of creation,'[102] and if inviolability is 'implicit' in the Genesis 2 'description of marital union',[103] Matthew 19 reaffirms the priority of those 'ageless' laws that 'from the beginning' (19:8) were 'simply part of the created order'.[104] For the prophet Malachi, this chronological priority

---

99   John Murray, *Divorce* (Philadelphia: the Committee on Christian Education, The Orthodox Presbyterian Church, 1953), 8.

100   In Mark's parallel passage (10:2–9) the Pharisees sound less certain, asking 'Is it lawful…' and also using ἐπιτρέπω rather than the ἐντέλλομαι.

101   Saldarini, *Matthew's Christian–Jewish Community*, 149.

102   Fretheim, 'Reclamation of Creation', 363.

103   Carmichael, *Origins*, 39.

104   Bruckner, *Implied Law*, 208.

was in some sense higher than even the 'primacy of morality' that the prophets proclaimed in relation to the laws of sacrifice. Whereas Amos could speak of God hating obedience to cultic laws when justice and righteousness have ceased (Amos 5:21–5), Malachi speaks of God's absolute settled hatred for divorce (Mal. 2:16);[105] it represents the abandonment of mercy that causes divine revulsion for sacrifice (Mal. 2:13–14). Jesus' statements in Matthew are continuous with that prophetic vision. He 'stands with neither Hillel nor Sahmmai nor with other proto-rabbis… Jesus stands with Malakhi (2:14–16)…and in line with Malakhi's admonition to "remember the Torah of Moses" [4:4]'.[106]

For many interpreters and Christians affected by divorce the crucial question is the meaning of the 'exception clauses'— 'except for sexual immorality' (Matt. 5:32; 19:9). Does πορνεία refer to incest[107] or to adultery?[108] Is it synonymous with עֶרְוַת דָּבָר (indecency/uncleanness) in Deuteronomy 24:1?[109] May someone who divorces on the basis of the exception remarry? Such questions are considered in exhaustive detail by some of the writers mentioned above,[110] but these issues are not directly relevant to the issue of the threefold division. Even supposing

---

105   The *English Standard Version* translates this verse as 'For the man who does not love his wife but divorces her, says the LORD…' but the accepted view that שָׂנֵא refers to God's hatred despite being third person masculine singular remains best. For a discussion of the issues see Andrew E. Hill, *Malachi: A New Translation with Introduction and Commentary* (New York: Doubleday, 1998), 249–51.

106   Sigal, *Halakah of Jesus of Nazareth*, 92–3.

107   Ben Witherington, 'Matthew 5.32 and 19.9—Exception or Exceptional Situation?' *NTS* 31 (1985), 571–6.

108   Dale C. Allison, 'Divorce, Celibacy and Joseph (Matthew 1.18–25 and 19.1–12),' *JSNT* 49 (1993): 3–10.

109   David Janzen, 'The Meaning of *PORNEIA* in Matthew 5.32 and 19.9:An Approach From the Study of Ancient Near Eastern Culture.' *JSNT* 80 (2000): 66–80.

110   See especially John Murray, *Divorce*, and Gordon J Wenham & William E. Heth, *Jesus and Divorce* (Carlisle: Paternoster Publishing, 1997).

divorce had been 'commanded' as Jesus' questioners claimed
(Matt. 19:7), it would not nullify the categories of the division
should an analysis such as Sigal's be correct:

> The simple way to read the text is that Jesus was opposed to divorce
> as was Malakhi, and that he regarded divorce for <u>porneia</u> as punitive,
> as did Moses and Jeremiah. Moses sought to circumscribe divorce by
> limiting it to <u>ervat dabar</u>, but the meaning of that term soon came
> under question. Jesus' definition of it was <u>porneia</u>.[111]

If divorce was 'punitive' (the merciful alternative to the death
penalty for adultery) and πορνεία defined עֶרְוַת דָּבָר, Jesus
would not be abrogating Deuteronomy 24:1, 'only exegeting
it'.[112] It would be on a par with the Pharisees coming and asking
'May we stone our children for any reason…Moses commanded
us to do so,' and for Jesus to respond in accordance with
Deuteronomy 21:18–21 that this was only to happen in cases
of acute rebellion. Such complicated hypotheses are, however,
unnecessary since Matthew 5:31–2, along with 19:3–12 present
Jesus as upholding the 'ageless' ordinance of marriage and the
moral primacy of the seventh commandment. He abrogates no
divorce laws because there was nothing to abrogate.

Oaths

Following on from divorce are Jesus' comments on oaths (5:33–7)
concerning which Carson makes the questionable assertion that
'it must be frankly admitted that here Jesus formally contravenes
OT law: what it permits or commands (Deut 6:13), he forbids.'[113]
Part of the rationale behind the prohibitions of 5:34–6 is that
'anything else comes from evil' (5:37), which if Carson is correct

---

111 Sigal, *Halakah of Jesus of Nazareth*, 95.

112 Ibid., 93.

113 Carson, *Matthew*, [Pradis Ver. 5.01.0035].

would not only imply that the law is evil, but that God himself
does evil since in Exodus and Deuteronomy it is God who most
frequently swears an oath.[114] The law itself never commands nor
encourages anyone to swear (שבע) an oath, although it regulates
their use in so far as anyone who takes an oath must keep it
(Num. 30:3) and swear by the name of the LORD (Deut. 6:13;
10:20). שבע indicates 'total obligation' such that the oath-
taker 'must regard him- or herself as entirely subject to the
god'.[115] Swearing by any other name would indicate idolatry or
apostasy, which the passage from Jeremiah 5 (mentioned above
concerning lust) also conveys. Furthermore, if Matthew 5:34–6
was a straightforward contravention of Mosaic Laws on oath
taking, 34b–6 would be nothing more than a rhetorical effect.
The text might as well read: 'Do not take an oath at all. Simply
say "Yes" or "No"; anything more than this comes from the
evil one.'[116] It is significant that what Jesus forbids in 34b–6 the
Mosaic Law did not permit in the first place. 'Do not take an
oath at all' ought to be interpreted in that context. Whether
the reference to oaths by heaven, earth, Jerusalem, or the head,
reflect a rabbinic view that such oaths are not binding, or whether
they were regarded as a substitution for God's name,[117] the law
did not permit such oaths. In Matthew they are symptoms of
hypocrisy that reveal an underlying desire to excuse lies and

114   Carson does note that God makes oaths and uses it as an argument
against Anabaptists and Jehovah's Witnesses. Ibid.

115   C. A. Keller, Art. שבע (1975), TLOT III (1997), 1296, quoted in Nathan
MacDonald, *Deuteronomy and the Meaning of 'Monotheism'* (Tubingen: Mohr
Siebeck, 2003), 106.

116   Davies and Allison make a similar observation: 34a 'makes 34b–6
redundant'. Davies and Allison, *Matthew*, Vol. I, 533.

117   For further discussion of these possibilities see Dennis C. Duling,
"'[Do not Swear...] by Jerusalem Because it Is the City of the Great King'"
(Matt 5:35),' *JBL* 110/2 (1991): 291–309, or Davies and Allison, *Matthew*, Vol.
I, 536.

avoid the 'total obligation' to the LORD required of the oath-
taker, which becomes clearer in the light of 23:16–22.

Even if someone wants to insist that Jesus was actually
forbidding something the law permitted, it would not represent
an 'advance', but a further recognition of the 'primacy of
morality', not least of the programmatic principles found in the
third and ninth commandments. Integrity and total submission
to God are more important than oath-taking, so if Matthew
is 'advocating simple truthfulness and trustworthiness'[118] he is
in harmony with the priorities the law itself establishes. This
approach to the law is likewise in continuity with the prophetic
message of 'mercy and not sacrifice'. Hosea, for example, counts
obedience to the command of Deuteronomy 6:13 with that
obedience which God may sometimes hate: '…swear not, "As
the LORD lives"' (Hos. 4:15). Matthew 5:33–7 is therefore not
new teaching, but an echo of the prophets.

Lex Talionis

After oaths comes the *lex talionis* (5:38–42), concerning which
Piper writes: 'The antithesis between this Old Testament legal
principle and Jesus' command is real. Taken absolutely they
exclude each other; they are contradictory. Jesus was in some sense
abolishing the *lex talionis*.'[119] This notion of abolition requires an
underlying presupposition that the purpose of the *lex talionis* was
to encourage precise reciprocity, such that if someone punched
an Israelite between the eyes he was required—were he still
standing—to return an instant blow. Snodgrass shows a better
understanding of its purpose, though he too makes unwarranted
assumptions:

118   Anthony J. Saldarini, *Matthew's Christian–Jewish Community* (Chicago:
University of Chicago Press, 1994), 153.
119   Piper, *'Love Your Enemies'*, 89.

> The fifth antithesis is an abrogation of the law if one ignores
> the function of the lex talionis in its context. But the moment
> that one admits that the purpose of the lex talionis was to limit
> revenge and to make sure that wrong doing was not ignored
> (Deut 19:19–21), then the statement of Jesus is not a violation of
> that function. Without playing with words, however, Jesus' teaching
> is a redirection, a paradigm shift. It asks that the disciples of the
> kingdom no longer stand on their rights; the concern is not for
> personal legal satisfaction. Instead, through hyperbole they are asked
> to implement the mercy code. If it is not a violation to be stricter
> than the law, it surely is not a violation to more loving than the law
> requires.[120]

The problem with this is that the *lex talionis* was not intended
to make Israelites 'stand on their rights', or to arouse concern
for 'personal legal satisfaction'. It was a murder and personal
injury sentencing guide for the justiciary (Exod. 21:22 and
Deut. 19:17–18 refer specifically to judges). Even supposing
it was a charter for personal vengeance, Jesus' recommended
response to financial litigation, to beggars and borrowers, would
not amount to 'a redirection' because the *lex talionis* did not
address such issues. Far from being antithetical to the law, the
call for generosity to beggars and borrowers is another echo of the
law (Lev. 25:35–8)—law that demanded not just willing lending,
but also unbegrudging debt cancellation (Deut. 15:7–11). And the
more general statement against vengeance would not flabbergast
anyone that was familiar with the Levitical command: 'You shall
not take vengeance or bear a grudge against the sons of your own
people…' (Lev. 19:18).

According to Jacob Milgrom 'the word "revenge" implies
extralegal retribution, which although forbidden to humans,
may be exacted by God',[121] but 'revenge' (נָקַם) is also used to

120   Snodgrass, 'Matthew and the Law', 122.
121   Jacob Milgrom, *Leviticus: A Book of Ritual Ethics*. (Minneapolis:
Fortress Press, 2004), 233.

speak of legal retribution in close context to the *lex talionis* (Exod. 21:20), so this is not correct. His next observation, following M. Greenberg, that it is a mark of a saint to commit his revenge to God (1 Sam. 24:12; Jer 15:15)[122] is well founded and further supported by the example of David's mercy to Shimei (2 Sam. 19:23). If it be objected that Matthew 5:39–42 moves on from the primitive old covenant morality of Jeremiah's cry for God to avenge, then we may wonder why the martyrs described in Revelation 6:10 are equally primitive. Those who react with mercy, leaving vengeance to God, are the meek who will inherit the earth (Ps. 37:11; Matt. 5:5). Matthew 5:39–42 is a call for such meekness. It is no more a 'paradigm shift' than Leviticus 19:18 or the example of David. Meekness and mercy were always meant to coexist with a penal code that demanded 'life for life'.

Again, even if an interpreter refuses to bend from the opinion that Matthew 5:39–42 'very severely restricts'[123] the use of the *lex talionis*, it would not necessarily prove an antithesis between Jesus and the law as restrictions may have existed due to conditions in Israel or because the perceived antithesis was in the law from the outset. In Overman's view, this section brings 'non-retaliation to the fore' and 'reflects the colonial situation of the Matthean community.'[124] This might be true especially if verse 41 alludes to civilians coerced into carrying Roman military luggage, and it could be that Roman rule excluded the penal directions of the Mosaic Code. More importantly, the *lex talionis* belonged to the 'statutes and ordinances' (חֻקִּים וּמִשְׁפָּטִים) that were to be observed 'in the land'. As with other requirements of the penal code, the *lex talionis* was not a mechanistic legal instrument. The likelihood that the death penalty for adultery could have been commuted to divorce is one example, and in

---

122 Ibid.

123 Wells and Zaspel, *New Covenant Theology*, 107.

124 Overman, *Church and Community in Crisis*, 84.

this context Matthew's designation of Joseph as just (δίκαιος) because he wanted to divorce Mary quietly (1:19) is noteworthy. It is unlikely he could have been described in such terms if by failing to seek Mary's execution he was flouting rigid legal requirements.[125] Only in the case of murder was mercy absolutely excluded (Num. 35:30–34). It makes little sense to suggest that Matthew 5:39–42 imposes new restrictions on a penological principle that was not 'obligatory always and everywhere', and which was always subject to potential restriction or 'abolition' by the mercy of meek and forgiving Israelites.

Love Your Enemies

With the call to 'love your enemies', the final verses of Matthew 5 bring together some themes from the previous verses. There is universal agreement that while the Mosaic Law commanded love of neighbour (Lev. 19:18) it never commanded anyone to hate their enemy.[126] This does not discourage Wells and Zaspel:

> It remains that "loving one's enemy" is a principle not immediately evident in any exposition of Moses (particularly in light of Deut. 23:3–6, etc.). This is plainly more than an articulation of the love command of Leviticus 19:18. It is an advance. Jesus extends the law's requirement. Simply put, Jesus demands more than Moses.[127]

What they seem to forget, however, is that Luke records Jesus' response to the question 'Who is my neighbour?' in a way that forbids convenient limitations of neighbour-

125   Allison makes a similar case in the context of divorce when he argues that the interpretation of the exception clauses must be consistent with Matthew's description of Joseph as just. Dale C. Allison, 'Divorce, Celibacy and Joseph (Matthew 1.18–25 and 19.1–12),' *JSNT* 49 (1993), 5.

126   Loader, *Jesus and the Law*, 178 n, 99; Schnackenburg, *Matthew*, 62; Luz, *Matthew 1–7*, 287.

127   Wells and Zaspel, *New Covenant Theology*, 107.

love (Luke 10:29–37). This will not surprise anyone familiar with the Pentateuchal references to 'neighbour' (רֵעַ). It speaks of neighbours who may also be enemies (Exod. 11:2; 32:27–8) and calls for acts of kindness towards enemies who must have been neighbours (Exod. 23:4). Although this text is often quoted as a Mosaic Law that calls for love of enemies,[128] Marius Reiser criticises its use because it 'does not refer to one's enemy himself, but to his cattle…The context is not about love either, but about unbiased justice.'[129] But neither justice nor animal welfare is the focus. If that were so, then why mention the enemy? The Pentateuch also assumes that people may hate their neighbours (Deut. 19:11), and records many laws (including Leviticus 19:18) that exist for no other reason than that neighbours may be, or become, enemies (Exod. 21:14–18; Lev. 19:13–19). Most people, at least, would consider it the act of an enemy if a neighbour steals their marriage partner (Lev. 18:20) or bears false witness against them (Exod. 20:16). The latter is exactly what will happen to the disciples when, like the prophets before them, they are persecuted by their neighbours (Matt. 5:11–12), even those of their own households (Matt. 10:36). Matthew 5:43–8 emphasises that such enemies and persecutors are to be the focus of their love and prayers, not those who were beyond the borders of their daily experience (like those in the example Wells and Zaspel reference from Deuteronomy 23:3–6).

This makes a statement like that of Eduard Schweizer rather puzzling when he argues that the call to pray for persecutors 'goes beyond the Old Testament, which makes no mention of prayer for those who do not share a bond of nature or common history.'[130] Who, according to the Old Testament, did not share such bonds?

128   For example, Eduard Schweizer, *The Good News According to Matthew*, trans. David E. Green. (London, SPCK, 1976), 132.

129   Marius Reiser, 'Love of Enemies in the Context of Antiquity', *New Testament Studies* 47.4 (2001), 420.

130   Schweizer, *Matthew*, 133.

Even if 'enemies' and 'persecutors' are taken out of the context of Matthew 5 so that family and neighbours are exchanged for the widest possible definition of 'Gentile nations', the Old Testament records prayers for their salvation also (e.g. Ps. 67).

Gundry argues that 'hate your enemies' was an imperatival paraphrase of Psalm 139:21–2: 'Matthew entertains no doubt that God inspired the psalmist, and such inspiration implies a command.'[131] While it is possible that 'hate your enemies' was 'an inference that was commonly drawn'[132] from Psalm 139, Gundry has no grounds for his speculative claim, and as Schweizer notes, 'the hatred there is not directed against a personal enemy, but against those who rebel against God and his ordinances'[133] (a valid observation in so far as the two are not always one). In the Old Testament, hatred of God's enemies and their actions (Ps. 119:128, 163) coexisted with the command to love others, just as they do in the New Testament (Luke 14:26; Rev. 2:6). Yet what that hatred entails requires careful exegesis in its original context and nowhere is it commanded.

Apart from the failure to consider properly the Mosaic laws, arguments for advance and abrogation in the command to love enemies ignores similar 'advance' in Old Testament passages mentioned earlier (such as those from Proverbs). It fails to explain why 'love for one's enemy is extolled (1 Sam. 24:19), and demanded in certain circumstances of everyday life.'[134]

Those six examples from Matthew 5:21–48 do not undermine the threefold division of the law. Jesus' statements are not antithetical to the law or representative of advance,[135] abolition,[136] and formal

131   Gundry, *Matthew*, 97.
132   Hagner, *Matthew 1–13*, Logos Library System.
133   Schweizer, *Matthew*, 132.
134   Ibid.
135   Wells and Zaspel, *New Covenant Theology*, 105.
136   Piper, *'Love Your Enemies'*, 89.

contravention;[137] they stand in 'co-ordination and continuity' with it. If anything, Jesus upholds several of the Ten Commandments (against murder, adultery, lies, and blasphemy) and his handling of other 'statutes and ordinances' from the Pentateuch recognises their non-universal jurisdiction.

SUMMARY

Matthew 5 is probably the key passage in any discussion of Jesus' attitude to the law since it records Jesus' declaration that he came not to 'abolish', but to 'fulfil'. Some of the scholarly definitions of these words determine that they mean the opposite of their natural sense. Theological frameworks and straitened contexts drive a 'whirlpool of conflicting interpretations' that produce over-refined word definitions. The best way out of this whirlpool is to interpret Matthew 5:17 in the ancient stream of biblical interpretation that sees Matthew interacting with Old Testament texts such as Jeremiah. Thus he presents Jesus as holding the same Pentateuchal assumptions about the law, sin, and covenant as the prophets, and as providing eschatological, soteriological, and moral fulfilment of the law in his person and teaching. Matthew shows us what fulfilment looks like; he does not demolish, abolish, advance, or reconstruct the Law of Moses. Many of the claimed antitheses in Matthew 5 are only so if one accepts unwarranted assumptions about the Mosaic Laws, whereas the teaching of Matthew 5:21–48 is co-ordinate and continuous with the law.

Yet again, viewed in isolation, none of the observations in the last two chapters force the conclusion that the 'moral law doth for ever bind all'. Taken together, however, the evangelists' attitudes to the law—implicit and explicit—along with Jesus' teaching confirm the categories described in chapters two and three. None

---

137   Carson, *Matthew*, [Pradis Ver. 5.01.0035].

of the arguments put forward by critics of the threefold division land a mortal blow to the ancient framework or compel us to accept that Jesus and the evangelisists broke away from the Old Testament view that some laws were a 'pattern', others were to be obeyed 'in the land', while the Decalogue was the controlling influence. The first chapter noted Ferguson's comment that Jesus' insistence that he fulfils rather than abolishes the law only makes sense given the premise of the threefold division.[138] In terms of the fully developed confessional expression of the threefold division, it would be premature to affirm that statement at this point. Nonetheless, it is possible to say that the premise of an embryonic threefold division in the Old Testament helps to make sense of Matthew 5 and other law-related parts of the Gospels in a way that is impossible if readers assume the law was an 'indivisible whole'. The Gospels do, however, hint at change since the rending of the temple veil that marked the end of Jesus' life signified change—at least for pattern laws and forms of cultic separation. The full extent of this change and its implications for the embryonic form will be the subject of the next two chapters. Did the apostles' attitudes to the law as recorded in the narrative of Acts and in the epistles terminate its progress or rather establish it as a fully developed Christian framework?

138   Ferguson, *Holy Spirit*, 164.

VI

THE LAW IN ACTS

Richard could not abide any fanatical legalism in his congregation. He once received a report that one of the brethren had been found to be a secret smoker. Now that was not the custom in that congregation. Without delay, the elders of the church convoked and decided to expel the man. Before passing the resolution, they summoned the culprit. As the proceedings began, Richard took out a packet of cigarettes, leisurely lit one up, and to the utter amazement of the elders, began to smoke. No one was expelled.

Ferenc Visky recounting a story about Richard Wurmbrand, with whom he shared a prison cell for several years in 1950's Romania.

According to the Gospels, Jesus' words and actions often left the future apostles bewildered. If Jesus was not asking them, 'Do you not yet understand?' (Mark 8:21), they were asking one another, 'What does he mean…?' (John 7:36; 16:18). When he announced his departure it did nothing to diminish their perplexity, but John records Jesus' assurance that once he has gone, the Paraclete will come to remind them of his words and enable them to comprehend 'all things' (John 14:26), which presumably included Jesus' teaching on the law and the prophets. Acts reports a post-resurrection reaffirmation of Christ's promise (Acts 1:5) and narrates the effect of its fulfilment (Acts 2:4–18; 4:8–12; 10:34–48). The epistles claim the Spirit's illumination (1 Cor. 2:6–12;

Eph. 3:4–5) and that the apostolic message was in continuity with that of Jesus and the prophets (1 John 1:1–5; 2 Pet. 3:1–3).

Much of twentieth century scholarship judged this conviction misplaced—Peter, Paul, James, and John were not in harmony with each other, far less Jesus or the prophets. Indeed, Paul did not even agree with himself. German scholarship even discovered that Paul was not Paul.[1] There may have been a time when conservative interpreters dismissed similar views with Luther-like contempt as 'what one can expect of crazy Germans'.[2] Today, however, scholars like Porter and Van Spanje give such arguments the courtesy of analysis and rebuttal, arguing against 'significant and sustainable contradictions'[3] or dismissing claims of Pauline inconsistency as 'absolutely unjustified'.[4] In any case, the first chapter of this book pointed out that supporters of the threefold division across ecclesiastical, geographical, and chronological borders held to a notion of textual coherence— 'unity and inerrancy' were 'unsurprising dogmas',[5] 'Scripture... one whole, homogenous work',[6] its teaching 'a single unified science',[7] and all its parts 'consent'[8] being 'immediately inspired by God'.[9] They accepted the threefold division while affirming that when New Testament writers claimed that the Holy Spirit enabled them to interpret Jesus Christ and the prophets who

---

1   Stanley E. Porter provides a brief history of how this position developed from F. C. Baur to Ernst Haenchen. Stanley E. Porter, *The Paul of Acts: Essays in Literary Criticism, Rhetoric, and Theology* (Tübingen: Mohr Siebeck, 1999), 187–9.

2   Martin Luther, *The Large Catechism*, trans. Robert H. Fischer (Philadelphia: Fortress Press, 1959), 3.

3   Porter, *Paul of Acts*, 205.

4   T. E. Van Spanje, *Inconsistency in Paul: A Critique of the Work of Heikki Räisänen.* (Tübingen: Mohr Siebeck, 1999), 252.

5   Young, *Biblical Exegesis*, 10.

6   Ibid., 97.

7   Aquinas, *Summa Theologiæ*, 2.

8   *WCF* I.V

9   *WCF* I.VIII

came before him, their conviction was well founded. Thus this investigation cannot proceed on an assumption that the New Testament writers are inconsistent, not only because of scholarly arguments to the contrary, but because the purpose of this book is to examine the biblical and theological basis for the threefold division within the framework of its proponents beliefs and common assumptions about Scripture.

The opening sentences of Acts introduce what follows as continuing from the author's previous account of 'all that Jesus began to do and teach' (Acts 1:1). It narrates the birth of the universal church and the trials of her early years. These included controversies over the law. A brief examination of some of those issues may indicate how the apostles viewed the Mosaic Law and provide a narrative background for some of the epistles.

Views on Luke's overall stance towards the law are as polarised as they are with respect to other biblical authors. Jacob Jervell, for example, is sure that Luke is deeply concerned about the law because it concerns the identity of the church. When the notion that Mosaic customs will be altered is attributed to Jesus, 'Luke sees it as patently false: therefore every criticism of the law is missing. This is done deliberately in order to show the position of the Torah in the church. Jesus did not alter anything, the law is permanently valid.'[10] Therefore 'Luke…stresses the Jewish Christians as being zealous for the law.'[11] A representative of the opposite pole is Craig Blomberg who thinks that Jervell seems to 'overemphasize Luke's interest in a law-keeping Christianity.'[12] This is all part of a '"pro-Jewish" trend in Lucan studies' that likes to 'jump around exegeting isolated texts apart from their

10   Jacob Jervell, *The Theology of the Acts of the Apostles* (Cambridge: Cambridge University Press, 1996), 56.

11   Ibid., 57.

12   Craig L. Blomberg, 'The Christian and the Law of Moses', in *Witness to the Gospel: The Theology of Acts*, I. Howard Marshall and David Peterson, eds. (Grand Rapids: Eerdmans, 1998), 398.

larger contexts and apart from the narrative flow of the plot of
the book.'[13] Had not Jervell fallen into this trap he would have
realised that 'no one was required to obey any command of the
Law for either salvation or Christian discipleship, apart from its
fulfilment in Christ.'[14] Neither of those extremes is satisfactory.
Jervell's claims rest on a misinterpretation of the place of
aliens under the Mosaic law, while Blomberg's agreement with
Weiser that according to Luke the Mosaic Law is 'a cultural
phenomenon'[15] is peculiar considering Luke's repeated references
to 'the Law of the Lord' (Luke 2:23–4, 39).

ECHOES OF SINAI

Before considering the Jerusalem decree—the most discussed
matter related to the law—it is worth noting some matters
relevant to issues discussed earlier in this book. Several times
in the narrative Luke meets charges of law-breaking against
Christians with a counterclaim that it is the Jews who are the
real antinomians, often breaking one or more commands of the
Decalogue. When the Jews charge Stephen with law-breaking
(Acts 6:13–14), the charge itself depends on them bearing false
witness, while Stephen charges the Jews with murder and failure
to keep the law throughout the generations (7:51–3). Unable
to resist Paul's arguments, the Jews conspire to murder him
(9:22–4). The Corinthian Jews accuse him of antinomianism
(18:12–13), yet they are merchants of violence (18:17). In Jerusalem
they make unsupported accusations (21:28–9) and only the
authorities' rapid intervention stops them murdering the apostle
(21:30–1). Therefore what Conzelmann sees happening in
Acts 23:3 is not a solitary episode: 'Luke is characterizing Judaism

13   Ibid., 399.
14   Ibid., 416.
15   Ibid., 410.

through its representatives—its relation to the Law is broken and hypocritical'.[16] The whitewashed priest acts in continuity with the false prophets in Ezekiel who took the LORD's name in vain with their whitewashing words and empty promises (Ezek. 13).

Luke could have accused the Jews of such moral failures without necessarily implying that Christians were the true law-keepers, but Acts includes several references, which, when combined with the examples above, suggest that Christian thinking presupposed the validity of the principles in the Decalogue:

I   The first commandment is reflected in Christian preaching which declares that only through one saviour can people be reconciled to the only God (Acts 4:11–12). Believers pray to this Sovereign LORD besides whom there is no other (Acts 4:24). Herod's willingness to grasp at equality with God triggered his ghastly end (Acts 12:22–3), which could have been avoided had he reacted like Paul and Barnabas in similar circumstances (Acts 14:11–15).

II The dawning of a new era does not bring changed attitudes to the second commandment whether in reference to Israel's past (Acts 7:42) or the Christian future (Acts 15:20, 29; 19:19). Intolerance of idolatry is not restricted to the believing community for Paul is grieved to see idols in a Gentile city (Acts 17:16).

III Taking the LORD's name in vain. See above (Acts 23:3).

IV Luke only ever presents the apostles as falling in line with traditional respect of Sabbath as a day of worship and prayer (Acts 13:14, 44; 16:13; 17:2; 18:4). The reference in Acts 4:24 and 14:15 to the LORD who made heaven and earth, and the sea, and all that is in them, is a precise quotation of the LXX wording in Exodus 20:11, τὸν οὐρανὸν καὶ τὴν

16   Hans Conzelmann, *Acts of the Apostles*, trans. James Limburg, A. Thomas Kraabel, and Donald H. Juel (Philadelphia: Fortress Press, 1972), 192.

γῆν καὶ τὴν θάλασσαν καὶ πάντα τὰ ἐν αὐτοῖς, which suggests a high degree of familiarity with the Sabbath commandment and ongoing acceptance of the view of divine transcendence that underpins the commandment.

V If Kaufmann and Braulik are correct in seeing the fifth commandment as finding its full expression in the Mosaic laws about respect for authority, then it may be worked out in the submission of Christians to rulers (Acts 23:5; 25:6–12) that do not set themselves above divine authority (Acts 5:29).

VI You shall not murder. See above (Acts 7:51–3; 9:22–4; 21:30–1).

VII The broad implications of the commandment against adultery are reflected, though not explicitly reiterated, in the Jerusalem Council's prohibition of sexual immorality (Acts 15:20).

VIII You shall not steal is not mentioned in any specific instance, although Peter's response to Ananias (Acts 5:4) suggests that his partial retention of the proceeds from the field was theft because it was no longer his own.

IX Bearing false witness is the root sin in the case of Ananias and Sapphira (Acts 5:1–11). False witnesses speak against Stephen (Acts 6:13), whereas Paul speaks the truth (Acts 26:25).

X On his departure from Ephesus, Paul claims that he has coveted nothing (20:33). This is widely seen as a reflection of Samuel's farewell address (1 Sam. 12:3–4),[17] but Samuel's words are a clearer echo of the eight commandment than the tenth. The keeping of the eighth, however, may well depend on the keeping of the tenth.

These observations suggest that if the law for Luke is 'a cultural phenomenon' that he must consider the nascent church to be guardian of both the culture and the phenomenon, in so far as they are represented in the principles of the Decalogue. No amount of attention to the narrative flow allows these examples to be interpreted to mean that Luke felt 'no one was required to obey any command of the law', unless we assume that Luke was remarkably good at hiding his feelings. This is true even of the Sabbath commandment despite Max Turner's efforts to continue the argument of *From Sabbath to Lord's Day* that although Jesus obeyed the fourth commandment, his 'messianic claim in relation to the Sabbath pointed to a transcendence of the institution'.[18] Jesus 'takes a position above it', though in a slightly ambiguous way that leaves the early church befuddled,[19] yet able to decide that the law 'was not to be imposed on the Gentiles and it was theologically irrelevant to the salvation of Jewish Christians.'[20] Turner acknowledges that there 'is very little direct evidence in Acts on the question of Sabbath observance' and observations that Christians were present in the synagogues 'do not take us far'.[21] For the anti-Sabbatarians, however, there is a long way to go, so even if 'direct evidence' is absent, 'we must work from inference.'[22] This would be dangerous, confesses Turner, were it not that he will recognize 'the sheer complexity of factors (some intangible) that impinge on the issue of Sabbath observance and the diversity of response that was inevitable as different situations weighted these factors differently.'[23]

This approach is no more satisfactory for Acts than it was for the Gospels. When Acts is plain about the Christian's obligations concerning food laws and circumcision it is startling if it should

18   Lincoln, 'A Biblical and Theological Perspective', 345.

19   Ibid., 364.

20   Max Turner, 'The Sabbath, Sunday, and the Law in Luke/Acts' in Carson, *Sabbath to Lord's Day*, 123–4.

21   Ibid., 124.

22   Ibid.

23   Ibid.

be so vague about what Turner rightly calls 'so fundamental, universal, and ingrained an institution as the Jewish Sabbath'.[24] He believes that 'the earliest Jewish Christians kept the whole law and were theologically committed to it'—a stance which, when coupled with the notion that Jesus was above the law, forces him to conclude that they went into 'retreat from Jesus stance with respect to the law.'[25] If it is hard to believe in a transfer from Sabbath to Lord's Day because it would mean, in Turner's view, that 'the most distinctive and highly controversial feature of the earliest church's practice has simply been totally ignored,'[26] it is surely harder to swallow the idea that the fourth word, engraved in the tablets of stone, was chiselled away without a murmur. Whether Luke-Acts was composed in 60 AD, 130 AD, or anywhere in between, it makes little sense to say that an author whose aim was to give his readers certainty concerning the things they had been taught (Luke 1:4) chose to record a radical revolution in the church's approach to Sabbath by forcing his readers to grapple with knotty intangibilities. Vermes' point applies here too—if Luke wanted to teach the end of the Sabbath he did 'a pitiful job'.[27] The 'sheer complexity' arises not from Luke's haziness, but from Turner declaring theologically irrelevant what Luke considered permanently relevant—the sanctification of one day in seven as a witness to the absolute transcendence of the Sovereign Lord who made heaven and earth, and the sea, with all that is in them. For him, and for the earliest Christians, there could be no retreat from this belief or the Sabbath observance that accompanied it because that would have been to retreat from Jesus' attitude to the law.

---

24   Ibid.
25   Ibid., 134.
26   Ibid., 135.
27   Vermes, *Jesus the Jew*, 13.

STATUTES AND ORDINANCES

Commentators on Acts find little worthy of comment concerning references to Mosaic laws that neither belong to the Decalogue nor are expressly cultic. Nestle-Aland, however, list a few possible references and allusions to such laws, some of which merit brief consideration.

Exodus 22:27 (BHS) and Acts 23:5

The clearest example comes in Paul's response to the assembly after calling the priest a whitewashed wall (Acts 23:1–5). He seems to quote Exodus 22:28: 'You shall not revile God, nor curse a ruler of your people.' Taken in isolation this appears to treat the laws in Exodus 22, which forbid everything from bestiality to usury, as if they were still binding. Although Conzelmann judges the apostle's reaction 'impossibly feeble' and 'unthinkable', it is 'appropriate to Luke's intent. Once again Paul shows himself as obedient to the Law.'[28] Fitzmyer counters that 'it is, indeed, quite thinkable' because of Paul's lengthy absence from Jerusalem,[29] but otherwise he agrees with Conzelmann, 'Paul shows again that he stands by what is prescribed in the Mosaic law.'[30] Those conclusions, however, miss the point of this citation. There is no suggestion of Paul withdrawing his remarks and he was well aware of a prophetic tradition that did not place speaking hard truths about failed leaders in the category of evil speech, so his response could be ironic and sarcastic. Calvin, following Augustine, called it a 'taunting excuse',[31] so Scott Spencer is standing in a long tradition when he writes that Paul is 'suggesting that the high

---

28   Conzelmann, *Acts*, 192.

29   Fitzmyer, *Acts*, 717.

30   Ibid., 718. Also Ernst Haenchen, *The Acts of the Apostles* (Oxford: Blackwell, 1971), 638.

31   John Calvin, *Acts*, BibleWorks 7.0.

priest's whitewashed demeanour has rendered him effectively "unrecognizable" as a faithful and true leader of God's people.'[32] This means that although the complete incident portrays Paul as someone who regards Ananias as a hypocritical law-breaker (see above regarding the third commandment, also Leviticus 19:15),[33] the reference to Exodus 22:28 is not meant to convey anything about his attitude to the law.

Deuteronomy 10:17 and Acts 10:34

Acts 10:34 records Peter's profession that 'God shows no partiality.' This follows the revelation that opened the way for him to visit Cornelius' without complaint (Acts 10:29). Even if Jews considered it 'unlawful' to visit Gentiles, he should not call any person unclean (Acts 10:28). According to Dunn, Peter has recognized the close correlation between food laws and the separation between Jew and Gentile that 'was clearly spelled out in Lev. 20.24–26'.[34] Perhaps; but it would be a mistake to follow the almost standard mistranslation of ἀθέμιτος in Acts 10:28 and conclude that Leviticus 20:24–6 debarred Jews from visiting Gentiles.[35] The passage in Leviticus records God's proclamation that he has set apart certain animals to be unclean to a people that he has set apart from other nations to be holy, and although this implies a 'close correlation',[36] it does not mean that others

32   F. Scott Spencer, *Acts* (Sheffield: Sheffield Academic Press, 1997), 212. Also Dunn who detects 'a sarcastic ring'. James D. G. Dunn, *The Acts of the Apostles* (Peterborough: Epworth Press, 1996), 304.

33   For discussion of Leviticus 19:15 see Fitzmyer, *Acts*, 717.

34   Dunn, *Acts*, 139.

35   'Unlawful' implies that Peter was talking about transgression of the Mosaic Law. The only other New Testament occurrence of the word is in 1 Peter 4:3 where it is most frequently translated by words such as 'abominable', 'detestable', 'unclean', or 'forbidden'. A similar translation may be more appropriate in Acts 10:28.

36   Dunn, *Acts*, 139.

were set apart to uncleanness on the grounds of nationality (even should Peter have thought so).[37] Though perplexed at first (Acts 10:17), Peter eventually sees things from the Pentateuch's standpoint and understands that no foods are intrinsically unclean; they are only set apart to uncleanness for as long as Israel is set apart, which can no longer be the case if all foods are now clean. The primary focus of the vision is therefore not dietary. Peter can no longer call things defiling or common that God has made clean (Acts 10:15), which in a later interpretation of the vision he identifies as Gentile hearts (Acts 15:9).[38] In this context, Peter's declaration of God's impartiality in Acts 10:34 draws out the implications of the Pentateuchal view that all animals are fundamentally clean—those who fear God and do what is right are acceptable to him irrespective of nationality (Acts 10:35).

That Peter has come to understand this not only through his vision, but also through reflection on the Pentateuch, becomes clear when he recalls Deuteronomy 10:17. He echoes not only the wording, but also the context, which Peter Craigie sees as 'a positive sermon on the negatively stated first commandment: "You shall have no other Gods before me."'[39] Israel had the stone tablets in the ark (Deut. 10:1–10), yet if they were to fear, love, serve, and obey God as he required (Deut. 10:11–13), they needed more than external symbols; he was primarily concerned that they had humble, tender, circumcised hearts (Deut. 10:16). Cornelius had such a heart; he displayed the love of God and neighbour that the law demanded (Acts 10:2) and therefore was acceptable to God (Acts 10:35). In any case, God's love was never absolutely exclusive: the 'God of gods and Lord of lords...loves

37 'The juxtaposition of the dietary prohibition and the holiness and separation requirements (v. 26) does not categorically mean that Israelites may not dine at the same table with others.' Milgrom, *Leviticus*, 259.

38 Fitzmyer, *Acts*, 546.

39 Peter C. Craigie, *The Book of Deuteronomy* (Grand Rapids: Eerdmans, 1976), 204.

the sojourner' (Deut. 10:17–18).[40] Even if the LORD loved the patriarchs and their seed 'above all peoples', it was not because they were a superior race;[41] the Lord of all chose to set his love upon their fathers (Deut. 10:15). When the sojourner enters the theatre of divine love, the LORD will love him too—'He shows no partiality'—and his people must imitate him (Deut. 10:19).

Peter's vision and speech show that he has now understood that if food distinctions have been abolished, national Israel is no longer the exclusive theatre of divine love. Reflection on the Pentatuech may have taught him that Jewish attitudes to Gentiles were not lawful in the first place, but the primary lesson was that God's love for people of all nations would now be expressed in a context unrestricted by national boundaries. Therefore, on the one hand, laws that symbolized Israel's distinctiveness no longer bind; on the other, the divine impartiality proclaimed in the law cannot be abolished and its demand for the love of the sojourner must have fuller expression. Indeed, from where Peter now stands, Deuteronomy's declarations of God's impartiality and love of sojourners may always have been indicative of the temporality and symbolic nature of separation laws.

Deuteronomy 23:21 and Acts 5:4

'Exactly what have they done wrong?'[42] asks Brian Capper concerning Ananias and Sapphira. Considering Peter's declaration recorded in Acts 5:4 it seems an unnecessary

40   The LXX translates גֵר (sojourner) with προσήλυτος, but the sojourner in ancient Israel may not always be the direct equivalent of the proselyte in the New Testament. For discussion of some of the issues involved see Max Wilcox, 'The "God-Fearers" in Acts – A Reconsideration' in *JSNT* 13 (1981), 102–22.

41   In this context, the *English Standard Version* is misleading when it goes out on a limb and translates the last words of Deuteronomy 10:15—כַּיּוֹם הַזֶּה— with 'as you are this day'.

42   Brian J. Capper, 'The Interpretation of Acts 5:4', *JSNT* 19 (1983), 117.

question: 'You have not lied to men but to God.' Given the
suggestion that Deuteronomy 23:21[43] stands behind the story, it
is, however, a question. Capper rightly rejects the idea that a vow,
or *korban*, is in the background because such a vow would have
been made before the sale, whereas Peter says the money was
still at Ananias' disposal after the sale (Acts 5:4).[44] Eventually,
he finds a parallel in the Dead Sea Scrolls and concludes that
'Ananias' crime falls awkwardly between embezzlement and
deception.'[45] It is unclear, however, why he takes Peter's initial
word as decisive, yet when in the next breath Peter identifies
Ananias' sin as lying, it is so inadequate that it requires a long-
drawn-out investigatory journey terminating at Qumran. Even
if Ananias had made a vow, slow payment is not the issue, but
underpayment. Theft and embezzlement may aggravate his sin,
but his primary fault is that he pretended to present the entire
proceeds of his sale, and therefore 'lied...to God'. Nestle-Aland's
suggestion that Acts 5:4 alludes to Deuteronomy 23:21 is therefore
questionable.

Deuteronomy 18:10–14 and Acts 19:19

In Braulik's and Kaufmann's Decalogue frameworks for the
laws of Deuteronomy, they see Deuteronomy 18 as dealing with
issues of authority and place it within the trajectory of the fifth
commandment concerning the honour of parents. The chapter
begins with laws about the place of the Levites (1–8) and ends
with laws about prophets—those who 'speak in the name of
the LORD' (15–22). Verses 9–14 fall in between and condemn
the 'abominable practices of the nations' that will result in their

43   'When you vow a vow to the LORD your God, you shall not be slow
to pay it: for the LORD your God will surely require it of you; and it would
be sin in you'.
44   Ibid., 119.
45   Ibid., 128.

expulsion from Canaan. Priest and prophet are God's appointed religious officers and mediators; Israel must not use alternative means of seeking to discern his will, such as divination, fortune-telling, interpreting omens, sorcery, wizardry, and necromancy.

This same contrast between God's appointed spokesmen and false prophets appears alongside the condemnation of magic and sorcery in Acts 19. Paul is God's appointed officer. He proclaims God's will for two years in the hall of Tyrannus (Acts 19:8–10) and God works miracles through him (Acts 19:10–11). When the sons of Sceva (a Jew, whose priesthood was more pagan than Jewish) fulfil the role of 'the prophet who presumes to speak a word in my name that I have not commanded him to speak' (Deut. 18:20; Acts 19:13–14), an evil spirit renders their words empty and them instantly recognizable as false prophets (Deut. 18:21–2; Acts 19:15). They escape with their lives, but little else (Deut. 18:20; Acts 19:16). The story of seven men fleeing naked and wounded from a city house cannot be embargoed; news of their misadventure leads to believers, who were once practitioners of magic, recognising their magic books as the literature of 'abominable practices' and throwing them on public bonfires (Deut. 18:9–12; Acts 19:18–19). Fitzmyer argues that 'Luke is trying to get across the idea that Christianity had nothing to do with magic, and that Jesus' name is no magical-incantation formula.'[46] This is at least part of his message, but if Deuteronomy 18 is in the background it conveys more than that. Luke earlier records Peter's claim in his Pentecost sermon that Deuteronomy 18:15—'The Lord your God will raise up for you a prophet like me...listen to him'—is fulfilled in Jesus Christ (Acts 3:22). He now places this fulfilment theme at the heart of Acts 19 so that even the evil spirit recognises Jesus and his messenger Paul (Acts 19:16), while Jesus' fulfilment of those laws

46   Fitzmyer, *Acts*, 646.

about God's communication through priest and prophet, rather than sorcery, is publicly acknowledged in the book-burnings.[47]

If this analysis is correct, then the laws in Deuteronomy 18 still function in the sub-structure of early Christian thought. They are not legally binding in the same way because their jurisdiction was in the land and they are fulfilled in Christ, but what the confessionists called the 'general equity' of the laws remains valid and therefore the Christians regard wizardry, necromancy, and false claims to speak in the name of Jesus Christ as no less displeasing to God than it was under the law.

Deuteronomy 28:29 and Acts 22:11

Following Deuteronomy's declaration of the laws that must be obeyed 'in the land' is a catalogue of blessings and curses that will accompany obedience or disobedience to those laws. Among those curses are madness, blindness, and confusion (Deut. 28:28). At first glance, the suggestion of a link between this verse and the conversion experience Paul recounts in Acts 22 might seem far fetched (especially if, as Craigie suggests, the Deuteronomic curse refers to tertiary syphilis)[48] yet the parallels are striking. 'All these curses' of Deuteronomy were guaranteed to fall not only upon disobedient Israel, but also upon those who persecuted them (Deut. 30:7). Not only is Paul blind and confused, but he gropes

---

47   For a discussion of how Luke develops this fulfilment theme in his gospel see David P. Moessner, *Lord of the Banquet: The Literary and Theological Significance of the Lukan Travel Narrative* (Harrisburg: Trinity Press International, 1989), especially pages 45–71. He argues that there is 'a profound correspondence in the calling, execution, and fate of the calling of the one who is the Prophet like Moses (Deut. 18:15–19), effecting a New Exodus for a renewed people of God', 60. Also (in relation to Acts 23): 'Luke presents Paul as following in the footsteps of his master in his journey-calling to witness to the Kingdom of God in suffering and affliction as he is rejected by an intractable people: like Jesus, he is to suffer the prophet's fate', 299.

48   Craigie, *Deuteronomy*, 344.

around in the dark 'at noonday' (Deut. 28:28–9; Acts 22:6; 10–11) having been confronted with his persecution of Jesus and the 'Way' (Acts 22:4; 7–8). It is therefore possible that Luke presents Paul's persecution of the church as bringing this curse upon his own head. This implies that the enemies of God are now Jews or Gentiles (Acts 26:17) who persecute the church and that the Deuteronomic blessings and curses no longer operate within their historical context. Even so, the divine justice administered in the blessings and curses endures, but submission to the Lord leads to the reversal of the curse for Paul (Acts 22:13) and those to whom he will minister (Acts 26:18).

THE APOSTOLIC DECREE

Not for the first time, we need to investigate a passage that is 'one of the most complicated in the New Testament'.[49] This time it is Acts 15, which gives an account of the Jerusalem Council and their response to those who claimed that circumcision was necessary for salvation. After much debate and an influential speech from James, the assembly decide to write with the following advice to the Gentile Christians in Antioch, Syria, and Cilicia:

> …it has seemed good to the Holy Spirit and to us to lay on you no greater burden than these requirements: that you abstain from what has been sacrificed to idols, and from blood, and from what has been strangled, and from sexual immorality. If you keep yourselves from these, you will do well. Farewell (Acts 15:28–9).

For Jervell, the only thing that makes this complicated is 'if the Decree is understood as liberation from the law'.[50] The opposite, he says, is the case:

---

49   Jervell, *Theology of the Acts*, 59.
50   Ibid.

...the Decree is necessary because the law demands it; the Decree expresses what Moses demands from Gentiles in order that they may live among Israelites (Acts 15:15–17). The background is what Leviticus 17–18 demands from the 'strangers' in Israel. The Decree is known from the synagogues as Moses is read there sabbath by sabbath, as happens all over the world. The Decree gives a common norm for Jews and Gentiles, grounding the unity of the church in the law...As the Decree is part of the Torah, the law remains valid for both Jewish and Gentile Christians.[51]

This widely-held view that Leviticus 17–18 lies behind the decree[52] may touch on some themes in the previous section, particularly the idea that moral continuity coincided with discontinuity in legal details to impact the way that Christians viewed Gentiles. It would certainly challenge the threefold division's assertion that only the Decalogue is binding. The next few pages will therefore consider the evidence for the Leviticus link.

From the beginning, Acts 15 is in no hurry to cooperate with this view, presenting the exegete with a bundle of textual problems. The translation of Acts 15:28–9 printed above depends on the Alexandrian text, one of whose representatives is $\mathfrak{P}^{45}$, a codex that in omitting 'sexual immorality' from Acts 15:20 narrows the decree to a dietary dictate.[53] Some find support for a similar omission from Acts 15:29 in other manuscripts,[54] but in his comprehensive

51   Ibid.

52   For example, Fitzmyer, *Acts*, 557; Richard Bauckham, 'James and the Gentiles (Acts 15.13–21)' in Ben Witherington, ed., *History, Literature, and Society in the Book of Acts* (Cambridge: Cambridge University Press, 1996), 172–5; Eric Franklin, *Luke: Interpreter of Paul, Critic of Matthew* (Sheffield: Sheffield Academic Press, 1994), 47–8.

53    $\mathfrak{P}^{45}$ comprised of the Gospels and Acts. It is the earliest example of a codex that includes such a large proportion of the text of the New Testament. For a more detailed description see Larry W. Hurtado, *The Earliest Christian Artifacts* (Grand Rapids: Eerdmans, 2006), 174–7.

54   Metzger identifies the texts that support this as 'Origen, contra Celsum, VIII:29, as well as vgms Vigilius and Gaudentius.' *Textual Commentary*, 380.

discussion of 𝔓⁴⁵, Royse writes that '𝔓⁴⁵ regularly omits from no discernible cause and with no discernible purpose'[55] and Origen's support for this reading in Acts 15:29 is 'extremely doubtful'.[56] For an interpreter who, despite this, holds the 𝔓⁴⁵ reading as authentic,[57] the link with Leviticus 17–18 becomes improbable due to the absence of the sexual immorality prohibition. Improbability gives way to impossibility if the Western text (D) is preferred since it omits 'what is strangled', reducing the decree to three moral prohibitions against idolatry, murder, and sexual immorality.[58] For Wilson, 'this unquestionably fits best into Luke's narrative',[59] but Metzger thinks it 'cannot be original, for it implies that a special warning had to be given to Gentile converts against such sins as murder, and that this was expressed in the form of asking them to "abstain" from it – which is slightly absurd!'[60] But is it? The epistles express similar sentiments (Jas. 4:2)[61] and Metzger's dismissal presupposes a weak interpretation of 'abstain' (ἀπέχω) or that any prohibition of idolatry and sexual immorality

---

55   James R. Royse, *Scribal Habits in Early Greek New Testament Papyri* (Leiden: Brill, 2006), 141.

56   Ibid., 147.

57   Royse lists several who argue for or against the 𝔓⁴⁵ reading (Ibid., 145–8), one of whom was Lagrange. He wrote concerning Acts 15:20: 'Nous pensons donc que pap. représente ici le texte authentique du décret.' M.-J. Lagrange, O.P. 'Le Papyrus Beatty des Actes des Apotres', *RB* 43 (1934), 169.

58   This is how it was understood by significant users of the Western text such as Tertullian ('On Modesty' chap. XII) and Cyprian ('Testimonies Against the Jews', Third Book, Head 119).

59   Wilson, *Luke and Law*, 101.

60   Metzger, *Textual Commentary*, 381. Similarly, Sanday writes '…it is indeed so pointless as to be incredible.' W. Sanday, 'The Text of the Apostolic Decree.' *Expositor*, October 1913, 298.

61   Not all interpreters take James' prohibition of murder as literal. For discussion of the issues involved and arguments in favour of a literal interpretation see Luke Timothy Johnson, *The Letter of James* (New York: Doubleday, 1995), 276–7; Ralph P. Martin, *James* (Nashville: Thomas Nelson Publishers, 1988), 140 n. b, 145–6.

must have been weaker than a prohibition of murder.[62] The
Western text also appends the words 'and do not do to others
what you would not wish them to do to you',[63] which may
reflect the connection between the double commandment and
the Decalogue (see previous chapter), raising the possibility
that the apostolic decree is another summarizing expression
of the Ten Commandments. Borgen's solution to the textual
problem is to say that there was no decree. The council was
only interested in discussing Christian proselytes and decided
to promulgate a traditional Jewish view of proselytes,[64] which
some 'actualized along the lines of Leviticus 17–18' (Alexandrian)
and others 'by emphasizing the pagan ethical vices, together
with idolatry' (Western).[65] This might address some issues
in Pauline studies,[66] but for now it is important to note the
possibility that elements of patristic teaching that leaned on the
Western text may have fed into the seventeenth century form
of the threefold division. An ethical interpretation would, for
example, have been in harmony with the views of Ireneaus, one
user of the Western text whose views were discussed in chapter
one. Similarly, it was natural for Tertullian to treat them as three
ethical prohibitions representative of 'pristine law' that 'will cease
[only] with the world'.[67] Nonetheless, the Alexandrian version
has prevailed, so for most interpreters the Leviticus connection
remains a possibility.

In his article on James and the Gentiles, Richard Bauckham

---

62   Other NT uses of ἀπέχω also carry no hint of tentativeness (1 Thess. 4:3,
5:22; 1 Tim. 4:3; 1 Pet. 2:11).

63   'καὶ ὅσα ἂν μὴ θέλωσιν ἑαυτοῖς γίνεσθαι ἑτέροις μὴ ποιεῖν'

64   Peder Borgen, 'Catalogues of Vices, The Apostolic Decree, and the
Jerusalem Meeting' in J. Neusner, ed., *The Social World of Formative Christianity
and Judaism* (Philadelphia, Fortress Press, 1982), 138.

65   Ibid., 139.

66   Franklin, *Luke*, 45–7, n. 3.

67   'On Modesty' chap. XII.

interacts with recent objections to the Leviticus link and provides
what is probably its most cogent defence. Leviticus 17–18 records
four prohibitions that apply to the sojourner (גֵּר). They match
the content and order of the prohibitions in Acts 15:29: 'Things
sacrificed to idols' (Lev. 17:8–9); 'blood' (Lev. 17:10, 12); 'what has
been strangled' (Lev. 17:13); and sexual immorality (Lev. 18:6–23).[68]
But why should they have been selected? Because, says Bauckham,
along with Amos 9:11–12, Jeremiah 12:16 has contributed to
Acts 15:16–18. Its use of the phrase בְּתוֹךְ עַמִּי (in the midst of my
people) is similar to phraseology found in the thematically linked
Zechariah 2:11 where the Lord says 'וְשָׁכַנְתִּי בְתוֹכֵךְ' (I will dwell
in your midst), which therefore parallels Amos 9:12.[69] The laws
in Leviticus 17–18 all apply to הגר הגר בתוכם (the sojourner in
the midst), so 'using the principle of gezērâ šawâ, these Gentiles
are those to whom the Torah refers in a *verbally corresponding
way*'[70] and 'the use of בתוך, as in Jer. 12.16 and Zech. 2.11/15 is the
principle of selection'.[71]

It is, however, a debatable hypothesis that gezērâ šawâ (II) lies
behind the apostolic decree. One of the rules of this method was
that the link word should be superfluous in one, but preferably

68   Bauckham, 'James and the Gentiles', 172–3.

69   Ibid., 175.

70   Bauckham takes his definition of gezērâ šawâ from Instone-Brewer
(Ibid., 176, n. 62) who defines it as 'the interpretation of one text in the light
of another text to which it is related by a shared word or phrase. The two texts
are often concerned with the same subject, but the existence of the same word
or phrase in two texts can suggest a relationship between them even if they are
concerned with completely unrelated subjects. This can also be seen as a result
of Nomological assumptions [reading Scripture as though it were a precisely
worded legal document], because the divine legislator would ensure that all
terms were used with complete consistency, so that the use of the same term
anywhere in the legal document would relate to its use anywhere else in the
same document.' David Instone-Brewer. *Techniques and Assumptions in Jewish
Exegesis before 70 CE* (Tübingen: J.C.B. Mohr (Paul Siebeck), 1992), 18.

71   Bauckham, 'James and the Gentiles', 176.

both texts.[72] This is not true of בתוך in the prophetic passages and in the Leviticus passages the preceding participle (גור) would also need to be superfluous.[73] If scribal tradition is the basis for the apostolic decree, Pragmatism[74] might provide a more convincing theory. Irrespective of scribal methodologies, however, the Leviticus link faces other difficulties, many of which are presented by Blomberg,[75] Pao,[76] Seifrid,[77] and Wilson,[78] but the primary reasons for rejecting Baukham's intricate hypothesis are as follows.

First, although he notes that the order is different in Acts 15:20 and 15:29[79] he makes no comment on the matter, even although it undermines his point that they are in the same order as Leviticus. If Luke treats the order so casually it is unlikely that he intended to show a link with Leviticus 17–18 on the basis of the order.

Second, Bauckham justifies the exclusion of other laws that use בתוך (Lev. 16:29; Num. 15:14–16, 29; 19:10) because they 'refer specifically to the temple cult',[80] yet by that same standard, Leviticus 17:8, 10, which he includes, should also be excluded.

Finally, his acknowledgment that 'there are other Mosaic laws'[81]

---

72   Instone-Brewer, *Techniques*, 49. He gives a good example where Ben Bag Bag links Numbers 28:2 and Exodus 12:6 (not 16:12) using שמר, "to guard/watch/keep" which can be said to be superfluous in both passages, so that the reason for its inclusion is to provide this link', 58.

73   Numbers 15:15 is the one case where הגר הגר occurs without בתוך or an indication of location. BHS suggest in the critical apparatus that אתכם, as in the following verse, is a necessary insertion. The LXX takes the same view with its use of ἐν ὑμῖν as do the major English translations by inserting 'with you'.

74   Instone-Brewer, *Techniques*, 21.

75   Blomberg, 'Christian and the Law', 408–10.

76   David W. Pao, *Acts and the Isaianic New Exodus* (Tübingen: Mohr Siebeck, 2000), 240–42.

77   M. A. Seifrid, 'Jesus and the Law in Acts.' *JSNT* 30 (1987), 48–9.

78   Wilson, *Luke and the Law*, 84–94.

79   Bauckham, 'James and the Gentiles', 173, n. 50.

80   Ibid., 176.

81   Ibid., 174. He cites the Sabbath commandment as the primary example.

that apply to the sojourner is a remarkable understatement. The sojourner (גֵּר) was subject to every requirement of the law and benefited from all its privileges.[82] He had no inheritance in the land and may have been poor or marginalized, but this only placed him alongside the Levite, the widow, and the fatherless (Deut. 14:29; 16:11; 26:12–13). There might have been a time prior to his circumcision when the sojourner had not yet come under the entire law (Exod. 12:48), but throughout the law the גֵּר is universally subject to the law.[83] For the apostolic council to have created a situation that left Christians thinking some of them were subject to the whole law and others only to a section of Leviticus unveiled by *gezērâ šawâ*, would have marked a swift departure not only from Peter's view that 'God shows no partiality' and makes no distinctions (Acts 15:8), but more remarkably, it would have amounted to an abandonment of the fundamental impartiality principle that underpinned all the Mosaic laws about the sojourner—'one law and one rule' for the native and the sojourner (Exod. 12:49; Lev. 7:7; Num. 15:15–16, 29); they are 'alike before the LORD'. When the sojourner theme appears elsewhere in the New Testament it is never a basis for distinctions.

82   He was subject to Passover laws (Exod. 12:19), could celebrate the Passover (Exod. 12:48–9; Num. 9:14), the Day of Atonement (Lev. 16:29), make offerings (Lev. 17:8–10; 22:18; Num. 15:14–16), and participate in the ceremony of the Red Heifer (Num. 19:10). The Sabbath was his to celebrate (Exod. 20:10) and he was bound not to take blood (Lev. 17:11–15), to keep sexual purity (Lev. 19:10), not to be idolatrous (Lev. 20:2) or blasphemous (Lev. 24:16). The sojourner was entitled to rest (Exod. 23:12), to a life free of oppression (Exod. 22:20; 23:9), to protection (Lev. 19:33–4), charity (Lev. 23:22), and equality (Lev. 24:22; Deut. 5:14).

83   Deuteronomy 14:21 is unlikely to represent a true exception. It is the only place where the LXX translates גֵּר with πάροικος rather than προσήλυτος when the law is referring to a foreigner in Israel. Unless this text was understood to refer to a time prior to the sojourner's circumcision, this suggests גֵּר was read in the light of its 56 other occurrences in the Pentateuch as a reference to the stranger (תּוֹשָׁב) rather than the sojourner.

In the new order, Gentiles are no longer strangers (Eph. 2:12–19); all Christians are sojourners together (1 Pet. 1:1; 2:11).

This discussion began with Jervell's claim that Acts 15 is only complicated 'if the Decree is understood as liberation from the law',[84] yet arguments for the Leviticus link are hardly a breeze. For Siefrid they are 'absurd'[85] because if Acts 15:28 requires no more burden except the demands of the decree, then though Gentiles must shun adultery, they are free to thieve and deceive. But is an embrace with complexity the only alternative to the Leviticus link? Not necessarily. The decree is complicated whether it is understood as liberation from the law or as promoting the abiding validity of the law because neither is the case. That the decree in Acts 15:28 is preceded by the claim that 'it seemed good to us' (ἔδοξεν), suggests that it no more depended on Levitical legal injunctions than the council's decision to send men with Paul and Barnabas (Acts 15:22, 25) or Luke's decision to write his gospel (Luke 1:3). According to Evans, this familiar Greek idiom rarely appears in the New Testament 'because it voiced the Greek humanist confidence in human reason and judgment.'[86] Although the decree guards against this by claiming collective responsibility with the Holy Spirit, the word does suggest a different process and basis than the simple appeal to what is written that Luke-Acts often cites as the basis for behaviour (Luke 2:23; 4:1–13; Acts 23:5) or belief (Acts 1:20; 13:29–33; 15:15–18). The passage does not tell us what Paul and Barnabas were saying in their arguments against those who insisted that circumcision was necessary for salvation (Acts 15:1–5), but the council stood with them in not upholding the plea of the Judean circumcisers. Even if Paul and Barnabas were arguing with the Judeans that the cultic elements in the apostolic decree could be set aside, that does not mean

84 Jervell, *Theology of the Acts*, 59.
85 Siefrid, 'Jesus and the Law', 49–50.
86 C. F. Evans, *Saint Luke* (London: SCM Press, 1990), 128.

Paul could not support the decree. The few requirements the council lays down are not meant to be an exhaustive ethical code, but temporary accommodations that would help to maintain peace in the church while the apostles worked to shape Christian thinking. It 'seemed good' not because a combo of casuistry and scribal tradition led their thoughts to Leviticus, but because unity was more important than absolute liberty.

In this sense, the apostolic decree is based on the general equity of Mosaic law; the second-greatest commandment required sensitivity towards the Judeans in this situation as much as it would require sexual purity in every situation. The decree represents not compromise, but compassion. It gives the church not a hermeneutic of biblical law, but an example of how Christians should behave whenever there is 'no small dissension' between parties who, despite mutual commitment to what is written, do not yet understand it in the same way.[87] 'It is in this mood,' writes Siefrid, 'that the decree is framed (15:25) and that

---

87 Despite differences in the detail and overall view of the law, this understanding of the decree intersects with the views of Franklin, *Luke*, 59; Wilson, *Luke*, 101; Seifrid, 'Jesus and the Law', 51–2; and F. F. Bruce who writes, 'While there was no more question of requiring Gentiles to submit to the ceremonial law, they would do well to behave considerately to their "weaker brethren" of Jewish birth, not all of whom could be expected immediately to acquire such an emancipated outlook on food-laws and the like as Peter and Paul. Therefore, without comprising the Gentiles' Christian liberty, James gave it as his considered opinion that they should be asked to respect their Jewish brethren's scruples...This would smooth the path of social and table fellowship between Christians of Jewish and Gentile birth.' *Commentary on the Book of Acts* (London: Marshall, Morgan & Scott Ltd, 1954), 311.

Ben Witherington offers a more nuanced view 'that what is being prohibited is the attending of temple feasts and all that they entail...The point is that the Mosaic Law, and not least the Ten Commandments, is already proclaimed throughout the Empire in syngagoues. The witness of Gentile Christians was important to James. They must not give Jews in the Diaspora the opportunity to complain that Gentile Christians were still practicing idolatry and immorality by going to pagan feast even after beginning to follow Christ.' *The Acts of the Apostles: A Socio-Rhetorical Commentary* (Grand Rapids: Eerdmans, 1998), 462–3.

Paul submits to James's request to perform a vow (21.20–24).'[88] And to this we can add Paul's circumcision of Timothy; it was 'a concession rather than an obligation.'[89] Those incidents, along with the three or four specifics of the apostolic decree are not therefore meant to address directly the issue of whether or not Mosaic laws are still binding.

SUMMARY

Interpreters of Acts mainly offer two extreme assessments of Luke's view of the law—total zeal for the law in meticulous detail or rejection of the law as a 'cultural phenomenon'. Either position challenges the hermeneutical framework of the threefold division, but neither convincingly.

Acts makes no naked proclamation that 'the moral law doth for ever bind all.' Nonetheless, the narrative portrays Christians as those whose praying, thinking, and acting presupposes the validity of the principles contained in the Decalogue, including the Sabbath. They obey the Ten Commandments while their persecutors deceive and kill.

The five citations and allusions to Mosaic laws vary in their relevance to the judicial laws of the threefold division. Paul's citation of Exodus 22:28 was sarcastic and Deuteronomy 23:21 does not underlie the story of Ananias and Sapphira, so neither Acts 5 nor Acts 26 convey that those laws are ever-binding. Peter's reminder that 'God shows no partiality' (Acts 10:34) recalls the wording and context of Deuteronomy 10:17. Divine impartiality endures in a context where the laws that symbolized Israel's distinctiveness no longer bind, so the love of sojourners has no limits. The account of Sceva's seven sons' embarrassing escapade in Acts 19 suggests that the laws of Deuteronomy 18 still

---

88   Siefrid, 'Jesus and the Law', 52.
89   Franklin, *Luke*, 65.

had a place, even if their landlocked jurisdiction and Christological fulfilment meant that it was the ethical principles rather than the legal details that affected Christian thinking. The curse of Deuteronomy 28:28–9 is not a statute, but the probable allusion to it in Acts 22 reflects similar themes of separations past and enduring justice. Viewed in the light of those examples, the confessional statement that the non-cultic laws from outside the Decalogue 'expired together with the state of that people [Israel], not obliging any other now, further than the general equity thereof may require,' is a defensible reflection of the approach in Acts. The legal specifics are set aside, but the moral equity abides because it rests in the lawgiver who shows no partiality.

Recent writers on Acts have largely assumed that the Jerusalem decree was based on Leviticus 17–18. This would suggest that the threefold division's proposition that all 'ceremonial laws are now abrogated' was contrary to Luke's account. On the other hand, if the injunction to abstain from sexual immorality was thought to be a reiteration of the seventh commandment it would uphold the proposition that 'the moral law doth for ever bind all.' The point of the apostolic decree, however, was not to uphold the Decalogue or any other part of the law. Compassion, shaped by an understanding of the principle of the second-greatest commandment means the apostles call upon Gentile converts to respect three laws that no longer bind and one that will always bind, yet the decree and other accounts of cultic obedience in Acts are legally neutral.[90] They neither undermine nor explicitly support the threefold division of the law.

90   In the context of cultic laws, it is worth noting that Acts 7:44 records Stephen's allusion to Exodus 25:40 and the idea that the tabernacle was made according to the pattern (τύπος). This theme will be discussed in a following section on Hebrews 8:5 as 'for both [Hebrews and Acts] the tabernacle...points to some kind of transcendent reality.' L. D. Hurst, *The Epistle to the Hebrews: Its background of thought* (Cambridge: Cambridge University Press, 1990), 97.

VII

THE APOSTLES AND THEIR EPISTLES

I am quite well. I shall be even better after death, if I keep the
commandments of God to the end.

John Huss (1369–1415) in a letter from prison.

The men who restated the threefold division in their theological
writings and confessions believed they were expressing orthodox
Christian doctrine that originated with the apostles and that was
preserved in their epistles. While Acts gives some indications of
how the apostles viewed the Mosaic Law, we must also consider
the threefold division in light of the epistles. In recent decades,
shifting standpoints have stimulated growth in the study of
Paul's attitude to the law, such that 'no area of Pauline studies
has undergone more sweeping revision',[1] yet no agreement has
emerged.[2] It is impossible to discuss exhaustively all the problems
within problems that receive repeated doctoral-dissertation-
length discussion in the Pauline scholarship industry, and even if
one managed to avoid drowning in its output, Hebrews, James,
Peter, and John still generate a sea of paper for the interpreter to
wade through.

1   F. Thielman, 'Law' in Gerald F. Hawthorne and Ralph P. Martin, eds.,
Dictionary of Paul and His Letters (Leicester: Inter Varsity Press, 1993), 529.

2   Ibid., 532.

There is a widespread perception that the debate surrounding the New Perspective on Paul (NPP) must touch on an issue such as the threefold division either because its tenets are hostile to Reformed theology or because its relatively conservative approach to the law might be supportive. While it is true that the NPP may take a view of justification where moral law is less significant with the result that the NPP is irreconcilable with traditional teaching on those issues,[3] it is neither possible nor necessary to do justice to those concerns here, not least because even reaching a basic definition of the NPP requires protracted discussion. In addition, interaction with the views of some of the key names associated with the NPP, such as Sanders and Dunn, feature at various points throughout this book.

'TYPICAL ORDINANCES' AND 'MORAL DUTIES'

In the remainder of this chapter I will consider whether key passages from the epistles that impinge on the threefold division show continuity or discontinuity with ideas that have already appeared in the Old Testament and the Gospels. This means drawing together some of the threads from earlier chapters, investigating the possible apostolic basis for the traditional categories and some interdependent theological ideas. Since Christians generally agree that ceremonial laws are no longer binding, we will deal with that category first. Having taken the Westminster Divines' formulation as the primary example of the threefold division, it is important to note that their use of 'ceremonial' did not reflect the application of 'anachronistic

---

3 Samples of the debate may be found in James D. G. Dunn, *The New Perspective on Paul* (Grand Rapids: Eerdmans, 2008); Simon J. Gathercole, 'What Did Paul Really Mean?' in *Christianity Today* (August 2007); Simon J. Gathercole, *Where Is Boasting? Early Jewish Soteriology and Paul's Response in Romans 1–5* (Grand Rapids: Eerdmans, 2002); Donald MacLeod, 'The New Perspective: Paul, Luther and Judaism.' *SBET* 22.1 (2004).

terms'[4] to the Mosaic Law. It was not a retrospective imposition of a category limited to a popular conception of what is 'cultic' or 'ritual', but a category they sought to define with the content of the law. Therefore it encompassed 'several typical ordinances; partly of worship, prefiguring Christ, His graces, actions, sufferings, and benefits; and partly of divers instructions of moral duties.'[5]

Copies and Shadows

The book of Hebrews leaves no doubt that for its unannounced author much of the Mosaic Law prefigured Christ and no longer served as a binding law code. It is inessential to determine if Moses should be numbered among the prophets[6] by whom God had spoken previously at various times and in various ways (Heb. 1:1) since what follows has immediate implications for God's revelation through Moses: God has now spoken by his Son, the heir, creator, and upholder of everything, in whom all the brilliance of deity converges (Heb. 1:2–3). This alone would mean that all previous revelation had been surpassed, but the critical event for the Mosaic Law is that God's son has made purification for sins. He has done what no son of Aaron could ever do—'sat down at the right hand of the Majesty on high' (Heb. 1:3). As much as this proclaims the Son's exaltation, it infers a task completed, the implications of which the author will spell out later (particularly 4:14–10:26): Never again will anyone

4   E. P. Sanders, *Paul* (Oxford: Oxford University Press, 1991), 91. He claims this is the case with the terms 'cultic' or 'ritual' law.

5   *WCF* XIX.III

6   See arguments for in Craig R. Koester, *Hebrews: A New Translation with Introduction and Commentary* (New York: Doubleday, 2001), 177, 183–5; John Owen, *An Exposition of the Epistle to the Hebrews with the Preliminary Exercitations* (London: T. Pitcher, 1790), 7. And against in Paul Ellingworth, *The Epistle to the Hebrews* (Grand Rapids: Eerdmans, 1993), 92–3.

need to stand before an altar or sprinkle blood on the mercy seat. To go against this is to refuse the God who has spoken his final word in his Son.

Chapter two discussed Aquinas' proposal that Deuteronomy 6:1 divides the law into moral, civil, and ceremonial. Had Aquinas found himself wanting to dig deeper than the Latin text, he might have built on his notion that Paul wrote Hebrews, in Hebrew, while Luke translated his work into flowing Greek,[7] to conclude that when Hebrews 9:1 and 9:10 use δικαιώματα to refer to 'regulations for worship' and 'external regulations' Luke was translating חֹק/חֻקָּה, which also underlies the 'ceremonies' he finds in Deuteronomy. This, however, would have added inconclusive linguistics to speculation. Only sometimes does חֹק/חֻקָּה refer to cultic law, the LXX twice translates other Hebrew terms for law with δικαίωμα in contexts that may not exclusively refer to cultic law (Deut 7:12; 33:10), and the New Testament does not restrict δικαίωμα to cultic matters (Rom. 1:32; Rev. 15:4).

Koester finds it unhelpful when interpreters like Attridge[8] suggest that Hebrews deals with the ritual law while Paul focuses on the ethical—Hebrews 9:19 refers to the entire law and sacrifices for sin included 'transgressions of the so-called ethical commandments'.[9] In contrast, Peterson criticizes Westcott for emphasising the ethical dimension because, for the writer of Hebrews, 'the Law's purpose is to regulate man's approach to God in a cultic sense.'[10] Neither extreme is satisfactory. Hebrews'

7   Thomas G. Weinandy, OFM, Cap., 'The Supremacy of Christ: Aquinas' *Commentary on Hebrews*', in Thomas G. Weinandy, OFM, Cap, Daniel A. Keating, and John P. Yocum, eds., *Aquinas on Scripture: An Introduction to his Biblical Commentaries* (London: T. & T. Clark, 2005), 223, n. 1.

8   Koester, *Hebrews*, 114, n. 239.

9   Ibid.

10   David Peterson, *Hebrews and Perfection: An Examination of the Concept of Perfection in the 'Epistle to the Hebrews'* (Cambridge: Cambridge University Press, 1982), 130.

reference to the new covenant (Heb. 8:10) would make little
sense if the writer views the law as exclusively cultic, and the late
Lord Bishop of Durham seems not to have been making a strictly
exegetical comment on Hebrews 7:19, but a broader theological
point that Hebrews must assume given its concept of sacrifice.[11]
Nonetheless, it is hard to dispute claims that Hebrews' focus
is on 'the cultic dimensions of the Torah'[12] or that it confines
itself 'almost exclusively to the priestly Torah, or cultic laws
of Leviticus.'[13] Even in 9:19 the point concerns ritual and the
author's reference to 'regulations'—δικαίωμα—in 9:1 and 9:10
as referring to the tabernacle and ceremonies is too specific to
be set aside as a rhetorical flourish. It represents a purposeful
demarcation of the laws relating to the tabernacle and sacrifice,
what *The Westminster Confession* calls 'typical ordinances'. When
the confession defines those ordinances as 'partly of worship',
its wording reflects Hebrews 9:1, which refers to 'regulations
for worship and an earthly sanctuary'.[14] The following verses
(Heb. 9:2–10) fill out the description with an account of the
tabernacle layout[15] and its priestly ministrations. These 'gifts
and sacrifices' were symbols (παραβολή), outward (σαρκός)
performances that could only be laid upon the people until

11   Brooke Foss Westcott, *The Epistle to the Hebrews* (London: Macmillan
& Co., 1903), 189. 'The very scope of the Law indeed was to define the
requirements of life, and to shew that man himself could not satisfy them.'

12   Harold W. Attridge, *The Epistle to the Hebrews* (Philadelphia: Fortress
Press, 1989), 204.

13   Susan Haber, 'From Priestly Torah to Christ Cultus: The Re-Vision of
Covenant and Cult in Hebrews', *JSNT* 28.1 (2005), 106.

14   *The Westminster Confession* does cite Hebrews 9 and their choice of
'ordinances' may reflect the preference for this term over 'regulations' in earlier
English translations of the Bible such as the King James Version.

15   Hebrews appears to vary from the Hebrew Old Testament account.
According to Gheorgita, a 'final solution to the alleged discrepancies in Heb. 9
is still to be found.' For a full discussion see Radu Gheorgita, *The Role of the
Septuagint in Hebrews: An Investigation of its Influence with Special Consideration
to the Use of Hab 2:3-4 in Heb 10:37-38* (Tübingen, Mohr Siebeck, 2003), 84–91.

Christ set things straight. This he has now done as 'high priest of the good things to come', ministering in the tabernacle that lies beyond this creation (Heb. 9:11). He sacrificed himself once for all (Heb. 9:26), which inevitably implies that those cultic regulations should no longer be laid upon anyone.

None of this means that when the author refers to 'food and drink and various baptisms' (Heb. 9:9) he is making 'a deprecatory reference to the purity laws of the Old Testament,'[16] not least because he was unlikely to belittle something through which he believed the Holy Spirit was declaring greater realities. Nor is it adequate to speak of his 'critique of the sacrifices',[17] to summarize his message as concerning the 'imperfection of the law and its sacrifices',[18] or to claim that 'implicit in Hebrews' denigration of the Levitical priesthood is an equally negative view of the Law.'[19] Such language is unduly pejorative and does not reflect the perspective of Hebrews, which does not see their 'weakness' and 'uselessness' (Heb. 7:18) as the result of divine short-sightedness, or of a God for whom it is 'impossible' to lie misleading the fathers by suggesting the impossible (Heb. 10:4). The law had not, as Lane argues, 'proven to be ineffective in achieving its purpose'.[20] That it could perfect nothing and no one (Heb. 7:19, 10:1) does not place Hebrews in dispute with the psalmist (Ps. 19:7). Like perfect tools that produce imperfect results when used for an unintended purpose, these regulations

16   Attridge, *Hebrews*, 243.

17   Lloyd Kim, *Polemic in the Book of Hebrews: Anti-Semitism, Anti-Judaism, Suppressionism?* (Eugene: Pickwick Publications, 2006), 176.

18   Ibid., 174. Kim's language is made all the more puzzling by his acknowledgement that when the author of Hebrews says 'it is impossible for the blood of bulls and goats to take away sin, he implies that they were never established in and of themselves for this purpose', 180.

19   Haber, 'From Priestly Torah to Christ Cultus', 116.

20   William L. Lane, *Hebrews 1-8*, WBC, ed. David A. Hubbard and Glenn W. Barker (General), Ralph P. Martin (New Testament), no. 47^A (Dallas: Word Books, 1991), 185.

could not produce perfect people; that was not their purpose. His point is not that the cultic laws were imperfect, but that they were perfect copies and perfect shadows of heavenly originals that would feature in the priestly work of Christ (Heb. 8:5, 9:23–4, 10:1).

How did he reach this conclusion? Not necessarily, as Kim claims, by starting with the solution and then identifying the problem, beginning with Jesus the perfect sacrifice and working backward to conclude that sacrifices were inadequate.[21] There would be nothing inherently wrong with such an approach, but it is more likely that he had a two-way thought process in which his understanding of the Old Testament informed his understanding of Jesus Christ. This becomes clear in Hebrews 10:5–9 where he uses a passage (Ps. 40:3–5) that typifies the Old Testament view of the primacy of morality over cult to support his view that God is ultimately unmoved by the blood of bulls and goats. The Pentateuch taught that 'sacrifice' is remedial obedience, not a casual alternative to 'mercy'. The prophets preached that sacrifice unaccompanied by obedience is hypocritical idolatry that God hates because it masks rebellion against him; he seeks humble obedience, not sheep and oxen. Hebrew's point, however, is not to launch an attack on hypocrisy, but to show that Jesus Christ supremely exemplified the primacy of morality by doing God's will, living the kind of life that God required and desired, a life that required no atoning sacrifice. Yet, paradoxically, the unique demands of God upon him meant that he would have to offer himself as a sacrifice 'once for all' (Heb. 10:10). His life proclaimed the desirability of doing God's will in contrast to the undesirability of sacrifice and burnt offering; his death proclaimed the abiding demands of mercy and morality, yet the end of sacrifice and offering. In using this strand of Old Testament teaching, Hebrews affirms, indeed

21   Kim, *Polemic in the Book of Hebrews*, 175.

depends upon prioritisation in the law and the treatment of 'ceremonial' laws as a distinctive component in the Mosaic code.

Also significant is the author's emphasis on the things prescribed by the law being copies (ὑπόδειγμα) and shadows (σκιά). Hebrews designates the tabernacle and its associated rituals as those shadows and copies (Heb. 8:5; 9:23; 10:1), not least because Moses was commanded to make everything 'according to the pattern' (Heb. 8:5) he saw on the mountain. According to Lee, ὑπόδειγμα signified not an 'example' (KJV) or a 'copy' (ESV, NIV), but only a 'glimpse'. The tabernacle and its ritual gave only 'a partial suggestion as distinct from a complete expression, a shadow as distinct from the reality of heaven…a rough reminiscence.'[22] This definition, however, adds a sense of blurriness that Hebrews does not unequivocally support. Something may give a partial expression or be a shadow without being 'rough', and other New Testament uses of ὑπόδειγμα suggest as much (John 13:15; Heb. 4:11). Even so, Hebrews 8:5 with its use of τύπος represents an exposition of Exodus 25:9 and 40 where תַּבְנִית ('pattern') suggests Moses saw a copy or plan of God's tabernacle rather than the original[23]—what Cassutto calls 'the likeness of the heavenly sanctuary'.[24] Rather like Ezekiel's vision of the 'appearance of the likeness of the glory of the Lord' (Ezek. 1:28), the tabernacle gave Israel a sight of the appearance of the likeness of the heavenly tabernacle, a view more remote than rough, more impenetrable than imprecise. Moving to Hebrews 10:1, the heavenly realities cast their shadow not only downwards, but also backwards. The ceremonial shadows proclaimed not only the existence of

22   E. Kenneth Lee, 'Words Denoting "Pattern" in the New Testament', *NTS* 8 (1961–2), 168.

23   See previous discussion on pages 107–113.

24   U. Cassuto, *A Commentary on the Book of Exodus*, trans. Israel Abrahams (Jerusalem: The Magnes Press, 1967), 327. Cassutto does not, as Propp incorrectly claims, suggest that Moses 'sees Yahweh's heavenly Tabernacle'. Propp, *Exodus 19–40*, 376.

'heavenly things', but also 'good things to come', namely the offering of Jesus, which would bring forgiveness and perfection to the sanctified (Heb. 10:10–15). When the good things come, there is a high priest, a sacrifice, and a holy place. He is greater than all who preceded him, his sacrifice is once for all, and the holy place is not made with hands. With the coming of reality, priests and sacrifice, along with the earthly tabernacle and all the laws that specifically proclaimed its existence in the midst of the people, must go. They were shadows and copies, something that cannot be said of the entire law. Of what could the second commandment against idolatry be a copy? Of what could the eighth commandment against theft be a shadow? Thus the people who have come to the 'heavenly Jerusalem' show that they are set apart to be holy, being marked not by what they eat or what they sacrifice, but by blameless behaviour, by obedience to those laws that were not 'shadows', and by a different kind of sacrifice (Heb. 12:12–13:16).

Hebrews is not the only epistle where those themes occur; Colossians 2:16–17 also brings together the vocabulary of shadows (σκιά) and things to come (μελλόντων). Questions concerning food and drink, a festival, a new moon or a sabbath are shadows of Christ. Martin judges that caution is in order before accepting a close link between those things and the Mosaic Law,[25] quoting with approval Moule's claim that in the union between Christ and the church 'all the great "realities" were found—pardon, sanctification, communion with God, etc.—of which ritual, whether Jewish or non-Jewish, was only a shadow.'[26] O'Brien is more specific suggesting that Paul is 'probably not' making direct reference to the Mosaic food laws or condemning the celebration of days unless observance is 'bound up with the

25 Ralph P. Martin, *Colossians: The Church's Lord and the Christian's Liberty* (Exeter: Paternoster Press, 1972), 90, n. 1.

26 Ibid., 91.

recognition of elemental spirits',[27] yet the 'things to come' must be interpreted from the standpoint of the Mosaic era—'Christ has arrived. The substance has already come. The regulations belonged to a transitory order, and have lost all binding force.'[28]

This variety of opinion stems in part from the view that Colossians is attacking an identifiable heresy or philosophy, variously defined as Jewish Gnosticism, Gnostic Judaism, Asectic Judaism, Hellenistic Syncretism, Hellenisitc Philosophy,[29] or Phrygian folk belief.[30] Swimming against the tide, Morna Hooker questions 'the theory that they are under attack by a specific group of teachers',[31] preferring to see Paul's teaching as a response to general pressure to conform to the ways of Colossian pagans and Jews, not least because Colossians makes no 'clear reference to the supposed error'.[32] The best that DeMaris can manage in response to Hooker is that the 'vast majority of scholars' disagree. This, however, would only be true if DeMaris qualified 'scholars' with 'recent' since (as he points out) this particular enterprise did not begin until 1879.[33] Scholars prior to the twentieth century,

27   Peter T. O'Brien, *Colossians, Philemon,*WBC, ed. David A. Hubbard and Glenn W. Barker (General), Ralph P. Martin (New Testament), no. 44 (Waco: Word Books, 1982), 138–9.
      Similarly Eduard Lohse, *Colossians and Philemon: A Commentary on the Epistles to the Colossians and to Philemon*, trans. William R. Poehlmann and Robert J. Karris (Philadelphia: Fortress Press, 1971), 115: 'The sacred days must be kept for the sake of "the elements of the universe," who direct the course of the stars', not because of any command of Torah.'

28   O'Brien, *Colossians, Philemon*, 140.

29   For a history of those ideas in the interpretation of Colossians see Richard E. DeMaris, *The Colossian Controversy: Wisdom in Dispute in Colossae* (Sheffield: JSOT, 1994), 18–40.

30   Clinton E. Arnold, *The Colossian Syncretism: The Interface Between Christianity and Folk Belief at Colossae* (Tübingen: J.C.B. Mohr, 1995).

31   Morna D. Hooker, *From Adam to Christ: Essays on Paul* (Cambridge: Cambridge University Press, 1990), 132.

32   Ibid., 134.

33   DeMaris, *Colossian Controversy*, 19, n.1.

particularly those who debated in the Jerusalem Chamber, would have had more sympathy with Hooker's demand for a 'clear reference' than with the hypothetical historicising of recent scholarship (even if those reconstructions would have enabled them to leap a hermeneutical hurdle by removing the passage from discussion of the threefold division). Pagan, Qumranian, Jewish, or other influences may have affected Colossian attitudes, but it is problematic to see the items in verse 16 as extra-Mosaic practices because they could not then function as shadows— something that becomes clear when commentators struggle to give a satisfying explanation of verse 17.[34] For this reason, the views mentioned above that non-Jewish ritual or syncretistic festivals were a shadow of Christian realities is untenable. The ritual practices of Israel's neighbours did sometimes encroach into Jewish worship, yet it would demand notable ingenuity to show, for example, that Colossians 2:16–17 viewed the use of cult prostitutes[35] or 'a magical/astrological interpretation of sabbaths'[36] as a shadow of things to come. It is also unlikely that Paul chose to attack a syncretised practice so indirectly that he focussed on the Mosaic component to the complete exclusion of any Pagan or folk elements. Verse sixteen therefore refers to Old Testament laws.

34   O'Brien, *Colossians, Philemon*, 138, 140: 'Paul is probably not referring to the OT food laws' yet shadow 'is to be interpreted from the period when the legal restrictions were enjoined; it is future from the standpoint of the OT.'

Arnold, *The Colossian Syncretism*, 221–2: 'In light of the present possibility of union with Christ, ritual observances, dietary regulations, and taboos motivated by fear of the hostile principalities and powers are wrong.'

DeMaris, *Colossian Controversy*, 63: 'Verse 17 simply registers his biting criticism of the praxis: the practices of v. 16 are a *mere* shadow; they obscure reality. Hence, the verse offers no clue as to what motivated the practices of v. 16.'

35   The practice was condemned by the prophets (Amos 2:7; Hos. 4:14). For further discussion see Helmer Ringgren, *Religions of the Ancient Near East*, trans. John Sturdy (London: SPCK, 1973), 167.

36   Arnold, *The Colossian Syncretism*, 218.

If this seems to produce a simple case of agreement with Hebrews and harmony with the teaching of the threefold division, where Colossians 2:16–17 refers to ceremonial laws as 'typical ordinances', then that is not the case. The first obstacle is that although 'food' could easily refer to Mosaic laws, 'drink' is judged to appear in only 'a few special cases'.[37] It is not clear, however, why Leviticus 11:34 should be a 'special case' and not an example of everyday uncleanness. In addition, 'drink offerings' were twice-daily accompaniments to the tabernacle offerings (Exod. 29:40–1), so 'drink' was not a peripheral component in the ceremonies of Israel. Nonetheless, Barth and Blanke are right to point out that βρῶσις and πόσις need not refer to specific foods so much as to the act of eating and drinking.[38] Other passages confirm this (Dan. 1:10 LXX; John 6:55), especially Romans 14:17, which brings the terms together following a discussion that focussed entirely on what is eaten, suggesting that it is reasonable to read Colossians 2:16 as referring in a general way to all dietary laws of the Old Testament.

The second difficulty is that although 'festival and new moon' could be a straightforward reference to the festivals prescribed in the law, 'sabbath' seems to refer to the fourth commandment, which raises the question, if it is a passing shadow then how can the category of law to which it belongs 'for ever bind all'? The nineteenth century Baptist expositor, Alexander MacLaren, attempted to resolve the problem by seeing this as a reference to the Jewish Sabbath, now replaced by the Lord's Day, which, in continuity with the pre-Mosaic principle of sabbath rest,

---

37   O'Brien, *Colossians, Philemon*, 138.

38   Markus Barth and Helmut Blanke, *Colossians: A New Translation with Introduction and Commentary*, trans. Astrid B. Beck (New York: Doubleday, 1994), 337. Also, Troy Martin, 'But Let Everyone Discern the Body of Christ (Colossians 2:17)', *JBL* 114/2 (1995), 255 n. 19: 'the words for eating and drinking here designate an activity.'

must be observed.[39] Perhaps he need not have worried because if De Lacey's view is typical of anti-sabbatarians, Colossians reveals 'that Paul could happily countenance Sabbath keeping; his attitude is that it, like many other things, does neither harm nor good.'[40]

It is not, however, self-evident that the fourth commandment is the target in Colossians. In the Mosaic Code, 'sabbath' could refer to more than the seventh day of the week. The Day of Atonement was a Sabbath (Lev. 23:32), as was every seventh year when the land lay fallow (Lev. 25:4). The prophets also illustrate that 'sabbath' does not always point strictly to the fourth commandment. God commanded Israel 'Keep *my* sabbaths' (Exod. 31:13; Lev. 19:3, 30; 26:2), but Hosea found himself responding to a situation in Israel where the holy days were so profaned that they had become uniquely '*her* sabbaths' (Hos. 2:11)—'days of Baal' (Hos. 2:13). God was going to bring their pluralism to an end—no more of their feast days, new moons, or sabbaths (Hos. 2:11). A simplistic equation between 'sabbath' and the fourth commandment is therefore inadequate, but what is most significant for the interpretation of Colossians 2:16 is that on the six other occasions where feasts, new moons, and sabbaths are grouped together in the Old Testament they are always bound up with offerings (1 Chron. 23:31; 2 Chron. 2:4, 8:13, 31:3; Neh. 10:33; Ezek. 45:17), suggesting that the term is concerned more with the sacrificial activity of those occasions than with the days themselves. This is clearest in Nehemiah 10:32 where the people oblige themselves to give a third part of shekel for the service of the house of God, which the expenditure breakdown in verse 33 details as outlays for showbread, offerings, sabbaths, new moons,

39   Alexander MacLaren, *The Epistles of St. Paul to Colossians and Philemon* (London: Hodder & Stoughton, 1892), 231–3.

40   D. R. De Lacey, 'The Sabbath/Sunday Question and the Law in the Pauline Corpus' in Carson, *Sabbath to Lord's Day*, 182–3.

and feasts. This only makes sense if sabbaths are not understood as a strict reference to the Decalogue commandment, where the rest enjoined was a universal command, not one exclusive to the Levitical order or one that carried financial obligations. In these contexts 'sabbaths' points not to the Sabbath commandment, but to ceremonial offerings and practices that were conducted on the Sabbath.[41] It is therefore most likely that just as the reference to food and drink designated an activity and served as shorthand for all the dietary laws, so feasts, new moons, and sabbaths serves as shorthand for the offerings and rituals common to those occasions. Taken together, all these things were the shadow of which Christ is the substance (σῶμα).

How σῶμα τοῦ Χριστοῦ should be translated is mired in controversy. Most translations take the expression as elliptical and supply the elided words, Troy Martin providing so many that he almost doubles the length of the verse.[42] For others, the issue is whether reality as opposed to shadow, the church, or both is in view.[43] The apparently literal use of σῶμα in the similar context of Hebrews 10:1–5 may raise the possibility of a similar meaning in Colossians,[44] but the primary issue for the threefold division is not the precise identification of σῶμα, but that Colossians 2:16–17 adopts standard expressions that delimit the ritual laws and views those laws as finding their true meaning with the coming of Christ.

---

41 For a discussion of what exactly happened on the Sabbath see Heather Mackay, *Sabbath and Synagogue: The Question of Sabbath Worship in Ancient Judaism* (Leiden: E. J. Brill, 1994), 11–42. Concerning non-priestly Jews her view is that 'the evidence of the Hebrew Bible alone, is solely of a faithfully observed and revered sabbath of rest. Only the sabbath of the priests include a set of rituals to be carried out in the Temple' (42). This would support the view that it is not the universally binding Decalogue commandment that texts such as Nehemiah 10:32–3 have in view.

42 Martin, 'Let Everyone Discern', 254.

43 O'Brien, *Colossians, Philemon*, 140–41.

44 A literal use already occurs in Colossians 1:22.

Identifying δόγμα

Paul's grounds for not allowing anyone to judge Colossian Christians on the basis of food or drink depended not only on them being shadows, but also on what he establishes in the preceding two verses (Col. 2:14–15): Christ has done away with χειρόγραφον—something that almost no English translations render in precisely the same way.[45] This troublesome noun signifies a handwritten document, a record of debt or of legal charges. It is followed by the dative τοῖς δόγμασιν, which points to regulations or decrees, and in doing so forces Barth and Blanke to rely on context (or perhaps theology) for their translation because 'the best grammatical solution' suggests the Mosaic Law has been wiped away (if the dative belongs to the verb).[46] Urging caution about seeing the law as the meaning of δόγμασιν, they connect it with the 'demands' of verse 16, only to explain those as an allusion to the law.[47] Dunn also rejects an identification of χειρόγραφον with the law, yet finds the 'awkward' τοῖς δόγμασιν 'leaves the precise relationship obscure' and the law is behind it somewhere.[48] One hundred years before Dunn, Abbot was less troubled about making a straightforward identification with the Mosaic Law, deciding that the difficult dative should be closely connected with χειρόγραφον.[49] John Calvin also identified the law, with the qualification that χειρόγραφον refers specifically

45   For example: 'the record of debt that stood against us with its legal demands' (ESV); 'the handwriting of ordinances that was against us, which was contrary to us' (KJV); 'the written code, with its regulations, that was against us and that stood opposed to us' (NIV).

46   Barth and Blanke, *Colossians*, 328–30.

47   Ibid., 338.

48   James D. G. Dunn, *The Epistles to Colossians and Philemon: A Commentary on the Greek Text* (Grand Rapids: Eerdmans, 1996), 165

49   T. K. Abbott, *The Epistles to the Ephesians and to the Colossians* (Edinburgh: T. & T. Clark, 1897), 255.

to ceremonies that leave us unable to deny our guilt, but Christ has 'effaced the remembrance of this obligation' and the debtor is set free. Those who urge observance of ceremonies detract from Christ's grace and 'restore to the *hand-writing* its freshness'.[50] This, he believed, was confirmed by Paul's only other use of δόγμασιν in Ephesians 2:15,[51] which some recent commentators call a clearer formulation.[52] How Colossians 2:14 should be translated will probably be a matter of interminable debate, but realistically, context, itself determined by other presuppositions such as the existence of a 'Colossian Heresy', will determine opinions. Working backwards from our interpretation of Colossians 2:16–17, and accepting that Ephesians 2:15 is expressing related ideas, it is reasonable to attempt an interpretation of the phrase as it is expressed in the old English translations: 'the handwriting of ordinances'.

This requires a diversion to Ephesians 2:14–15, which proclaims that Christ, our peace, has broken down the dividing wall of hostility between Jew and Gentile, having abolished in his flesh 'the law of commandments in ordinances'. But what does the dividing wall signify? According to Yee, 'the mass of NT scholarly opinion'[53] considers Ephesians 2:14–18 (approximately)[54] to be comprised of reworked hymnic material. Lincoln belongs to that mass. He presents a reconstructed hymn in which the dividing wall refers to 'a cosmic wall' between heaven and earth—an idea that appears in pre-Ephesian Judaism and post-

---

50   John Calvin, *Commentaries on the Epistles of Paul the Apostle to the Philippians, Colossians, and Thessalonians*, trans. John Pringle (Edinburgh: Calvin Translation Society, 1851), 188.

51   Ibid., 189.

52   Dunn, *Colossians and Philemon*, 165; Lohse, *Colossians*, 109, n. 107.

53   Tet-Lim N. Yee, *Jews, Gentiles and Ethnic Reconciliation: Paul's Jewish Identity and Ephesians* (Cambridge: Cambridge University Press, 2005), 127.

54   No unanimity exists on the extent of the hymnic form.

Ephesian Gnosticism.[55] Not everyone is willing to accept such conjectured reconstructions. Yee outlines 'severe criticism'[56] of the hymnic theory and Moritz claims that the scholarly mass behind the notion has been greatly exaggerated.[57] It is, in any case, not clear how an original 'cosmic wall' could relate to a wall dividing Jew and Gentile. Other unsatisfactory proposals for the dividing wall refer it to the temple curtain or to the temple wall that formed a barrier to Gentiles. In the context of these verses, however, it is not possible to avoid a connection with the Mosaic Law: the breaking down of the wall and the abolition of the 'law of commandments in the sphere of [its] ordinances'[58] coincide. But what is the scope of the legal material and what is its relationship to the wall? Was it the wall of hostility or was it simply the Jews 'wrong conception and use of the law'[59] that brought hostility?

Consistent with the anti-Sabbatarian views he expressed in *From Sabbath to Lord's Day*, Lincoln is hostile to the idea that anything other than the whole law could be in view, dismissing any identification of ceremonial law as a 'dogmatic gloss'.[60] The lengthy phrase, τὸν νόμον τῶν ἐντολῶν ἐν δόγμασιν, expresses a sense of the entire law's oppressiveness; the whole

---

55   Andrew T. Lincoln, *Ephesians,*WBC, ed. David A. Hubbard and Glenn W. Barker (General), Ralph P. Martin (New Testament), no. 42 (Waco: Word Books, 1990), 128–9, 141.

56   Yee, *Jews, Gentiles and Ethnic Reconcoliation*, 128–31.

57   Thorsten Moritz, *A Profound Mystery: the Use of the Old Testament in Ephesians* (Lieden: E. J. Brill, 1996), 25–9.

58   This is the translation proposed by Joosten because one of the functions of the preposition ἐν is to delimit the sphere in which a process is accomplished. Jan Joosten, 'Christ a-t-il aboli la loi pour réconcilier Juifs et Païens?' *ETR* 80 (2005): 95–102. (I was unable to obtain a hardcopy of this article, but I am grateful to Professor Joosten for sending me a copy by email.)

59   Harold W. Hoehner, *Ephesians: An Exegetical Commentary* (Grand Rapids: Baker Academic, 2002), 374.

60   Lincoln, *Ephesians*, 142.

law created division that could only be removed if Christ dealt with its cause—'the law itself'.[61] Lincoln (along with Hoehner),[62] however, applies his own 'dogmatic gloss'. The unquestioned rules that 'apply to every time and place'[63] and the 'self-understood' things of legal history[64] did not divide Jew and Gentile. Differences between the civil laws of Israel and those of surrounding nations, for example in the comparative humaneness of Mosaic penology,[65] did not create partition any more than Singapore's now-relaxed ban on chewing-gum created a dividing wall between Singaporeans and the rest of the world.[66] Israel learned that her experience of receiving the law was unique (Deut. 4:33), but Ephesians is concerned with content that divides and not the mode of its revelation. What did separate Jew from Gentile was those laws, categorized by the theme of separation, that were specifically ordained to signify Israel's separation to God and regulate their approach to a God whose separation was signified by the inner veil (Exod. 26:33; Lev. 20:24–6).

Joosten thinks it improbable that the whole law would be abolished in order to reconcile Jew and Gentile as that would have forced a totalitarian regime upon Jews—Christ cannot be drawn in the image of Antiochus IV Epiphanes (1 Mac. 1:41–3).[67] Antiquity bears witness to social laws as a source of enmity, so

61   Ibid.

62   Hoehner, *Ephesians*, 376.

63   Carmichael, *Law and Narrative*, 314.

64   Daube, 'Self-understood', 128.

65   The Code of Hammurabi provides examples: Hands cut off for striking one's father, a nurse's breast to be cut off over contractual disagreements, and different standards for rich and poor. See: James B. Pritchard, 'The Code of Hammurabi', *Ancient Near Eastern Texts* (Princeton, Princeton University Press, 1969), 175, laws 195, 194, 203–5.

66   'Singapore to partly lift gum ban' Available from news.bbc.co.uk/2/hi/uk_news/3512498.stm; accessed 10 June 2008.

67   Joosten, 'Christ a-t-il aboli la loi'.

Ephesians has in view 'expansions' of the law that 'do not appear in the Torah, but they were decreed by the sages. Historically, they make their first appearance in the intertestamental literature.'[68] While this theory sounds plausible, Joosten's elaboration of a parallel[69] between Ephesians 2 and Acts 10 eventually highlights the weakness of identifying δόγμασιν as extra-Mosaic laws, since, as he points out, 'It is God himself who changes the law in abolishing the clauses concerned.'[70] If, however, decrees of the sages were the ordinances in view then it is more likely that Ephesians would simply adopt the dismissive stance recorded elsewhere (Isa. 29:13; Matt. 15:9; Heb. 13:9) rather than creating the strange situation where 'une initiative divine' is required to abolish laws that, not being of divine origin in the first place, did not exist in the divine economy. The abolition of such laws may be a necessary consequence of the argument in Ephesians 2, yet they fall not as targets, but as collateral damage (for which no apology will follow).

Yee agrees that Ephesians does not speak of the whole law. He prefers to develop his understanding from verses 11–13 and focus on circumcision as the law to which the Jews rally as their boundary marker.[71] The enmity this has created does not lie with the law itself; it is the 'human attitude that perverted the gifts of God into signs of separation and exclusiveness.'[72] It is possible that Ephesus witnessed such perversions of the law, nonetheless, the laws bound up with Israel's separateness were signs of Israel's

---

68 Ibid. 'Elles ne figurent pas dans la Torah, mais elles ont été édictées par les sages. Historiquement, elles font leur apparence pour la première fois dans la littérature intertestamentaire.'

69 He describes this in terms of mutual illumination rather than literary: 'les deux textes s'illuminent mutuellement.'

70 '...c'est Dieu lui-même qui change la loi en abolissant les clauses concernées.'

71 Yee, *Jews, Gentiles and Ethnic Reconcoliation*, 150, 160.

72 Ibid., 160–61.

separation by design, not by perversion. Indeed, the laws were not the gifts, but signs of the gift, which Leviticus unashamedly attributes to the elective generosity of God: 'I…separated you' (Lev. 20:24–6). The Gentiles were at one time 'separated', 'alienated', and 'far away' from God (Eph. 2:12–13), not because of Jewish perversity, but because God did not choose them. Only the God who made this separation could remove it, which he did in Christ Jesus, removing the wall, making the two one, bringing peace and undifferentiated reconciliation with God to Gentiles who were 'far off' or to Jews who were 'near' (Eph. 2:14–18). This meant that, like Peter in Acts 10, the Ephesian Christians had to grasp that the abolition of food distinctions went together with God's expansion of his household (Eph. 2:19). Jewish-Gentile enmity has to go because the inner veil has gone—both have access to the Father by one Spirit (Eph. 2:18); Israel is no longer separated to God—he will dwell in the midst of one undivided temple (Eph. 2:19–22); Christ has discharged the law of commandments in ordinances—he has eliminated the separation to which they bore witness.

Putting Ephesians 2 and Colossians 2 side by side, it appears that they are dealing with the same type of laws. Ephesians emphasises more the aspect of separation of Jew and Gentile that was concomitant with the cultic laws, Colossians stresses the previously outstanding demand for satisfaction of sin's debt of which the sacrifices were a constant reminder, but both epistles depend on the argument that Christ's work means such laws no longer bind. To restore them would be to attempt to reinstate the dividing wall and negate the peace with God that Jew and Gentile share together. To insist on the reinstatement of any of the laws that regulated Israel's approach to the God behind the veil would be to act as if the sacrificial system's call for atonement had not been answered, restoring 'to the *hand-writing* its freshness', and marking a return to the shadows.

As a balance to this, it is worth noting an epistolary echo of the policy highlighted in our discussion of the apostolic decree, which, though not crucial to the independent categorisation of ceremonial laws, gives further insight into the apostolic approach. The Jerusalem Council laid down temporary accommodations, motivated by compassion, which gave the church an example of how Christians should behave when they are at variance over their understanding of what is written. Hebrews, Ephesians, and Colossians express their absolute conviction that the shadows of ceremonial observance and cultic separation have fled away. Romans 14 also gives this view a double restatement (v. 14, 20) and forbids the imposition of food and festival regulations (v. 3), but in the context of a chapter where the emphasis is on showing love (v. 15) for Jewish brothers who feel unable to jettison their observance of those customs. The whole argument represents a partially inverted application of the long-established principle of the primacy of morality over cult: in such situations the summarizing second-greatest commandment, which he has just quoted in Romans 13:9, requires temporary observance of cultic regulations, not because they have ceased to be shadows, but because peace and mutual edification are primary (v. 19).

This does not mean, however, that such a principle could be applied without restriction. Ongoing apostolic adherence to the primacy of morality is not in question. In fact, it may underpin 1 Corinthians 13 where Paul describes the loveless multilinguist as an unpleasant racket. Although his mention of gongs and cymbals could allude to the din of pagan worship in Corinth,[73] such conclusions presuppose that the primary requirement to picking up on the apostle's references is a detailed knowledge of Corinthian culture, whereas the Old Testament background to his thought is of greater relevance. Even if the cymbal

73   Gordon D. Fee, *The First Epistle to the Corinthians* (Grand Rapids: Eerdmans, 1987), 632; Leon Morris, *The First Epistle of Paul to the Corinthians* (Leicester: Inter-Varsity Press, 1985), 178.

(κύμβαλον) 'was an "instrument" expressly associated with the pagan cults',[74] is it not significant that it is primarily associated with temple worship (e.g. LXX 1 Chron. 15:16, 19, 28; Ezra 3:10; Ps. 150:5)? And given Amos' expression of divine contempt for such noise (Amos 5:21–4), is this not a more likely allusion in Paul's opening comment? However gifted someone may be, if they have not love, their life is an offering no more acceptable to God than was all the sacrifice and music of temple worship when it was unaccompanied by mercy; mercy that was ultimately no different to the love that Paul describes in this chapter. Yet, such neigbour love could not go beyond temporary observance of food and festivals to encompass sacrifice. Hebrews is adamant in its warnings that the sacrifice of Christ was a 'once for all' offering (Heb. 7:27; 10:12) and there must be no drawing back from worship that approaches God on that basis (Heb. 10:36–9). The writer would not have offered ongoing sacrifice as an option for the 'weak' of Romans 14 (Heb. 10:18); the only alternative to the blood of Jesus is raging fire (Heb. 10:26–7).

'A Lamb without Blemish'

In a previous chapter I argued that Jesus' fulfilment of the law and the prophets in Matthew 5:17 was eschatological, soteriological, and moral. He fulfilled the law by his person and teaching, by his obedience, and in making his followers obedient. These interrelated themes emerge again when the apostolic writings refer to Jesus' death in language that recalls the Mosaic sacrificial system. His perfect moral fulfilment of the law meant that he was the one to whom the sacrifices pointed and who had ransomed his people to live holy lives. Large sections of Hebrews (7:26–8; 9:1–10:39) and several texts in the epistles repeat those themes (1 Pet. 1:13–19; 2:21–4; 1 Cor. 5:7; Gal. 4:4–5; Eph. 5:2; 1 John 2:2;

---

74   Fee, Corinthians, 632.

4:10; Rev. 5:6, 12; 7:14; 13:8). They are too numerous to examine in individual detail, but the examples from 1 Peter bring the key fulfilment themes together, so they may serve as a sample.

The immediate problem with the passages from 1 Peter is that they (particularly chapter two) are widely regarded as being rooted in—'probably the most contested chapter in the Old Testament'[75]—Isaiah 53, which describes the grief-bearing, sorrow-carrying servant who is wounded, crushed, and chastised for others. Sinless, yet silent, he goes like a lamb to the slaughter, making an offering for guilt, bearing iniquity, causing many to be found righteous. Controversy surrounds several issues in the passage, such as the identification of persons, but key disputes relevant to this subject focus on sin-offering and vicarious suffering. Immanuel Kant is generally credited with promoting the idea that guilt is non-transferable,[76] which resulted in interpreters finding the idea of *Stellvertretung* (place-taking) 'theologically simply unthinkable'[77] and proposing various solutions.[78] Even if Kant's 1793 publication marked some kind

75   Brevard S. Childs, *Isaiah* (Louisville: Westminster John Knox Press, 2001), 410.

76   See discussion in Bernd Janowski, 'He Bore Our Sins' in Bernd Janowski and Peter Stuhlmacher eds., *The Suffering Servant: Isaiah 53 in Jewish and Christian Sources,* trans. Daniel P. Bailey (Grand Rapids: Eerdmans, 2004), 50–52. Also Daniel P. Bailey, 'Concepts of *Stellvertretung* in the Interpretation of Isaiah 53' in William H. Bellinger, Jr. and William R. Farmer, *Jesus and the Suffering Servant: Isaiah 53 and Christian Origins* (Harrisburg: Trinity Press International, 1998), 232–4.

77   Otfried Hofius, 'The Fouth Servant Song in the New Testament Letters' in Janowski and Stuhlmacher, *The Suffering Servant,* 172. Hofius' view is not based only on Kantian presuppositions but on his exegesis of Psalm 51.

78   Hofius chooses '"*inclusive* place-taking" (German: *inkludierende Stellvertretung*). Christ takes the place of sinners in such a way that he does not displace them (as in the substitutionary model) but rather encompasses them as *persons* and affects them in their very being.' Ibid., 173. Morna D. Hooker argued for '*representative suffering* rather than *vicarious suffering*' in her article 'Did the Use of Isaiah 53 to Interpret His Mission Begin with Jesus?' in Bellinger and Farmer, *Jesus and the Suffering Servant,* 98.

of hermeneutical watershed, the question arose well before his day. In the previous century we find John Owen seeking to provide exegetical support for his argument that 'it is not contrary to the nature of divine justice…that in sundry cases some persons should suffer punishment for the sins and offences of others.'[79] The passages Owen expounds[80] do at least make the point that Scripture's presentation of divine government presents the same stumbling block for anyone who recoils at notions of substitution. To his catalogue might also be added Genesis 15:6, which presents the same difficulty in reverse with God in some sense counting Abraham to be what he was not—righteous.[81]

The crucial question for the threefold division concerns the background to Isaiah 53—does it lie in the Mosaic Law? According to Spieckermann it is impossible to find a 'prefabricated' prehistory for the fourth servant song.[82] He builds on Zimmerli's claim that Ezekiel influences the language of Isaiah 53, but his leading reason for rejecting the link is that Leviticus was 'in all probability written after Isaiah 53'.[83] This would have been mildly startling to those who throughout church history have accepted the threefold division. Many of them, not least the Westminster Divines, would also have rejected Hofius' rule that the Old Testament texts 'may not and must not be understood' as having 'an *excess* of meaning that remained concealed from the original authors and bearers of the tradition' such that 'the fourth

79   Owen, *Glory of Christ*, 139.

80   Exod. 20:5, Lam. 5:7, 2 Kgs 23:26-7, Luke 11:50-51, Gen. 9:25, 2 Sam. 21:9-14; 24:15-17, 1 Kgs 21:29.

81   This appears to be the sense of חָשַׁב in Genesis 15 and the two following occurrences in Genesis—Rachel and Leah counted foreigners by their own father (31:15) and Tamar counted a prostitute by Judah (38:15).

82   Herman Spieckermann, 'The Conception and Prehistory of the Idea of Vicarious Suffering in Janowski and Stuhlmacher, *The Suffering Servant*, 16.

83   Ibid., 3.

Servant Song acquires a sense that was *not* originally its own.'[84] They would have seen Jesus to be taking a rather different view (Matt. 13:17; Luke 10:24), one that Peter adopted (1 Pet. 1:10–12) and which controlled his use of Isaiah 53. From that perspective it is not difficult to see Peter viewing the cultic law through the lens of Isaiah 53 so that Isaiah's revelation shortens the shadows that will disappear when the Son rises.

The mere acceptance of a link between 1 Peter, Isaiah 53, and the Mosaic Law does not, however, automatically show that the idea of substitution is a common thread. Along with others influenced by the atonement theology of Gese[85] (long 'considered an assured result in Tübingen')[86] Spieckermann precludes the possibility that Leviticus suffers any notion of the transfer of sins.[87] In his chapter on the atonement, Gese is determined to establish a gulf between the concept of atonement and Leviticus 16:21–2. This leads to the contradictory theory that Aaron's performance with the scapegoat depicts not a 'transferal of sins, but a continuation of the subject in a delegated succession',[88] yet represents 'a removal of sin. It is a rite of elimination.'[89] How removal can take place without transfer and how the positive idea of continuation (he cites 27:18, 23; Deut. 34:9) can be applied to sin is unclear. More significantly, the activity of atonement does not finish (as Mary Douglas claims)[90] when the tabernacle and its furnishings are atoned for (Lev. 16:20), but

---

84   Hofius, 'The Fourth Servant Song', 188.

85   Harmut Gese, *Essays on Biblical Theology*, trans. Keith Crim (Minneapolis: Augsburg, 1981), 93–116.

86   Bailey, 'Concepts of *Stellvertretung*', 243.

87   Spieckermann, 'Conception and Prehistory', 2–4.

88   Gese, *Essays*, 105.

89   Ibid., 122.

90   Mary Douglas, 'The Go-Away Goat' in Rolf Rendtorff and Robert A. Kugler, eds., *The Book of Leviticus: Composition and Reception* (Leiden: Brill, 2003), 128.

with the return of the men from outside the camp (Lev. 16:26–8).
The live goat is central to proceedings throughout. Aaron must
'make atonement upon it' (Lev. 16:10), which is inseparable
from the unavoidable transfer of 'all of Israel's sins, ritual and
moral alike, of priests and laity alike'[91] to the substitute.[92] Far
from being 'unthinkable', 'place-taking' is central to Leviticus
and the substitution concept expressed in Isaiah 53 might not
have come as a complete shock to the Aaronic line. Once this
is granted, a general adoption and development of Mosaic Laws
on sacrifice appears likely in Isaiah 53. It is no more necessary to
identify precise 'analogy between a slain animal and the suffering
servant'[93] in Isaiah than it is to identify precise analogies when the
book of Hebrews applies sacrificial theology to Christ. From the
perspective of New Testament declarations about prophecy and
Isaiah's own proclamations of God-wrought incomprehension
(Isa. 6:4–6), some measure of mystery might be expected. That
all the language of sin bearing, substitution, and offering is rolled
into the fourth Servant Song was sufficient reason for Christians
to hear it as Isaiah's orchestration of a Mosaic theme.

The fulfilment of ceremonial law described in 1 Peter depends
first on Christ's moral fulfilment of the law when he is described
as the lamb without blemish or spot (1 Pet. 1:19). The lamb (ἀμνός)
need not be tied to the Passover lamb but can be taken as a general
reference to the scores of Pentateuchal references to sacrificial
lambs, all of which had to be unblemished (ἄμωμος). This
vocabulary is not restricted to the physical condition of animals, it
also conveys the idea of moral purity and law-keeping, especially
throughout the Psalms (Ps. 15:2; 18:22–3, 30; 19:7, 13; 37:18) and
elsewhere in the New Testament (Heb. 9:14). First Peter 2:22–3

91   Milgrom, *Leviticus 1–16*, 1044.

92   For further discussion of transference in the text and in the wider ANE
see Milgrom, *Leviticus 1–16*, 1041–3. Also Frank H. Gorman, Jr., *The Ideology of
Ritual: Space, Time and Status in the Priestly Theology* (Sheffield: JSOT, 1990).

93   Childs, *Isaiah*, 418.

goes on to expound the lamb metaphor with its description of Christ in language that reflects Isaiah's characterisation of the silently suffering servant (Isa. 53:7, 9). His perfection was not restricted to speech or reactions—he simply 'committed no sin', making him an acceptable offering to God, which he became when he 'bore our sins in his body on the tree' (1 Pet. 2:24). His wounding on the cross brings healing that is simultaneous with those who have wandered from God and his laws[94] returning to him and coming back under his oversight (1 Pet. 2:25). Their former wanderings were futile and ignorant, but Christ has redeemed them with his 'precious blood' (1 Pet. 1:14, 18–19). In the Pentateuch, return to God implies obedience (Deut. 30:2, 8, 10); in Peter, it is an implication and an imperative. The basis for his renewed proclamation of the divine command, 'Be holy as I am holy' (1 Pet. 1:15–16), rests upon Christ bearing the sin of others and becoming the sacrificial lamb whose blood buys their freedom. He is the example of the kind of holiness they must emulate in speech and conduct (1 Pet. 2:1, 11–25). In this way Peter presents Christ as the fulfiller of the sacrifices and offerings of the Old Testament. This does not amount to tracing intricate lines from the details of Mosaic legislation to specific aspects of the work of Christ. Instead, it represents a general gathering up of the sacrificial laws where broad themes, such as substitution and redemption, find their fulfilment in Christ Jesus. Whatever the nuances of particular passages, this extensive rather than intensive approach to Christ's fulfilment of the law is representative of the New Testament as a whole. The Westminster Divines were not misrepresenting its teaching when they claimed that God gave 'ceremonial laws…prefiguring Christ, His graces, actions, sufferings, and benefits'. Although his fulfilment of those laws was primarily soteriological, it depended upon his

---

94   This is frequently the meaning of πλαναω (e.g. Deut. 4:19, 11:28, 13:5, 30:17; Ps. 58:3, 119:10).

moral fulfilment of the whole law, and this combined moral and soteriological fulfilment demands and achieves eschatological fulfilment in the Christ-likeness of his chosen and holy people.

'Divers instructions of moral duties'

One final feature of the confessional explanation of the ceremonial category focuses on the law's demand for moral obedience. Even if the threefold division categorizes certain laws as essentially ceremonial, it recognises a moral aspect to those laws and treats them as subservient to morality. While proof-texts do not reveal the sole basis for confessional statements, they do give some indication of what various 'instructions of moral duties' might point to. *The Westminster Confession's* references to 1 Corinthians 5:7 and 2 Corinthians 6:17 suggest that the divines primary focus was the implied moral demands of ceremonial law rather than ethical stipulations that appeared within laws categorized as ceremonial.

First Corinthians 5 records Paul's response to the Corinthian's willingness to judge the apostolic leaders while they were unwilling to judge a man who was in a sexual relationship with his stepmother. This evil has flourished in the soil of their boasting and conceit (1 Cor. 5:2, 6) and verses 6b–8 record the apostle's call to the church to make a clean break with ways of thinking and behaviour that marked what they were, rather than what they are:

> Do you not know that a little leaven leavens the whole lump? Cleanse out the old leaven, so that you may be a new lump—as you are unleavened. For Christ, our Passover, has been sacrificed. Therefore let us celebrate the festival, not with the old leaven, the leaven of malice and evil, but with the unleavened bread of purity and truth.

This recalls the story of the Passover in Exodus 12 and assumes a close connection between Passover and the Feast of

Unleavened Bread. For seven days following the Passover, the Israelites were to eat unleavened bread and to ensure that their homes were leaven-free (Exod. 12:15). The idea that unleavened bread was simply 'bread made without yeast' (NIV) is slightly misleading since leaven was a lump of dough kept over from the previous day that would be added to the next batch of dough causing the bread to rise.[95] Although the Passover had to be eaten 'in haste' (Exod. 12:11) it is unlikely that the bread had to be unleavened for that reason; time-saving in the kitchen does not seem to have affected the Passover menu in other ways.[96] Leaven may have been 'a metaphor for evil and corruption',[97] yet this does not mean as Segal suggests that unleavened bread was a sign warning that neglect of ritual cleanness 'might be fraught with grave consequences in the ensuing year',[98] or that the practice (at harvest time) was motivated by 'the avoidance of impurity'.[99] It is more likely that the break in continuity symbolized simply that—discontinuity and a break with the past for Israel.[100] God's command, 'Observe the Feast of Unleavened Bread for on this very day I brought you out of the land of Egypt' (Exod. 12:17), suggests that the unleavened bread was to be a repeated reminder that at the Passover they had broken their links with Egypt and were to live in marked discontinuity with its ways, a theme that is explicitly repeated elsewhere in the Pentateuch (Lev. 18:3).

It is this symbolism that re-emerges in 1 Corinthians. Christ

95   See W. Dommershausen, 'לֶחֶם leḥem' in TDOT, vol. 7, 522.

96   For a summary of scholarly theories about the origins and development of Passover see Tamara Prosic, *The Development and Symbolism of Passover until 70 CE* (London: T&T Clark International, 2004), 19–32. 'There is,' she concludes, 'hardly any consensus among scholars.' 32.

97   Mary Douglas, *Leviticus as Literature* (Oxford, Oxford University Press, 1999), 164.

98   J. B. Segal, *The Hebrew Passover from the Earliest Times to A.D. 70* (London: Oxford University Press, 1963), 169.

99   Ibid., 180.

100   See John L. Mackay, *Exodus* (Fearn: Mentor, 2001), 213–4.

has been sacrificed as their Passover so they must now celebrate
the feast and cleanse out the old leaven. This is not an exclusive
reference to the immoral man,[101] nor is stamping out sexual
immorality 'the burden of the entire epistolary unity (vv. 1, 13)'[102]
since the old leaven is defined as all 'malice and evil'. Even a little
of this was too much; it leavens the whole lump. This does not
mean that the 'sinister side to fermentation'[103] that Mary Douglas
and others observe couples with a notion of sin's contagiousness
to determine Paul's argument, not least because it might then
make good sense to leave the world (1 Cor. 5:10). The point is
that just as there must be absolute discontinuity between the old
dough and a new lump for bread to be unleavened, so there must
be a clean break between the Corinthians and their former ways.
Everything that belongs to their old way of life must go, not least
the 'arrogance' and 'boasting' that infects the Corinthian church
and makes it an incubator for immorality. Just as Egyptian ways
were incongruous in Israel after the Passover, evil ways had no
place in the church after the sacrifice of Christ, our Passover.
Contagion was not the issue—they really were unleavened,
but they had to become what they were. Cleansing out the 'old
leaven' would also produce right acting in the case Paul mentions;
'purity and truth' would testify to their redemption and mark
them out as 'a new lump'.

In referring to Passover and unleavened bread, 1 Corinthians
assumes that not a jot or tittle has passed from the laws concerning
those feasts in terms of their fundamental significance. The
record of the annual reminder to God's people of discontinuity
between what they were and what they are becomes a constant
reminder. The festival continues not in observation of the ancient

---

101   As argued by Raymond F. Collins, *First Corinthians* (Minnesota,
Liturgical Press, 1999), 214. Also John Paul Heil, *The Rhetorical Role of Scripture
in 1 Corinthians* (Atlanta: Society of Biblical Literature, 2005), 97.

102   Ibid., 215.

103   Douglas, *Leviticus*, 164.

forms, but in the steady pursuit of the substance to which the forms pointed. A similar approach materializes in other passages that cite or allude to the law such as 2 Corinthians 6:14–18 or 1 Peter 1:16 where the aim is to promote the distinctiveness and moral purity signified by the ritual forms rather than to promote observance of the forms themselves. In this, the apostolic writers seek to preserve inviolate the core significance of the ritual laws, while at the same time maintaining that they are no longer binding. It is in recognition of this that the confessional formulation included in its definition of ceremonial laws 'divers instructions of moral duties'.

Section Summary

Christians almost universally agree that the ceremonial laws of the Mosaic Law are no longer binding, sometimes because they take them to be part of an indistinguishable mass of redundant legislations, sometimes because, like the Westminster Divines, they see them as a definable category of 'typical ordinances'. Justification for acceptance of this long-established categorisation emerges in the apostolic writings' delimitation of certain laws as copies and shadows and in Ephesians' recognition of a category of law that created a separation now abolished in Christ. That ceremonial laws prefigured Christ is reflected in the New Testament's proclamation of Christ as a substitute who provided extensive fulfilment of the law. Although those laws are now abrogated, Christ gives new voice to their call for moral purity and holiness.

'JUDICIAL LAWS'

Apart from a vociferous troop of theonomists who argue that Mosaic civil law is applicable in all ages, most Christians accept that the judicial laws are no longer binding. Those who disagree

296 FROM THE FINGER OF GOD

with theonomists, are unlikely to take issue over the nature of
God, but concerning 'the way in which the Old Testament is
applied to people today.'[104] Bahnsen reasoned that 'something
that was sinful in the Old Testament is likewise sinful in the New
Testament',[105] so all 'standing laws' remain morally binding today
'unless they are rescinded or modified by further revelation.'[106]
He used the term 'standing laws' to distinguish laws enshrined in
the Mosaic code from commands that applied on one occasion.
A great mass of Christian teachers down through the ages would
agree that all 'standing laws' remain binding, except that for
them the 'standing laws' would be the Ten Commandments. This
book has argued that the church had biblical and theological
justification for viewing judicial laws as having temporal standing
'in the land'. It is not necessary to repeat those arguments here or
to discuss theonomy in detail, only to ask if the apostolic writings
agree with those earlier conclusions. This means discussing New
Testament use of judicial laws and wider theological issues that
might have an impact on Christian attitudes to laws that were
outside the Ten Commandments, yet not explicitly shadows or
ceremonies. That such laws fall into a category of 'judicial law'
happens almost by default in that the epistles deal distinctly with
ceremonial laws and with the Decalogue, yet have very little to
say about the remainder of the Mosaic Law.

The Westminster Confession of Faith reflects this, giving only 35
out of 532 words on the law to judicial law. While not providing
an exhaustive basis for their view that judicial laws 'expired' with
the ancient Israelite state, their proof-texts may once more give
some hints as to their reasoning. In selecting Genesis 49:10, they

104   Dan G. McCartney, 'The New Testament Use of the Pentateuch:
Implications for the Theonomic Movement' in William S. Barker and W.
Robert Godfrey, eds., *Theonomy: A Reformed Critique* (Michigan: Academie
Books, 1994), 129.
105   Bahnsen, *By This Standard*, 44.
106   Ibid., 345–6.

again chose a text that leaves scholars searching for words. It is, according to Moran, 'perhaps the most famous *crux interpretum* in the entire Old Testament.'[107] The text records Jacob's promise to Judah that the sceptre and staff would not depart from Judah 'until Shiloh come'. Although there are many interpretative difficulties with this text[108] and with the place of Shiloh in Scripture,[109] the promise has a long history of Messianic interpretation and would have been interpreted in this way by the Westminster Divines. While the Messianic interpretation of the text merits investigation—especially the link with Ezekiel 21:32(27) along with the possibility of a connection between Ezekiel 21:31(26) and the Magnificat (Luke 1:52)—it is not vital to their argument. The crucial point is that they saw the coming of the Messiah as having an impact upon Judah as ruler and lawgiver,[110] such that laws specifically related to the 'body politic' under his sceptre had expired. This is a necessary implication of some previous conclusions in this book. If Matthew 5 presents Christ's fulfilment of the law as partly eschatological so that Jeremiah's new covenant promises are partly fulfilled when Emmanuel causes the law to be written on the hearts of 'disciples of all nations', then the law has now permanently breached the borders of Israel. Unless the Messiah had defined his reign as rule over a new global super-state, then whatever portion of the law specifically regulated Judah's body politic no longer had the same function. With the Messiah's coming, the 'statutes and ordinances' that were to be

---

107   W. L. Moran, 'Gen 49,10 and its Use in Ez 23,32', *Biblica* 39 (1958), 405.

108   For a comprehensive discussion see Victor P. Hamilton, *The Book of Genesis: Chapters 18–50* (Grand Rapids: Eerdmans, 1995), 658–61.

109   A summary of nineteenth and twentieth century discussion of Shiloh can be found in Donald G. Schley, *Shiloh: A Biblical City in Tradition and History* (Sheffield: Sheffield Academic Press, 1989), 11–99.

110   'Lawgiver' translates חקק in the Polel throughout the Authorized Version. Modern versions prefer 'sceptre' or 'staff' except in the case of Isaiah 33:22 where 'lawgiver' remains almost universal.

obeyed 'in the land' had now fulfilled what Galatians describes as their protective and tutelary role (Gal. 3:19, 24). This approach is reflected throughout the epistles in three ways: submission to secular authorities, memorial and foretoken in judicial laws, and the application of general equity.

Submit Yourselves

On three occasions in the epistles, Christians are urged to submit themselves to ruling authorities. God has established the governing authorities; they are his servants and ought not to be the objects of Christian rebellion (Rom. 13:1–2) at any level of government (1 Pet. 2:13–14). Submission to rulers and authorities means obedience to their statutes and laws (Titus 3:1), including acceptance of their penal doctrines (Rom. 13:4). How absolute or not such submission was meant to be has been a matter of debate within commentaries[111] and during various turbulent periods of church history when Christians have judged rulers to be placing themselves above the law.[112] Irrespective of those controversies, however, and despite the presumption that rulers will uphold good and punish evil (Rom. 13:3–4; 1 Pet. 2:14), it is an unavoidable conclusion that rather than campaigning for Moses-inspired judicial reform, the epistles called upon Christians to submit themselves to national laws that were not patterned on the judicial laws of Israel. This is not to say they would have disapproved of rulers, Christian or not, constructing

---

111   For a summary see Robert Jewett, *Romans* (Minneapolis: Fortress Press, 2007), 785.

112   One example is the Scottish Covenanters' armed struggle with Charles I, defended by Samuel Rutherford, one of the Scottish Commissioners to the Westminster Assembly, in *Lex, Rex*. Rutherford placed '*rex* firmly under *lex*', John Coffey, *Politics, Religion and the British Revolutions: the Mind of Samuel Rutherford* (Cambridge: Cambridge University Press, 1997), 152.

laws and penalties inspired by the Mosaic civil code, only that they accepted that those laws were of temporal jurisdiction 'in the land' and not a universal manual on statecraft.

Expired yet Speaking

Jesus' statement that 'not an iota, not a dot, will pass from the law until all is accomplished' (Matt. 5:18) included laws that no longer had jurisdiction, notably laws about gathering manna that remained embedded in a law code that would stand until the end of time despite the passing of their period of enforcement. 'Built-in obsolescence' meant that their abiding relevance was in memorial and foretoken. This approach resurfaces in Hebrews when the author treats the penalties of the Mosaic Law as an abiding warning against the serious consequences of failing to heed divine revelation. If disobedience to the Mosaic Law brought punishment on Israelite law-breakers (Heb. 2:2), how will we escape if we ignore the revelation of God in Christ (Heb. 2:3–4)? Although he recognises the Mosaic punishments as 'just' (ἔνδικος), his point is not that they stand as an ever-binding penal code,[113] but that if transgressors got what they deserved then, it is doubly certain they will get what they deserve now. Hebrews 10:28–9 repeats the theme, placing emphasis not so much on the increased certainty of punishment as on the increased severity of a punishment worse than physical death. That Hebrews uses such *a fortiori* arguments in these cases is no controversial assertion. It highlights two of very few epistolary references to the Mosaic civil code and shows that in Hebrews the judicial laws, or at least their penalties, had an abiding relevance. Somewhat like Abel (Heb. 11:4), though expired, they still speak.

---

113 'The use of aorists (cf. ἔλαβεν) may implicitly suggest…that the Law's validity belongs to the past.' Ellingworth, *Hebrews*, 138.

General Equity

The Westminster Divines asserted that although the judicial laws had expired, their 'general equity' still stands. In this connection, they referred to 1 Corinthians 9:8–10, which cites Deuteronomy 25:4, a law that forbids the muzzling of an ox while it treads grain. Paul's interpretation of this passage 'has drawn more attention from scholars than the point he draws from it.'[114] The reason for this is that Paul's point is plain: the apostles have a right (which he declines) to benefit from their labour. On the other hand, his route from the threshing floor to Corinth and from ox to apostle is not immediately transparent, particularly if the discussion starts from the presupposition that Deuteronomy 25:4 is purely concerned with animal welfare. This presupposition brings many interpreters to conclude that Paul's exegesis of the text is allegorical,[115] or even that his commitment to a Jewish conviction that God is concerned with loftier matters left him with the hermeneutical principle that 'detailed prescriptions of the law are to be allegorically expounded'.[116] Similar assumptions lead Old Testament commentators to conclude that since the immediate context of Deuteronomy 25 (and beyond) is preoccupied with matters relating to social justice and family law that verse 4 'has no connection with its immediate context',[117] or that its connection is merely 'prosidic'.[118] If, however, Keil

114   David E. Garland, *1 Corinthians* (Grand Rapids: Baker, 2003), 409.

115   Martin Luther, *Luther's Works* (28), ed. Hilton C. Oswald (Saint Louis: Concordia Publishing House, 1973), 348; William Barclay, *The Letters to the Corinthians* (Edinburgh: Saint Andrew Press, 1965), 88; James Moffatt, *The First Epistle of Paul to the Corinthians* (London: Hodder and Stoughton, 1938), 117.

116   Hans Conzelmann, *1 Corinthians* (Philadelphia: Fortress Press, 1975), 155.

117   A. D. H. Mayes, *Deuteronomy* (London: Oliphants, 1979), 327–8. Also Craigie, *Deuteronomy*, 313.

118   Duane L. Christensen, *Deuteronomy 21:10–34:12*, WBC, ed. Bruce Metzger, David A. Hubbard, and Glenn W. Barker (General), John D. W. Watts (Old Testament), no. 6B (Nashville: Thomas Nelson, 2002), 602.

THE APOSTLES AND THEIR EPISTLES

and Delitzsch were correct that it was never intended to 'apply merely literally', then allegorical interpretation is non-existent in 1 Corinthians. For Richard Hays, Paul's exegesis does not depend on allegorical methodology; allegory is an 'accidental effect', a by-product of his hermeneutical conviction that Scripture was written 'for us' (1 Cor. 9:10), which makes him read the Mosaic commandment as addressed directly to Gentile believers.[119] In a later work, Hays prefers to speak of 'figurative' or 'metaphorical' rather than 'allegorical' readings, highlighting Paul's insistence that God is really concerned about humans and suggesting that the context in Deuteronomy brought Paul to view the text as concerned with economic justice.[120]

That God is not concerned about oxen is the plain assertion of 1 Corinthians, but what does this mean? Does God simply not care about animal welfare or is the focus on the intended recipients of Scripture (as Luther seemed to think)?[121] Instone-Brewer judges that Paul is arguing from the standpoint of accepted views that the benefit to the ox was incidental to the benefit that man would get from obeying this law.[122] Praising God for his compassion to animals was also forbidden in synagogue worship.[123] If, however, the Psalms featured in synagogue worship this is a surprising prohibition since, as Luther points out, the psalmist suggests God is concerned about all things (Ps. 36:6).[124] We might also expect that if this were a standard Jewish assumption that when Jesus spoke of the Father's care for birds and lilies (Matt. 6:26–30)

119   Richard B. Hays, *Echoes of Scripture in the Letters of Paul* (New Haven: Yale University Press, 1989), 166.

120   Richard B. Hays, *First Corinthians* (Louisville: John Knox Press, 1997), 151.

121   God 'did not give Scripture to oxen and they cannot preach Scripture. They cannot quote Moses and what he wrote for them.' Luther, *Works* (28), 348.

122   D. Instone-Brewer, '1 Cor 9.9–11: A Literal Interpretation of "Do not Muzzle the Ox".' *NTS* (38) 1992, 557.

123   Ibid., 556.

124   Luther, *Works* vol. 28, 348.

his hearers would have been as surprised as Paul's might have been unsurprised. Given such examples,[125] it is improbable that Paul bases his argument on the presupposition that God does not care about animals before going on to conclude with his contemporaries that 'an "ox" in scripture implied any labourer, of any species of animal, including human.'[126] Although Luther's interpretation of Paul's comment paved the way for unbridled allegory—the preacher is the ox, the chaff he threshes are worldly people and the grain he produces are the saints[127]—his focus on the intended recipients of Scripture gets closer to the point. Paul's question is not a way of saying that God could not care less about oxen. God does care about the welfare of animals, but any revelation he has made concerning animal welfare is not directed to animals. God was not 'thinking about doing something'[128] with oxen when he gave the law. Whether they heard the law or not made no difference. It was therefore 'for us'. Paul's focus is on God's purpose in referring to oxen in the context of Deuteronomy 25, a purpose, which despite a general assumption to the contrary, was broader than literal animal welfare.

Unlike most Old Testament exegetes who assume that Deuteronomy 25:4 is a stray law, Carmichael gives a coherent argument for seeing the precept as immediately connected with the levirate law that follows (Deut. 25:5–10). Just as an ox should not be denied its portion from the treading, Israelites should not be denied their portion in the land:

> This denial is the chief concern of the levirate law. A man who dies childless is denied the continuation of his name in the land. This means that his house, his estate, his fields, his place in the land disappear. They are absorbed in the brother's estates. The surviving

125   Also Ps. 136:25, 147:9; Prov. 12:10; Matt. 10:29. And Matthew 12:11 implies Jews in Jesus' day thought God cared about animals more than the Sabbath.
126   Instone-Brewer, '1 Cor 9.9–11', 564.
127   Luther, *Works* vol. 28, 348.
128   '30.39 μέλει' in *Louw-Nida Greek-English Lexicon*.

brother therefore gains without labor, whereas it should be that the one who labors gains, as in the proverbial example of the unmuzzled ox....The brother's refusal to raise a male heir to his dead brother is motivated by his unwillingness to lose his acquired possessions....

If the reference to the unmuzzled ox is designed to direct attention to the human world...Muzzling, as an allusion to the human world, may symbolize the concept of silencing a person, a concept that is the concern of the levirate law, which speaks metaphorically of an Israelite's name being wiped out. In short, D's penchant for clever lines of association and his use of literal and nonliteral meanings suggest that the prohibition concerning the unmuzzled ox is placed before levirate law to serve as an introduction.[129]

It is not necessary to accept Carmichael's claim that Deuteronomy 25:4 is proverbial to see that it could be connected with the levirate laws by a common theme of rightful rewards and integrity in dealings. Tables presented in an earlier chapter[130] show that according to the Decalogue sub-structure of the Mosaic Law, Deuteronomy 25:4 comes on the turning point between the ninth and tenth commandments, linking integrity and contentment. It is likely that Paul is picking up on these themes in 1 Corinthians 9, presenting what he believes is God's purpose in Deuteronomy. It is therefore not surprising that 1 Timothy 5:18 cites the same law and immediately follows with a statement that could well allude to Deuteronomy 24:14–15: 'the labourer deserves his wages.'[131] What God cares about are the deeper principles woven into the legal narrative and Paul seeks to express those principles. On the one hand, there must be honesty expressed in workers receiving a just reward; on the other hand he

129   Calum M. Carmichael, *The Laws of Deuteronomy* (Ithaca: Cornell University Press, 1974), 239–40.

130   See tables on pages 97, 98, and 100.

131   Complications surround this phrase. Does the opening 'For the Scripture says' include this or only the reference to the ox? If it includes the second phrase, is it a citation of Luke 10:7? Is Paul treating Jesus' words as Scripture?

will express contentment fulfilling his apostolic responsibilities
while forgoing those rights (1 Cor. 9:15). Interpreted in this way,
the law of Deuteronomy 25:4 is not misplaced and nor does its
citation in 1 Corinthians 9 depend on allegorical interpretation.
It provides a vivid example of what the Westminster Divines
understood by 'general equity'. The law about the ox did not
demand specific application in the steadings of seventeenth
century England, but the principles of fairness, integrity, and
contented fulfilment of every duty were always obligatory.

The Corinthian epistles and 1 Timothy provide a further
example of how the undergirding principles of a Mosaic
judicial law remain relevant. In 1 Timothy 5:19 the requirement
for two or three witnesses immediately follows the citation of
Deuteronomy 25:4 and is applied specifically to elders, while in
2 Corinthians 13:1 it has a more general application. The text
behind the New Testament references is Deuteronomy 19:15,
although Deuteronomy 17:6 repeats the stipulation. Except for
Héring, who thinks that in 1 Corinthians the interpretation has an
'almost allegorical sense',[132] most interpreters see fewer difficulties
than with the busy ox. They accept the complication that leads
Héring to his position, namely that the two or three witnesses
are made up by the third of Paul's visits (2 Cor. 13:1) rather
than by two or three individual witnesses of specific offenses.[133]
While the logic of this interpretation could be supported by the
close proximity of witnesses to his visit in verse 1, the argument
that in Judaism the rule about witnesses could be understood
as a requirement to forewarn offenders of punishment[134] is
not a convincing reason to transpose 'warnings' for 'witnesses'.

132   Jean Héring, *The Second Epistle of Saint Paul to the Corinthians*
(London: Epworth Press, 1967), 99.

133   Furnish takes this view and calls several notable writers to his
defence (Chrysostom, Calvin, Lietzmann, Windisch, Bruce, and Barrett).
Victor P. Furnish, *II Corinthians* (New York: Doubleday, 1984), 575.

134   Ibid.

According to Matthew's record, even those clamouring for penal consequences were sticklers for literal obedience to this rule (Matt. 26:60). In addition, the kind of offences that should be the subject of discipline in Corinth were neither minor nor certain to have been witnessed by Paul (2 Cor. 12:20–21). It might be that when offences are 'flagrant and out in the open' that there is 'little need to set up an "inquisition"',[135] but it does not follow that normal standards of evidence can therefore be abandoned. Paul is doing nothing more than reiterating the standard of evidence by which people must be judged when the Corinthian church disciplines its members.

1 Timothy presents a more straightforward case of judicial procedure and, as William Fuller has shown, the wider passages (1 Tim. 5:19–21; Deut. 19:15–20) have 'extensive parallels' between 'the ethico-legal situations', the effect the judgment should have on observers, the warnings against partiality, and in a triad of persons involved in the exercise of justice.[136] In Guilding and Braulik's outlining of the Decalogue sub-structure of Mosaic Law, Deuteronomy 19:15–21 comes under the influence of the sixth commandment. An intent to preserve life and protect individuals from the unjust wounding or death that could follow malicious testimony (Deut. 19:16) is the burden of the laws about evidence. Where it is proven that someone gave false evidence, he must suffer the penalty that his testimony would have brought upon his victim—'life for life...' (Deut. 19:18–21). Similarly in 1 Timothy, impartiality and correct judgment mattered (1 Tim. 5:21), not merely so that standards of evidence as philosophic ideals might be maintained, but to preserve the reputations of elders. They had to be selected carefully and to

---

135   Ralph P. Martin, *2 Corinthians,* WBC, ed. Bruce M. Metzger, David A. Hubbard, and Glenn W. Barker (General), Ralph P. Martin (New Testament), no. 40 (Dallas: Word Books, 1986), 469.

136   J. William Fuller, 'Of Elders and Triads in 1 Timothy 5.19–25.' *NTS* (29) 1983, 260.

keep their lives pure (1 Tim. 5:22). If the church were to accept the uncorroborated testimony of individual witnesses the danger was that malicious accusations could destroy elders in the church.

Brian Rosner claims that the law is the last thing on Paul's mind when he calls on Timothy to 'keep these things' (1 Tim. 5:21): 'It is not the Law of Moses that Christians are called to heed…but his own apostolic directions.'[137] Unless we are to believe that 'these things' are 'apostolic directions' that exclude the previous three verses (1 Tim. 5:18–20), Rosner's argument is untenable. We may debate how Paul uses the law, but that his 'apostolic directions' in these verses are rooted in biblical law is unquestionable. Following his directions here means preserving continuity with the fundamental principle behind a particular Mosaic law—a principle summarized in the sixth commandment. In this case, that requires literal application of rules about evidence to the church; the details of the judicial process no longer apply but the number of witnesses must not change.

This law and the theology of *The Westminster Confession* have had an impact beyond the church, not least in influencing standards of evidence in Scottish law. In contrast to English law, which only requires a plurality of witnesses in 'some exceptional cases'[138] such as speeding and perjury,[139] Scottish law deems uncorroborated testimony insufficient,[140] at least 'to the fact to be established' if not 'each circumstance'.[141] Viscount

137   Brian S. Rosner, 'Paul and the Law: What he Does not Say.' *JSNT* (32) 2010, 413.

138   D. W. Elliot, *Phipson and Elliot Manual of the Law of Evidence* (London: Sweet & Maxwell, 1980), 155.

139   Colin Tapper, *Cross and Tapper on Evidence* (London: Butterworths, 1995), 250–52.

140   David H. Sheldon, *Evidence: Cases and Materials* (Edinburgh: W. Green & Son Ltd., 2002), 78–123. Also W. J. Lewis, *Manual of the Law of Evidence in Scotland* (Edinburgh and Glasgow: William Hodge & Company, Ltd, 1925), 245–50.

141   George Tait, *A Treatise on the Law of Evidence in Scotland* (Edinburgh: John Anderson & Co., 1824), 435–6.

Stair, a probable signatory of the National Covenant and the Solemn League and Covenant[142] whose view of law in general reflected that of the Westminster Divines,[143] wrote in a work that 'laid an imperishable foundation for the law of Scotland':[144]

> In all controversies witnesses are adhibited to determine, as a common rule amongst all nations; which is confirmed by the word of God, "In the mouth of two or three witnesses let every word be established:" where, by every word, is understood every allegeance to be proved. For it is not meant that words should only be proved by witnesses, but that things so proved, being proponed by words written or spoken, if a just conclusion be thence inferred. But words of the mind, or thoughts, cannot be proved by witnesses, unless they be expressed by words, or other sufficient signs.[145]

The notable exception to this principle is expressed in the 'Moroov Doctrine', which allows evidence on one charge to corroborate evidence on another.[146] Ironically, this legal doctrine probably has its origins in a successful case against a parish minister for attempting to suborn false evidence.[147] More recently, the Free Church of Scotland considered allowing the doctrine to be used in church courts, but concluded the idea is 'not clearly found

142   David M. Walker, *Viscount Stair: Glasgow, European City of Culture Stevenson Lecture* (Glasgow: University of Glasgow, 1990), 4.

143   Ibid., 8. Walker does not mention the Westminster Divines, but the theological ideas he lists are some of those mentioned earlier in this thesis.

144   Ibid., 14. Quoting words on a memorial to Stair in Glasgow University.

145   James Viscount of Stair, *The Institutions of the Law of Scotland Deduced from its Originals and Collated with the Civil and Feudal Laws and with the Customs of Neighbouring Nations,* vol. 1 (Edinburgh: Thomas Clark, M.DCCC. XXVI), Title XLIII, 'Probation by Witnesses', 766.

146   See Peter K. Vandore, 'The Moorov Doctrine' in *The Juridical Review* (1974), 30–55, 179–95. In response to a recent call from Scotland's Lord Advocate, Elish Angiolini, for the doctrine to be extended, the infamous advocate, Donald Findlay, QC, said any weakening in the need for corroboration would constitute 'a dangerous attack on Scotland's legal system'. Shan Ross, 'Scots rape laws "worst in the world".' in *The Scotsman,* 5 March 2008.

147   Sheldon, *Evidence,* 115.

in Scripture and cannot be clearly deduced from it'.[148] The Westminster Divines and Viscount Stair would have agreed.

Section Summary

The way that the epistles deal distinctly with ceremonial laws and with the Decalogue means that 'judicial law' exists almost by default. The apostolic demand that Christians obey the laws of their land cannot coexist with the idea that the judicial laws of Israel remain binding. Nonetheless the penalties of the judicial laws still warn of the consequences of disobedience and still bear testimony to the fundamental principles upon which they are based. The structure of the Mosaic Law suggests that those principles are expressed in the Decalogue. Apostolic application of this 'general equity' sometimes meant literal application of a judicial law, but not always.

'A PERFECT RULE OF RIGHTEOUSNESS'

For many contemporary Christians, especially some evangelicals, the threefold division's most controversial claim is that the moral law is 'a perfect rule of righteousness' that 'doth for ever bind all.' The issues that take up the remainder of this chapter are whether the epistles affirm, develop, or undermine some of the earlier scriptural acknowledgments of the Decalogue's distinctiveness. Do they overturn the view that it is perpetually binding?

Negativity Towards the Law

If the epistles are in any sense negative about the law that may appear to pose a greater problem for the category of moral

148 'Report of the Committee to Review Disciplinary Procedures', *Reports to the General Assembly of the Free Church of Scotland: 2008*, 135.

law than for the ceremonial and judicial categories, which the threefold division holds to be abrogated. Although few in recent discussion of the apostolic approach to the law have been inclined to describe the epistles as unremittingly hostile to the Mosaic Law, many have seen Paul as liable to blow hot or cold, either due to development in his views or to plain inconsistency.[149] Like historians, perhaps theologians should not expect 'complete intelligibility…from the foreign lands of the past',[150] but it should certainly be expected of both that before branding a historical figure inconsistent 'we ought first to consider whether we may not in some way have misunderstood what he said.'[151] Most famous for charging Paul with holding a view of the law 'full of difficulties and inconsistencies'[152] is Heikki Räisänen whose approach, says Kruse, 'sticks in the throats of conservatives'.[153] If that is true, it might seem ironic that some of Räisänen's views are charitable to the threefold division: the Law of Moses 'consists of different elements that are of different value' and the threefold divisions of Justin and Ptolemy take an approach to the law that is 'more logical than Paul's'[154] and 'in purely intellectual terms…

149 Many recent works on Paul and the Law provide a summary of those scholarly arguments as they have developed over the last century or so. See Brice L. Martin, *Christ and the Law in Paul* (Leiden: E. J. Brill, 1989), 39–55; Stephen Westerholm, *Perspectives Old and New on Paul: The "Lutheran"Paul and His Critics* (Grand Rapids: Eerdmans, 2004), 164–70; Colin Kruse, *Paul, the Law and Justification* (Leicester: Apollos, 1996), 28–42.

150 Quentin Skinner, *Visions of Politics: Volume 1: Regarding Method* (Cambridge: Cambridge University Press, 2002), 56.

151 Ibid., 55. Skinner takes Machiavelli's discussion of liberty and monarchy as an example: 'In his *Discorsi* Machiavelli affirms that liberty is possible only under a *repubblica*. But he also affirms that Rome lived in *libertà* under her early kings. What then does he believe? Does he or does he not think that liberty and monarchy are incompatible?'

152 Heikki Räisänen, *Paul and the Law* (Tübingen: J. C. B. Mohr, 1987), 264.

153 Kruse, *Paul*, 40.

154 Räisänen, 224.

clear and far more impressive'.[155] In fact, all the non-Pauline writers he surveys are more consistent than Paul.[156] The literature he selects is so diverse that generalisations are difficult,[157] but if those writings are so obviously clearer it is surprising that those with which Paul was familiar did not improve his own thinking and that those later theologians who treated Paul's writings as authoritative were not left in confusion. For some of them, as for 'conservatives', reaching agreement with Räisänen would be almost impossible since he regards Colossians, Ephesians, and the Pastorals as Deutero-Pauline,[158] while they regarded their views as consistent with a wider canon.

This question of consistency is but one of 'a constellation of interrelated "problems" as fixed and stable as the stars in the night sky' that make up the 'scholarly construct' of 'Paul's view of the law',[159] and although hermeneutical star-gazing might also make us ask 'What is man?' it will only distract from the questions of this book. For that reason, anyone who wants to conduct a meticulous study of the arguments for and against Räisänen's views may immerse themselves in his writings and in Van Spanje's extended response.[160] In any case, the basic accusation of Pauline inconsistency sometimes depends on a view of consistency that effectively renders all Scripture inconsistent. Francis Watson argues that Paul's inconsistencies are in the Torah itself and his 'view of the law' is simply his reading of the law so any contradictions in his view derive from the Pentateuch:[161]

155   Ibid., 226.

156   Ibid., 228.

157   Colossians, Ephesians, Pastorals, Hebrews, James, the Gospels, Revelation, Acts, Ignatius, Barnabas, Marcion, Justin, Ptolemy, Kerygma Petrou. Ibid., 203–27.

158   Ibid., 201–7.

159   Francis Watson, *Paul and the Hermeneutics of Faith* (London: T & T Clark, 2004), 274–5.

160   Van Spanje, *Inconsistency in Paul.*

161   Watson, *Paul,* 275, n. 5; 514, 520.

Paul remains committed to scriptural coherence, but his antithetical hermeneutic puts it under severe strain. Or rather, as he himself might prefer to think, his hermeneutic is based on the *discovery* of the tension-laden dynamics of the scriptural narrative itself, in its diachronic unfolding – a discovery that serves to illuminate the logic of the gospel. Scriptural dissonance is both uncovered by the gospel and resolved by it, since its theological function is to testify to the gospel.[162]

This produces an 'Evangelical Paul' according to one reviewer[163] and a 'decontextualized Paul' according to another,[164] both which charges Watson rejects.[165] Irrespective of his arguments, the idea that Scripture has a 'tension-laden dynamic' is suggested by various biblical passages, but for reasons logically prior to the detailed interpretations that feature in Watson's five hundred pages of exegesis. In one of his earlier works, Räisänen rightly observed that one of the characteristics of prophetic utterance in 'ancient Hebrew thought' was that it could have a lethal effect, causing hardening by proclamation, so that a proclamation such as that of Isaiah 6:9–10 is 'very similar to a curse'.[166] Such a view of divine revelation appears elsewhere in the prophets (Jer. 5:21–3; Hos. 6:5; Ezek. 12:2–3; Zech. 7:11–12). The Isaiah text also mirrors themes found in the Pentateuch: the hardening of Pharaoh's heart comes as a God-ordained response to the voice of the LORD (Exod. 4:21; 5:2; 7:13 etc.) and in Deuteronomy 29:1–3 where the 'deprivation of the receptive heart and the production of an

162   Ibid., 24.

163   Douglas A. Campbell, 'An Evangelical Paul: A Response to Francis Watson's *Paul and the Hermeneutics of Faith.*' *JSNT* 28.3 (2006), 339, 346.

164   Christopher D. Stanley, 'A Decontextualized Paul? A Response to Francis Watson's *Paul and the Hermeneutics of Faith.*' *JSNT* 28.3 (2006), 353–62.

165   Francis Watson, 'Paul the Reader: An Authorial Apologia.' *JSNT* 28.3 (2006), 363–73.

166   Heikki Räisänen, *The Idea of Divine Hardening: A Comparative Study of the Notion of Divine Hardening, Leading Astray and Inciting to Evil in the Bible and the Qur'an* (Helsinki: Finish Exegetical Society, 1976), 60–61.

obdurate heart can be thought of as one and the same process.'[167]
Similarly, the Psalms intertwine revelation with hardening: Israel's
refusal to receive the blessing of the revelation of the Decalogue
at Sinai (Ps. 81:8–11) results in deeper hardening and God giving
them up to the devices of their thrawn hearts (Ps. 81:12), though
not without hands still outstretched (Ps. 81:13–16; cf. Isa 65:2).
Isaiah 6:9–10 appears in each of the Gospels, normally with
the Parable of the Sower (Matt. 13:13; Mark 4:12; Luke 8:10;
John 12:40), but one of the most interesting reappearances of
this Old Testament theme comes in John 15. Jesus, the true vine,
speaks of his Father taking away every dead branch and pruning
every healthy branch (John 15:2), while assuring the disciples
that they are already clean because of the words he has spoken
to them (John 15:3). It is a common assumption that pruning
refers to suffering in the sense of Hebrews 12:4–11,[168] but the
use of καθαίρει in verse 2 and καθαροί in verse 3 suggests that
cleansing and pruning are the work of one instrument—'διὰ τὸν
λόγον'.[169] In this way, John 15:2 reflects the Old Testament idea
that the same divine revelation that brings growth and blessing
also brings destruction and curse to the fruitless and unyielding.
Given the prominence of this theme in Scripture and in the
teaching of Jesus, it is highly improbable that Paul or any other
apostle could have had a one-dimensional view of the law. To
assume that he should present it (or any future revelation) as
either unmixed blessing or curse is unreasonable. It is valid to
expect tension in the epistles and unnecessary to demand that

167   Craig A. Evans, *To See and Not Perceive: Isaiah 6.9-10 in Early Jewish
and Christian Interpretation* (Sheffield: Sheffield Academic Press, 1989), 51.

168   'At the most, it is reminiscent of purifications and trials undergone
by the disciples.' Rudolf Schnakenburg, *The Gospel According to John*, vol. 3
(Tunbridge Wells: Burns & Oates, 1982), 98; D. A. Carson, *The Gospel According
to John* (Leicester: Inter-Varsity Press, 1991), 514.

169   For a fuller discussion see Jan G. van Der Watt, *Family of the King:
Dynamics of Metaphor in the Gospel According to John* (Leiden: Brill, 2000), 39.

every assertion about the Decalogue raise no queries. Coherence and consistency do not require the elimination of every tension.

Deuteronomy and Isaiah feature once again when Paul expresses the hardening theme in Romans 9–11 and 2 Corinthians 3,[170] the latter being particularly significant with its references to Horeb and the giving of the Decalogue. Predictably, scholars concerned with the Corinthians passage are keen to stress its all-surpassing difficulty,[171] but it is at least clear that Paul views Israel as hardened and unable to understand the old covenant unless they turn to Christ (2 Cor. 3:14–16). The law itself has been instrumental in this deadly holocaust, which cannot end without the intervention of the life-giving Spirit (2 Cor. 3:6–8). He makes several contrasts between the old and new covenants. The old is a ministry of death and condemnation carved in stone; the new a ministry of the Spirit, of life and righteousness written in human hearts (2 Cor. 3:3, 6–7). The old had a fading glory; the new has a greater and enduring glory (2 Cor. 3:7–11).

Rather than being a negative assessment of the moral content of the Decalogue, or of the typological and eschatological content of the law as a whole, these comments proclaim the law's impotence to bring life and permanent glory. The letter kills because the life-giving Spirit is not active with the ministers of the old covenant to remove the veil and reveal the transforming glory of the Lord to whom every reading of Moses bears witness (2 Cor. 3:6, 15–18). Furnish's claim that this does not amount to rejection of the law, only of 'that way of using the law which presumes that its "letter" provides a sure way to righteousness and life,'[172] finds affirmation in the widespread recognition that the

---

170 Evans, *To See and not Perceive*, 83–9.

171 Stockhausen quotes A. T. Hanson to make the point: 'The Mount Everest of Pauline texts as far as difficulty is concerned.' Carol Kern Stockahusen, *Moses' Veil and the Glory of the New Covenant: The Exegetical Substructre of II Cor. 3,1–4,6* (Roma: Editrice Pontificio Istituto Biblico, 1989), 32.

172 Furnish, *II Corinthians*, 200.

words of Ezekiel and Jeremiah underpin the passage (Jer. 31:33; Ezek. 11:19–20; 36:26–7).[173] There is no radical difference in the words inscribed in stone or written in human hearts. Watson argues that Paul takes Moses' return with the first and second pair of tablets as two sides of one event. The identical tablets, one pair bound up with Moses' glorified face and the other with death and plague upon the idolatrous people, meant that 'the glory and the killing belong together.'[174] While this is possible, his later comment that in the new order 'the second tablet of the Decalogue no longer represents a "ministry of death" or of "condemnation"'[175] is not absolutely convincing. The contrast is not in the absolute transformation of the Decalogue; glory and killing still belong together even in the new order since the law still 'kills' those who read it with a veil. Indeed, the ministry of the new covenant produces its own holocaust (2 Cor. 2:15–16). The law only ceases to be a ministry of condemnation and death when through Christ the veil is removed and the Spirit of the living God disperses the shadows, bringing life to law-inscribed hearts. The great contrast is in the extent and effects of the Spirit's ministry, which can only be greater and far more glorious because of Christ's work. This passage is not hostile to the Decalogue or to the law as a whole, only to the idea that it can bring life without the Spirit or be read without reference to Christ. The combination of negative and positive ideas reflects not Pauline inconsistency, but established biblical themes, possibly even of the 'glory and killing' within Exodus 31–4 itself.

Paul's writings are not the only place where interpreters find negativity or mixed sentiments towards the law. Some believe that Hebrews expresses similar or greater hostility. The epistle also leans on the Jeremiah and Ezekiel passages mentioned above,

173   Stockhausen, *Moses' Veil*, 73–82; Furnish, *II Corinthians*, 195–6; Martin, *2 Corinthians*, 45, 53.

174   Watson, *Paul*, 289.

175   Ibid., 312.

but for Michael Morrison it is simple: 'A change in priesthood implies a change *in the law*; they stand or fall together.'[176] Hebrews 8:13 proclaims the law's demise and in the second half of chapter 10 the 'author states bluntly that the law is obsolete.'[177] It is not simply that Morrison overestimates Hebrews' bluntness; everything in the epistle is stacked against the law. Even the new covenant quotation from Jeremiah 31 serves little purpose other than to prove that the old is obsolete: 'The author does not do anything with the details of Jer 31—he says nothing about law in the heart, God being their God, or everyone knowing the Lord (he even omits most of those details when he quotes Jer 31 again in Heb 10:16–17).'[178]

This statement, however, is only true because Morrison eliminates forgiveness of sin from the list of elements found in the new covenant promise of Hebrews 8. In fact, Hebrews 10 repeats two out of four of these elements, specifically that God will write his laws on their hearts and forgive their lawlessness, so Morrison's trivialisation of the new covenant references to law and his unwillingness to explain how lawlessness can exist in the absence of law are unsatisfactory. Similarly, specific reference to the law cannot be avoided by appealing to the Hebrew text of Jeremiah 31:33 and reading תּוֹרָה in the widest possible sense so that νόμους in Hebrews 8:10 and 10:16 embraces 'ideas of guidance, direction and instruction'[179] rather than being a specific reference to the law. On other occasions in Jeremiah that record God speaking of 'my law' (תּוֹרָתִי) the immediate context suggests

176   Michael D. Morrison, *Who Needs a New Covenant? Rhetorical Function of the Covenant Motif in the Argument of Hebrews*, Princeton Theological Monograph Series 85 (Eugene: Pickwick Publications, 2008), 56.

177   Ibid., 57.

178   Ibid., 60.

179   This seems to be the significance of Bruce's footnote on the original wording of Jeremiah 31. F. F. Bruce, *Commentary on the Epistle to the Hebrews* (London: Marshall, Morgan & Scott, 1964), 172, n. 54.

the law promulgated on Horeb (Jer. 9:12; 16:11). Jeremiah's new covenant has not broadened the concept so that torah has become an undefined and fluid body of teaching. It is 'the same commandments as at Sinai',[180] 'at minimum…the Ten Commandments'[181] that will be written on the hearts of Israel. The passages in Hebrews reflect such an understanding and Lane is correct that the newness is 'not in newness of content',[182] but it is left to a more ancient commentator to draw the parallels:

> Expositors generally and properly observe, that here is an allusion to the giving of the law on mount Sinai, in the *first* covenant. For then the law, (that is, the *ten words*) was written in tables of stone; not so much to secure the outward letter of them, as to represent the hardness of the people's hearts to whom they were given. This event God promises to prevent under the new covenant by writing these laws now *in our hearts*, which he wrote before only in *tables of stone*; that is, he will effectually work that obedience in us which the law requires…[183]

The allusion with Sinai is less generally observed today, yet it remains valid since the only laws that God inscribes are the Ten Commandments and Hebrews provides no good reason to assume that the words inscribed on human hearts represent a redrafted morality. One idea that remains observed is Owen's assertion that the new covenant brings new obedience, although it is often overstated as a promise 'to change hearts and minds so that people no longer fall into sin'[184] or as something that 'guarantees obedience on the part of the people'[185] who make up the Christian church. Like Corinthians, Hebrews assumes an ongoing struggle

---

180   Walter Brueggemann, *A Commentary on Jeremiah: Exile and Home-coming* (Grand Rapids: Eerdmans, 1998), 293.

181   Jack R. Lundbom, *Jeremiah 21–36* (New York: Doubleday, 2004), 468.

182   Lane, *Hebrews 1–8*, 209.

183   Owen, *Hebrews*, vol 3 (Pitcher edition), 449.

184   Koester, *Hebrews*, 391.

185   Thomas McComiskey, *The Covenants of Promise* (Nottingham: IVP, 1985), 85.

with sin (Heb. 12:1–4) and does not abandon the established view that divine revelation may encounter hardened hearts (Heb. 3:8, 15; 4:7). The idea that the new covenant 'is called new because it gives a new heart, a new nature and a new spirit'[186] suggests that those things could not have been experienced before Christ, yet Hebrews does not view new covenant believers' obedience as qualitatively superior to that of Abraham or any other saint in the cloud of witnesses.

This idea that the new covenant is permanent because individual obedience is guaranteed depends on the almost universal understanding that the better promises of Hebrews 8:6 are those contained in the covenant itself (Heb. 8:10–12), but this results in the idea that the covenant promises were enacted upon themselves. Given that the new covenant quotation occurs in a section that stresses the superiority of Christ's priestly ministry, is it not more coherent to view the promises referred to in Hebrews 8:6 as those made to Christ? In which case, the covenant is 'better' not only because he is its mediator who has made a 'once for all' sacrifice, but because it is established upon the promises of everlasting priesthood made to Christ, by God (Heb. 7:21–2). The promises within the new covenant are fulfilled because the covenant itself is enacted upon these 'better promises'.[187] The Levitical priests received no such promises; their sin-marred priesthood was temporary. Christ's priesthood is eternal and effective. God has made an oath and 'will not change his mind', so Christ cannot fail as high priest and mediator of the new covenant. In Owen's exposition, the contrast remains one between the individuals under the respective covenants

---

186   Henry T. Mahan, *Bible Class Commentary on Hebrews* (Darlington: Evangelical Press 1989), 37.

187   This interpretation is also an alternative to the view that there is nothing new in the new covenant (Bruce cites Duhm as an example: Bruce, *Hebrews*, 172, n. 52) or that 'new' is meant in irony (see reference to Wilber Wallis in John Fischer, 'Covenant, Fulfillment & Judaism in Hebrews.' *ETR* 13 (1989)).

whereas the tables of stone could be reflective of the hard hearts of both ages. Such hearts always needed the removal and replacement that Ezekiel spoke of, so that the divine inscription of the principles of the Decalogue would be a delight rather than bondage, but the only means by which that was ever achieved and the only guarantee that it will continue in the people of God is in the mediator of the new covenant. Its newness and superiority lies in him. Far from expressing hostility towards the law or commanding a blunt assertion that the law is obsolete, he confirms that the laws inscribed in stone do not pass away.

An Ineffaceable Inscription

Theologians throughout the centuries have spoken of 'natural law' being written on human hearts. The idea, though not the phrase, is found in *The Westminster Confession* and is part of their argument for claiming that the moral law is ever-binding. If, however, 'natural law' is understood as the morals enshrined in the Decalogue, does not this make redundant the new covenant promise that God would write his law on the hearts of Israel? The key passage from the epistles that touches on this issue is Romans 2:14–15,[188] which many have understood to speak of such 'natural law'. But what if rather than referring simply to Gentiles, Paul is talking about Gentile Christians? This is the view of several recent writers, such as Ito,[189] Wright,[190] and Jewett.[191] Gathercole backs them up with claims of a 'distinguished heritage',[192] but the most distinguishing feature of its heritage is some extraordinary

188   This is also one of the proof texts referred to in WCF *XIX*.I.

189   Akio Ito, 'Romans 2: A Deuteronomistic Reading', *JSNT* 59 (1995), 21–37.

190   N. T. Wright, 'The Law in Romans 2' in James D. G. Dunn, ed., *Paul and the Mosaic Law* (Grand Rapids: Eerdmans, 2001), 131–150.

191   Jewett, *Romans*, 213.

192   S. J. Gathercole, 'A Law unto Themselves: The Gentiles in Romans 2.14–15 Revisited', *JSNT* 85 (2002), 29.

gaps: it skips from 'Ambrosiaster' to Augustine, who flip-flopped on the issue, before leap-frogging fifteen centuries and reappearing in the works of several twentieth century Germans,[193] notably Karl Barth.[194] Gathercole's defence is the most comprehensive and he summarises his argument as follows:

> First, having established the logical connection between Rom. 2:13 and 2.14, it will be argued that the phrase τὰ τοῦ νόμου refers to the Torah in a comprehensive sense. Thus, the justification promised to the doers of the Torah in 2.13 belongs to those who τὰ τοῦ νόμου ποιῶσιν. This obedience does not take place 'by nature', as φύσει belongs grammatically to the first clause in 2.14, and does not modify the 'doing of the Law'. With regard to Rom. 2.15, it will be argued that the three components of the 'work of the Law written on the heart', the 'conscience', and the 'thoughts accusing' and even 'defending' constitute features of a Christian believer.[195]

This argument claims the advantage of seeing the same people—justified Gentiles—in verse 14 as in verse 13.[196] Although some who take Gentiles in a general sense do connect verse 14 more directly with verse 12,[197] this is not universally the case,[198] so affirmation of the logical connection does not lead inexorably to the Christian-Gentile view,[199] or to the inconceivable conclusion

---

193   Ibid., 29–30.

194   'The Gentiles whom in 2.14–15 Paul mentions in contrast to the Jews are simply the Gentile Christians.' Maico M. Michielin, ed., *A Shorter Commentary on Romans by Karl Barth* (Aldershot: Ashgate, 2007), 20.

195   Gathercole, 'A Law unto Themselves', 30.

196   Ibid., 32.

197   James D. G. Dunn, *Romans 1-8,* WBC, no. 38ᴬ (Dallas: Word, 1988), 98; Joseph Fitzmyer, S.J., *Romans* (New York: Doubleday, 1993), 309; John Murray, *The Epistle to the Romans* (London: Marshall, Morgan & Scott, 1967), 72.

198   'He now states what proves the former clause.' Calvin, *Romans, .*

199   The reverse is also true since Jewett, who is aware of Gathercole's article, says 'the γάρ ("for") of v. 14 indicates an argumentative connection with the foregoing thesis concerning the impartial judgment of God in v. 11.' Jewett, *Romans,* 213.

that 'the doers of Torah to be justified are actually not hearers of Torah at all.'[200] Where were those Gentile Christians who were not 'hearers of Torah at all'? How did they avoid the Psalms, the Prophets, the teachings of the Sermon on the Mount, and every debate about the law? Could it really be that Gentile Christians listening to Paul's letter were about to hear the law for the first time as the reader came to Romans 2:21–2 or 13:9? Even if they were, Paul's argument depended on them being doers rather than hearers, so he was about to make it instantaneously redundant.

Although the discussion concerning φύσει (by nature) is hampered by its limited use in Scripture, the observation that it 'qualifies *identity*, rather than *behaviour*'[201] is defensible, yet not conclusive. The 'problem' that the traditional placement of φύσει means the 'accomplishment of Torah that leads to justification seems to take place spontaneously "by nature"'[202] is created by Gathercole's interpretation of the link between verse 13 and 14[203] rather than being a problem that actually exists in the traditional approach. Even supposing φύσει modifies the first clause and the text is translated 'Gentiles, who do not have the law by nature, do what the law requires', Gentiles in general could still be in view. If Gentiles 'do not have the law by nature' the implication is that the Jews do have the revealed law 'by nature', which only makes sense if 'by nature' applies to Jews born after the giving of the law and if Jews and Gentiles were judged equal in this respect before Horeb. Detached from the second clause, 'by nature' would no longer be synonymous with the 'law written in their hearts' of verse 15—Jew and Gentile could have had the law written on their hearts from the beginning. Gathercole also makes the point that 'it would be unparalleled in Paul's thought to say

200   Gathercole, 'A Law unto Themselves', 33.
201   Ibid., 36.
202   Ibid., 35.
203   '...the syllogism runs: "Those who do Torah (2.13) will be justified... the Gentiles do Torah...therefore the Gentiles will be justified.' Ibid., 32.

that Gentiles had the spontaneous natural ability to carry out even *elements* of Torah.'[204] But so what? Why should any biblical writer's thought require two or three parallels within their own writings for it to be affirmed as their thought? More to the point, it would be unparalleled in Paul's thought to say that anyone — Jew or Gentile—had shown a 'spontaneous natural ability' to obey the law. The outlook changes, however, when Gathercole's unwarranted addition of spontaneity and ability is removed from the definition of φύσει,[205] since it is highly improbable that Paul's thought did not include the idea that all people, in some sense, 'by nature do what the law requires'—the concept is too firmly established in the Old Testament. New Testament commentators and scholars, however, tend to neglect the basic idea of pre-Sinai law, which is evident in discussions of Romans 2:14–15 where the focus is almost entirely on the possibility of an allusion to Jeremiah 31:33.[206] If their analysis is correct, whether τὰ τοῦ νόμου need[207] or need not[208] be understood grammatically as referring to a limited number of laws does not matter; should 'Jeremiah and Paul only differ in their temporal perspective,'[209] the reference must be to the Decalogue (as discussed above) rather than to Torah in a 'comprehensive sense'.

204   Ibid., 37.

205   It is unreasonable to paste the definition 'spontaneous natural ability' into the arguments of those who view Romans 2:14 as referring to Gentiles in general. This is not how they would define φύσει in translation and ideas about common grace or human depravity may influence theological definitions.

206   Fitzmyer, *Romans*, 311; Dunn, *Romans 1–8*, 100; Jewett, *Romans*, 215. That Fitzmyer and Dunn refer to Jeremiah suggests that it is not correct that 'Reference (or not) to Jer. 31 on Paul's part in Rom. 2.15 is the key boundary-marker dividing those who see the Gentiles as Christian and those who do not'; Gathercole, 'A Law unto Themselves', 41, n. 72.

207   'Again, the phrase *ta tou nomou*, lit., "the (things) of the law," means some of the precepts of the law, not necessarily all that is prescribed by the Mosaic law.' Fitzmyer, *Romans*, 309.

208   Gathercole, 'A Law unto Themselves', 34.

209   Ibid., 41.

An alternative suggestion from Ito is that Paul also alludes to Deuteronomy 30:14 where Moses says to Israel, 'the word is very near you, in your mouth, and in your heart, that you may do it.'[210] According to Gathercole, 'Ito is almost certainly wrong'[211]— too certainly to merit refutation—but perhaps his idea deserves consideration. Although Deuteronomy 30:14 may reflect the terminology of Deuteronomy 6:6,[212] Moses' words amount to more than a comment on the 'educational process' indicating that 'Torah is to be memorized'.[213] Perhaps the seventeenth century commentator, Matthew Henry, was reflecting more widely held opinions when he found in Deuteronomy 30:14 a reference to 'the law of nature, which would have been found in every man's heart, and every man's mouth, if he would but have attended to it.'[214] His interpretation may have been designed to account for the contrast between Deuteronomy 6 as a command that God's words be *upon* their hearts (עַל־לְבָבֶךָ) and Deuteronomy 30 as a statement that God's word is *in* their hearts (וּבִלְבָבְךָ). The difference between the prepositions עַל and בְּ should not be overemphasized since עַל can convey the same meaning as בְּ,[215] but בְּ ordinarily suggests a greater degree of internality. Unless we assume that Deuteronomy 30 intends to convey that by the time Moses spoke those words the internalization of the law had been achieved, then Henry may have been correct—in a statement that reflected the Pentateuch's overall view of humanity, Moses was reminding Israel that the laws that had come to them from Sinai were not alien to them, but 'self-understood' norms that were already in their hearts.

---

210   Ito, 'Romans 2', 26.
211   Gathercole, 'A Law unto Themselves', 41, n. 72.
212   Mayes, *Deuteronomy*, 370.
213   Christensen, *Deuteronomy 21:10–34:12*, 743.
214   Matthew Henry, *Commentary on the Whole Bible*, BibleWorks 7.0.
215   For example, 'And they took in [בְּ] their hands…' (Deut. 1:25) and '… the two tablets of the covenant were in [עַל] my two hands' (Deut. 9:15).

Paul's Old Testament allusion may, however, not be to any specific text, but rather to those norms, which, contrary to Schreiner, means that Paul was not plundering the Greeks.[216] This book has already discussed and largely accepted the arguments for the Ten Commandments being regarded as a 'regiving' of 'self-understood', 'ageless', pre-Sinai rules, the full range of which are 'implied and operative' in Genesis 1 to Exodus 18. The idea that the Decalogue is distinct because it is not a distinct historical development is part of a Scripture-wide presupposition that its contents were 'self-understood' from the beginning. It is reflected in areas such as the prophetic disregard for national boundaries when they condemned transgressions of the Decalogue. Given the extent to which the text of the Old Testament operates with this presupposition, it is more likely that Paul is doing the same rather than appealing directly to Jeremiah 31:33 or Deuteronomy 30:14. No approach to Romans 2:14–15 is without difficulty, but accepting a wider Pentateuchal background to Paul's thought avoids the complications of the Gentile-Christian understanding and the contradictions that arise from bringing the new covenant promise into either understanding.[217]

From this perspective, Paul is answering 'the question arising from verse 12, namely: If the Gentiles are without the law, how can they be regarded as having sinned?'[218] The answer is that the work of the law is written on their hearts. This also makes sense of verses 15b–16, which, whenever the accusing and defending may commence, is an unambiguous reference to the

216 'Paul borrows here the popular Greek conception of a natural law written on the heart.' But also 'the focus must be on the moral norms of the Mosaic law.' Thomas R. Schreiner, *Romans* (Grand Rapids: Baker, 2003), 122 and 122, n. 8.

217 For example: 'This detail also brings the Gentile Christians into close proximity with Jewish Christians, in that both have a law written on their hearts, though in differing manners.' Jewett, *Romans*, 215.

218 Murray, *Romans*, 72. Also Fitzmyer, *Romans*, 312.

final judgment. The idea that Christians will find themselves in inner turmoil on 'that day' is not compatible with the wider New Testament picture of joy and guiltlessness (1 Cor. 1:8). It is unbelieving Gentiles who 'suppressed the truth' (Rom. 1:18) that will find themselves in turmoil when the searcher of hearts exposes an inscription of his law upon their hearts that reason could not erase and darkness could not hide (Rom. 1:21). He has no partiality (Rom. 2:11), so although Jew and Gentile will be judged according to the same 'ageless' standard, that day will see 'many Gentiles faring better than many Jews',[219] not because the Gentiles have an excuse (Rom. 1:20), or because they already have what the new covenant brings, but because the Jews' possession, knowledge, and perversion of the law has increased their accountability (Rom. 2:17–24). On this understanding of Romans 2, *The Westminster Confession's* opening statements on the law (19:1–2) represent a coherent and justifiable expression of apostolic doctrine.

Sin and Judgment

What is sin? Answering that question in *The Guardian*, Julian Baggini gives a dictionary-style definition:

Sin n. (obs.): Something young people do not know or care about.[220]

So obsolete has sin become that it 'is as alien to the contemporary mind as fetching water from a well, darning your own socks or finding Demis Roussos sexy.'[221] The Catholic Catechism's definition of sin as 'humanity's rejection of God and opposition to him' is simply nonsensical to 'the godless', while the church

---

219   Dunn, *Romans 1–8*, 106.
220   Julian Baggini, 'What is sin?' *The Guardian*, 9 May 2006.
221   Ibid.

itself is responsible for the situation that 'what actually counts as sinful behaviour…is not clear.'[222]

While Baggini's observations about society might be valid, the primary definitions of sin in standard dictionaries remain as far removed from his definition as the *Westminster Shorter Catechism's* definition is from that of the *Catholic Catechism*:

> sin … transgression of God's known will or any principle or law regarded as embodying this (*Collins*).[223]

> sin … An act which is regarded as a transgression of the divine law and an offence against God… (*OED*)[224]

> Sin is any want of conformity unto, or transgression of, the law of God (*WSC* 14).

That the Westminster Divines had this much in common with the editors of substantial dictionaries may not be indicative of Puritan influences on the publishers, but it may reveal the extent to which biblical definitions of sin—specifically perhaps the Authorized Version's translation of 1 John 3:4 as 'sin is transgression of the law'—shape concepts of sin in Western society. The purpose of this section is to discuss those issues of sin and judgment as they relate to the threefold division. Does the claim that the Ten Commandments represent a distinct and programmatic category of 'ageless' moral law, to which every child of Adam must give 'personal, entire, exact, and perpetual obedience',[225] receive confirmation in the way that the epistles define sin? Is the claim that Jew and Gentile will be judged according to the same standard only a necessary implication of the preceding approach to Romans 1–2 or does it have wider support in the epistles?

222   Ibid.
223   *Collins Dictionary of the English Language* (London & Glasgow: Collins, 1986), 1423.
224   *The Oxford English Dictionary*, vol. 15 (Oxford: Clarendon Press, 1989), 504.
225   *WCF* XIX.I.

According to Kalogeraki, in Jewish literature contemporary to
1 John, 'it goes without saying that sin is basically conceived of
as the infringement of God's commandments.'[226] In the epistle
and the Gospel the core of sin is rejecting Christ.[227] While the
Gospel does not reject other shades of meaning, conflicts in the
community mean 'sin needs redefining' in the epistle so it is
'expanded and obtains moral dimensions'.[228] Regardless of views
on the Gospel–epistle links, a previous chapter in this book
rejected the picture of John's Gospel as a moral wasteland. Distinct
emphases in either text need not be equated with a redefinition
of sin. It seems more likely that for both it could go 'without
saying' that sin is breaking God's commandments.

But what does the epistle say? The answer cannot be
determined by contemporary Jewish literature or the Authorised
Version translation of 1 John 3:4, only by examination of the
text. What the old version renders as 'transgression of the law',
the modern translations render as 'lawlessness' (ESV, NIV). The
word is ἀνομία and there is little doubt that in this context it
denotes disregard for the law rather than being 'without the
law', so it remains true that 'almost all exegetes of recent times
have translated it as: violation of the law, scorn for the law, or
illegality.'[229] It is difficult to translate it any other way without
following the examples of de la Potterie[230] or Schnackenburg[231]
and providing a less literal, more interpretative rendition. In any

226   Despoina M. Kalogeraki, *The Concept of Sinlessness and Sinfulness in
the First Letter of John: with reference to the paradox encountered in 1:6–10/3:6-10*
(Thessaloniki: ΕΚΔΟΣΕΙΣ, 2007), 98.

227   Ibid., 192.

228   Ibid., 194.

229   Ignace de la Potterie, S. J. and Stanislaus Lyonnet, S. J., *The Christian
Lives by the Spirit* (New York: Society of St. Paul, 1971), 38.

230   '...sin is iniquity'. Ibid., 55.

231   'We would therefore suggest that *anomia* should be translated "evil"
rather than "lawlessness".' Rudolf Schnackenburg, *The Johannine Epistles*, trans.
Reginald and Ilse Fuller (Tunbridge Wells: Burns & Oates, 1992), 171.

case, holding to the more literal translation does not always mean holding to the literal understanding so that sin is transgression of the law. In many cases the redefinition of ἀνομία follows on from other presuppositions. According to Schnackenburg, the author is not moving away from antinomianism because 'though he speaks continually of keeping the commandments (2:3, 4; 3:22, 24; 5:2), he never fights for a rehabilitation of the law'[232] and the commandments are not 'just a general code of law, even if it be the venerable Decalogue…it is the teaching of Christ himself, not only by word but also by the example of his life.'[233] Could it not be, however, that the author feels no need to rehabilitate the law because, like the Gospel writers, he saw no cleavage between the Decalogue and Christ's teaching or example?

If presuppositions about the law prompt some exegetes to move away from a literal translation of ἀνομία, reconstructions of the 'Johannine Community' and views of the context influence others. In a community riven by false teachers claiming sinlessness,[234] their 'delusion' itself makes them guilty of 'lawlessness'.[235] Should it be Antichrist secessionists who find sin inconsequential[236] then 'their attitude to sin constitutes the iniquity [ἀνομία]'.[237] Despite differences in expression, Bultmann and Brown, in common with many other interpreters,[238] hold that 1 John 3:4 must be interpreted in the light of 1 Thessalonians 2:3–12 so that sin is

232   Ibid.

233   Ibid., 99.

234   Rudolf Bultmann, *Johannine Epistles*, trans. R. Philip O'Hara with Lane C. McGaughy and Robert W. Funk (Philadelphia: Fortress Press, 1973), 50–51.

235   Ibid., 49.

236   Raymond E. Brown, *Epistles of John* (New York: Doubleday, 1982), 399.

237   Ibid., 427.

238   For example, Schnackenburg, *Johannine Epistles*, 171; de la Potterie, *The Christian Lives*, 44–55; David Rensberger, *1 John* (Nashville: Abingdon Press, 1997), 90; Stephen S. Smalley, *1,2,3 John*, WBC, ed. David A. Hubbard and Glenn W. Barker (General), Ralph P. Martin (New Testament), no. 51 (Waco: Word Books, 1984), 155.

viewed in a particular eschatological context. Some also claim that the connection between ἀνομία and law in the LXX is non-existent or weak,[239] but to argue that ἀνομία has nothing to do with νόμος is as perverse as arguing that law-breaking has nothing to do with law. Apart from scores of examples where ἀνομία only makes sense if law is assumed, the LXX does make several direct connections,[240] but proving or disproving this link is of little importance given the eventual definitions of sin that those who prefer the eschatological perspective arrive at:

> The act of sin (John seems to be saying) involves a rebellious alignment with the devil, rather than with God in Christ (cf. vv 8, 10). It implies not merely breaking God's law, but flagrantly opposing him (in Satanic fashion) by so doing.[241]

> Perpetrators of sin declare that they are secret allies and colleagues of Satan. They submit to the power of Christ's adversary (vv. 7–8) and prove themselves to be genuine children of the devil (vv. 9–10).[242]

> Sin as the Iniquity is opposed to Jesus who was revealed to Israel as the Lamb of God who takes away the sin of the world (John 1:29).[243]

> ...the author of the Fourth Gospel nowhere mentions a series of individual sins, such as stealing, murder, adultery, etc. We might say that he rises to a higher level, from which he can encompass everything in one glance and reduce it all to one...man's negative response in his meeting with Christ.[244]

The question is how does any of this go beyond the traditional translation and interpretation that sees sin as breaking God's law? Does the rest of Scripture view 'merely breaking God's law' as something less than flagrant opposition? Are 'perpetrators of sin'

239   de la Potterie, *The Christian Lives*, 40–41; Smalley, *1,2,3 John*, 154.
240   Leviticus 26:43; Deuteronomy 31:29; 2 Samuel 22:23–4; Jeremiah 36:23.
241   Smalley, *1,2,3 John*, 155.
242   Schnackenburg, *Johannine Epistles*, 171.
243   Brown, *Epistles of John*, 427.
244   de la Potterie, *The Christian Lives*, 54.

normally allies of Christ? Is sin friendly to Jesus? Why does it take us to a 'higher level' to reduce sin to rejection of Christ? In the end, none of these redefinitions add anything to the traditional definition of sin, but are subsumed within it. If sin is breaking whatever laws God has made binding at a specific point in time, then there are sufficient examples within the New Testament of the application of Mosaic Laws to include what those writers have proposed. If it is legitimate to interpret 1 John from the standpoint of 1 Thessalonians then receiving Christ represents obedience to the first and second commandments rather than a transcending of their demands (1 Thess. 1:9–10). Elsewhere, the implication is that acknowledgment of Jesus Christ is one and the same with obedience to the summarising first and greatest commandment (1 Cor. 8:4–6).[245] The Johannine writings give no reason to think that the law or laws of which sin is the transgression would be understood as anything less or something more refined than the commandments of the Decalogue.

This definition of sin is not restricted to 1 John; the epistle of James makes a similar statement. A following section will discuss James 2:8–12 in more detail, but the point to note now is that in verse 9 sin is synonymous with transgression of the law. In the first example, the transgression is showing partiality, but this is failure to obey the second greatest commandment (v. 8) and no less sin than murder and adultery (v. 11). Sinlessness requires perfect keeping of the whole law (v. 10). To James may be added Pauline texts that only make sense if sin is transgression of the law—Romans 3:20 with its statement that the knowledge of sin comes through the law or Romans 7:7 with its autobiographical account of that principle.

245 'To the extent that this echoes the *Shema*, we should also hear the echo of that text's call to "love the Lord your God with all your heart and with all your soul and with all your might" (Deut. 6:5)....All of this has a direct bearing on the question of idol meat: this one God of Israel is "a jealous God" who is well known to have no tolerance of idolatry.' Hays, *First Corinthians*, 140.

So does it go 'without saying' in the epistles that sin is breaking God's laws? 1 John 3:4 and these examples ensure that it does not. Nonetheless, it probably could go 'without saying', since so much depends on that basic assumption, not only in the epistles, but throughout Scripture. An exhaustive exploration and uncovering of that assumption is beyond the scope of this book, but it is fair to say that the confessionists were justified in claiming biblical grounds for defining sin as transgression of the law. Accordingly, law was a fundamental component of their theological framework since God's wrath and curse on sin brought death and misery to sinners[246] that could only be removed through Christ being made under the law and undergoing the miseries that others deserved.[247] But is their definition now obsolete? In so far as law is defined by the Decalogue, critics of the threefold division might need to say yes. For the divines, to sin was to break those laws irrespective of one's place in time—pre-lapsarian or post-lapsarian, pre-Sinai or post-Sinai, pre-Pentecost or post-Pentecost. Whether it was Adam's eating the forbidden fruit, Cain's fratricide, Nadab and Abihu's liturgical innovation, or Demas' love of this world, they all constituted transgressions of the Decalogue. Righteousness was not a fluctuating ideal; sin was not a roughly defined problem. If, however, the law is a unity and the whole law is abrogated, of what law is sin a transgression? If James (along with Paul and Jesus) envisages 'new law' that 'expands, and deepens, the demands of the "old" law'[248] does that not mean that the only lawgiver and judge (Jam. 4:2) employs a double standard? It is one thing to say that a new era of revelation means new applications of the law, but something else to say that the law, and consequently sin, have expanded.

246   *WCF* VI.VI.

247   *WCF* VIII.IV; *WSC* 27.

248   Ralph P. Martin, *James,* WBC, ed. David A. Hubbard and Glenn W. Barker (General), Ralph P. Martin (New Testament), no. 48 (Nashville: Thomas Nelson, 1988), 67.

One of the implications of seeing the law that was laid down in the Decalogue as a fixed moral code is that it must therefore be the standard by which all people in every age will be judged. Much of the exegetical and theological argument in the preceding chapters leads to that conclusion. In the epistles, the ideas that the Decalogue is written on the fleshy hearts of Christians, that it remains inscribed on the stony hearts of unbelievers, and that all sin constitutes transgression of the Ten Commandments, logically require that final judgment be according to that standard. If the moral norms to be enforced on that day remain 'self-understood' it should not be surprising if many references to the final judgment make no mention of the legal standard that will be employed.[249] The earlier discussion of Romans 2 introduced the subject of universal judgment according this 'ageless' standard, but do the epistles say anything that suggest an alternative ethical code tips the scales of eternal justice? Sometimes forthcoming judgment is explicitly predicted for transgressions of the Decalogue such as adultery (Heb. 13:4), but generally, judgment is according to 'deeds' (1 Pet. 1:17; Jude 15; Rev. 20:12–13), 'whether good or evil' (2 Cor. 5:10). Although the deeds remain unspecified, the language in these cases may echo Jeremiah 17:10 where the LORD searches hearts and gives every man 'according to his ways, according to the fruit of his deeds'. Unlike its parallel passage of Psalm 1, Jeremiah 17 makes no direct mention of the law, yet its opening words recall Sinai's tablets of stone, perhaps suggesting that the sin inscribed on Judah's heart is defined by the Ten Words that will be the measure of the blessed and cursed man alike. In two of those New Testament echoes explicit reference to the law is never far away (1 Pet. 1:16; 2 Cor. 3), but even so, the idea that final judgment will be according to that standard remains an implicit assumption rather than something the authors felt they had to spell out.

There are also two examples in the epistles where a litany of iniquities are met with an unvarying response of judgment. First, Romans 1:24–2:11, which lists several literal transgressions of the Decalogue—covetousness, murder, lies, and disobedience to parents (Rom. 1:29–30)—and various offences that break other Mosaic Laws, which a previous chapter on the Pentateuch has shown may depend on the Decalogue and to which the principles uncovered in Paul's use of judicial laws may also apply. While Romans 1 may not in any literary sense be based on the Decalogue, none of those death-deserving deeds (Rom. 1:32) go beyond established or plausible applications of its commandments. The second example is 1 Peter 4:1–5, which lists one literal transgression—idolatry (1 Pet. 4:3)—and several implied. It may seem that some of those, such as drunkenness, go beyond the Decalogue, but as Elliot points out, the only other place οἰνοφλυγίαις occurs (in its verbal form) is in Deuteronomy 21:20 where it characterizes the behaviour of a son who dishonours his parents.[250] Similarly, in 1 Peter drink-fuelled orgies do not represent an uncharacteristic and isolated indiscretion; they are built-in features of Gentile enslavement to human passions that show no concern for future judgment or the 'will of God' (1 Pet. 4:2, 5).

Returning to Romans 2, we meet with a plain statement that final judgment will be according to the law: 'it is not the hearers of the law who are righteous before God, but the doers of the law will be justified' (v. 13). 'The vexation this text has caused in the history of interpretation is an interesting study in its own right.'[251] Nonetheless, the vexatious issue of how judgments

250   John H. Elliot, 1 Peter (New York: Doubleday, 2000), 723.
251   Klyne R. Snodgrass, 'Justification by Grace – to the Doers: An Analysis of the Place of Romans 2 in the Theology of Paul.' NTS 32 (1986), 73.

according to works might sweetly comply with Romans 3:20 or the doctrine of justification is not an immediate concern.[252] The crucial point is that people will stand or fall in the final judgment on the basis of whether or not they have conformed to the law, and it is not a triviality that when Romans 2:21–2 expands the argument that the examples of tutelary hypocrisy are restricted to transgressions of the seventh, eighth, and second commandments.[253] Even so, as with most of the epistles' references to the final judgment this does not constitute an explicit proclamation that the Ten Commandments are the measure of sin or standard of final judgment, but explicit proclamations are redundant when an assumption is so widespread in Scripture that its rejection would require proclamation no less explicit than rejection of the creation account or the exodus from Egypt. There is nothing in the epistles' approach to sin and judgment that suggests a moral or legal basis that goes beyond the Decalogue or narrows its field of application. The question of what 'law' Romans 2:13 has in mind and what 'will of God' 1 Peter 4:2 wishes

252   Snodgrass' article seeks to reconcile those ideas: 'Judgment according to works is not the contradiction of justification by faith, but its presupposition.' Ibid., 86.

253   'The fourth query…moves beyond the Ten Commandments' claims Jewett, and refers to Josephus' call that none blaspheme the gods that others revere. Jewett, *Romans*, 228–9. Interestingly, John Calvin took a similar approach to the mass, advising those who had turned from Roman Catholicism to cease attending, yet objecting to any 'display of contempt' for the mass that might be regarded as 'sheer impiety against God.' John Calvin, *Selected Works of John Calvin*. ed. and trans. Henry Beveridge (Grand Rapids: Baker Book House, 1983), 407. The accusation of Romans 2:22 could, however, refer to the Jerusalem temple. Dunn, *Romans 1–8*, 114. Irrespective of these arguments, it seems more likely that the parallel with the previous examples points to hypocrisy that constitutes a direct breach of the second commandment.

It is also worth noting that Nestle-Aland cite Psalm 50:16–21 with its reminiscence of Horeb (discussed on pages 134–139 of this thesis) as an allusion in Romans 2:21. Nestle-Aland, *Novum Testamentum Graece*, 787. Also Keil & Delitzch on Psalm 50: 'What Jahve says in this passage is exactly the same as that which the apostle of Jesus Christ says in Rom 2:17–24.'

to uphold is ultimately determined by exegetical conclusions and theological presuppositions such as those identified earlier in this book. If ceremonial law has been abrogated and judicial laws have expired then it is not those laws. If prophets, and possibly psalmists, viewed God as judging peoples that did not have the Decalogue according to its moral precepts then not only might this be reflected in Romans, but for God to be just would he not have to judge peoples 'without the law' by that standard regardless of their place in history? Coupled with those conclusions and presuppositions is an expectation, namely that if the 'law' or the 'will of God' is summed up in the Decalogue, then the epistles will uphold its precepts or call for obedience to its commands from Christians and unbelievers alike. It is the purpose of the following section to find out if that expectation will be met.

A Strengthened Obligation

The Westminster Divines were persuaded the moral law was binding upon all—'justified persons and others'.[254] For all, it served as a guide, as a means to convince people of sin and their need of Christ. For believers, even if they were not under the law as a 'covenant of works',[255] the law's promises were an encouragement and its prohibitions a restraint on sin. Christ's coming into the world strengthened rather than weakened obligation to obey the law.[256] These things they believed not only because of how they understood Jesus' teaching in the Sermon on the Mount and the Gospels, but also because they saw it reaffirmed in the epistles.

In chapter four, I concluded that Jesus' references to the two greatest commandments, in particular his response to the scribe,

254   *WCF* XIX.V.
255   *WCF* XIX.VI.
256   *WCF* XIX.V.

confirm that he gave the highest place to the commandments of the Decalogue and it was 'with good reason' that the two great commandments were considered a précis of the Decalogue. This link between the two great commandments and the Decalogue makes partial re-emergence in the epistles. It is partial primarily because the first great commandment gets no verbatim citation, which of course does not mean the apostles considered it abrogated—the *Shema* with its love command is interwoven into various passages. Gerhardsson sees it appearing in several passages as part of a synthesis where the love commands are exemplified in Christ, whom we must imitate.[257] In 1 Corinthians 8, Wright finds Paul using a 'Christianized *Shema*' to reassert monotheism and argue for the primacy of love: 'The love of God—the fulfilled *Shema*—is the central characteristic of the true people of God.'[258] James 2:18–22 provides another example where the apostle maintains the logic of the *Shema*—'his basic creed'[259]—in insisting that faith without works is dead. Regardless of these arguments, the answer to the question, did the apostles believe people should love God with all their heart, mind, and soul? is obvious. It may be less obvious that they believed that obligation still summarised the abiding demands of the Decalogue, yet the overall picture that has been established of the church's approach to the law means a blunt proclamation is not required to support the conclusion that the apostolic writers viewed the first great commandment in this way.

Critics of the threefold division might object to this, yet their

257   Birger Gerhardsson, *The Shema in the New Testament* (Lund: Novapress, 1996), 283. He mentions Philippians 2:6–11, Romans 15:1–3, and 1 Corinthians 10:33–11:1.

258   N. T. Wright, *The Climax of the Covenant: Christ and the Law in Pauline Theology* (Edinburgh: T&T Clark, 1991), 132.

259   Peter H. Davids, 'James's Message: The Literary Record' in Bruce Chilton and Jacobs Neusner, eds., *The Brother of Jesus: James the Just and His Mission* (Louisville, Westminster John Knox Press, 2001), 68.

own works show that previous conclusions about Jesus and the law cannot be placed in exegetical quarantine. That views of Jesus' attitude to the law in the Gospels influences exegesis of the epistles is inevitable. Moo, for example, in his interpretation of James 2:8 suggests that 'royal law' is not the clear reference to Mosaic law that it appears to be;[260] it 'may well extend beyond the Mosaic law as fulfilled and reinterpreted by Jesus to include the teaching of Jesus.'[261] He also notes James' recognition that the second greatest commandment that 'stands at the heart of the NT ethical code goes back…to Jesus' teaching'[262] in Matthew 22:37–40.[263] Not that this is universally accepted—Dibelius sees no link with Jesus' comments on the greatest commandments, so 'royal law' is not the love commandment, but simply '*the* law'.[264]

Neither Moo's reluctance to define 'royal law' as the law, nor Dibelius' unwillingness to link it with the love commandment are at home in James 2. If the two great commandments summarise the Decalogue it makes no difference whether or not 'royal law' refers specifically to the love commandment. And unless James' exclusive citation of two Decalogue commandments (Jas. 2:11) is hermeneutically adiaphorous, he himself appears to accept the summarising approach.[265] If he does not, then he is unlike

260   Douglas J. Moo, *The Letter of James* (Leicester: Apollos, 2000), 111. His argument against the threefold division appears in 'The Law of Christ', 320–1.

261   Moo, *James*, 112.

262   Ibid.

263   Similar views are expressed by several other commentators. Martin, *James*, 67; Johnson, *James*, 231.

264   Martin Dibelius, *James*, Michael A. Williams trans. (Philadelphia: Fortress Press, 1976), 142.

265   This also suggests Painter is correct when he says that 'it would be unwise to reject the picture, built up elsewhere, of James and the Jerusalem church as law observant.' John Painter, 'Who Was James?' in Chilton and Neusner, *The Brother of Jesus*, 54. (The 'picture' Painter has in mind reveals an intertextual relationship with Matthew and 'this Petrine Gospel', 54–5.)

Paul who makes a similarly exclusive citation of four Decalogue commandments before making the unambiguous statement that they and 'any other commandment, are summed up in this word: "Love your neighbour as yourself."' (Rom. 13:9). Fitzmyer begins his explanation of 'any other commandment' by saying that the 'immediate sense' of the phrase is 'of the Decalogue' before going on to say that this extends 'in a more remote sense...to any legal system, Roman, ecclesiastical, civil, etc.'[266] Jewett takes the same approach,[267] but despite Paul's earlier call for submission to authorities (Rom. 13:1), it would be a significant leap for him to see every law ever enacted as a derivative of neighbour love. Ecclesiastics—to say nothing of empires and states—could not claim to have produced a *corpus juris* of unblemished love. Love of neighbour might demand settled disobedience to certain ecclesiastical and civil laws, yet love could never be divorced from the commandments Paul cites in Romans 13:9.[268] In the light of Paul's approach to ceremonial and judicial laws, the 'immediate sense' is the only sense, so that in the context of Romans 13 'any other commandment' is most likely to have brought to mind the command to honour parents or the command not to bear false witness.[269]

It is not necessarily problematic, however, if 'any other commandment' implies that the first four commandments are also summed up in the command to love neighbour rather than the command to love God; a wooden first greatest commandment/ first table and second greatest commandment/second table equation has not been universally held. A previous chapter

266 Fitzmyer, *Romans*, 679.

267 Jewett, *Romans*, 812.

268 Schreiner makes this point and argues that this passage in Romans indicates that Paul made a distinction between moral and ritual law. Thomas R. Schreiner, 'The Abolition and Fulfillment of the Law in Paul.' *JSNT* 35 (1989), 59.

269 Jewett presents a variety of reasons for Paul's selectivity at this point. See Jewett, *Romans*, 810–12.

showed that most exegetes have been content to accept a more general equation between the two, recognising that love for God and love for neighbour are indivisible. This is evident even within particular Decalogue commands, notably the Sabbath commandment. Although in the New Testament the idea is expressed most explicitly in 1 John 4:19–20, it is a necessary implication of the fulfilment language of Romans 13:8 and also of the final reference to the second greatest commandment in Galatians 5:14.

The basic definitions of πληρόω featured in the earlier discussion of Matthew 5:17 (and Appendix 2) where Jesus' fulfilment of the law was seen as eschatological, soteriological, and moral. How πληρόω is understood in that context influences conclusions about its equally-debated meaning in Romans and Galatians.[270] Witherington (following Longenecker) argues that it is Christ's fulfilment that is in view:[271] He fulfilled the law making 'it possible for his followers to see the fulfillment of the Law and its requirements in their own lives simply by following his example…'[272] It is difficult to reconcile this with Witherington's keenness to preserve Paul from contradiction[273] and the significant point that Galatians 5:14 'does not say the Christian is fulfilling the law'.[274] Unqualified transfer of the contextually-defined meaning of πληρόω from Matthew to the epistles does not work, and while a very theological interpretation

270 'Just as in the parallel passage by Matthew, to "fulfill" the law means to accomplish its original intent and purpose.' Jewett, *Romans*, 809. 'Paul is almost certainly following…language already established in the Jewish Christian debate with the Pharisees (cf. Matt 5:17–20).' Dunn, *Romans 9–16*, 777. 'The language here reflects Matthean convictions…' Ben Witherington III, *Grace in Galatia: A Commentary on St Paul's Letter to the Galatains* (Edinburgh: T&T Clark, 1998), 383.

271 Witherington, *Galatians*, 382.

272 Ibid., 384.

273 Ibid., 380.

274 Ibid., 382.

might identify Christ as the 'one' in Romans 13:8, initially it is preferable to expect the same meaning in both passages. The idea that πληρόω means 'summed up' (NIV) is widely dismissed,[275] and probably rightly because that is an assumption in the extended contexts rather than the immediate meaning of πληρόω. Nor is the point to establish a contrast with Jewish observance of the law as 'doing' (ποιέω – Gal. 5:3) and to point to 'a decisive difference between law and love'.[276] Whatever objections Paul may have had to Jewish 'doing', he was neither excluding this from his concept of fulfilling the law nor sundering law from love—'the one who loves another has fulfilled the law…love is the fulfilling of the law' (Rom. 13:8, 10)—and Dunn's definitions of 'properly perform' or 'exhaustively complete'[277] make most sense in Romans and Galatians.

In Barclay's opinion 'Paul chose this vocabulary partly because of its *ambiguity*!' and to leave 'unclear the status of the rest of the commandments'.[278] If the conclusions in the earlier parts of this chapter are correct, Paul was not ambiguous about ceremonial or judicial law, and their status is not ambiguous in the framework established so far. To fulfil the love commandment after the torn veil means to fulfil the moral laws of the Decalogue, so if any ambiguity exists it is only with respect to the first commands of the Decalogue, but in reality there is no ambiguity. Paul could not conceive of fulfilment of the law that excluded love for God any more than he could conceive of lawless anarchy unaccompanied by hatred of God (Rom. 1:30). For these reasons, the indivisibility of love for God and neighbour are necessary

275 J. Louis Martyn, *Galatians* (New York: Doubleday, 1997), 488; Hans Dieter Betz, *Galatians* (Philadelphia: Fortress Press, 1979), 274–5; Witherington, *Galatians*, 383; John M. G. Barclay, *Obeying the Truth: A Study of Paul's Ethics in Galatians*, John Riches, ed. (Edinburgh: T&T Clark, 1988), 137–8.

276 Betz, *Galatians*, 275. Also Martyn, *Galatians*, 197.

277 Dunn, *Romans 9-16*, 777.

278 Barclay, *Obeying the Truth*, 140.

implications of Paul's fulfilment language, yet as Augustine pointed out long ago there may also have been a practical reason:

> Since in fact love is only made perfect through the two commands of love of God and neighbour, why is it that in both letters the Apostle mentions only the love of neighbour, unless it is because people can lie about their love of God, since it is put to the test less often, but they are more easily found guilty of not loving their neighbour when they behave wickedly towards others….in a question of works of righteousness it is usually enough to mention just one of them, but it is more appropriate to mention the one on the basis of which a person is more easily found guilty.[279]

In other words, Augustine sees Paul using logic slightly similar to that of James—failure to keep one law means failure to keep the whole law (Jam. 2:10)—so that the God-then-neighbour order of the law when it makes its demands is reversed to a neighbour-then-God order when it seeks to secure conviction.

It is not possible to enter into the detailed debate concerning the Christian's relationship to the law that surrounds passages like Galatians 5, other than to note that the ambition to frame Paul's language as descriptive rather than prescriptive ends up producing overly fine distinctions: believers' fulfilment of the law 'happens quite naturally' and 'not by submitting to that law',[280] or they are not 'obligated to it' yet 'their conduct coincidentally displays the behavior that Mosaic Law prescribes.'[281] This is a strange dichotomy. That someone 'coincidentally' keeps a law does not mean he feels no obligation to submit to it. If such love of God and neighbour happens so naturally, why do the epistles frequently stress believers' obligations to exhibit behaviour that the law requires? Rather than reading the passages above

---

279   Eric Plumer, *Augustine's Commentary on Galatians: Introduction, Text, Translation, and Notes* (Oxford: Oxford University Press, 2003), 207.

280   Witherington, *Galatians*, 381.

281   Ibid. He is quoting Thielman at this point.

as promoting practically meaningless distinctions, it is better to view them as apostolic acceptance and reuse of the principle that the two greatest commandments are a précis of the Decalogue, the fulfilment of which is a strengthened obligation for Christians (and therefore everyone else).

A Rest Remains

On several occasions the epistles call for behaviour that accords with the Decalogue without actually quoting any of it (1 Cor. 6:18; 10:14; Col. 3:5–10; 1 Tim. 1:8–11; Eph. 5:1–5). Of these perhaps the most relevant is 1 Timothy since it is often thought to echo each of the Ten Commandments.[282] The most prominent example where a single commandment is quoted in the context of an ethical exhortation appears in Ephesians 6:1–3, which is hard to interpret in any other way than as an immediate call for obedience to the fifth commandment. Not that no one is willing to try—De Lacey in particular is at pains to ensure that the initial call for children to obey their parents stands aloof from the fifth commandment: the link between 'it is right' and verse 2 'should not be overemphasized',[283] quoting the commandment is 'far from being [the author's] *primary* motivation' because the imperative is not grounded in the commandments but in the calling and new life of Ephesians 4.[284] One of De Lacey's fellow-contributors to *From Sabbath to Lord's Day*, Andrew Lincoln, is equally reluctant to accept the link: 'from what we know of the universality with which the obedience of children to parents was upheld, it is far more likely that the writer's appeal is to this general sense of what was fitting and right, to which he

---

282   Luke Timothy Johnson, *The First and Second Letters to Timothy* (New York: Doubleday, 2001), 169–71; George W. Knight III, *The Pastoral Epistles: A Commentary on the Greek Text* (Grand Rapids: Eerdmans, 1992), 83–5.

283   De Lacey, 'The Sabbath/Sunday Question', 193, n. 126.

284   Ibid., 178.

then gives further biblical support.'²⁸⁵ Ironically, both of those approaches may strengthen the link between the command in verse 1 and the commandment in verse 2 since the Decalogue itself grounds its imperatives in redemption (Exod. 20:2) and its 'self-understood' commands are synonymous with 'this general sense'. Doubtless, it is right to obey parents for those reasons, but it is hardly unthinkable that the author thought it δίκαιος because for him God's commandments were the primary measure of what is right (cf. Rom. 7:12). It is not only the commandment that is still valid; the promise attached to it also holds good.²⁸⁶ Lincoln finds it misplaced: the promise 'would be alien to the Paul who expected an imminent parousia, even if this Paul had come to terms with his own death before that event. It is more likely to have been penned by a Jewish Christian follower....'²⁸⁷ This promise need not have been alien to any Paul, however, especially if it was never meant to be understood as holding out threescore and ten years to those who successfully avoided the death penalty for dishonouring their parents.²⁸⁸ It is preferable to see it within the general remit of the land promise first made to Abraham and repeated throughout Deuteronomy (1:8; 6:10; etc.). Although that promise of a 'resting place' and an 'inheritance'

285   Andrew T. Lincoln, *Ephesians*, WBC, ed. David A. Hubbard and Glenn W. Barker (General), Ralph P. Martin (New Testament), no. 42 (Texas: Word Books, 1990), 403.

286   Why this is called 'the first commandment with a promise' is much debated. Hoehner's commentary provides an up-to-date list of the various possibilities and supports the well-established view that it is the first commandment with a specific promise. See Hoehner, *Ephesians*, 790–91.

287   Lincoln, *Ephesians*, 406.

288   Durham takes such a view: 'These words must be read in the light of such texts as Exod 21:15, 17; Lev 20:9; and Deut 21:18–21, 27:16....The addition to the fifth commandment has a double meaning: while appropriate honor accorded father and mother could contribute for a number of reasons to the length of one's days in Yahweh's land, a lack of respect for them could just as certainly mean an abrupt end to those days.' Durham, *Exodus*, 292.

(Deut. 12:8–9) was viewed as in some sense fulfilled in the days of Joshua (Josh. 21:43–5; 23:1), David (2 Sam. 7:1), and Solomon (1 Kgs. 5:4), psalmists and prophets still looked for greater, ongoing, or renewed fulfilment (Ps. 37; Isa. 60:21; 61:7, Jer. 24:6–7; 32:41, Ezek. 37:24–8). In the New Testament, Jesus shares that outlook (Matt. 5:5) while the preacher in Hebrews takes the example of those who failed to enter Canaan (3:1–19) before declaring that the promise still stands (4:1, 6); Joshua's day saw only a token fulfilment (4:8). The promise of rest was and is the gospel (4:2, 6); those who believe enter that rest with the God who has rested from his works (4:3, 10). In Romans, this promise of land and rest sweeps away geographic boundaries: 'For the promise to Abraham or to his descendants that he would be heir of the world...' (Rom. 4:13). It still holds good, awaiting fulfilment in the renewal of the cosmos: 'Just as Abraham's earliest descendants were promised a land and received it, so the future descendants of Abraham will one day share Abraham's inheritance of a world that has been conquered by the Prince of Peace.'[289] Read from this eschatological perspective, Ephesians 6 is saying—imminent parousia or death—that those who obey their parents will receive the promised inheritance (Eph. 1:11). It is not that obedience to the fifth commandment is presented as the way to eternal life, but rather it is part of that new life with its 'true righteousness', which is made manifest in the wholesale conformity to God's commandments described from Ephesians 4:24 to 6:9.

This interpretation of the fifth commandment in Ephesians also has implications for how the fourth commandment is interpreted. This book has noted that rejection of the threefold division has often gone hand-in-hand with anti-Sabbatarianism. It is also clear that attitudes to the Sabbath, whether those of the Westminster Divines or of anti-Sabbatarians, are largely shaped by conclusions or expectations arising out of Jesus' attitude to the

---

289   McComiskey, *Covenants of Promise*, 55.

law. Therefore, specific arguments that Jesus did not undermine the Sabbath, that Acts records no retreat from Jesus' attitude, and that epistolary references to feasts, new moons, and sabbaths served as shorthand for the offerings and rituals common to those occasions, along with other arguments that have supported the threefold division, inevitably leave the fourth commandment no less valid than any other of the Ten Words.

In *From Sabbath to Lord's Day*, however, Lincoln raises the further issue of eschatology. His argument, which is mainly dependent on Hebrews 3:7–4:13, maintains that Jesus' fulfilment of the concept of rest tied up with the Sabbath means that the 'already' outweighs the 'not yet' so that the Old Testament physical rest has become 'salvation rest': 'Believers in Christ can now live in God's Sabbath that has already dawned.'[290] But in what way is this rest new for the individual believer? Is it qualitatively superior to the salvation rest that the Psalmist knew (Ps. 116:7)?[291] These questions are complex, as are the exegetical issues in Hebrews 4, but it is not necessary to discuss them in detail.[292] The important point is that even assuming a high degree of typology in the fourth commandment, it is the same basic theme that is explicit in the fifth commandment, and the degree of eschatological fulfilment of that theme is no greater in one than the other. The degree of 'already' that Lincoln sees can indeed only be reconciled with Ephesians 6:1–3 if the promise should not be there, but the promise is in the text because the author sees its fulfilment as sufficiently 'not yet' that both the promise and the moral law that accompanies it are still binding.

290   A. T. Lincoln, 'Sabbath, Rest, and Eschatology in the New Testament' in Carson, *Sabbath to Lord's Day*, 214–5.

291   מָנוֹחַ signifies a resting place. It is the opposite of wilderness wanderings (Deut. 28:65) and exile (Lam. 1:3).

292   The variety of opinion Lincoln cites shows that accepting or rejecting the point of view he presents will not necessarily determine views of the Sabbath (see his comment on Jewett). Lincoln, *Sabbath to Lord's Day*, 213–4.

The promise is being cumulatively fulfilled and it is not, as Lincoln argues, the 'you have come' of Hebrews 12:22 that marks the end of the Sabbath;[293] 'things that have been made' (Heb. 12:27), including the cycle of work and rest, will not be removed until the 'yet once more' of Hebrews 12:26. The degree of 'already' in anti-Sabbatarian theology amounts to an over-realized eschatology. It may not, as used to be thought of the Thessalonians,[294] have led them to abandon work, but as Craigie noted, the fourth commandment brings a 'double obligation' of working for six days and resting on the seventh.[295] The epistles' relative silence on the Sabbath suggests not that this obligation has been overturned, but that as surely as the Creator remains transcendent so it remains binding.

Secondary Texts and Interrelated Themes

One of the stated aims towards the beginning of this discussion on the epistles was to draw together some of the threads that appeared earlier. It was never possible to weave every thread into the narrative, to discuss every interrelated theological issue, or to investigate every passage in the epistles that concerns the law. The objective has been to focus on matters having a direct impact on the threefold division. Those threads and texts will not have been subject to uniform interpretations within the communities shaped by *The Westminster Confession*, or the *Thirty Nine Articles* and *Irish Articles* with their near-identical formulations. When the field is expanded to include all who have adopted the

293   Ibid., 211.

294   For a discussion see Colin R. Nicholl, *From Hope to Despair in Thessalonica: Situating 1 and 2 Thessalonians* (Cambridge: Cambridge University Press, 2004), 157–79.

295   Craigie, *Deuteronomy*, 156. If or how the Sabbath commandment understood in this way might have influenced texts that deal with work, such as those in 1 and 2 Thessalonians, may be a topic worthy of investigation.

threefold division within the last eighteen hundred years even greater diversity will emerge. Nonetheless, before summarising this chapter, it is worth describing briefly how some of those things have been understood within *The Westminster Confession*'s framework and also noting how a few writers within that tradition interpreted statements about the law.

Many of the Old Testament features highlighted as pointing to the Decalogue's distinctiveness are assumed in the epistles. No one doubted that the Decalogue was given in the form of direct speech (Heb. 12:19). Regardless of views on the place of the Decalogue, that morality has primacy over cult for the apostles is uncontroversial; like the prophets they never showed hostility towards obedience to the Ten Commandments or suggested that God could hate such obedience. Sometimes they depended on prophetic texts that themselves depended on the Decalogue (Ezek. 28:2–9 in 2 Thess. 2:4 and Acts 12:22; Jer. 2:11 in Rom. 1:23).[296] The epistles also echo directly Jesus' sayings (Jam. 5:12; 2 John 9), while their emphasis on morality that goes beyond external conformity follows his teaching such that their own is likewise not antithetical to the law, but in co-ordination and continuity with it.

Some texts, such as 1 Corinthians 7:9 with its insistence that keeping the commandments of God is what counts were not discussed because the debate about whether or not ἐντολῶν θεοῦ signifies the Decalogue[297] is secondary when what commandments are to be obeyed has already been determined by the hermeneutical framework established in the light of more explicit passages. The same applies to the frequent references to obeying commandments in the Johannine epistles, or when Revelation speaks of the saints as those who 'keep the commandments of God' (Rev. 12:17; 14:12). Unless such passages

---

296   Nestle-Aland, *Novum Testamentum Graece*, 795, 798.
297   See De Lacey, 'The Sabbath/Sunday Question', 176–7.

clearly point to a different meaning they are interpreted by whatever interpretive framework is consciously or unconsciously in place rather than being of architectonic significance.[298]

The Westminster Confession begins its lengthy explanation of the implications of moral law binding all with the statement that 'true believers be not under the law as a covenant of works, to be thereby justified or condemned'.[299] It is in this sense that passages such as Romans 6:14–15 that might otherwise be interpreted as proclaiming absolute freedom from the law are understood. 'You are not under law but under grace' therefore points not to the Mosaic economy but to moral law 'as a covenant of works' or something to be fulfilled in order to be justified. To be 'dead to the law' (Rom. 7:4–6; Gal. 2:19) is to be free from that impossible burden.[300] Believers are dead to the hope of justification by works

---

298   Moo highlights the inevitability of this: 'A deluge of books and articles [on the Mosaic law] has examined virtually every conceivable perspective. Yet nothing even approaching a consensus has emerged. Several factors account for the radically different conclusions reached by biblical scholars and theologians, the most important of which is the diverse theological and hermeneutical frameworks that are used to order and arrange the various texts. Theological confessional allegiances—Lutheran, Reformed, dispensational, etc.—thus dictate which texts are given precedence and used to interpret others.' Moo, 'The Law of Christ', 320.

299   *WCF* XIX.VI.

300   Despite leaving the Church of Scotland, one to become an itinerant and the other to become a Baptist, brothers, Robert and James Haldane interpreted Romans and Galatians in line with their Reformed tradition: 'To the moral law exclusively, here and throughout the rest of the chapter, the Apostle refers.…Dead to the law means being freed from the power of the law, as having endured its curse. It has ceased to have a claim on the obedience of believers, in order to life, though it still remains their rule of duty.' Robert Haldane, *Exposition of the Epistles to the Romans,* vol. II (London: Hamilton, Adams, and Co, M.DCCC.XXXVIII), 106–7. 'Thus the believer is dead to the law, that he may live unto God. In the matter of justification, he has no more confidence in the best work which he ever performed, than in the greatest sin he ever committed.' J. A. Haldane, *An Exposition of the Epistle to the Galatians* (Edinburgh: William Whyte and Co, 1848), 87.

because Christ 'is the end of the law' (Rom. 10:4), yet the 'law is holy' and 'good' (Rom. 7:12; 1 Tim. 1:8) so it remains a 'rule of life'[301] for all. Those who are justified have been convicted of the moral law's unmet requirements (Rom. 7:7) and given a clear 'sight of the need they have of Christ, and the perfection of His obedience'.[302] Christ put himself 'under an authoritative and unchangeable, but by them violated Moral Law, to fulfil, as their representative, all its commandments, and endure, as their substitute, all its curse'.[303] His full and final settlement of their debt means they bear no further liability and the righteous requirement of the law is fulfilled in them (Rom. 8:4).[304] Justification means that the 'obedience and satisfaction of Christ' is imputed to them.[305] Such interpretations are not only an outcome of the threefold division as a hermeneutical framework—the theology of substitutionary atonement is only coherent on the basis of such a view of moral law. As Hugh Martin pointed out, a move away from this approach means that more than a theology of law comes undone.[306]

SUMMARY

In this chapter I aimed to draw together some of the threads from earlier chapters, investigating the possible basis for the

301   Ibid.

302   *WCF* IX.VI.

303   Martin, *Atonement*, 273.

304   'It is eloquent of the apostle's view of the place of the law of God in the life of the believer that he should conceive of the holiness, which is the end promoted by the redemptive work of Christ, as the fulfilment of the ordinance of God's law....The term "fulfilled" expresses the plenary character of the fulfilment which the law receives and it indicates that the goal contemplated in the sanctifying process is nothing short of the perfection which the law of God requires.' Murray, *Romans*, 283.

305   *WCF* XI.I.

306   See Chapter One.

traditional categories and some interdependent theological ideas within the epistles ascribed to the apostles. Of all the assertions in the threefold division, the idea that ceremonial laws no longer bind is probably the least controversial in the Christian church. Hebrews' delineation of some laws as 'copies and shadows', Colossians adoption of standard expressions to define ritual laws, and Ephesians reference to the 'law of commandments in ordinances' all point to a category of law that prefigured Christ and his work. When Peter speaks of Christ as the lamb without blemish it amounts to a view of Christ's fulfilment that is again moral, soteriological, and eschatological. First Corinthians' reference to the Passover and unleavened bread also brings all three together when it promotes the moral purity signified in the ritual forms rather than the forms themselves. In its explanation of ceremonial law, *The Westminster Confession* reflects the content of those passages.

The category of judicial law exists because of the way that the epistles categorize ceremonial laws, deal with the Decalogue, and accept that the laws intended for observance 'in the land' have expired with the Messiah's coming. Only from that perspective can apostles call on Christians to submit themselves to authorities. Yet that does not mean that the judicial laws are irrelevant—their penalties still warn of the consequences of disobedience and their undergirding moral principles remain binding.

The view that the Decalogue is ever-binding may seem to face an immediate challenge from epistolary statements that appear negative or inconsistent about the law. That the Old Testament does not view the effects of divine revelation as universally positive suggests that 'tension' in the epistles reflects the Old Testament. This emerges particularly in 2 Corinthians 3 where the combination of negative and positive ideas does not point to inconsistency. That divine revelation kills and makes alive, wounds and heals, is reflected in the apostolic approach to the law. The notion that the author of Hebrews is hostile to the law is particularly insubstantial; the law to be written on new-covenant hearts is the same law that was written on the stone tablets. It is also written on the stony hearts of those in Romans who 'by nature' do what the law requires, not necessarily because Paul is making an appeal to Jeremiah 31, but because he too viewed the Ten Commandments as the ageless standard by which all will be judged. To sin is to transgress those precepts for 'sin is transgression of the law'; to love God and neighbour is to live in accord with those laws. This includes the fourth commandment, the eschatological fulfilment of which is no more fully realised than for the fifth commandment. These conclusions suggest a basic continuity with the categories and ideas identified in the Old Testament and Gospels, demonstrating that the categories of the threefold division along with the practical-theological conclusions of *The Westminster Confession* cannot be dismissed as a convenient imposition on the New Testament texts.

VIII

THE END OF THE WHOLE MATTER

> If you love me, you will keep my commandments.
>
> *Jesus Christ*

The preacher wrote, 'Of making many books there is no end, and much study is a weariness of the flesh' (Eccles. 12:12). But for him, the end of the whole matter was this: 'Fear God and keep his commandments, for this is the whole duty of man. For God will bring every deed into judgment, with every secret thing, whether good or evil' (Eccles. 12:13–14).

For Reformed theologians and their theological forerunners, this was likewise the end of the whole matter. The threefold division of the law was a practical-theological framework that briefly expounded this whole duty of man in the Christian era and affirmed the standard by which God would judge every deed good or evil. Its advocates believed that it was rooted in the text of Scripture, read as a coherent, consenting, and unified whole. In the light of recent rejection of this belief, I set out to investigate the biblical and theological grounds for the threefold division, concluding that Scripture as a whole develops the Pentateuch's categorization of some laws as a pattern, others as statutes to be obeyed 'in the land', and the Decalogue as universally binding moral law. This embryonic form of the threefold division makes its mark throughout Scripture, for example, in the primacy of morality over cult and in the Gospels' proclamation of Jesus, not as the abolisher of law, but as the one who provides eschatological, moral, and soteriological fulfilment of the law. The apostolic writings confirm those basic categories: pattern laws were 'copies and shadows', the laws of 'the land' give way to the decrees of earthly kings, and the Decalogue still spells out what it means to love God and neighbour.

The nature of the threefold division means that this book has interacted with several theological disciplines. This inevitably uncovers other areas that could be the subject of extended study within the confines of those disciplines. For example, I referred to many works in the field of biblical theology and devotees of that methodology might want to discuss more exhaustively some of the intertextual observations and interpretations I have suggested.

In the the first chapter I sought to uncover the historical roots of the threefold division, concluding that no one individual is its author and that its adoption by figures such as Justin Martyr and Thomas Aquinas reflects its status as the 'orthodox position'. Given that Stylianopoulos wrote a doctoral dissertation seeking to prove a threefold division in Justin Martyr alone, such research could likely be repeated for other church fathers. There may also be scope to trace in meticulous detail the historical route and development of the division from the second century to Aquinas or from Aquinas to Westminster.

Another example comes from systematic theology itself, particularly Hugh Martin's question about the relationship between atonement and moral law, mentioned in chapter one. He was sure that conserving the distinctiveness of moral law and 'the Westminster doctrine, which is the Catholic doctrine, of Atonement'[307] went together. Martin's discussion goes beyond exegetical theology into areas of moral philosophy, but it is interesting that some staunch defenders of penal substitution are also likely to either reject the Decalogue as moral law and a 'perfect rule of righteousness' or to adhere to the New Perspective with its unfixed 'boundary markers'.[308] So once more, here is Martin's question: 'What instrumentality or efficiency towards any thing like this can possibly be ascribed to the Incarnation of God's Son, if there be no strictly moral and authoritative juridical law?'[309]

In the article quoted in chapter one, Carson noted that recent works on penal substitution have forced readers to 'take note that historic Christian confessionalism will not roll over and play dead'.[310] If the source of Christian confessionalism is Scripture—read as a coherent, progressive, and self-interpreting whole—then the threefold division of the law need not roll over and die. No single passage of Scripture clearly states the threefold division of the law. It cannot be demonstrated by simplistic appeal to a particular Scripture, only by a progressive reading of the Old and New Testaments as the coherent source of Christian theology. Theologians, churchmen, and believers who read Scripture in that way were justified in receiving the ancient threefold division of the law as the 'orthodox position'. They did not yield blind allegiance to an untested ecclesiastical dogma, but gave thoughtful acceptance to the threefold division of the law with its practical-theological implications. They embraced it as catholic doctrine because it is biblically and theologically valid. They were right to do so. And we are not ashamed to follow.

---

307   Martin, *Atonement*, 255.

308   John Piper has a lengthy discussion of N. T. Wright endorsing Steve Chalke's book, *The Lost Message of Jesus*, yet claiming to defend penal substitution. See John Piper, *The Future of Justification: A Response to N. T. Wright* (Wheaton: Crossway Books, 2007), 47–53.

309   Martin, *Atonement*, 274.

310   Carson, 'Doctrine of Penal Substitution.'

APPENDIX 1

A summary of Georg Braulik's findings in 'Die Ausdrücke für 'Gesetz' im Buch Deuteronomium' (The Expressions for 'Law' in the Book of Deuteronomy), *Biblia* 51 (1970), 44–64.

1. When the first expression, בְּרִית (covenant), is used with reference to Horeb, as opposed to the patriarchal covenants, it refers specifically to the Horeb revelation and the Decalogue (Deut. 4:13, 23; 5:2–3; 9:9, 11, 15; 10:8; 17:2; 29:24; 31:9, 16, 20, 25–6) or to an oath to keep that covenant (Deut. 29:8, 11, 13, 20).

2. דְּבָרִים (words) sometimes describes the Decalogue (Deut. 4:10, 13, 36; 5:5, 22; 9:10; 10:2, 4), but is also used to refer to the rest of the Mosaic law (Deut. 1:18; 6:6; 11:18) as is דְּבָר (word) (Deut. 4:2; 13:1; 30:14). In Deuteronomy 15:15; 24:18, 22 and 12:28 דָּבָר and דְּבָרִים mean the single preceding law, while in 28:14 דְּבָרִים probably means the whole Mosaic law including the Decalogue.

3. דֶּרֶךְ (way—as in course of life) defines the Decalogue (Deut. 5:33; 9:12, 16; 13:6) or the entire law including the Decalogue (11:28; 31:29).

4. In Deuteronomy 16:12 the word חֻקִּים (statutes, decrees) refers to cultic regulations and in 17:19 to the regulations governing future kings. In all other places חֻקִּים is the whole Mosaic Law both inside (Deut. 4:40; 6:17; 26:17; 27:10) and outside (Deut. 4:6; 6:24) a series of law words.

5. The singular חֻקָּה (statute) is never used but the plural and suffixed חֻקֹּתָיו is used in series with other words for law and thus means all the individual laws of Moses.

6. In the majority of cases (Deut. 5:31; 6:1, 25; 7:11; 8:1; 11:8, 22; 15:5; 17:20; 19:9; 27:1; 30:11) מִצְוָה (commandment) defines the entire law of Moses. The exceptions are Deuteronomy 26:13 and 31:5 where it refers to arrangements specified in the context. In six places מִצְוֹת refers to the Decalogue (Deut. 5:10, 29; 6:17; 7:9; 8:2; 13:5) but in all other places it covers the entire Mosaic code.

7. מִשְׁמֶרֶת (charge, injunction) occurs only in Deuteronomy 11:1. It is in series with other law words and covers the whole law. When used outside the double expression חֻקִּים וּמִשְׁפָּטִים (statutes and judgements), מִשְׁפָּטִים (Deut 7:12; 8:11; 11:1; 26:17; 30:16) defines the whole of Moses law promulgation.

8. The double expression itself (חֻקִּים וּמִשְׁפָּטִים) forms an inclusion around the Deuteronomic paranesis (5:1–11:32) and around the law corpus (12:1–26:16). In 4:14 it is used in contrast with the Decalogue to delimit the laws which Moses himself had to pass on and teach to the people.

9. עֵדֹת (testimony) is used only three times, in Deuteronomy 4:45, 6:17, and 20. Despite the word's connection with the Ark in Exodus 25:22 it should not be equated with the Decalogue only, but with the whole law.

10. Finally, תּוֹרָה (torah) is used only with three exceptions in the 'Rahmenteueen'. Its range of meaning covers not only the contents of the paranesis and legal corpus found in 5–26 and 28, but also the entire book of Deuteronomy 1–32.

APPENDIX 2

DEFINING πληρόω – 'TO FULFIL'

This survey is not meant to be exhaustive and it is impossible to pigeon-hole the following exegetes too precisely, but the pages that follow describe and discuss the five primary approaches to πληρόω.

(a) In his book, *Jesus–Jesuah*, Gustaff Dalman sought 'to illumine the background, and depict the environment in which our Lord's words were uttered'.[1] Largely, this involved examining extra-biblical usage of New Testament words and seeking to apply the fruits of this to the interpretation of Jesus' words. He saw the idea of confirmation as most prominent in Matthew's use of πληρόω:

> Scripture is either confirmed or annulled according to whether its ordinances are kept or not…A Law teacher is a confirmer (fulfiller) of the Law when he gives the proper interpretation of the letter of it, according to the standard set by the Law itself, and hence by God, so that the letter preserves its validity and is confirmed also by those who, in instruction or practice, follow the interpretation of that teacher.[2]

Unless 'confirm' refers to the individual's submission to ordinances and laws of Scripture, it is difficult to make sense of Dalman's concept. Laws are not confirmed or annulled so much by the compliance of those under them, as they are by the execution of penalties upon those who rebel against them. Nonetheless,

1 Dalman, *Jesus–Jeshua*, xi.
2 Ibid., 58.

some writers follow Dalman and argue that πληρόω should be translated 'confirm' in Matthew 5.

In recent times, the most vociferous advocate of 'confirm' has been Greg Bahnsen. He dismissed the possibility that πληρόω could mean 'put an end to', 'replace', 'supplement', 'personally obey', or 'cause to be better kept', concluding that πληρῶσαι stands in strong opposition to καταλῦσαι and must therefore mean 'confirm'. His translation, he believed, was backed by Septagintal and other New Testament use of πληρόω, as well as famous preachers and scholars.[3] Ultimately, it is the theonomic worldview that dominates Bahnsen's lexicography, since for him the crucial point is that this confirmation of the law must not be restricted to the broad principles, but extended to every jot and tittle: 'Jesus, the awaited Messiah, rectifies the fallen standard of the law; he confirms its exhaustive details and restores a proper conception of kingdom righteousness.'[4] This view does not, as Bahnsen supposes, reflect the Reformed tradition. His understanding of the nature of confirmation and the conclusions he reaches differ from those of Reformed theology, not least in that his interpretation cannot make sense without reading 'ethical stipulations' into τοὺς προφήτας.

The most comprehensive rejection of 'confirm' as a legitimate translation of πληρόω comes from Vern Poythress, who shows that the semantic evidence Bahnsen presents is weak and the standard lexica are correct in supplying 'fulfil'.[5] Just as the English word 'fulfil' may imply 'confirm' in some contexts, πληρόω could be translated 'confirm' and make sense within its context, but that does not justify listing 'confirm' as a new sense.[6] The only case where 'confirm' is a plausible rendering is

3   Bahnsen, Theonomy in Christian Ethics, 50.
4   Ibid., 86.
5   Poythress, Shadow of Christ, 363–4.
6   Ibid., 366.

in 1 Kings 1:14 (LXX) where Nathan says to Bathsheba, 'While you are still speaking with the king, I will come in and confirm your words.' This translation, however, should be second choice because one of the standard renderings of πληρόω is 'complete', which could be what Nathan had in mind.[7] To accept 'confirm' as a legitimate translation would be to proceed on the basis of 'a queer, unexplainable exception'.[8]

Carson claims 'not a few writers, especially Jewish scholars, take the verb to reflect the Aramaic verb *qum* ("establish," "validate," or "confirm" the law)'.[9] He raises three objections to this, only the third of which deals specifically with πληρόω:

> The LXX never uses *pleroo* ("fulfil") to render *qum* or cognates (which prefer *histanai* or *bebaioun* ["establish" or "confirm"]). The verb *pleroo* renders *male* and means "to fulfil." In OT usage this characteristically refers to the "filling up" of volume or time, meanings that also appear in the NT (e.g., Acts 24:27; Rom 15:19). But though the NT uses *pleroo* in a number of ways, we are primarily concerned with what is meant by "fulfilling" the Scriptures…
>
> In a very few cases, notably James 2:23, the NT writers detect no demonstrable predictive force in the OT passage introduced…Most NT uses of *pleroo* in connection with Scripture, however, require some teleological force…even the ambiguous uses presuppose a typology that in its broadest dimensions is teleological, even if not in every detail.[10]

This analysis is correct and provides further reasons to reject 'confirm' as a translation, but the prevalence of 'predictive force' in New Testament uses of πληρόω ought to inform rather than control the exegesis of Matthew 5:17–19. How it is used elsewhere cannot negate the force of 'I have not come to abolish', which, along with the end envisioned for the law in the Old Testament

---

7   Ibid., 369–70.
8   Ibid., 377.
9   Carson, *Matthew*, [Pradis Ver. 5.01.0035].
10 Ibid.

itself, must define the fulfilment promised in Matthew 5:17. It is also noteworthy that in no New Testament use of πληρόω, concerning Scripture is abolition the end implied. Even in Philippians 4:19, where πληρόω appears concerning 'need', the concept of abolition does not fit, if for no other reason because 'need' could be fulfilled, yet recurring. Thus Bahnsen and others could have made their point without their unnecessary resort to the translation 'confirm'.

(b) In his discussion of the Sermon on the Mount, Robert Banks argues that Jesus' teaching is not on the same level as the Old Testament law, neither affirming nor abrogating it, but surpassing it.[11] This hypothesis may shape his definition of πληρόω, which he says 'includes not only an element of discontinuity (that which has now been realised transcends the Law) but an element of continuity as well (that which transcends the Law is nevertheless something to which the Law itself pointed forward).'[12] David Wenham challenges Banks' view:

> The contrast in v. 17b, "I came not to abolish but to...," favours this view: "abolish–fulfil/establish" are a more natural pair of opposites than "abolish–fulfil/transcend". And the subsequent context also favours this interpretation: the fact that Jesus is the fulfiller of the law leads on to the practical "therefore" of v. 19: Jesus' followers are to uphold not abolish the law.[13]

That alone is a satisfactory basis on which to dismiss Bank's definition, but the identification of an element of discontinuity, in that that which is fulfilled has been transcended, is open to challenge simply because it would be another 'queer, unexplainable exception'. The lexica do not suggest 'transcend' as a possible translation of πληρόω and there are no biblical applications of the word to Old Testament texts that would

11 Banks, *Jesus and the Law*, 189.
12 Ibid., 210.
13 Wenham, 'Jesus and the law', 93.

imply disengagement from that which is fulfilled.¹⁴ Whether or
not there is a sense in which Jesus transcends the law, 'to surpass'
is not the meaning of πληρόω. Bank's emphasis on Jesus' teaching
also leads to a depersonalisation of Jesus' words such that he
should have said something like: 'I have not come to abolish the
law or the prophets, but to fulfil them by my teaching.'

(c) Banks is on common ground with several other exegetes
with the second half of his definition—the law itself pointed
forward to its fulfilment by Jesus (or his teaching). Davies and
Allison, for example, write: 'When Jesus declares, "I came...
to fulfil", he means that his new teaching brings to realization
that which the Torah anticipated or prophesied: its "fulfiller"
has come.'¹⁵ As with Banks, their focus on Jesus' teaching as
that which fulfils lacks obvious support from Matthew 5:17
where Jesus speaks of himself: '*I* came...to fulfil.' Davies and
Allison do suggest that the subject of this teaching is that Jesus
is the 'fulfiller', but the degree of circularity in that renders their
argument impenetrable. If the teaching realizes that which the
law anticipated and prophesied, does it not therefore fulfil the
law? Perhaps their following statement is intended to clarify:

> ...he who fulfils the law and the prophets displaces them in so far as
> he must become the centre of attention: the thing signified (Jesus) is
> naturally more important than the sign (the law and the prophets)
> pointing to it. This is why Matthew's book is firstly about Jesus, not
> about the law and the prophets. Secondly, if the law is fulfilled, it
> cannot on that account be set aside. Fulfilment can only confirm the
> Torah's truth, not cast doubt upon it.¹⁶

14 Timothy and Barbara Friberg, *Analytical Lexicon to the Greek New
Testament* (BibleWorks 6); J. P. Louw and E. A. Nida, *Louw-Nida Greek-
English Lexicon of the New Testament Based on Semantic Domains*, 2nd Edition
(BibleWorks 6); Frederick William Danker, *Greek-English Lexicon of the New
Testament and Other Early Christian Literature*, Third Edition (BibleWorks 6).
15 Davies and Allison, *Matthew*, Vol. I, 487.
16 Ibid.

This more clearly identifies Jesus himself as the fulfiller, but it is of little help in defining πληρόω because the same thing can be said of God in the Old Testament. The lawgiver was more important than the law, yet that did not displace it; the prophets strove to make the LORD the centre of attention, but that did not make them redundant. Certainly, he who fulfils is the focus, but that has no bearing on the continuity or discontinuity of the law.

Carson shares this view 'that Jesus fulfills the Law and the Prophets in that they point to him, and he is their fulfillment'; it 'has been well set forth by Banks'.[17] This means he sees πληρόω having the same meaning in Matthew 5:17 as it does in the formula quotation of 1:22 or the Exodus event of 2:15. The words and events of the Old Testament pointed to Jesus and prophesied of him.[18] More explicitly, 'in the light of the antitheses' Matthew 5:17 'insists that just as Jesus fulfilled OT prophecies by his person and actions, so he fulfilled OT law by his teaching.'[19] This does not do away with the Old Testament, but means that whatever continuity and significance it has is rooted in Jesus and his teaching.[20] For Carson the 'inevitable' conclusion is that if the antitheses are understood 'in the light of this interpretation of vv. 17–20', then Jesus is primarily 'showing the direction in which it points, on the basis of his own authority', which may have the effect of 'intensifying' or 'annulling' elements of the law.[21]

Like the previous writers, Carson emphasises Jesus' fulfilment of the law 'by his teachings', in contrast to the prophecies, which are fulfilled 'by his person and actions'. He settles on

17   Carson, *Matthew*, [Pradis Ver. 5.01.0035].
18   Ibid.
19   Ibid.
20   Ibid.
21   Ibid.

this interpretation 'in light of the antitheses', yet he wishes to interpret the antitheses 'in the light of this interpretation', which may explain why his conclusion is unwarranted. Matthew 'insists' on no such dichotomy between the fulfilment of law and prophets in 5:17.

According to Carson, the main objection to his view 'is that the use of "to fulfil" in the fulfillment quotations is in the passive voice, whereas here the voice is active.' Without explaining why, he declares it 'doubtful whether much can be made out of this distinction',[22] but perhaps this objection deserves more attention. In Matthew's fulfilment quotations, πληρόω always refers to Scriptures from the prophets (1:22; 2:15, 17, 23; 4:14; 8:17; 12:17; 13:35; 21:4; 26:54–6; 27:9), whereas in 5:17 the reference is to the law and the prophets. Likewise in 3:15, the only other place where πληρόω is used in the active voice, there is a possible reference to the law (to be discussed shortly). In the fulfilment quotations, prophecies are realized in the life of Jesus by the God of providence, a fact of which Jesus may (26:54–6) or may not be conscious (1:22; 2:15, 17), whereas in 3:15 and 5:17 Jesus himself wittingly fulfils. Therefore, even if the word has the same core meaning in 5:17 as in the formula quotations, the voice and the object of πληρόω may give a certain nuance to the definition that affects the overall conclusions.

Hagner objects to this view that πληρόω refers to Jesus' life and salvific acts as the fulfilment of prophecy on the grounds that it is 'unrelated to the context [which he defines as 5:17–48], where the deeds of Jesus are not in view', only his teaching.[23] On its own, that is not a compelling reason to dismiss the approach of Banks and Carson. It would not be foreign to the context for Jesus to teach about how he fulfils the law and to explain the implications of that. The context does not require that the

---

22   Ibid.
23   Hagner, *Matthew 1–13*, Logos Library System.

fulfilment itself be exclusively in terms of his teaching. In any case,
Jesus' teaching is so integral to his life and acts that it can hardly
be treated separately from what he is and does. Indeed, elsewhere
in Matthew his teaching is expressly mentioned as part of the
fulfilment (13:35). Such a comprehensive view of Jesus' fulfilment
is expressed in the traditional description of his work as prophet,
priest, and king, 'both in his humiliation and exaltation'.[24]
Overall, while this understanding of fulfilment has weaknesses it
cannot be dismissed outright, but two other possibilities must be
considered before determining its usefulness.

(d) Perhaps the least popular way of reading πληρόω is
as a reference to Jesus' obedience to the law. Several writers
dismiss this with little discussion and on various grounds:
Hagner because the word 'is never used in Matthew to describe
obedience to the law',[25] Carson because it 'misses the point',[26]
and Carter for a variety of reasons.[27]

Before joining this chorus of dismissal it is worth considering
the arguments of Ulrich Luz. Unlike others, his translation of
'abolish' is not determined by 'fulfil', but the reverse. When Greek
and Hellenistic Jewish texts use καταλύω concerning νόμος, 'the
meaning wavers between "abolish" in the sense of "invalidate"
and "abolish" in the sense of "not to keep", "break".'[28] This, he
thinks, does not fit in with the view expressed by Banks and

24   WSC, Q 23.
25   Hagner, Matthew 1–13, Logos Library System.
26   Carson, Matthew, [Pradis Ver. 5.01.0035].
27   πληρόω 'means more than simply "do" or obey the scriptures...Nor
can it mean that Jesus brings into being something that was only promised
or foreshadowed in the past....Jesus fulfils the scriptures by implementing or
accomplishing God's previously revealed, salvific will in his proclamation of
God's empire and in his actions....Jesus recognizes and implements scripture
as a binding authority. Interpreted in relation to Jesus, the scriptures are the
authoritative source of the justice or righteousness (5:20) which he teaches (cf.
5:21–43).' Carter, Matthew and the Margins, 141.
28   Luz, Matthew 1–7, 264.

Carson (c). It is 'especially deeds, and not the teaching, of Jesus'
that Matthew has in view. The reminiscence of Matthew 3:15 is
also important as it concerns Jesus' actions when he submitted
to John's baptism in order to 'fulfil all righteousness.'[29] Luz does
not want to exclude the idea of prediction, but 'praxis is prior to
teaching.'[30]

Although 4 Maccabees 5:33[31] appears to confirm his comment
that καταλύω can convey transgression of laws rather than
abolition, some of the examples[32] he cites in an earlier article[33]
are less convincing. Furthermore, this sense is not recognised in
the lexica and the analysis of biblical usage earlier in this chapter
suggests that the ideas of 'destruction' or 'cessation' are what is
normally intended.

Luz' suggestion about Matthew 3:15 is uncommon, but not
unique. Jay Adams argues that the baptism event is about Jesus'
submission to the Mosaic Law, as were his circumcision, going to
the Passover, and observance of Jewish feasts.[34] He quotes from Ben
Rose who explains Jesus' baptism as fulfilment of Leviticus 8:6–7,
which required him to be sprinkled as 'a ceremonial act of His

29   Ibid.

30   Ibid., 265.

31   'οὐχ οὕτως οἰκτίρομαι τὸ ἐμαυτοῦ γῆρας ὥστε δι' ἐμαυτοῦ τὸν
πάτριον καταλῦσαι νόμον'; 'I do not so pity my old age as to break the
ancestral law by my own act' (RSV).

32   'εὖ οἶδ' ὅτι πάντα μᾶλλον αἱρήσονται παθεῖν ἢ καταλῦσαί τι τῶν
πατρίων'; '...I know very well that they would choose to suffer anything
whatever rather than a dissolution of any of the customs of their forefathers'
(Josephus, Ant. 16:35).

'...μισεῖν γὰρ ἔλεγον τὸν ἑαυτῶν βασιλέα καταλύσαντα μὲν τὰ πάτρια
ξένων δ' ἐραστὴν ἐθῶν γενόμενον'; '...for they said that they hated their
own king for abrogating the laws of their forefathers, and embracing foreign
customs' (Josephus, Ant. 20:81).

33   Ulrich Luz, 'Die Erfüllung des Gesetzes bei Matthäus', *Zeitschrift für
Theologie und Kirche* 75 (1978), 398–435.

34   Jay E. Adams, *The Meaning and Mode of Baptism.* (Philipsburg:
Presbyterian and Reformed, 1975), 17.

ordination to the priesthood'; Numbers 4:3, 47, which required
him to be thirty years old; Exodus 28:1, which required him to
be called of God; and Numbers 8:6–7, which required him to be
sprinkled with water by one already a priest, an office which John
inherited from his father (Exod. 29:9; Num 25:13).[35] In response
to the obvious problem that Jesus was not of the tribe of Levi,
Adams turns to Wilbur A. Christy who solves the problem with
the idea that the laws relating to the Aaronic priesthood are to be
applied directly to Jesus' Order of Melchizedek.[36]

This argument found in Adams' work is simplistic. The idea
of an uncomplicated transference of Levitical regulations to the
priesthood of Jesus lacks biblical evidence, and in any case it is
doubtful that Jesus fulfilled all the requirements in the passages
cited by Rose. Was he, for example, clothed with coats, sashes,
and capes 'as the LORD commanded Moses' (Lev. 8:13)? Did
he shave his body (Num. 8:7)? And, if he did all those things,
we might expect the gospel writers to record protests from
Jesus' opponents that one of the tribe of Judah should make
himself a Levite. Furthermore, if specific commandments
required Jesus' baptism then John's response would have been to
immediately accept Jesus' request rather than seeking to resist.

Luz is sure 'the baptism by John obviously is not commanded'
in the Old Testament law, but equally persuaded that δικαιοσύνη
in Matthew 3:15 'means a requirement of law which is to be
fulfilled'—something for which he finds support in patristic
writers. It is, however, 'not only' the Old Testament law that
is in view, but 'the entirety of the divine will as the Matthean
Jesus interprets it.'[37] The text is 'only indirectly' Christological
when πληρόω is understood as 'actualize' and when it is seen
as pointing to 5:17. Other Christological interpretations are

35   Ibid., 17–18.
36   Ibid., 19.
37   Luz, *Matthew 1–7*, 178.

'eisegesis'.[38] His interpretation, however, is hard to follow: the baptism is not commanded in the law, yet it is a requirement of law, and not only of the law, but of the entire divine will.

Luz leans on Benno Przybylski's study of the righteousness words in Matthew, which concludes that the righteous (δικαιος) 'are basically those who obey the law',[39] and δικαιοσύνη is always 'seen as God's demand upon man. Righteousness refers to proper conduct before God'[40] and not to a divinely gifted righteousness.[41] So, for example, in Matthew 5:20 'the righteousness that is to exceed that of the scribes and the Pharisees is a righteousness that is representative of an extremely meticulous observance of the law.'[42] When it comes to Matthew 3:15, John and Jesus' act of baptism carries out 'the total will of God'. It is part of what it means to fulfil all righteousness. Without this act, God's revealed will would be left undone.[43] But what does Przybylski mean by this? What, specifically, would be left undone? This question he leaves unanswered.

Donald Hagner acknowledges that Przybylski's conclusions are in some cases 'incontestable', but takes him to task on what he sees as forced consistency. He rejects not only the idea of Jesus' baptism as submission to the law, but also of it as submission to God in a general sense:

> No writer is obligated to use a word consistently; the meaning of a word must be determined from its immediate context and not be imposed upon a text in the name of lexical consistency. If δικαιοσύνη has a range of meanings, there is then no reason why Matthew may not have used the word in different senses...It is difficult to

38   Ibid., 178–9.
39   Benno Przybylski, *Righteousness in Matthew and his World of Thought.* (Cambridge: Cambridge University Press, 1981), 103; Luz *Matthew 1–7*, 177, n. 30.
40   Ibid., 99.
41   Ibid., 84–5, 90.
42   Ibid., 83.
43   Ibid., 94.

FROM THE FINGER OF GOD

understand submission to John's baptism as submitting to God's demand. There is no divine commandment either in the OT or in the Gospels to submit to John's baptism. Submission to that baptism then can hardly in itself be thought of as an act of righteousness.[44]

This is a legitimate observation, yet it is reasonable to give logical priority to 'lexical consistency' and only to reject the elsewhere 'incontestable' understanding of δικαιοσύνη as related to God's demands upon man, if it is incompatible with the context. Despite the absence of a specific baptism commandment, can Jesus' submission be regarded as a neutral act like sleeping or eating food? Is there some sense in which Jesus and John could have been acting in obedience to the law? If 'to fulfil all righteousness' does not mean to fulfil some specific law, what does it mean? Hagner offers a salvation-history solution:

> Since Matthew, as nearly all admit, has a salvation-historical perspective, there is no reason to exclude the possibility that he can understand δικαιοσύνη here not as moral goodness but as the will of God in the sense of God's saving activity. That is, by the baptism and its main point—the accompanying anointing by the Spirit—John and Jesus together ("for us") inaugurate the fulfillment of God's saving purposes, "the saving activity of God".[45]

This, however, drives an unnecessary wedge between moral goodness and God's saving activity. Even if Matthew 3:15 should not be understood as strict legal obedience, God's saving purpose cannot be something less than to produce moral goodness in the objects of his saving activity.

(e) Staying with Hagner, we can now discuss the final and perhaps commonest way of understanding πληρόω in Matthew 5:17. Hagner is one of those who claim that Jesus fulfils the law and the prophets by giving them an authoritative interpretation: 'Jesus defines righteousness by expounding the

44   Hagner, *Matthew 1–13*, Logos Library System.
45   Ibid.

true meaning of the law' and 'fulfil' is best understood in that sense. His interpretation is definitive. He does not destroy the law, but preserves it, bringing 'out its meaning in a definitive manner'.[46] Loader shares this approach:

> The focus is not so much on Jesus doing God's will, but on Jesus causing God's will to be done....The emphasis here is on Law in particular and upholding it and giving instruction so that it is rightly fulfilled. The focus in the context is not on Jesus replacing the Law.[47]

> Matthew presents it rather as a matter of Jesus upholding the integrity of the Law and the Prophets by giving them authoritative interpretation.[48]

> Jesus does not set aside Law, but fulfils the Law and the Prophets in a way that leaves them still valid, but no longer as the ultimate source of authority: he is.[49]

According to Carson, the idea that πληρόω means 'Jesus "fills up" the law by providing its full, intended meaning…requires an extraordinary meaning for pleroo'.[50] Hagner dismisses Carson's objection on the grounds that it is 'unrelated to the context' of Matthew 5:21–48, which is Jesus' teaching.[51] In addition, it is hard to see how this differs significantly from Carson's own view that Jesus primarily shows the direction in which the Law points 'on the basis of his own authority' even if final conclusions about the purpose of the law may differ.

Snodgrass and Wright move in the same direction as Hagner and Loader, but they are more specific, finding the locus of 'Jesus causing God's will to be done' in the lives of his followers:

---

46   Ibid.
47   Loader, *Jesus' Attitude towards the Law*, 167.
48   Ibid., 168.
49   Ibid., 168 n. 66.
50   Carson, *Matthew*, [Pradis Ver. 5.01.0035].
51   Hagner, *Matthew 1–13*, Logos Library System.

Jesus did not come to set aside or nullify the scriptures; rather his purpose was to affirm them and bring them to reality. Possibly the word 'accomplish' is a suitable translation and would also serve well in the similar construction at 3:15. Matthew's point is that Jesus came so that people would live according to the Scriptures.

5:17 expresses that Jesus' purpose was not to destroy the scriptures, but to bring them to actuality in people's lives…as long as their lives continue on this earth the law has validity (Snodgrass).[52]

His followers…deep, heartfelt keeping of God's laws would be a sign to the nations…Jesus wasn't intending to abandon the law and the prophets. Israel's whole story, commands, promises and all, was going to come true in him….He was the salt of the earth. He was the light of the world…embodying the way of self-giving love which is the deepest fulfilment of the law and the prophets (Wright).[53]

If the meaning of πληρόω ought to be determined primarily by the context of Jesus' teaching in Matthew 5 (Hagner), and not primarily by wider Matthean and New Testament usage (Carson) then those scholars have reasonable grounds to see Jesus fulfilling the law in himself, his teaching, and in the lives of the followers.

Should the detailed argument of Adams be rejected, the vagueness of Przybylski or Luz prove unsatisfactory, and the dichotomizing of Hagner be unnecessary, what is the alternative? In chapter five of this book I tried to answer this question and to provide a valid alternative, namely that we get closer to Matthew's understanding of πληρόω if we interpret it not in these restricted contexts, but in light of Matthew's interaction with Old Testament passages, particulary Jeremiah 31. In that wider context, Jesus' fulfils the law not just in one way, but in his person and teaching (c), by his obedience (d), and in making his followers obedient (e).

52 Snodgrass, 'Matthew and the Law', 115–16.
53 N. T. Wright, *Matthew for Everyone. Part I, Chapter 1–15.* (London: SPCK, 2002), 40–1.

BIBLIOGRAPHY

———. *A New Catechism: Catholic Faith for Adults.* London: Search Press, 1967.

Abbott, T. K., *The Epistles to the Ephesians and to the Colossians.* Edinburgh: T. & T. Clark, 1897.

Adam, A. K. M., Fowl, Stephen E., Vanhoozer, Kevin J., Watson, Francis. *Reading Scripture with the Church: Toward a Hermeneutic for Theological Interpretation.* Grand Rapids: Baker Academic, 2006.

Adams, Jay E. *The Meaning and Mode of Baptism.* Philipsburg: Presbyterian and Reformed, 1975.

Allbee, Richard A. 'Asymmetrical Continuity of Love and Law between the Old and New Testaments: Explicating the Implicit Side of a Hermeneutical Bridge, Leviticus 19.11–18.' *JSOT* 31.2 (2006), 147–66.

Alexander, T. Desmond. *From Paradise to the Promised Land.* Carlisle: Paternoster, 1995.

Alexander, and Rosner, Brian S. eds., *New Dictionary of Biblical Theology.* Leicester: Inter-Varsity Press, 2000.

Allen, Leslie C. *Psalms 101–150.* Word Biblical Commentary, ed. David A. Hubbard and Glenn W. Barker (General), John D. W. Watts (Old Testament), no. 21. Waco: Word Books, 1983.

Allison, Dale C. 'Mark 12:28–31 and the Decalogue.' *The Gospels and the Scriptures of Israel,* eds Craig A. Evans and W. Richard Stegner. Sheffield: Sheffield Academic Press, 1994.

———. *The New Moses: A Matthean Typology.* Edinburgh: T&T Clark, 1993.

———. 'Divorce, Celibacy and Joseph (Matthew 1.18–25 and 19.1–12).' *Journal for the Study of the New Testament* 49, (1993): 3–10.

Alston, Wallace M. Jr. & Welker, Michael eds., *Reformed Theology:*

*Identity and Ecumenicity II – Biblical Interpretation in the
Reformed Tradition.* Grand Rapids: Eerdmans, 2007.

Alt, Albrecht. *Essays on Old Testament History and Religion.* Oxford:
Basil Blackwell, 1966.

Andersen, Francis I. and Freedman, David Noel. *Amos: A New
Translation with Introduction and Commentary.* New York:
Doubleday, 1989.

Aquinas, Thomas. *On Law, Morality, and Politics,* eds Richard
J. Regan and William P. Baumgarth. Indianapolis: Hacket
Publishing Company, 1988.

———. *Summa Theologiæ: A Concise Translation.* ed. Timothy
McDermott. London: Eyre and Spottiswode, 1989.

Arnold, Clinton E. *The Colossian Syncretism: The Interface Between
Christianity and Folk Belief at Colossae.* Tübingen: J.C.B. Mohr
(Paul Siebeck), 1995.

Asiedu-Peprah, Martin. *Johannine Sabbath Conflicts As Juridical
Controversy.* Tübingen: Mohr Siebeck, 2001.

Attridge, Harold W. *The Epistle to the Hebrews.* Philadelphia: Fortress
Press, 1989.

Avgvstini, S. Avreli. *Catechizandis Rvdibvs,* trans. Joseph Patrick
Christopher. Washington DC, The Catholic University of
America, 1926.

Bacchiocchi, Samuele. *Divine Rest for Restlessness: A Theological Study
of the Good News of the Sabbath for Today.* (Rome: Pontifical
Gregorian University Press, 1980).

Bahnsen, Greg L. *Theonomy in Christian Ethics.* Nutley: The Craig
Press, 1977.

———. *By This Standard.* Tyler: Institute for Christian Economics, 1985.

———. 'The Prima Facie Acceptability of Postmillennialism.' *The
Journal of Christian Reconstruction* 3 no. 2 (1976–77): 48–105

Balentine, Samuel E. *The Torah's Vision of Worship.* Minneapolis:
Fortress Press, 1999.

Balla, Peter. *Challenges to New Testament Theology: An Attempt to
Justify the Enterprise.* Tübingen, Mohr Siebeck, 1997.

Banks, Robert. *Jesus and the Law in the Synoptic Tradition.* Cambridge: Cambridge University Press, 1975.

Barclay, John M. G. *Obeying the Truth: A Study of Paul's Ethics in Galatians*, Riches, John. ed. Edinburgh: T&T Clark, 1988.

Barclay, William. *The Letters to the Corinthians.* Edinburgh: The Saint Andrew Press, 1965.

Barker, William S. and Godfrey, W. Robert. *Theonomy: A Reformed Critique.* Michigan: Academie Books, 1994.

Barr, James. *Fundamentalism.* London: SCM Press Ltd, 1995.

———. *The Concept of Biblical Theology: An Old Testament Perspective.* London: SCM Press, 1999.

Barth, Karl. *Church Dogmatics* (vols. 1–3). Edinburgh: T. & T. Clark, 1961.

Barth, Markus and Blanke, Helmut. *Colossians: A New Translation with Introduction and Commentary.* Beck, Astrid B., trans. New York: Doubleday, 1994.

Barton, John. *Ethics and the Old Testament.* Harrisburg: Trinity Press International, 1998.

———. *Amos's Oracles against the Nations: A study of Amos 1.3–2.5.* Cambridge: Cambridge University Press, 1980.

Bartor, Asnat. 'The "Juridical Dialogue": A Literary Judicial Pattern.' *Vetus Testamentum* LIII, 4 (2003): 445–64.

Bauer, David R. and Powell, Mark Allan eds. *Treasures New and Old: Contributions to Matthean Studies.* Atlanta: Scholars Press, 1996.

Bauckham, Richard. *The Gospels for All Christians.* Grand Rapids: Eerdmans, 1998.

Bayes, Jonathan F. *The Threefold Division of the Law.* Newcastle: Christian Institute, 2005.

Beale, G. K., ed. *The RIGHT Doctrine from the WRONG Texts.* Grand Rapids: Baker, 1994.

Beecher, Willis Judson. *The Prophets and the Promise.* Grand Rapids: Baker, 1963.

Beckwith, Roger T. *Calendar and Chronology, Jewish and Christian: Biblical, Intertestamental and Patristic Studies.* Leiden: E. J. Brill, 1996.

Beckwith, Roger T. and Scott, Wilfrid. *This Is the Day: The Biblical*

Doctrine of the Christian Sunday in its Jewish and Early Church Setting. London: Marshall, Morgan & Scott, 1978.

Behr, John. *The Formation of Christian Theology Volume 1: The Way to Nicea*. New York: St Vladimir's Seminary Press, 2001.

Bell, Richard H. *No One Seeks for God: An Exegetical and Theological Study of Romans 1.18–3.20*. Tübingen: Mohr Siebeck, 1998.

Bellinger, William H. Jr. and Farmer, William R. *Jesus and the Suffering Servant: Isaiah 53 and Christian Origins*. Harrisburg: Trinity Press International, 1998.

Bergen, Richard Victor. *The Prophets and the Law*. Cincinnati: Hebrew Union College Press, 1974.

Betz, Hans Dieter. *Galatians*. Philadelphia: Fortress Press, 1979.

Brown, Charles Thomas. 'Beyond Obedience: Jesus and the Law in Matthew 5:17–20.' MAT diss., Catholic Theological Union at Chicago, 1991.

Blomberg, Craig L. 'The Law in Luke–Acts.' *Journal for the Study of the New Testament* 22 (1984): 53–80.

———. 'The Christian and the Law of Moses' in *Witness to the Gospel: The Theology of Acts*. I. Howard Marshall and David Peterson, eds. Grand Rapids: Eerdmans, 1998: 397–416.

Bocker, Hans Jochen. *Law and the Administration of Justice in the Old Testament and Ancient East* trans. Jeremy Moiser. London: SPCK, 1980.

Bockmuehl, Markus. 'Matthew 5. 32; 19. 9 in the Light of Pre-Rabbinic Halakah.' *New Testament Studies* 35 (1989): 291–5.

Booth, Robert P. *Jesus and the Laws of Purity in Mark 7*. Sheffield: JSOT Press, 1986.

Boyarin, Daniel. *A Radical Jew: Paul and the Politics of Identity*. Berkeley, University of California Press, 1994.

Braulik, Georg. 'Die Ausdrücke für 'Gesetz' im Buch Deuteronomium.' *Biblia* 51 (1970): 39–67.

———. *The Theology of Deuteronomy: Collected Essays of Georg Braulik* trans. Ulrika Lindblad. N. Richland Hills: BIBAL Press, 1994.

Bright, John. 'The Apodictic Prohibition: Some Observations.' *Journal of Biblical Literature* 92 (1973): 185–204.

Brin, Gershon. *Studies in Biblical Law: From the Hebrew Bible to the Dead Sea Scrolls.* Sheffield: Sheffield Academic Press, 1994.

Broadhead, Edwin K. 'Mk 1,44: The Witness of the Leper.' *Zeitschrift für die Neutestamentliche Wissenschaft* 83 (1992): 257–65.

Brown, Raymond E. *The Epistles of John.* New York: Doubleday, 1982.

Bruce, F. F. *Commentary on the Book of Acts.* London: Marshall, Morgan & Scott Ltd, 1954.

———. *Commentary on the Epistle to the Hebrews.* London: Marshall, Morgan & Scott, 1964.

Bruckner, James K. *Implied Law in the Abraham Narrative: A Literary and Theological Analysis,* Journal for the Study of the Old Testament Supplement Series 335, ed. David J. A. Clines and Philip R. Davies. Sheffield: Sheffield Academic Press, 2001

Brueggemann, Walter. *A Commentary on Jeremiah: Exile and Homecoming.* Grand Rapids: Eerdmans, 1998.

Bultmann, Rudolf. *The Johannine Epistles,* trans. R. Philip O'Hara with Lane C. McGaughy and Robert W. Funk. Philadelphia: Fortress Press, 1973.

Buttrick, George Arthur, ed. *The Interpreter's Dictionary of the Bible.* New York: Abingdon Press, 1962.

Byrskog, Samuel. *Jesus the Only Teacher: Didactic Authority and Transmission in Ancient Israel, Ancient Judaism and the Matthean Community.* Stockholm: Almqvist & Wiksell International, 1994.

Calvin, John. *The Gospel according to St John 1–10.* Edinburgh: The Saint Andrew Press, 1959.

———. *Commentaries on the Epistles of Paul the Apostle to the Philippians, Colossians, and Thessalonians.* trans. John Pringle. Edinburgh: Calvin Translation Society, 1851.

———. *A Harmony of the Gospels: Matthew, Mark & Luke* (vol. 1–3), Carlisle: Paternoster Press, 1995.

——— *Institutes of the Christian Religion.* Grand Rapids: Eerdmans, 1970.

———. *Genesis.* Edinburgh: Banner of Truth, 1975.

———. *Sermons on Deuteronomy,* Edinburgh: Banner of Truth, 1990.

———. *Selected Works of John Calvin.* ed. and trans. Henry Beveridge. Grand Rapids: Baker Book House, 1983.

Campbell, Douglas A. 'An Evangelical Paul: A Response to Francis Watson's *Paul and the Hermeneutics of Faith.*' *JSNT* 28.3 (2006), 337–51.

Campbell, Iain D. *On the First Day of the Week: God the Christian and the Sabbath.* Leominster: Day One Publications, 2005.

Capper, Brian J. 'The Interpretation of Acts 5:4.' *Journal for the Study of the New Testament* 19 (1983), 117–131.

Carmichael, Calum M. *Law and Narrative in the Bible.* New York: Cornell University Press, 1985.

——. *The Laws of Deuteronomy.* Ithaca: Cornell University Press, 1974.

——. *The Origins of Biblical Law: The Decalogues and the Book of the Covenant.* New York: Cornell University Press, 1992.

——. *The Spirit of Biblical Law.* Athens: University of Georgia Press, 1996.

Carter, Warren. *Matthew and the Margins: A Socio-Political and Religious Reading.* Sheffield: Sheffield Academic Press, 2000

Carson, D. A., et al., ed. *New Bible Commentary: 21st Century Edition.* Leicester: IVP, 1994.

Carson, D. A., ed. *From Sabbath to Lord's Day.* Academie: Grand Rapids, 1982.

Carson, D. A., O'Brien, Peter T. and Siefrid, Mark A., eds., *Justification and Variegated Nomism, Volume I, The Complexities of Second Temple Judaism.* Tubingen: Mohr Siebeck, 2001.

——. *Justification and Variegated Nomism, Volume II, The Paradoxes of Paul.* Tubingen: Mohr Siebeck, 2004.

Carson, D. A., and John Woodbridge, eds. *Hermeneutics, Authority and Canon* Leicester: IVP, 1986.

Carson, D. A. *The Gospel According to John.* Leicester: IVP, 1991.

——. *The Sermon on the Mount.* Grand Rapids, Baker Book House, 1978.

Casselli, Stephen J. 'The Threefold Division of the Law in the Thought of Aquinas.' *WTJ* 61:2 (1999), 175–207.

Cassuto, U. *A Commentary on the Book of Exodus,* Israel Abrahams, trans. Jerusalem: The Magnes Press, 1967.

Childs, Brevard S. *Biblical Theology in Crisis.* Philadelphia: The Westminster Press, 1970.

——. *Biblical Theology of the Old and New Testaments: Theological Reflection on the Christian Bible.* London: SCM, 1992.

——. *Exodus.* London: SCM, 1974.

——. *Isaiah.* Louisville: Westminster John Knox Press, 2001.

——. *Old Testament Theology in a Canonical Context.* London: SCM, 1985.

Chilton, Bruce and Evans, Craig A. *Jesus in Context: Temple Purity and Restoration.* Leiden: Koninklijke Brill, 1997.

Chilton, Bruce and Neusner, Jacobs, eds. *The Brother of Jesus: James the Just and His Mission.* Louisville, Westminster John Knox Press, 2001.

Christensen, D. L., ed. *A Song of Power and the Power of Song.* Winona Lake: Eisenbrauns, 1993.

——.*Deuteronomy 1–11.* Word Biblical Commentary, ed. David A. Hubbard and Glenn W. Barker (General), John D. W. Watts (Old Testament), no. 6A. Dallas: Word Books, 1991.

——. *Deuteronomy 21:10–34:12,* Word Biblical Commentary, ed. Bruce Metzger, David A. Hubbard, and Glenn W. Barker (General), John D. W. Watts (Old Testament), no. 6B. Nashville: Thomas Nelson, 2002.

Clines, David J. A. *Interested Parties: The Ideology of Writers and Readers of the Hebrew Bible.* Sheffield: Sheffield Academic Press, 1995.

Cochrane, Arthur C. *Reformed Confessions of the Sixteenth Century.* London: SCM Press, 1966.

Coffey, John. *Politics, Religion and the British Revolutions: The Mind of Samuel Rutherford.* Cambridge: Cambridge University Press, 1997.

Collins, G. N. M. *The Heritage of Our Fathers—The Free Church of Scotland: Her Origin and Testimony.* Edinburgh: Knox Press, 1976.

Collins, John J. *Encounters with Biblical Theology.* Minneapolis: Augsburg Fortress, 2005.

Collins, Raymond F., *First Corinthians.* Minnesota, Liturgical Press, 1999.

Conzelmann, Hans. *Acts of the Apostles*, James Limburg, A Thomas
     Kraabel, and Donald H. Juel trans. Philipadelphia: Fortress
     Press, 1972.

Craigie, Peter C. *Deuteronomy*. Grand Rapids: Eerdmans, 1976.

———. *Psalms 1–50*. Word Biblical Commentary, ed. David A.
     Hubbard and Glenn W. Barker (General), John D. W. Watts
     (Old Testament), no. 19. Waco: Word Books, 1983.

Cranfield, C. E. B. *The Gospel According to Mark*. Cambridge:
     University Press, 1963.

———. 'St. Paul and the Law.' *SJT* 17 (1964), 43–68.

———. '"The Works of the Law" in the Epistle to the Romans.' *JSNT*
     43 (1991), 89–101.

Cromartie, Michael. ed. *A Preserving Grace: Protestants, Catholics, and
     Natural Law*. Grand Rapids: Eerdmans, 1997.

Crossley, James G. 'Halakah and Mark 7.4: "and beds".' *Journal for the
     Study of the New Testament* 25.4 (2003), 433–47.

Crüsemann, Frank. *The Torah*. Edinburgh: T & T Clark, 1996.

Cunningham, Harold G. 'God's Law, "General Equity" and the
     Westminster Confession of Faith.' *Tyndale Bulletin* 58.2 (2007),
     289–312.

Dalman, Gustaff. *Jesus–Jeshua: Studies in the Gospels*, trans. Paul P.
     Leverhoff. London: SPCK, 1929.

D'Angelo, Mary Rose. *Moses in the Letter to Hebrews*. Missoula:
     Scholars Press, 1979.

Daube, D. *Biblical Law*. Cambridge: University Press, 1947

———. *The New Testament and Rabbinic Judaism*. London: The Athlone
     Press, 1956.

———. 'The Self-understood in Legal History.' *The Juridical Review* 18
     (1973): 126–34.

Davies, Eryl W. *Prophecy and Ethics: Isaiah and the Ethical Traditions of
     Israel*. Sheffield: JSOT Press, 1981.

Davies, G. I. *Hosea* Grand Rapids: Eerdmans, 1992.

Davies, W. D. and Allison, Dale C., *A Critical and Exegetical
     Commentary on the Gospel According to Matthew, Vol. I*.
     Edinburgh: T. & T. Clark, 1988.

———. *A Critical and Exegetical Commentary on the Gospel According to Matthew, Vol. II*. Edinburgh: T. & T. Clark, 1991.

Day, John. *Psalms*. Sheffield: Sheffield Academic Press, 1990.

de la Potterie, Ignace, S. J. and Lyonnet, Stanislaus, S. J., *The Christian Lives by the Spirit*. New York: Society of St. Paul, 1971.

Delitzsch, F. *Isaiah*, Commentary on the Old Testament in Ten Volumes, C. F. Keil and F. Delitzsch, vol. VII. Grand Rapids: Eerdmans, 1978.

DeMaris, Richard E. *The Colossian Controversy: Wisdom in Dispute in Colossae*. Sheffield: JSOT, 1994.

Deming, Will. 'Mark 9. 42–10. 12. Matthew 5. 27–32, and B. Nid. 13b: A First Century Discussion of Male Sexuality.' *New Testament Studies* 36 (1990): 130–41.

Derrett, J. Duncan M. 'Law in the New Testament: the Syro-Phoenician Woman and the Centurion of Capernaum.' *Novum Testamentum* 15 (1973): 161–86.

Dibelius, Martin. *James*, Michael A. Williams trans. Philadelphia: Fortress Press, 1976.

Douglas, Mary. *Leviticus as Literature*. Oxford: Oxford University Press, 1999.

Down, M. J. 'The Sayings of Jesus About Marriage and Divorce.' *Expository Times* 95 (1984): 332–4.

Duling, Dennis C. '"[Do not Swear…] by Jerusalem Because it Is the City of the Great King" (Matt 5:35).' *Journal of Biblical Literature* 110/2 (1991): 291–309.

Dumbrell, W. J. *Covenant and Creation*. Carlisle: Paternoster, 1997.

———. 'The Logic of the Role of the Law in Matthew V 1–20.' *Novum Testamentum* 23 (1981): 1–21.

Duncan, J. Ligon III. *What About Theonomy?* Jackson: Unpublished Article, 1993.

Dunn, James D. G. *Jesus, Paul and the Law: Studies in Mark and Galatians*. London: SPCK, 1990.

———. *The Epistles to Colossians and Philemon: A Commentary on the Greek Text*. Grand Rapids: Eerdmans, 1996.

———. *Romans 1-8*, Word Biblical Commentary, ed. David A.

Hubbard and Glenn W. Barker (General), Ralph P. Martin (New Testament), no. 38[A]. Dallas: Word Books, 1988.

——. *The New Perspective on Paul*. Grand Rapids: Eerdmans, 2008.

——. 'Jesus and Purity: An Ongoing Debate.' *New Testament Studies* 48 (2002), 449–67.

——. *The Acts of the Apostles*. Peterborough: Epworth Press, 1996.

——. *Paul and the Mosaic Law*. Grand Rapids: Eerdmans, 2001.

Durham, John I. *Word Biblical Commentary: Exodus*. Waco: Word, 1987.

Dyrness, William. *Themes in Old Testament Theology*. Carlisle: Paternoster, 1998.

Eaton, John H. *Kingship in the Psalms*. (Sheffield: JSOT Press, 1986).

Edelman, Diana Vikander. *King Saul in the Historiography of Judah*. Sheffield: JSOT Press, 1991

Eichdrot, Walther. 'The Law and the Gospel: The Meaning of the Ten Commandments in Israel and for Us.' *Interpretation* 11 (1957): 23–40.

——. *Theology of the Old Testament*. London: SCM Press, 1961.

Ellingworth, Paul. *The Epistle to the Hebrews*. Grand Rapids: Eerdmans, 1993.

Elliot, D. W. *Phipson and Elliot Manual of the Law of Evidence*. London: Sweet & Maxwell, 1980.

Elliot, John H. *1 Peter*. New York: Doubleday, 2000.

Emmerson, Grace I. *Hosea: An Israelite Prophet in Judean Perspective*. Sheffield: JSOT Press, 1984.

Eskenazi, Tamara C., Harrington, Daniel J. and Shea, William H., eds. *The Sabbath and Christian Tradition*. New York: Crossroad, 1991.

Esler, Philip F. *New Testament Theology: Communion and Community*. Minneapolis: Fortress Press, 2005.

Evans, C. F. *Saint Luke*. London: SCM Press, 1990.

Evans, Craig A. *To See and Not Perceive: Isaiah 6.9-10 in Early Jewish and Christian Interpretation*. Sheffield: Sheffield Academic Press, 1989.

Evans, Craig A. and Porter, Stanley E., eds. *The Historical Jesus*. Sheffield: Sheffield Academic Press, 1995.

Evans, Craig A. and Stegner, W. Richard, eds. *The Gospels and the Scriptures of Israel.* Sheffield: Sheffield Academic Press, 1994.

Fisher, Edward. *The Marrow of Modern Divinity.* Fearn: Christian Focus Publications, 2009.

Fairbairn, Patrick. *The Revelation of Law in Scripture.* Edinburgh: T. & T. Clark, MDCCCLXIX.

Fee, Gordon D. *The First Epistle to the Corinthians.* Grand Rapids: Eerdmans, 1987.

Feinberg, John S., ed. *Continuity and Discontinuity.* Wheaton: Crossway Books, 1988.

Ferguson, Sinclair. *The Holy Spirit.* Leicester: IVP, 1996.

Firmage, Edwin B., Bernard G. Weiss, and John W. Welch. *Religion and Law: Biblical–Judaic and Islamic Perspectives* Winona Lake: Eisenbrauns, 1990.

Fischer, John. 'Covenant, Fulfillment & Judaism in Hebrews.' *ETR* 13 (1989).

Fitzmyer, Joseph, *The Acts of the Apostles.* New York: Doubleday, 1998.

——. *Romans.* New York: Doubleday, 1993.

Fowl, Stephen E. *Engaging Scripture: A Model for Theological Interpretation.* Oxford: Blackwell, 1988.

——. *The Theological Interpretation of Scripture: Classic and Contemporary Readings.* Oxford: Blackwell, 1977.

Fowl, Stephen E. and Jones, Gregory L., *Reading in Communion: Scripture and Ethics in Christian Life,* London: SPCK, 1991.

France, R. T. *The Gospel According to Matthew: An Introduction and Commentary.* Leicester, Inter-Varsity Press, 1985.

Franklin, Eric. *Luke: Interpreter of Paul, Critic of Matthew.* Sheffield: Sheffield Academic Press, 1994.

Frend, W. H. C. *The Rise of Christianity.* Philadelphia: Fortress, 1984.

Fretheim, Terence E. 'The Reclamation of Creation: Redemption and Law in Exodus', *Interpretation* 45, 354–65.

Friedmann, Daniel. *To Kill and Take Possession: Law Morality, and Society in Biblical Stories.* Peabody: Hendricksen Publishers, 2002.

Froehlich, Karlfried. *Biblical Interpretation in the Early Church.* Philadelphia: Fortress, 1984.

Fuller, J. William. 'Of Elders and Triads in 1 Timothy 5.19–25.' *NTS* (29) 1983, 258–63.

Furnish, Victor P. *II Corinthians*. New York: Doubleday, 1984.

Gaebelein, Frank E. ed. *Expositors Bible Commentary*, [Pradis Ver. 5.01.0035] (Grand Rapids: Zondervan, 2002).

Gaffin, Richard B. *Calvin and the Sabbath*. Fearn: Mentor, 1998.

Galinski, Myer. *Pursue Justice: The Administration of Justice in Ancient Israel*. London: Nechdim Press, 1983.

Garland, David E. *1 Corinthians*. Grand Rapids: Baker Academic, 2003.

Gathercole, Simon J. *Where Is Boasting? Early Jewish Soteriology and Paul's Response in Romans 1–5*. Grand Rapids: Eerdmans, 2002.

——. 'What Did Paul Really Mean?' *Christianity Today*, August 2007: 22–8.

——. 'A Law unto Themselves: The Gentiles in Romans 2.14-15 Revisited', *JSNT* 85 (2002), 27–49

Geisler, Norman L. 'Dispensationalism and Ethics.' *Transformation* 6 no. 1 (1989): 7–14

Gerhardsson, Birger. *The Shema in the New Testament*. Lund: Novapress, 1996.

Gese, Harmut. *Essays on Biblical Theology* trans. Keith Crim. Minneapolis: Augsburg, 1981.

Gheorgita, Radu. *The Role of the Septuagint in Hebrews: An Investigation of its Influence with Special Consideration to the Use of Hab 2:3-4 in Heb 10:37-38*. Tübingen, Mohr Siebeck, 2003.

Gibbs, Jeffrey A. 'Israel Standing with Israel: the Baptism of Jesus in Matthew's Gospel (Matt 3:13–17)', *CBQ*, 64

Gibbs, Lee W. 'The Puritan Natural Law Theory of William Ames'. *Harvard Theological Review* 64 (1971): 37–57.

Goldberg, Steven. *Bleached Faith: the Tragic Cost when Religion is Forced into the Public Square*. Stanford: Stanford Law Books, 2008.

Goppelt, L. 'τύπος as the Heavenly Original according to Ex. 25:40.' In *Theological Dictionary of the New Testament* VIII, 256–9. Grand Rapids: Eerdmans, 1972.

Gordon, Robert. P., ed. '*The Place Is Too Small for Us*': *The Israelite Prophets in Recent Scholarship*. Winona Lake: Eisenbrauns, 1995.

Gordon, T. David. 'Critique of Theonomy: A Taxonomy.' *Westminster Theological Journal* 56 (1994): 23–43.

Gorman, Frank H., Jr. *The Ideology of Ritual: Space, Time and Status in the Priestly Theology*. Sheffield: JSOT, 1990.

Goulder, Michael D. *The Psalms of Asaph and the Pentateuch: Studies in the Psalter, III*. Sheffield: Sheffield Academic Press, 1996.

Grant, Robert M. 'The Decalogue in Early Christianity.' *Harvard Theological Review* XL, no. 1 (January 1947): 1–17.

Green, Joel B. and Turner, Max, eds. *Between Two Horizons: Spanning New Testament Studies and Systematic Theology*. Cambridge. Eerdmans, 2000.

Greidanus, Sidney. *The Modern Preacher and the Ancient Text*. Leicester: IVP, 1988.

——. 'The universal dimension of law in the Hebrew scriptures.' *Sciences Religieuses/Studies in Religion* 14/1 (1985): 39–51.

Guest, Deryn; Goss, Robert E.; West, Mona; and Bohache, Thomas, eds. *The Queer Bible Commentary*. London: SCM Press, 2006.

Guilding, A. E. 'Notes on the Hebrew Law Codes.' *Journal of Theological Studies* XLIX (1948): 43–52.

Gundry, Robert H. *Matthew: A Commentary on His Literary and Theological Art*. Grand Rapids: William B. Eerdmans, 1982.

Gunton, Colin E., Holmes, Stephen R. and Rae, Murray A. *The Practice of Theology: A Reader*. London: SCM Press Ltd, 2001.

Gurtner, Daniel M. *The Torn Veil: Matthew's Exposition of the Death of Jesus*. Cambridge: Cambridge University Press, 2007.

Haber, Susan. 'From Priestly Torah to Christ Cultus: The Re-Vision of Covenant and Cult in Hebrews.' *JSNT* 28.1 (2005), 105–124.

Haenchen, Ernst. *The Acts of the Apostles*. Oxford: Blackwell, 1971.

Hagner, Donald A. *Matthew 1–13*. Word Biblical Commentary, ed. David A. Hubbard and Glenn W. Barker (General), Ralph P. Martin (New Testament), no. 33A., [Libronix System 2.1c], (Bellingham, 2000–4).

384   BIBLIOGRAPHY

Haldane, J. A. *An Exposition of the Epistle to the Galatians.* Edinburgh: William Whyte and Co, 1848.

Haldane, Robert. *Exposition of the Epistles to the Romans,* vol. II. London: Hamilton, Adams, and Co, M.DCCC.XXXVIII.

Halpern, Baruch and Hobson, Deborah W., eds. *Law and Ideology in Monarchic Israel.* Sheffield: Sheffield Academic Press, 1991.

Hamilton, Victor P., *The Book of Genesis: Chapters 18–50.* Grand Rapids: Eerdmans, 1995.

Hanson, R. P. C. 'Notes on Tertullian's Interpretation of Scripture.' *JTS* 22 (1961), 273–9.

Harrelson, Walter. 'Karl Barth on the Decalogue.' *Sciences Religieuses/Studies in Religion* 6/3 (1976–77): 229–40.

Harrington, Daniel J. (S.J.) *The Gospel of Matthew.* Collegeville: Liturgical Press, 1991.

———. 'The New Covenant', *America,* 27 March 2006, 31.

Harris, R. Laird, Gleason L. Archer Jr., and Bruce K. Waltke, eds. *Theological Wordbook of the Old Testament.* Vol. 1&2. Chicago: Moody Press, 1980.

Hawthorne, Gerald F. and Martin, Ralph P. eds., *Dictionary of Paul and His Letters.* Leicester: Inter Varsity Press, 1993.

Hays, Richard B. *Echoes of Scripture in the Letters of Paul.* New Haven: Yale University Press, 1989.

———. *First Corinthians.* Louisville: John Knox Press, 1997.

Hecht, N. S., Jackson, B. S., Passamaneck, S. M., Piattelli, D., and Rabello, A. M. *An Introduction to the History and Sources of Jewish Law.* Oxford: Clarendon Press, 1996.

Heil, John Paul. *Ephesians: Empowerment to Walk in Love for the Unity of All in Christ.* Atlanta: Society of Biblical Literature, 2007.

———. *The Rhetorical Role of Scripture in 1 Corinthians.* Atlanta: Society of Biblical Literature, 2005.

Hendriksen, William. *Mark.* Edinburgh: Banner of Truth, 1975.

Hepner, Gershon. 'Abraham's Incestuous Marriage with Sarah a Violation of the Holiness Code.' *Vetus Testamentum* LIII, 2 (2003): 143–55.

Héring, Jean. *The Second Epistle of Saint Paul to the Corinthians.* London: Epworth Press, 1967.

Heron, Alsadair I. C., ed. *The Westminster Confession in the Church Today.* Edinburgh: The Saint Andrew Press, 1982.

Hertzberg, Hans Wilhelm. *I & II Samuel.* London: SCM Press Ltd, 1960.

Heschel, Abraham Joshua. *The Sabbath: its meaning for modern man.* New York: Noonday Press, 1998.

Hesselink, I. John. *Calvin's Concept of the Law.* Allison Park: Pickwick Publications, 1992.

Heylyn, Peter. *The History of the Sabbath.* London: Printed for Henry Seile, and are to bee fold at the Signe of the Tygers-head in Saint Pauls Churchyard, 1636.

Hill, Andrew E. *Malachi: A New Translation with Introduction and Commentary.* New York: Doubleday, 1998.

Hodges, Louis Igou. 'A Defense of the Tripartite Understanding of the Law Articulated in 'The Westminster Confession of Faith'.' *Evangelical Philosophical Society.* November 1990.

Hoehner, Harold W. *Ephesians: An Exegetical Commentary.* Grand Rapids: Baker Academic, 2002.

Hooker, Morna D. *A Commentary on the Gospel According to St. Mark.* London: A & C Black, 1991.

———. *From Adam to Christ: Essays on Paul.* Cambridge: Cambridge University Press, 1990.

Holland, Tom. *Contours of Pauline Theology: A Radical New Survey of the Influences on Paul's Biblical Writings.* Fearn: Mentor, 2004.

House, Paul R. *The Unity of the Twelve.* Sheffield: Sheffield Academic Press, 1990.

Hultgren, Arland J. 'The Double Commandment of Love in Mt 22:34–40'. *Catholic Biblical Quarterly* 36. (1974): 373–8.

Hurst, L. D. *The Epistle to the Hebrews: Its background of thought.* Cambridge: Cambridge University Press, 1990.

Hurtado, Larry W. *The Earliest Christian Artifacts.* Grand Rapids: Eerdmans, 2006.

Instone-Brewer, David. *Techniques and Assumptions in Jewish Exegesis before 70 CE*. Tübingen, J.C.B. Mohr (Paul Siebeck), 1992.

——. '1 Cor 9.9–11: A Literal Interpretation of "Do not Muzzle the Ox".' *NTS* (38) 1992, 554–65.

Isidore of Seville, *The Etymologies of Isidore of Seville*. trans. Stephen A. Barney, W. J. Lewis, J. A Beach, and Oliver Berghof. Cambridge: Cambridge University Press, 2006.

Ito, Akio. 'Romans 2: A Deuteronomistic Reading.' *JSNT* 59 (1995), 21–37

Jackson, Bernard S. 'The Ceremonial and the Judicial Biblical Law as Sign and Symbol'. *Journal for the Study of the Old Testament* 30. (1984): 25–50.

Janowski, Bernd and Stuhlmacher, Peter eds. *The Suffering Servant: Isaiah 53 in Jewish and Christian Sources*. trans. Daniel P. Bailey. Grand Rapids: Eerdmans, 2004.

Janzen, David. 'The Meaning of *PORNEIA* in Matthew 5.32 and 19.9: An Approach From the Study of Ancient Near Eastern Culture.' *Journal for the Study of the New Testament* 80, (2000): 66–80.

Jeanrond, Werner G. *Theological Hermeneutics: Development and Significance*. London: MacMillan, 1991.

Jensen, Joseph. *The Use of tôrâ by Isaiah: His Debate with the Wisdom Tradition*. Washington, D.C.: The Catholic Biblical Association of America, 1973.

Jervell, Jacob. 'The Law in Luke-Acts'. *Harvard Theological Review* 64 (1971): 21–36.

——. *The Theology of the Acts of the Apostles*, Cambridge: Cambridge University Press, 1996.

Jewett, Robert. *Romans*. Minneapolis: Fortress Press, 2007.

John Paul II. *Keeping the Lord's Day Holy: Apostolic Letter DIES DOMINI of the Holy Father John Paul II*. London: Catholic Truth Society, 1998.

Johnson, Luke Timothy. *The Letter of James*. New York: Doubleday, 1995.

——. *The First and Second Letters to Timothy*. New York: Doubleday, 2001.

Johnson, Marshall D. 'Reflections on a Wisdom Approach to Matthew's Christology'. *Catholic Biblical Quarterly* 36 (1974): 44–64.

Johnstone, William. 'The 'Ten Commandments': Some Recent Interpretations' *Expository Times* 100 (1989), 453–61.

Jones, Gwilym II. *The Nathan Narratives*. Sheffield: JSOT Press, 1990.

Joosten, Jan. 'Christ a-t-il aboli la loi pour réconcilier Juifs et Païens?' *ETR* 80 (2005): 95–102.

Jubilee Policy Group. 'Relational Justice: a new approach to penal reform'. *Insight*. Cambridge: Jubilee, 1994.

Kaiser, Otto. *Isaiah 1–12*. London: SCM Press Ltd, 1983.

Kaiser, Walter C. *Toward Old Testament Ethics*. Michigan: Zondervan, 1983.

———. *The Uses of the Old Testament in the New*. Chicago: Moody Press, 1985.

———. 'God's Promise Plan and His Gracious Law'. *Journal of the Evangelical Theological Society* 33 no. 3 (19--): 291.

Kalogeraki, Despoina M. *The Concept of Sinlessness and Sinfulness in the First Letter of John: with reference to the paradox encountered in 1:6–10/3:6-10*. Thessaloniki: ΕΚΔΟΣΕΙΣ, 2007.

Kanagaraj, Jey J. 'The Implied Ethics of the Fourth Gospel: A Reinterpretation of the Decalogue'. *Tyndale Bulletin* 52.1 (2001): 33–60.

Karlberg, Mark W. 'Reformed Interpretation of the Mosaic Covenant'. *Westminster Theological Journal* 43 (1980): 1–56.

Kaufmann, Yehezkel. *The Religion of Israel: From its Beginnings to the Babylonian Exile*, trans. Moshe Greenberg, London: George Allen & Unwin Ltd, 1961.

Kaufman, Stephen A. 'The Structure of the Deuteronomic Law'. *Maarav* 1 no. 2 (1978–79): 105–58.

Kaye B. N., and Wenham G. J. eds. *Law, Morality and the Bible*. Leicester: IVP, 1978.

Kazen, Thomas. *Jesus and Purity Halakhah: Was Jesus Indifferent to Purity?* Stockholm: Almqvist & Wiksell International, 2002.

Keerankeri, George. *The Love Commandment in Mark: An Exegetico-*

Theological Study of Mk 12,28–34. Roma: Editrice Pontificio Istituto Biblico, 2003.

Keil, C. F. and Delitzsch F. *The Pentateuch*. Biblical Commentary on the Old Tesatament, vol II. Edinburgh: T & T Clark, MDCCCLXIV.

Kelly, Seán P. *Matthew's Gospel and the History of Biblical Interpretation*. Lewiston: Mellen Biblical Press, 1997.

Kevan, Ernest F. *The Grace of Law*. London: The Carey Kingsgate Press, 1964.

Kilgallen, John J., S.J. 'The Matthean Exception-Text', *Biblica* 61 (1980), 102–5.

Kimball, Charles A., *Jesus' Exposition of the Old Testament in Luke's Gospel*. Sheffield: Sheffield Academic Press, 1994.

Klawans, Jonathan 'Idolatry, Incest, and Impurity: Moral Defilement in Ancient Judaism.' *Journal for the Study of Judaism* XXIX, 4 (1998), 391–415.

Kline, Meredith G. *The Treaty of the Great King: The Covenant Structure of Deuteronmy*. Grand Rapids: Eerdmans, 1963.

———. *By Oath Consigned - A Reinterpretation of the Covenant Signs of Circumcision and Baptism*. Grand Rapids: Eerdmans, 1968.

———. 'Comments on an Old-New Error'. *Westminster Theological Journal* 41 (1978): 172–89.

Knight, George A. F. 'The Lord is One.' *Expository Times* 79 (1967/68) 8–10.

Knight, George W. III, *The Pastoral Epistles: A Commentary on the Greek Text*. Grand Rapids: Eerdmans, 1992.

Knowles, Michael. *Jeremiah in Matthew's Gospel: The Rejected-Prophet Motif in Matthaean Redaction*. Sheffield: JSOT Press, 1993.

Koester, Craig R. *Hebrews: A New Translation with Introduction and Commentary*. New York: Doubleday, 2001.

Kretzmann, Norman and Stump, Eleonore, eds. *The Cambridge Companion to Aquinas*. Cambridge: Cambridge University Press, 1993.

Kruse, Colin. *Paul, the Law and Justification*. Leicester: Apollos, 1996.

Kugel, James L. ed. *Studies in Ancient Midrash*. Harvard University Centre for Jewish Studies, 2001.

Kupp, David D. *Matthew's Emmanuel: Divine Presence and God's people in the First Gospel*. Cambridge: Cambridge University Press, 1996.

Laansma, Jon. *'I Will Give You Rest': The Rest Motif in the New Testament with Special Reference to Mt 11 and Heb 3–4*. Tübingen: Mohr Siebeck, 1997.

Lacoste, Jean-Yves. *Encyclopedia of Christian Theology*, vols. 1–3. New York: Routledge, 2005.

Lagrange, M.-J. 'Le Papyrus Beatty des Actes des Apotres.' *RB* 43 (1934), 161–71.

Lane, William L. *Hebrews 1-8*, WBC, ed. David A. Hubbard and Glenn W. Barker (General), Ralph P. Martin (New Testament), no. 47A. Dallas: Word Books, 1991.

Lee, E. Kenneth. 'Words Denoting "Pattern" in the New Testament.' *NTS* 8 (1961–2), 166–73.

Lee, Patrick. 'Permanence of the Ten Commandments: St. Thomas and His Modern Commentators', *Theological Studies* 42.3 (1981) 422–43.

Letham, Robert. *The Westminster Assembly: Reading its Theology in Historical Context*. Phillipsburg: P&R Publishing, 2009.

Letis, Theodore P., *The Ecclesiastical Text: Text Criticism, Biblical Authority, and the Popular Mind*. Fairhill: The Institute for Renaissance and Reformation Biblical Studies, 2000.

Lewis, W. J. *Manual of the Law of Evidence in Scotland*. Edinburgh and Glasgow: William Hodge & Company, Ltd, 1925.

Levenson, Jon D. 'The Theologies of Commandment in Biblical Israel.' *Harvard Theological Review* 73 (1980): 17–33.

———. *Sinai and Zion: An Entry into the Jewish Bible*. Chicago: Winston Press, 1985.

Levering, Matthew. *Biblical Natural Law: A Theocentric and Teleological Approach*. Oxford: Oxford University Press, 2008.

Levine, Amy-Jill with Blickenstoff, Marianne, eds. *A Feminist*

Companion to Matthew. Sheffield: Sheffield Academic Press, 2001.

Levine, Baruch A. *Leviticus.* New York: The Jewish Publication Society, 1989.

Levinson, Bernard M. 'Textual Criticism, Assyriology, and the History of Interpretation: Deuteronomy 13:7a as a Test Case in Method.' *Journal of Biblical Literature* 120/2 (2001): 211–43.

Levison, John R., *Portraits of Adam in Early Judaism: From Sirach to 2 Baruch.* Sheffield: JSOT Press, 1988.

Lindars, Barnabas ed. *Law and Religion.* Cambridge: James Clark & Co, 1988.

Lincoln, Andrew T. *Ephesians,* Word Biblical Commentary, Hubbard, David A. and Barker, Glenn W. eds. (General), Martin, Ralph P. (New Testament), no. 42. Waco: Word Books, 1990.

Lioy, Dan. *The Decalogue in the Sermon on the Mount.* New York: Peter Lang, 2004.

Loader, William R. G., *Jesus' Attitude towards the Law: A Study of the Gospels.* Tübingen: Mohr Siebeck, 1997.

Lohfink, Norbert. *Theology of the Pentateuch: Themes of the Priestly Narrative and Deuteronomy* trans. Linda M. Maloney. Minneapolis: Fortress Press, 1994.

Lohse, Eduard. *Colossians and Philemon: A Commentary on the Epistles to the Colossians and to Philemon.* trans. William R. Poehlmann and Robert J. Karris. Philadelphia: Fortress Press, 1971.

Longenecker, Richard N. *Paul, Apostle of Liberty.* Grand Rapids: Baker, 1980.

——. *Word Biblical Commentary - Galatians* Dallas: Word Books, 1990.

Lundbom, Jack R. *Jeremiah 21–36.* New York: Doubleday, 2004.

Luther, Martin. *The Large Catechism,* trans. Robert H. Fischer. Philadelphia: Fortress Press, 1959.

——. *Luther's Works,* vol. 28, ed. Hilton C. Oswald. Saint Louis: Concordia Publishing House, 1973.

Luz, Ulrich. *Matthew 1–7: A Commentary.* trans. Wilhelm C. Linss. Edinburgh: T&T Clark, 1990.

——. *Matthew 1–7*. Minneapolis: Fortress Press, 2007.

——. 'Die Erfüllung des Gesetzes bei Matthäus', *Zeitschrift für Theologie und Kirche* 75 (1978), 398–435.

——. 'Intertexts in the Gospel of Matthew', *Harvard Theological Review* 97:2 (2004), 119–137.

Matlock, Michael D. 'Obeying the First Part of the Tenth Commandment: Applications from the Levirate Marriage Law.' *JSNT* 31.3 (2007), 295–310.

McBride, S. D. Jr. 'The Yoke of the Kingdom: An Exposition of Deut. 6:4–5.' *Interpretation* 27 (1973) 273–306.

McCarthy, D. J. 'Notes on the Love of God in Deuteronomy and the Father-Son Relationship between Yahweh and Israel.' *Catholic Biblical Quarterly* 27 (1965): 144–7.

McComiskey, Thomas. *The Covenants of Promise* Nottingham: IVP, 1985.

MacDonald, Nathan. *Deuteronomy and the Meaning of 'Monotheism'*, Tubingen: Mohr Siebeck, 2003.

MacLeod, Donald. 'The New Perspective: Paul, Luther and Judaism'. *SBET* 22.1 (2004), 4–31.

——. 'How Right Are the Justified?' *SBET* 22.2 (2004), 173–95.

McKay, Heather A. *Sabbath and Synagogue: The Question of Sabbath Worship in Ancient Judaism*, Leiden: E. J. Brill, 1994.

McKay, J. W., 'Man's Love for God in Deuteronomy and the Father/ Teacher – Son/Pupil Relationship.' *Vetus Testamentum* XXII, (1972): 426–35.

Mackay, John L. *Exodus*. Fearn: Mentor, 2001.

MacKenzie, Donald. 'The Judge of Israel,' *VT* 17:118–21

Mahan, Henry T., *Bible Class Commentary on Hebrews*. Darlington: Evangelical Press 1989.

Marcus, Joel. *Mark 1–8*. New York: Doubleday, 2000.

Martin, Brice L. 'Matthew on Christ and the Law.' *Theological Studies* 44 (March 1983): 53–70.

——. *Christ and the Law in Paul*. Leiden: E. J. Brill, 1989.

Martin, Hugh. *The Atonement: In Its Relations to the Covenant, the*

Priesthood, the Intercession of Our Lord. Edinburgh, Lyon and
    Gemmell, 1877.

Martin, Ralph P. *James.* Nashville: Thomas Nelson Publishers, 1988.

——. *Colossians: The Church's Lord and the Christian's Liberty,* (Exeter:
    Paternoster Press, 1972).

Martin, Troy. 'But Let Everyone Discern the Body of Christ.' *JBL*
    114/2 (1995): 249–55.

Martyn, J. Louis. *Galatians.* New York: Doubleday, 1997.

Matera, Frank J. *New Testament Ethics: The Legacies of Jesus and Paul.*
    Louisville: Westminster John Knox Press, 1996.

Mayes, A. D. H. *Deuteronomy.* London: Oliphants, 1979.

Meier, John P. 'The Historical Jesus and the Historical Law: Some
    Problems within the Problem.' *Catholic Biblical Quarterly* 65
    (2003): 52–79.

——. *Law and History in Matthew's Gospel: A Redactional Study of Mt.
    5:17–48.* Rome: Biblical Institute Press, 1976.

Metzger, Bruce M. *A Textual Commentary on the Greek New Testament.*
    Stuttgart: Deutsche Bibelgesellschaft, 2002.

Meyer, Heinrich A. W. *Commentary on Galatians*

Meyer, Jason C. *The End of the Law: Mosaic Covenant in Pauline
    Theology.* Nashville: B & H Publishing Group, 2009.

Michaels, J. R., *1 Peter.* Word Biblical Commentary, ed. David A.
    Hubbard and Glenn W. Barker (General), Ralph P. Martin
    (New Testament), no. 49., [Libronix System 2.1c], (Bellingham,
    2000–4).

Milgrom, Jacob. *Leviticus: A Book of Ritual Ethics.* Minneapolis:
    Fortress Press, 2004.

——. *Leviticus 1–16.* New York; Doubleday, 1991.

Millar, J. Gary. *Now Choose Life.* Studies in Biblical Theology, series
    ed. D. A. Carson, no. 6. Leicester: Apollos, 1998.

Miller, James. E 'Sexual Offences in Genesis'. *JSOT* 90 (2000), 41–53.

Miller, Patrick D. 'The Place of the Decalogue in the Old Testament
    and Its Law'. *Interpretation.* (1989): 229–42.

Miller, Patrick D., Jr., Hanson, Paul D. and McBride, S. Dean, eds.
    Ancient Israelite Religion. Philadephia: Fortress Press, 1987.

Mills, Mary E. *Biblical Morality: Moral perspectives in Old Testament Narratives.* Aldershot: Ashgate Publishing, 2001.

Moessner, David P. *Lord of the Banquet: The Literary and Theological Significance of the Lukan Travel Narrative.* Harrisburg: Trinity Press International, 1989.

Moffatt, James. *The First Epistle of Paul to the Corinthians.* London: Hodder and Stoughton, 1938.

Mohrlang, Roger. *Matthew and Paul: a comparison of ethical perspectives.* Cambridge: Cambridge University Press, 1984.

Moran, W. L. 'Gen 49,10 and its Use in Ez 23,32.' *Biblica* 39 (1958): 405–25.

Moritz, Thorsten. *A Profound Mystery: The Use of the Old Testament in Ephesians.* Lieden: E. J. Brill, 1996.

Morris, Leon. *The First Epistle of Paul to the Corinthians.* Leicester: Inter-Varsity Press, 1985.

Morrison, Michael D., *Who Needs a New Covenant? Rhetorical Function of the Covenant Motif in the Argument of Hebrews.* Princeton Theological Monograph Series 85. Eugene: Pickwick Publications, 2008.

Motyer, J. A. *The Prophecy of Isaiah.* Leicester: Inter-Varsity Press, 1993.

———. *The Revelation of the Divine Name.* London: Tyndale Press, 1959.

Murray, Ian H. *The Puritan Hope.* Edinburgh: Banner of Truth, 1971.

———. *Lloyd-Jones: Messenger of Grace.* Edinburgh: Banner of Truth Trust, 2008.

Murray, John. *Divorce.* Philadelphia: The Committee on Christian Education, The Orthodox Presbyterian Church, 1953.

———. *Principles of Conduct.* London: Tyndale, 1957.

———. *The Epistle to the Romans.* London: Marshall, Morgan & Scott, 1967.

———. 'The Adamic Administration' *Collected Writings of John Murray.* Edinburgh: Banner of Truth, 1977.

———. *The Covenant of Grace.* Phillipsburg: P&R, 198-

———. 'The Work of the Westminster Assembly', *The Presbyterian Guardian*, vol. 11 (1942).

Neusner, J. *et al.* eds. *The Social World of Formative Christianity and Judaism*. Philadelphia: Fortress Press, 1982).

Neyrey, Jerome H. 'The Idea of Purity in Mark's Gospel.' *Semeia* 35 (1986), 91–128.

Nicholl, Colin R. *From Hope to Despair in Thessalonica: Situating 1 and 2 Thessalonians*. Cambridge: Cambridge University Press, 2004.

Nicholson, E. W. 'The Decalogue as the Direct Address of God'. *Vetus Testamentum*. Vol. XXVII, Fasc. 4 (1977): 422–33.

Niehaus, Jeffrey J. *God at Sinai*. Carlisle: Paternoster, 1995.

Noll, Mark A., Bebbington, David W., and Rawlyk, George A. (eds.), *Evangelicalism: Comparative Studies of Popular Protestantism in North America, the British Isles, and Beyond, 1700–1990*. Oxford: Oxford University Press, 1994.

Nolland, John. *Luke 18:35–24:53*, Word Biblical Commentary, ed. Bruce M. Metzger, David A. Hubbard and Glenn W. Barker (General), John D. W. Watts (Old Testament), Ralph P. Martin (New Testament) no. 35c. Nashville: Thomas Nelson, 1993.

North, Gary. *Tools of Dominion*. Tyler: Institute for Christian Economics, 1990.

O'Brien, Peter T. *Colossians, Philemon*. Word Biblical Commentary, David A. Hubbard and Glenn W. Barker (General), Ralph P. Martin (New Testament), eds. no. 44. Waco: Word Books, 1982.

O'Donovan, O. M. T. 'Towards an Interpretation of Biblical Ethics'. *Tyndale Bulletin* 27 (1996): 58–61.

Osborn, Eric Francis. *Justin Martyr*. Tübingen, J. C. B. Mohr, 1973.

Overman, J. Andrew. *Church and Community in Crisis: The Gospel According to Matthew*. Valley Forge: Trinity Press International, 1996.

Owen, John. *An Exposition of the Epistle to the Hebrews with the Preliminary Exercitations*. London: T. Pitcher, 1790.

——. *An Exposition of the Epistle to the Hebrews* Vol. III. Edinburgh: Johnstone and Hunter, 1854.

——. *The Glory of Christ*. Fearn: Christian Focus Publications, 2004.

Pancaro, Severino. *The Law in the Fourth Gospel*. Leiden: E. J. Bill, 1975.

Pannenberg, Wolfhart. *Systematic Theology*. Vols. 1–3. Edinburgh: T & T Clark Ltd, 1991.

Pao, David W. *Acts and the Isaianic New Exodus*. Tübingen: Mohr Siebeck, 2000.

Parker, Kenneth L., *The English Sabbath: A study of doctrine and discipline from the Reformation to the Civil War*. Cambridge: Cambridge University Press, 1988.

Parry, Ken; Melling, David J.; Brady, Dimitri; Griffith, Sidney H. & Healy, John F. eds., *The Blackwell Dictinary of Eastern Christianity*. Oxford: Blackwell, 1999.

Patrick, Dale. *Old Testament Law*. London: SCM, 1985.

——. 'The First Commandment in the Structure of the Pentateuch', *VT* 45, 107–18.

Paul, Shalom M. *A Commentary on the Book of Amos*. Minneapolis: Fortress Press, 1991.

Payne, J. Barton. *The Theology of the Older Testament*. Grand Rapids: Zondervan, 1972.

Pelikan, Jaroslav. *The Christian Tradition: A History of the Development of Doctrine*. Volume 1. The Emergence of the Catholic Tradition (100–600). Chicago: University of Chicago Press, 1971.

Pennington, Jonathan T. *Heaven and Earth in the Gospel of Matthew*. Leiden: Koninklijke Brill, 2007.

Perkins, Pheme. *Love Commands in the New Testament*. New York: Paulist Press, 1982.

Perowne, J. J. Stewart. *The Book of Psalms: A New Translation with Introductions and Notes Explanatory and Critical*. London: Bell & Daldy, 1868

Peterson, David. *Hebrews and Perfection: An Examination of the Concept of Perfection in the 'Epistle to the Hebrews'*. Cambridge: Cambridge University Press, 1982.

Phillips, Anthony. *Ancient Israel's Criminal Law – A New Approach to the Decalogue*. Oxford: Basil Blackwell, 1970.

———. 'A Fresh Look at the Sinai Pericope – Part 1'. *Vetus Testamentum* XXXIV no. 1 (1984): 39–52.

———. 'A Fresh Look at the Sinai Pericope – Part 2'. *Vetus Testamentum* XXXIV no. 3 (1984): 282–94.

Philo. *De Decalogo* Vol. VII *The Leob Classical Library* trans. F. H. Colson. London: William Heinemann Ltd, MCMXXXVII.

Piper, John. *'Love Your Enemies': Jesus love command in the synoptic gospels and in the early Christian paranesis: A history of the tradition and interpretation of its uses.* Cambridge: Cambridge University Press, 1979.

———. *The Future of Justification: A Response to N. T. Wright.* Wheaton: Crossway Books, 2007.

Plumer, Eric. *Augustine's Commentary on Galatians: Introduction, Text, Translation, and Notes.* Oxford: Oxford University Press, 2003.

Porter, Stanley E. *The Paul of Acts: Essays in Literary Criticism, Rhetoric, and Theology.* Tübingen: Mohr Siebeck, 1999.

Porter, Stanley E. & Evans, Craig A., eds. *The Pauline Writings.* Sheffield: Sheffield Academic Press, 1995.

Poythress, Vern. *The Shadow of Christ in the Law of Moses.* Brentwood: Wolgemuth & Hyatt, 1991.

Pritchard, James B. *Ancient Near Eastern Texts.* Princeton: Princeton University Press, 1969.

Propp, William C. *Exodus 19–40: A New Translation with Introduction and Commentary.* New York: Doubleday, 2006.

Prosic, Tamara. *The Development and Symbolism of Passover until 70 CE.* London: T&T Clark International, 2004.

Przybylski, Benno. *Righteousness in Matthew and his world of thought.* Cambridge: Cambridge University Press, 1981.

Räisänen, Heikki. *Jesus, Paul and Torah: Collected Essays.* Sheffield: JSOT Press, 1992.

———. *Paul and the Law.* Tübingen: J. C. B. Mohr, 1987.

———. *The Idea of Divine Hardening: A Comparative Study of the Notion of Divine Hardening, Leading Astray and Inciting to Evil in the Bible and the Qur'an.* Helsinki: Finish Exegetical Society, 1976.

Rebdtorff, Rolf. *The Canonical Hebrew Bible: A Theology of the Old Testament.* tr. David E. Orton. Leiden: Deo Publishing, 2005.

Rendtorff, Rolf and Kugler, Robert A. eds. *The Book of Leviticus: Composition and Reception.* Leiden: Brill, 2003.

Regev, Eyal. 'Moral Impurity and the Temple in Early Christianity in Light of Ancient Greek Practice and Qumranic Ideology.' *Harvard Theological Review* 97:4 (2004) 383–411.

Reiser, Marius. 'Love of Enemies in the Context of Antiquity', *New Testament Studies* 47.4 (2001), 411–27.

Rensberger, David. *1 John.* Nashville: Abingdon Press, 1997.

Ridderbos, Herman. *The Epistle to the Galatians.* Grand Rapids: Eerdmans, 1954.

Ridderbos, Jan. *The Bible Student's Commentary - Deuteronomy.* Grand Rapids: Zondervan, 1984.

Ringgren, Helmer. *Religions of the Ancient Near East.* trans. John Sturdy. London: SPCK, 1973.

Roberts, Alexander, and James Donaldson, eds. *The Ante-Nicene Fathers: Translations of the Writings of the Fathers down to A Z.D. 325,* vol. I-III. Edinburgh: T & T Clark, 1986.

Robertson, O. Palmer. *The Christ of the Covenants.* Phillipsburg: P&R 1980.

——. *The Christ of the Prophets.* Awaiting Publication.

——. 'Current Reformed Thinking on the Nature of Divine Covenants' *Westminster Theological Journal* 40: 63–76.

Robinson, Bernard P., 'Jeremiah's New Covenant: Jer 31,31-34', *Scandinavian Journal of the Old Testament* vol. 15 no. 2 (2001), 181–204.

Rodd, Cyril S. *Glimpses of a Strange Land: Studies in Old Testament Ethics* Edinburgh: T & T Clark, 2001

Rogerson, John W., Davies, Margaret, & Carroll R., M. Daniel, *The Bible in Ethics: The Second Sheffield Colloquium.* Sheffield: Sheffield Academic Press, 1995.

Rohls, Jan. *Reformed Confessions: Theology from Zurich to Barmen,* trans. John Hoffmeyer. Louisville: John Knox Press, 1997.

Rosner, Brian S. ed., *Understanding Paul's Ethics: Twentieth Century Approaches*. Grand Rapids: Eerdmans, 1995.

Rosner, Brian S., 'Paul and the Law: What he Does not Say.' JSNT 32 (2010): 405–19.

Royse, James R., *Scribal Habits in Early Greek New Testament Papyri*. Leiden: Brill, 2006.

Rushdoony, Rousas J. *God's Plan for Victory*. Fairfax: Thoburn Press, 1980.

Saldarini, Anthony J. *Matthew's Christian–Jewish Community*. Chicago: University of Chicago Press, 1994.

Sailhamer, John H. 'The Mosaic Law and the Theology of the Pentateuch' *Westminster Theological Journal* 53 (1991): 241–61.

Sanday, W., 'The Text of the Apostolic Decree.' *Expositor*, October 1913, 289–305.

Sanders, E. P. *Jesus and Judaism*. London: SCM Press Ltd, 1985.

———. *Paul*. Oxford: Oxford University Press, 1991.

———. *Paul and Palestinian Judaism: A Comparison of Patterns of Religion*. London: SCM Press Ltd, 1977.

———. *Jewish Law from Jesus to the Mishnah*. London: SCM Press Ltd, 1990.

Sanders, Jack T. *Ethics in the New Testament: Change and Development*. Philadelphia: Fortress Press, 1975.

Sandys-Wunsch, John and Eldredge, Laurence. 'J. P. Gabler and the Distinction Between Biblical and Dogmatic Theology: Translation, Commentary, and Discussion of His Originality', *Scottish Journal of Theology* 33.1 (1980): 133–58.

Sariola, Heikki. *Markus und das Gesetz: Eine redaktionskritische Unterschung*. Helsinki: Suomalainen Tiedeakatemia, 1990.

Sawyer, John F. A. ed., *Reading Leviticus: A Conversation with Mary Douglas*. Sheffield: Sheffield Academic Press, 1996.

Schaefer, Konrad. *Psalms*. BERIT OLAM: Studies in Hebrew Narrative & Poetry, ed. David W. Cotter. Collegeville: The Liturgical Press, 2001.

Schaff, P. *Creeds and Confessions of Christendom*.

Schley, Donald G. *Shiloh: A Biblical City in Tradition and History.*
Sheffield: Sheffield Academic Press, 1989.

Schnakenburg, Rudolf. *The Gospel According to John*, vol. 3. Tunbridge
Wells: Burns & Oates, 1982.

——. *The Johannine Epistles*, trans. Reginald and Ilse Fuller.
Tunbridge Wells: Burns & Oates, 1992.

Schreiner, Thomas R. *The Law & Its Fulfillment*. Grand Rapids: Baker,
1993.

——. *Romans*. Grand Rapids: Baker Academic, 2003.

——. 'The Abolition and Fulfillment of the Law in Paul.' *JSNT* 35
(1989), 47–74.

Segal, Ben-Zion and Levi, Gershon eds. *The Ten Commandments in
History and Tradition*. Jerusalem: The Magnes Press, The Hebrew
University of Jerusalem, 1990.

Seifred, M. A. 'Jesus and the Law in Acts.' *JSNT* 30 (1987), 39–57.

Schnackenburg, Rudolf. *The Gospel of Matthew*. Grand Rapids,
Eerdmans, 2002.

Schweizer, Eduard. *The Good News According to Matthew,* trans. David
E. Green. London, SPCK, 1976.

Shaw, Robert. *The Reformed Faith*. Lochcarron: Christian Focus
Publications, 1980.

Shemesh, Yael. 'Rape is Rape is Rape: The Story of Dinah and
Shechem (Genesis 34)' *Zeitschrift für die alttestamentlich
Wissenschaft* 119 (2002): 2–21.

Segal, J. B. *The Hebrew Passover from the Earliest Times to A.D. 70.*
London: Oxford University Press, 1963.

Sheldon, David H. *Evidence: Cases and Materials*. Edinburgh: W.
Green & Son Ltd., 2002.

Siefrid, M. A., *Jesus and the Law in Acts. JSNT* 30 (1987), 39–57.

Sigal, Phillip. *The Halakah of Jesus of Nazareth According to the Gospel
of Matthew*. Lanham, University Press of America, 1986.

Sim, David C. 'The Gospel for All Christians? A Response to Richard
Bauckham.' *Journal for the Study of the New Testament* 84, (2001):
3–27.

Singer, Isidore. Managing ed. *The Jewish Encyclopaedia*. New York &
    London: Funk & Wagnalls Company, 1903.

Skinner, Quentin. *Visions of Politics: Volume 1: Regarding Method*.
    Cambridge: Cambridge University Press, 2002.

Smalley, Stephen S. *1,2,3 John*. WBC, ed. David A. Hubbard and
    Glenn W. Barker (General), Ralph P. Martin (New Testament),
    no. 51. Waco: Word Books, 1984.

Snodgrass, Klyne R. 'Justification by Grace – to the Doers: An
    Analysis of the Place of Romans 2 in the Theology of Paul.' *NTS*
    32 (1986), 72–93.

Soggin, J. Alberto. *The Prophet Amos*, trans. John Bowden, 1987.
    London: SCM Press Ltd, 1987

Soll, Will. *Psalm 119: Matrix, Form, and Setting*. Washington: The
    Catholic Biblical Association of America, 1991.

Spencer, F. Scott. *Acts*. Sheffield: Sheffield Academic Press, 1997.

Stair, James Viscount of. *The Institutions of the Law of Scotland
    Deduced from its Originals and Collated with the Civil and Feudal
    Laws and with the Customs of Neighbouring Nations*, vol. 1.
    Edinburgh: Thomas Clark, M.DCCC.XXVI.

Staniloae, Dumitru. *The Experience of God*. Translated and Edited
    by Ioan Ionita and Robert Barringer. Brookline: Holy Cross
    Orthodox Press, 1994.

Stanley, Christopher D. 'A Decontextualized Paul? A Response to
    Francis Watson's *Paul and the Hermeneutics of Faith*.' *JSNT* 28.3
    (2006), 353–62

Stockhausen, Carol Kern. *Moses' Veil and the Glory of the New
    Covenant: The Exegetical Substructre of II Cor. 3,1–4,6*. Roma:
    Editrice Pontificio Istituto Biblico, 1989.

Stuart, Douglas. *Hosea - Jonah*. Word Biblical Commentary, ed. David
    A. Hubbard and Glenn W. Barker (General), John D. W. Watts
    (Old Testament), no. 31. Waco: Word Books, 1987.

Strickland, Wayne G. ed. *The Law, the Gospel and the Modern
    Christian: Five Views*. Grand Rapids: Zondervan, 1993.

Stylianopoulos, Theodore. *Justin Martyr and the Mosaic Law*.
    Missoula: Society of Biblical Literature, 1975.

Sylva, Dennis D. 'The Temple Curtain and Jesus' Death in the Gospel of Luke.' *Journal of Biblical Literature* 105/2 (1986): 239–50.

Tait, George. *A Treatise on the Law of Evidence in Scotland.* Edinburgh: John Anderson & Co., 1824.

Tapper, Colin. *Cross and Tapper on Evidence.* London: Butterworths, 1995.

Tate, Marvin E. *Psalms 51–100.* Word Biblical Commentary, ed. David A. Hubbard and Glenn W. Barker (General), John D. W. Watts (Old Testament), no. 20. Dallas: Word Books, 1990.

Terrien, Samuel. *The Psalms: Strophic Structure and Theological Commentary.* Grand Rapids: Eerdmans, 2002.

Theodoret of Cyrus. *Commentary on the Psalms 73–150.* trans. Robert C. Hill. Washington: The Catholic University of America Press, 2001.

Urbach, Ephraim E. *The Sages: Their Concepts and Beliefs.* Translated from the Hebrew by Israel Abrahams. Jerusalem: The Magnes Press, The Hebrew University of Jerusalem, 1975.

Van der Ploeg, J. 'Studies in Hebrew Law.' *Catholic Biblical Quarterly* 12 (1950): 248–59, 416–27; 13 (1951): 28–43, 296–9.

Van der Watt, Jan G. 'Ethics and Ethos in the Gospel According to John.' *Zeitschrift für die Neutestamentliche Wissenschaft* 97 (2006): 147–76.

——. *Family of the King: Dynamics of Metaphor in the Gospel According to John.* Leiden: Brill, 2000.

Van Ness, Daniel W. *Crime and its Victims.* Leicester: IVP, 1986.

Van Spanje, T. E. *Inconsistency in Paul: A Critique of the Work of Heikki Räisänen.* Tübingen: Mohr Siebeck, 1999.

Vandore, Peter K. 'The Moorov Doctrine' in *The Juridical Review* (1974), 30–55, 179–95.

Vasholz, Robert I., *Leviticus.* Fearn: Mentor, 2007.

Vermes, Geza. 'The Decalogue and the Minim.' In *In Memoriam Paul Kahle: Beiheft zur Zeitschrift für die alttestamentliche Wissenschaft,* 232–40. Berlin: Verlag Alfred Töpelmann, 1968.

——. *The Religion of Jesus the Jew.* London: SCM Press, 1993.

Von Rad, Gerhard. *Genesis.* London: SCM, 1972.

Victor, Peddi. 'A Note on חק in the Old Testament.' *Vetus Testamentum* XVI (1966): 358–61.

Walker, David M. *Viscount Stair: Glasgow, European City of Culture Stevenson Lecture.* Glasgow: University of Glasgow, 1990.

Watson, Francis. *The Open Text: Directions for Biblical Studies.* London: SCM Press Ltd, 1993.

———. *Paul and the Hermeneutics of Faith.* London: T & T Clark, 2004.

———. 'Paul the Reader: An Authorial Apologia.' *JSNT* 28.3 (2006), 363–73

Weinandy, Thomas G., OFM, Cap, Keating, Daniel A., and Yocum, John P. eds. *Aquinas on Scripture: An Introduction to his Biblical Commentaries.* London: T. & T. Clark, 2005

Weinfeld, M. 'The Origin of the Apodictic Law: An Overlooked Source.' *Vetus Testamentum* XXIII, fasc. 1 (1973): 61–75.

Weisheipl, James A. *Friar Thomas D'Aquino: His Life, Thought, and Work.* New York: Doubleday, 1974.

Weiss, Herold. 'The Sabbath in the Synoptic Gospels.' In *New Testament Backgrounds,* 109–123. Sheffield: Sheffield Academic Press, 1997.

Wells, Tom and Zaspel, Fred. *New Covenant Theology.* Frederick: New Covenant Media, 2002.

Wenham, David. 'Jesus and the law: an exegesis on Matthew 5: 17-20.' *Themelios* 4 (1979): 92–6.

Wenham, Gordon. J. *The Book of Leviticus.* Michigan: Eerdmans, 1979.

———. *Genesis 1–15.* Waco: Word Books, 1987.

———. *Story as Torah: Reading the Old Testament Ethically.* Edinburgh: T&T Clark, 2000.

———. 'Matthew and Divorce: An Old Crux Revisited.' *Journal for the Study of the New Testament* 22 (1984): 95–107.

———. 'Gospel Definitions of Adultery and Women's Rights.' *Expository Times* 95 (1984): 330–32.

Wenham, Gordon J. and Heth William E. *Jesus and Divorce.* Carlisle: Paternoster Publishing, 1997.

Westcott, Brooke Foss. *The Epistle to the Hebrews*. London: Macmillan & Co., 1903

Westerholm, Stephen. *Preface to the Study of Paul*. Grand Rapids: Eerdmans, 1997.

———. *Perspectives Old and New on Paul: The "Lutheran Paul and His Critics"*. Grand Rapids: Eerdmans, 2004.

Whitelam, Keith W. *The Just King: Monarchical Judicial Authority in Ancient Israel*. Sheffield: JSOT Press, 1979.

Wiles, M. F. *The Divine Apostle*. Cambridge: Cambridge University Press, 1967.

———. 'St Paul's Conception of Law'. *The Churchman* LXIX (1955–6): 144–52.

Williams, Michael D. *This World Is not My Home: The Origins and Development of Dispensationalism*.

Williams, Rowan. *On Christian Theology*. Oxford: Blackwell, 2000.

Wilcox, Max. 'The "God-Fearers" in Acts – A Reconsideration' in *Journal for the Study of the New Testament* 13 (1981), 102–22.

Wilson, S. G. *Luke and the Law*, Cambridge: Cambridge University Press, 1983.

Witherington, Ben. 'Matthew 5.32 and 19.9—Exception or Exceptional Situation?' *New Testament Studies* 31 (1985): 571–6.

———. *The Acts of the Apostles: A Socio-Rhetorical Commentary*. Grand Rapids: Eerdmans, 1998.

———. *The Gospel of Mark: A Socio-Rhetorical Commentary*. Grand Rapids: Eerdmans, 2001.

———. ed., *History, Literature, and Society in the Book of Acts*. Cambridge: Cambridge University Press, 1996.

———. *Grace in Galatia: A Commentary on St Paul's Letter to the Galatians*. Edinburgh: T&T Clark, 1998.

Witte, John Jr., *Law and Protestantism: The Legal Teachings of the Lutheran Reformation*. Cambridge: Cambridge University Press, 2002.

Wojciechowski, Markus. 'The Touching of the Leper (Mark 1,40–45) as a Historical and Symbolic Act of Jesus.' *Biblische Zeitschrift* 33 (1989): 114–19.

Wolfson, Henry Austryn. *Philo: Foundations of Religious Philosophy in Judaism, Christianity and Islam.* Vol. 2. Cambridge, Massachusetts: Harvard University Press, 1948.

Wright, Christopher J. *Deuteronomy.* New International Biblical Commentary, ed. Robert L. Hubbard Jr. and Robert K. Johnston, no. 4. Peabody: Hendrickson, 1996.

———. *Living as the People of God.* Leicester: IVP, 1983.

———. *Walking in the Ways of the Lord.* Leicester: Apollos, 1995.

Wright, N. T. *Jesus and the Victory of God.* Minneapolis: Fortress Press, 1996.

———. *Matthew for Everyone. Part I, Chapter 1–15.* London: SPCK, 2002.

———. *The Climax of the Covenant: Christ and the Law in Pauline Theology.* Edinburgh: T&T Clark, 1991.

Yang, Yong-Eui. *Jesus and the Sabbath in Matthew's Gospel.* Sheffield: Sheffield Academic Press, 1997.

Yee, Tet-Lim N. *Jews, Gentiles and Ethnic Reconciliation: Paul's Jewish Identity and Ephesians.* Cambridge: Cambridge University Press, 2005.

Young, Frances M. *Biblical Exegesis and the Formation of Christian Culture.* Cambridge: Cambridge University Press, 1997.

Internet Resources

Aquinas, Thomas. Summa Theologica www.knight.org/advent/ summa/ 07/09/97

Augustine. LETTER LXXXII. ccel.wheaton.edu/pager. cgi?file=fathers/NPNF1-01/augustine/letters/v2.4.html&from=L ETTERLXXXII&up=fathers/NPNF1-01/. 17/09/97

C. W. Conrad, Active, Middle, and Passive: Understanding Ancient Greek Voice. http://www.ioa.com/~cwconrad/Docs/ UndAncGrkVc.pdf 18/01/06

Leo the Great, 'A Homily on the Beatitudes'. http://www.newadvent. org/fathers/360395.htm 04/04/06.

SCRIPTURE INDEX

18 71, 185
18:1–13 97
18:1–29 185
18:3 293
18:5 150
18:6–19:14 174
18:6–23 258
18:14–30 97
18:20 235
18:22–3 95
18:30 157
19 97, 102, 104
19:3 277
19:3–4 157
19:10 260
19:13–19 235
19:15 248
19:16 91
19:16–17 95
19:17 223
19:18 232, 234
19:19 117
19:30 277
19:32 95
19:33–4 260
19:34 157
19:36 157
20 71
20:2 260
20:17 78
20:24 184, 186, 189, 282, 284
20:24–6 184, 186, 248, 282, 284
20:25 184, 189
21:7 226
22:6 178
22:18 260
23 97
23:22 157, 260
23:32 277
24:15 95
24:16 125, 260
24:22 157, 260
25:2–8 92
25:4 277

25:23ff. 117
25:35–8 232
26:1–12 157
26:2 277
26:11–12 204
26:43 328

NUMBERS

4:3 366
4:47 366
8:6–7 366
8:7 366
19:13 113
25:13 366
30:3 230
35:30–34 234
35:33–4 185
9:14 260
15:14–16 259, 260
15:15 259
15:15–16 260
15:29 259, 260
19:10 259, 260
28:2 259

DEUTERONOMY

1:8 342
1:18 355
1:25 322
4:2 355
4:6 355
4:10 209, 355
4:13 83, 84, 93, 108, 355
4:13–4 106
4:14 104, 356
4:16 64
4:16–18 111
4:19 291
4:23 355
4:26 84
4:32–3 57
4:33 80, 282
4:33-9 80

4:36 355
4:40 355
4:45 356
5:1–11:32 101, 217, 356
5:2–3 355
5:5 81, 138, 355
5:10 356
5:14 260
5:21 74
5:22 81, 83, 86, 87, 143, 355
5:29 85, 356
5:31 104, 356
5:33 85, 86, 355
6 322
6:1 31, 106, 108, 109, 268, 356
6:4 51, 139
6:4–9 157
6:5 329
6:6 203, 208, 355
6:10 342
6:13 229, 230, 231
6:17 355, 356
6:20 356
6:24 355
6:25 356
7:7 86
7:9 356
7:11 356
7:12 268, 356
7:25 159
7:25–6 86
8:1 356
8:2 356
8:3 219
8:11 356
8:16–19 219
8:19–20 86
9:4–6 86
9:9 81, 355
9:10 83, 355
9:11 355
9:12 64, 81, 355
9:15 322, 355
9:16 355

GENERAL INDEX

INDEX OF HEBREW AND GREEK TERMS

(with brief definition in particular contexts)

INDEX OF NAMES AND AUTHORS

The Marrow of Modern Divinity

Edward Fisher

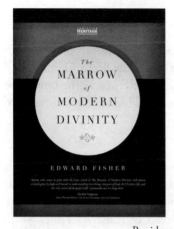

The Marrow emphasizes biblical, evangelical doctrines such as the sovereignty of God in the covenant of grace, the free offer of the gospel, assurance in Christ as the essence of faith, and sanctification by grace rather than by the law. Thomas Boston loved these grace-filled doctrines and discovered that they strengthened his hold on the precious gospel that he lived and preached.

Philip G Ryken
President, Wheaton College, Wheaton, Illinois

Anyone who comes to grips with the issues raised in *The Marrow of Modern Divinity* will almost certainly grow by leaps and bounds in understanding three things: the grace of God, the Christian life, and the very nature of the gospel itself. I personally owe it a huge debt.

Sinclair B. Ferguson,
Senior Minister, First Presbyterian Church, Columbia, South Carolina

An intriguing book, penned as dialogue between a minister (Evangelista), a young Christian (Neophytus), a legalist (Nomista) who believes Christianity is a set of rules to be obeyed and Antinomista who thinks it's okay to sin because God will forgive him anyway, *The Marrow of Modern Divinity* remains tremendously relevant for our world today. This newly laid out and eagerly awaited edition includes explanatory notes by the famous puritan Thomas Boston, an Introduction by Philip Ryken and an historical Introduction by William Vandoodewaard.

ISBN 978-1-84550-479-3

Christian Focus Publications
publishes books for all ages

Our mission statement –

STAYING FAITHFUL
In dependence upon God we seek to impact the world through literature faithful to His infallible Word, the Bible. Our aim is to ensure that the LORD Jesus Christ is presented as the only hope to obtain forgiveness of sin, live a useful life and look forward to heaven with Him.

REACHING OUT
Christ's last command requires us to reach out to our world with His gospel. We seek to help fulfil that by publishing books that point people towards Jesus and help them develop a Christ-like maturity. We aim to equip all levels of readers for life, work, ministry and mission.

Books in our adult range are published in three imprints.
Christian Focus contains popular works including biographies, commentaries, basic doctrine and Christian living. Our children's books are also published in this imprint.
Mentor focuses on books written at a level suitable for Bible College and seminary students, pastors, and other serious readers. The imprint includes commentaries, doctrinal studies, examination of current issues and church history.
Christian Heritage contains classic writings from the past.

Christian Focus Publications, Ltd
Geanies House, Fearn, Ross-shire,
IV20 1TW, Scotland, United Kingdom
info@christianfocus.com
www.christianfocus.com